In and Out of Church

In and Out of Church

The Moral Arc of Spiritual Change in America

Steven M. Tipton

ROWMAN & LITTLEFIELD
Lanham • Boulder • New York • London

Published by Rowman & Littlefield
An imprint of The Rowman & Littlefield Publishing Group, Inc.
4501 Forbes Boulevard, Suite 200, Lanham, Maryland 20706
www.rowman.com
86-90 Paul Street, London EC2A 4NE

British Library Cataloguing in Publication Information Available

Library of Congress Cataloging-in-Publication Data

Names: Tipton, Steven M., author.
Title: In and out of church : the moral arc of spiritual change in America / Steven M. Tipton.
Description: Lanham : Rowman & Littlefield, [2024] | Includes bibliographical references and index.
Identifiers: LCCN 2024027925 (print) | LCCN 2024027926 (ebook) | ISBN 9781538197042 (cloth) | ISBN 9781538197059 (paperback) | ISBN 9781538197066 (ebook)
Subjects: LCSH: Ex-church members--United States. | Religion and sociology--United States. | United States--Church history.
Classification: LCC BR526 .T68 2024 (print) | LCC BR526 (ebook) | DDC 306.6/773--dc23/eng/20240708
LC record available at https://lccn.loc.gov/2024027925
LC ebook record available at https://lccn.loc.gov/2024027926

™ The paper used in this publication meets the minimum requirements of American National Standard for Information Sciences—Permanence of Paper for Printed Library Materials, ANSI/NISO Z39.48-1992.

For Silas and Niels

Contents

Preface

Why are so many Americans leaving church? Half no longer belong to a congregation. A quarter now say they are unchurched, up from one in six a decade ago and one in twelve a generation ago, led by more than a third of young adults. Where have they gone, and what are they doing instead? What moves them? What should we make of it? And what can we learn from those who have stayed or returned, and from congregations that have sparked their continuing commitment or renewed participation?[1]

After decades of drift and several long years of grievous pandemic that closed church doors and crowded the internet, the time has come to weigh these questions more deeply and answer them more carefully. We need to open a keener moral inquiry into the arc of spiritual change in America. We need to probe a thicker cultural account of intergenerational religious influence, inspiration, and formation that we practice today in forms of ritual action, sacred expression, and moral community that reach far beyond the pews.[2]

This is a book voiced by spiritually attuned, morally articulate young adults adrift from the churches and temples of their childhood yet immersed in currents of spiritual practice and imagination now shifting the shape and course of American religion. In heartfelt dialogue with their baby boom parents, these millennials mull how and why they got here in terms that open up and fill in the "spiritual but not religious" profile sketched by surveys of "religious nones." This book brings these numbers to life and makes moral sense of this sketch of individuals leaving church by setting their story within the larger cultural drama of multiplex modern society and quicksilver selfhood in search of authentic fulfillment in caring community.

This inquiry into spiritual and religious change engages Americans in and out of church across three generations. It heeds postwar baby boomers who have stayed in the mainline churches of their childhood, switched to other churches or faiths, drifted away from organized religion to "nothing in particular," or embraced new "spiritual practices" and joined new spiritual movements. How has this touched and textured the religious lives of their children and grandchildren, particularly the millennials who are the likeliest to be unchurched? How do their offspring in turn tell the story of their own maturing faith, growing doubt, dawning de-conversion, or unfolding spiritual journey? How are they bringing up their own children in light of the religious formation, confusion, and change they experienced in their families of origin and cultural communities, their schooling and politics?[3]

Who are your best friends, we can ask, and what do you do, feel, and go by in common with them? We can link this practical line of moral and social inquiry with more nuanced institutional analysis, lit by case studies of congregating across generations of family and friends in communities that are unusually responsive to young adults. We need to see how congregations enact particular practices of love and work at the heart of becoming adult—caring companionship and courtship, responsibility in calling and career, compassionate concern lived out as a spouse, parent, friend, and citizen. We need to hear how congregations understand why young adults leave church, and why they decide to respond as they do. We need to explore how "organized religion" can un-organize itself to reach the next generation and beyond.[4]

In and Out of Church takes the reader inside an evangelical "almost megachurch" mushrooming from Presbyterian roots in Silicon Valley, then it joins three Methodist congregations thriving across class and color lines in Atlanta. It shows how these churches reach out to unchurched young adults and hold on to their own as they come of age by "putting belonging before believing and behaving." These congregations lift up spiritual experience beyond the pews and challenge conventions of "organized religion" in ways that many "spiritual *and* religious" churchgoers have now come to embrace and pray pastors to heed.[5]

This book focuses on exemplary congregations in two metropolitan areas, Silicon Valley and Atlanta, rich in unchurched young adults and representative of their widening social range. These churches are no less rich in their cultural range of contrast and continuity across religious traditions, sacramental and evangelical, megachurch and mainline. All of them feature remarkable lay participation and organizational innovation, vivid theological imagination, and felt moral urgency. At the same time, conversation and reflection among members of these congregations encompass others they know in and out of church who have pursued spiritual paths of their own. These range from mindfulness meditation and peer-counseling groups through yoga and aerobics classes, fine arts and community projects, to daily regimens of self-care devoted to personal wellness. They are linked in turn to spiritual seekers and followers committed to alternative religious groups, athletic or aesthetic disciplines, psychotherapeutic circles to realize human potential, and political movements to bring about social change.[6]

This study concentrates on mainline and evangelical Protestantism—in counterpoint to Catholic, Jewish, and Black Church voices—situated in metropolitan suburbs at the cultural crossroads of spiritual change in American religion. Silicon Valley and metro Atlanta hardly represent American society at large, or small-town "middle America" in particular. But they distinctly and vividly represent the cultural dynamics and social landscape of individualizing spiritual change among Americans today. Given its social scope and scale, this book does not and cannot map the full range and diversity of American religion lived out in practice and outlined in national surveys. But it does dig deep into changes in spiritual ideals, ritual experience, and moral understanding, changes that radiate outward from the epicenter of this new religious frontier through our mass media, music, and popular culture as a whole. It asks, "Why so?" to elicit the cultural meaning and moral drama of institutions enacted in everyday practices and social relationships in and out of church. This kind of moral and social inquiry broadens and complements "how-to" questions posed by more church-specific research on congregational ministry, worship, and outreach aimed at bringing young people back to church.[7]

Survey research on "faith in flux," done over decades among the growing ranks of Americans who leave church, particularly "spiritual but not religious" young adults, proves informative and provocative but also limited in what it reveals.[8] It centers on attitudinal data drawn from individuals, typically identified in terms of conventional categories of "religious preference," such as "evangelical, fundamentalist, liberal, or moderate Protestant," data that is then correlated with a range of interacting demographic and social variables such as age, gender, race, income, education, and political partisanship to profile who is moving in or out of which kind of church.[9] Precisely because these data are individual and attitudinal, causally overdetermined and cohort-bound, they reveal only glimpses of the underlying reasons and overarching meaning of individual action and attitude, including the culturally constituted paradoxes we share and contest in moral principle and practice.

But from the statistical skeleton of survey analyses we can flesh out the interplay of generational and family dynamics in firsthand stories of religious and spiritual change. In their nuanced complexity and narrative coherence such stories can help us see beyond the numbers of churched and unchurched Americans counted into either/or categories. These numbers in turn come to life and come together in the stories that follow. We can see why religious "nones are not all created equal," since some who claim no religious preference leave church forever, and others only for a season.[10] Some quit fully and "stop believing," while "liminal" others only edge away and often return to the fold. Some declare themselves lifelong "atheists," and others allow they are "agnostics," if only for the time being. Still others identify with "nothing in particular" in terms of denominational doctrine or membership, organized religion or faith tradition. But some of them still go to church or temple. Some "unattached believers" choose "no religion." But they "believe in God," and they practice their own spiritual beliefs in their own way.

Indeed the shifting categories used in various surveys over decades to classify those religiously affiliated and disaffiliated can cloud or confuse exactly who is in or out of church, where they stand, what they do there, and why they stay, leave, or return. So I parse these shifting categories and distinguish these varied surveys throughout the text and notes of chapter 1 to specify the statistical varieties of what it means to leave church. In chapter 2, I trace stories of spiritual change in and out of church across lines of religious participation, practice, belief, belonging, membership, preference, and identification, both within and beyond the bounds of faith drawn by bodies of worship.

Instead of trying to reduce "leaving church" to the either/or action or agree/disagree opinion of individuals, chapters 1 and 2 together open up a wider moral vista of shifting stances toward religious institutions in light of personal spiritual beliefs seen as cultural convictions and moral judgments. Growing convictions of freedom of conscience and thinking for yourself are rooted in revivalist and republican traditions of American culture, argues chapter 3, rather than simply being suffused by the warm glow and Romantic resonance of self-expressive individualism today, which permeate the stories of chapter 2.

Chapter 3 illuminates these personal stories of spiritual change through a cultural conversation situated in social space and historical time. It unfolds through American religious institutions and ideals seen as a moral drama centered on *why* we have come to understand religious meaning and practice differently today, both in and out of church. How do overarching, underlying visions of selfhood and society come to be contested and shift shape as commonsense to guide the way we live and the way we pray, here and now? Only by reflecting on the contrasting cultural traditions of our shared moral visions and vocabularies can we make sense of such changes in what we feel and do, for example, in seeking to realize selfhood in sensitive spiritual touch with the moment, others, and nature. Only thus can we discern why congregations respond in kind or not, for example, when it comes to "putting belonging before believing and behaving," or reimagining what it means to ask, "From what and for what do we want to be saved?" This cultural conversation and moral dialogue span chapters 2 and 3, and they unfold through the congregational cases in chapters 4 and 5.

Interwoven with ethnography, cultural interpretation of the moral drama of American institutions frames the whole of this inquiry and leads to its conclusions. Chapter 6 weighs our overarching moral visions of quicksilver selfhood in spiritual community, and our underlying ideals of church, sect, and modern mysticism. It shows how their dynamic interplay shapes the continuity and change of American religion in a world of protean possibility and paradox, no longer united by biblical covenant or perfected by providential progress, yet no more divided by conflicts of individual freedom and fairness than bound by the interdependence of our common fate.

However enriched we grew as a people of plenty after World War II and however divided we have become through decades of economic inequality and political polarization since then, Americans continue to rehearse and contest this moral drama we share. As unique individuals with equal rights, we think for ourselves and pursue happiness in a free society. We grow up as doers and joiners who go out and get involved to make our dreams come true. We seek to live out our faith and find spiritual fulfillment to reintegrate religion with the authenticity of everyday life affirmed without doubt or despair. In this moral sense, "we" make up a cultural communion of all souls that spans religious denominations and traditions, not only an elect of all saints that marks off one sect from another. We the faithful inhabit religious institutions indebted to dissenting Protestants who conceived a church of come-outers gathered into a priesthood of all believers, no less than we the people inhabit a democracy indebted to revolutionary republicans who conceived the self-government of all citizens in a society devoted to voluntary association.

Survey data confirm that relatively few unchurched Americans see themselves as fervent atheists or strict agnostics. Instead, most still believe in God, or a "Higher Power of some sort," in predominantly personalized, immanent ways, and most still pray or commune with this Spirit in do-it-yourself practice along their own intimate paths. Exploring these varied rites and beliefs offers an apt point of departure for a much thicker, more nuanced intergenerational narrative of spiritual innovation as well as exodus and drift from mainline churches in particular since the 1960s. Such exploration promises deeper insight into why these changes have taken place. It yields no single recipe for church renewal, no silver bullet for church growth. It leads instead to much more specific examples of how flourishing communities of faith can embrace their own offspring by engaging their autonomy—and bring their spirit into the body of congregational life, not to grow its numbers but to inspire its communion among members one of another.

✤

STANDPOINT AND METHODS

The methods and questions that this moral and social inquiry pursues arise from a sociology of morality that couples interpretive sociology of culture with comparative philosophical and religious ethics to show how particular persons situated in social space and historical time make moral sense of their lives and their world, and how they do it within communities of shared discourse and practice.[11]

Conversations with more than two hundred persons shape this story, including eighty who took part in recorded interviews, sixty quoted in its pages, and uncounted others in and out of churches in Silicon Valley and metropolitan Atlanta, extending over six years of participant-observation fieldwork from 2017 to 2022. This ethnographic fieldwork concentrated on the four congregations featured in chapters 4 and 5 of this volume. It focused on their exemplary understanding and practice of engagement with young adults in worship, preaching, teaching, and a range of service projects, small groups, and big events—from weddings and funerals to film festivals and singles dances. This fieldwork also included more than a dozen other congregations as comparative cases tied into these intergenerational stories of religious upbringing and leaving church.

Most recorded interviews ran for two to three hours, some ran as short as an hour, and a few continued for as long as six hours at a single sitting. Many consisted of a single session, and some extended to one or more follow-up sessions, particularly those with parents and offspring (featured in chapter 2); and with key ministers and lay leaders (featured in chapters 4 and 5), some of them interviewed several times per year. Most interviews were conducted as one-on-one conversations. A handful were done with married couples, church colleagues, or co-pastors.

All the names of informants and interviewees in this book are pseudonyms, and any similarities of these names to actual persons are purely coincidental. In some cases, I excised or changed specific descriptive details to preclude personal identification, while profiles remain consistent in socially representative terms, for example in identifying a source as a youth minister, seniors minister, or lay leader of a congregation; or as a lawyer, manager, teacher, social worker, or psychotherapist. I asked all interviewees for, and was granted, recorded oral and written releases before interviews. I coded and keyed all interviews to actual names on lists held in confidence and stored separately from the interview tapes, digital files, and transcripts, according to standards for such ethnographic research overseen by Emory University's institutional review board, which approved this project.

NOTES

1. Jeffrey M. Jones, "U.S. Church Membership Falls Below Majority for First Time," Gallup Poll Social Series, March 29, 2021, http://www.news.gallup.com/poll/341963; Gregory A. Smith et al., "America's Changing Religious Landscape," Pew Research Center, May 12, 2015.

2. Robert N. Bellah, "Religious Evolution," *American Sociological Review* 29, no. 3 (1964): 358–74; Steven M. Tipton, "Social Differentiation and Moral Pluralism," in *Meaning and Modernity*, ed. Richard Madsen et al. (Berkeley: University of California Press, 2002), 15–40, 278–81; and Claude S. Fischer, *To Dwell among Friends* (Chicago: University of Chicago Press, 1982).

By July 4, 2022, COVID-19 had infected some 87 million Americans, according to the Centers for Disease Control and Prevention, and had taken the lives of 1,015,998—one in 330—leaving more than one in three Americans grieving the loss of a parent, grandparent, child, sibling, friend, colleague, or neighbor. See Jordan Allen et al., "Coronavirus in the U.S.: Latest Map and Case Count," *New York Times*, July 4, 2022; and Julie Bosman et al., "Who I Lost," *New York Times,* March 6, 2021. Net declines of in-person attendance and sunk costs of getting online during the COVID-19 pandemic compelled many churches to weigh hybrid options to continue providing online services, small groups, and outreach activities, reports Diana Kruzman in "Houses of Worship Grapple with the Future of their Online Services," *Religious News Service*, February 14, 2022. One in three US millennials tunes in to digital spiritual or religious activities at least monthly, but only one in twenty does so exclusively, reports Sarah Wilkins-LaFlamme, "Digital Religion among U.S. and Canadian Millennial Adults," *Review of Religious Research,* 64 (2022): 225–48.

3. Cf. Steven M. Tipton, *Getting Saved from the Sixties* (Berkeley: University of California Press, 1982); Richard Madsen, "The Archipelago of Faith," *American Journal of Sociology* 114, no. 5 (2009): 1263–1301; Duane F. Alwin, "Cohort Replacement and Changes in Parental Socialization Values," *Journal of Marriage and Family*, 52 (1990): 347–60; Michael Walzer, *Thick and Thin: Moral Argument at Home and Abroad* (Notre Dame, IN: University of Notre Dame Press, 1994); Robert Wuthnow, *After the Baby Boomers* (Princeton, NJ: Princeton University Press, 2007); and Christian Smith, *American Evangelicalism* (Chicago: University of Chicago Press, 1998).

4. Mark Chaves, *Congregations in America* (Cambridge, MA: Harvard University Press, 2004); Charles Taylor, *Modern Social Imaginaries* (Durham, NC: Duke University Press, 2004); and Charles Taylor, *A Secular Age* (Cambridge, MA: Harvard University Press, 2007). For formulating the need of organized religion to un-organize itself, I am indebted to an anonymous reader's review.

5. Cary Funk and Gregory A. Smith, "'Nones' on the Rise: One-in-Five Adults Have No Religious Affiliation," Pew Research Center, October 9, 2012, 23, survey questions 73a–g.

6. Tipton, *Getting Saved from the Sixties*, chs. 2–4; Robert N. Bellah, Richard Madsen, William M. Sullivan, Ann Swidler, Steven M. Tipton, *Habits of the Heart: Individualism and Commitment in American Life* (Berkeley: University of California

Press, 2008); Leigh Stein, "The Empty Religions of Instagram," *New York Times*, March 6, 2021.

7. Cf. Jim Davis and Michael Graham with Ryan P. Burge, *The Great Dechurching: Who's Leaving, Why Are They Going, and What Will It Take to Bring Them Back?* (Grand Rapids, MI: Zondervan, 2023); Jennifer M. McClure Haraway, *No Congregation Is an Island: How Faith Communities Navigate Opportunities and Challenges Together* (Lanham, MD: Rowman & Littlefield, 2023); Allen T. Stanton, *Reclaiming Rural: Building Thriving Rural Congregations* (Lanham, MD: Rowman & Littlefield, 2021); and related professional research on the model of consulting and publishing programs pioneered by the Alban Institute to aid mostly mainline congregations.

8. Luis Lugo et al., "Faith in Flux: Changes in Religious Affiliation in the U.S.," Pew Research Center, 2009; Cary Funk and Gregory A. Smith, "'Nones' on the Rise."

9. Michael Hout, "American Religion, All or Nothing at All," *Contexts* 16 (2017): 78–80; Michael Hout and Claude S. Fischer, "Why More Americans Have No Religious Preference: Politics and Generations," *American Sociological Review* 67 (2002): 165–90; Michael Hout and Claude S. Fischer, "Explaining Why More Americans Have No Religious Preference," *Sociological Science* 1 (2014): 423–47; Darren E. Sherkat, *Changing Faith: The Dynamics and Consequences of Americans' Shifting Religious Identities* (New York: NYU Press, 2014); Aaron Gullickson, "The Diverging Beliefs and Practices of the Religiously Affiliated and Unaffiliated in the United States," *Sociological Science* 5 (2018): 361–79.

10. Ryan P. Burge, *The Nones* (Minneapolis: Fortress Press, 2021), 95–122.

11. See Tipton, "Social Differentiation and Moral Pluralism"; Tipton, *Getting Saved from the Sixties*, chs. 1, 5; and Bellah et al., *Habits of the Heart*, chs. 2, 3.

Acknowledgments

For their sharp insight and good counsel in helping me shape this work through successive drafts, I am indebted to my longtime collaborators and friends Ann Swidler, Richard Madsen, and William Sullivan. I am likewise indebted to my Emory University colleagues, particularly to E. Brooks Holifield and Russell Richey, for their close critical reading of the penultimate draft. For their generous, vital support of this project, I thank Dean Jan Love of Candler School of Theology; and Chris Coble, Jessicah Duckworth, and their colleagues at the Lilly Endowment. For insightful assistance in researching this study I thank Kristyn Sessions. For expert aid in preparing the final manuscript I thank Ulrike Guthrie. For superb editing, I thank Richard Brown, Victoria Shi, Samuel Withers, their colleagues, and reviewers at Rowman & Littlefield Publishers. To the churchgoers, church leaders, and church leavers whose stories bring this book to life, I am most grateful. To Kristin, who nurtured this book while writing her own, I give thanks for sustaining our life together.

Chapter 1

Faith in Flux

Americans are leaving church. Over the past generation more and more US adults claim no religious affiliation, with the young leading the way.[1] Why so? Why have they left? Where have they gone, and what are they doing instead of attending worship and saying prayers, singing hymns and hearing sermons, confessing sins and creeds, sharing the bread of life and joy of fellowship? Taking a walk in the park, talking of love, or arguing politics. Going for a run, strumming a guitar, stretching deep in yoga class, or sitting still in meditation. Meeting friends for brunch in a neighborhood café. Lingering over coffee and the Sunday paper at home, turning on the game, or simply sleeping in.

Are the unchurched so different from their parents or predecessors of a generation ago? Are they indeed spiritual but not religious? Are they somehow better or worse for leaving church? Freer, truer, and more authentic? Or less responsible, conscientious, and caring? In terms of their own opinions and attitudes, elicited in polls and surveys this chapter probes, they are being true to themselves in leaving churches that fail to meet their genuine spiritual needs. Organized religion, they charge, too fervently pursues money, power, and politics. It imposes too many rules and claims too much truth in the name of God. Churches may do good for others, they concede, but you need not go to church to be a good person or raise good children. These charges may hit or miss the mark, as diverse churchgoers see it, but this exodus raises questions not only for religious leaders but for all Americans. Are we all better or worse off as a result? Are we richer in spiritual self-awareness and social tolerance or poorer in moral community and cultural capital? More open-minded or empty-hearted?

In this chapter, we will count the numbers of those leaving or staying in church, switching or returning. We will weigh the proportions of those in polls who agree with this or that reason, motive, or cause for doing so, with an eye to the actual complexity and variety of religious affiliation and disaffiliation in America today. In the following chapters, we will hear the voices of the unchurched telling their own stories in their own words, images, and visions of what it means to live a good life in a good society. Across generations they reflect on their religious upbringing at home and in childhood churches, their own spiritual journeys in and out of church, and how they are raising their children as believers but not belongers, both or neither. We will hear, too, from ministers and members of exemplary congregations on what leads young adults in and out of church, how churches can and should respond, and the promise and peril of what lies ahead.

RELIGIOUS NONES

Three in ten American adults now claim no religious affiliation, up from one in six a decade ago and one in a dozen in 1990, to rival the numbers of Roman Catholics and evangelical Protestants as the largest US religious groups. The quickening pace of this nearly fourfold increase in a generation comes mostly from a larger slice of each cohort identifying with "nothing in particular" by way of a religious tradition, institution, or body of worship. Led by adults under age thirty, "religious nones" in all include more than one in three millennials (born between 1981 and 1996), compared to one in eight of those leading the baby boom (born between 1946 and 1954) and one in twenty of those born in the 1930s.[2]

A third of self-identified political "liberals" declared themselves "nones" in 2012, compared to one in six "moderates" and one in twelve "conservatives." By 2019 one in three Democrats identified as "nones" and most Democrats reported attending religious services seldom or never, compared to only one in six Republicans identified as "nones" and most attending services at least monthly. Led by millennials, two-thirds of Americans now say they attend religious services only a few times a year or less. Just one-third say they attend monthly or more often, compared to half of Americans a decade ago.[3]

Fewer than half of Americans now belong to a congregation, down from two-thirds for much of the twentieth century, with most of the decline coming in the last decade or so in step with more adults reporting no religious identification. But even those who do identify with a particular faith are now less likely to belong to a congregation, leaving only two belongers for every three believers instead of three in four twenty years ago. Fewer than one in ten adults with "no religious preference" say they belong to a church.[4] One in four American adults now say they never attend services, compared to one in nine a generation ago, including almost all the "nones" who identify as "atheists" and "agnostics," and half who identify as "nothing in particular." The faithful attend church no less often, slowing gradual declines in overall rates of monthly attendance. But now there are fewer faithful in the population, as more unchurched young adults replace churchgoing members of older generations.[5]

THINK FOR YOURSELF

This trend arises in the 1960s, when politically liberal young adults born early in the baby boom grew much less likely than earlier cohorts to attend traditional religious services, and much more likely to adopt countercultural ideals of authentic self-expression and greater personal liberty to "be yourself" and "do your own thing." Tracing lines of causal influence linking political and religious identity through ideology or opinion can be complicated and contested. But deeper changes in moral vision and practical virtue have clearly led younger Americans away from the pews. Shifts in our institutionally shared sense of selfhood, social relationship, and way of life have inspired successive generations to heed spreading spiritual convictions of personal autonomy and freedom of choice in religious practice, belief, and belonging. You can be counted as a religious "none," if you so choose, and now you are freer to say so in public without affirming atheism or denying spirituality.[6]

Since World War II more parents have raised their children to "think for yourself" instead of obeying authority.[7] Although younger Americans continue to "believe in God or a higher power," they have grown more convinced that individuals should form their own religious beliefs independently of religious institutions. They should express and fulfill themselves spiritually instead of keeping the faith by upholding denominational loyalties and orthodox creeds. The unchurched grow more distant from organized religion, seen as a cornerstone of dutiful moral authority and practice at odds with the spiritual freedom to be yourself and its political parallels.[8] At the same time, they grow less trusting that other institutions—job markets, colleges, business, and government—will reliably and fairly heed their voices, serve their interests, and reward their efforts. Unchurched Americans who come from families with weak religious attachments and low participation to begin with more often identify as "nothing in particular" in terms consistent with their looser connections to school, work, civic involvement, and political activity than do self-identified atheists and agnostics as well as churchgoers.[9]

WHY LEAVE?

Why do people choose to leave church? Which people? Which churches? Once the answer seemed simple. More educated young adults, more single than married with children, more cosmopolitan than local, and more countercultural than conventional. Now it's not so either-or. Religious "nones" continue to be concentrated among educated, liberal single White males under thirty, notably the tenth of American adults who identify as atheists or agnostics. But the rising ranks of "nones" now prove more diverse, especially the fifth of all adults who identify as "nothing in particular." They account for at least three in five of all "nones," split evenly between women and men. They count as the fastest-growing US religious group over the past decade, as White Protestants and Catholics in particular struggled to hold their own. They more often include Blacks and Hispanics as well as Whites, those over fifty as well as under, those without college degrees as well as graduates, those earning less and more than the median wage, and residents of the South and Midwest as well as the West and Northeast.[10]

The distinctive profile of African Americans underscores these clear generational trends. Black millennials tend to be *less* religious than their elders by standard measures. But they remain significantly *more* religious than other Americans of their generation. They follow national trends of a fourfold increase of "nones" over the past generation but at lower levels. Only 5 percent of Black Americans versus 7 percent of Whites said they were unaffiliated in 1980, only 12 percent versus 16 percent in 2007, and only 21 percent versus 27 percent in 2020. Most Black "nones" describe themselves as "nothing in particular," with only one in a hundred identifying as an atheist and two as agnostic, compared to 3 and 4 percent of all "nones" in the United States. Indeed, three in four Black "nones" say religion plays at least a somewhat important role in their lives. Nearly half say religion is *very* important. That triples the sixth of all US "nones" who say so, and it equals the half of mainline Protestants who say so.[11]

While men still prove likelier than women to leave church, and Whites likelier than Blacks or Hispanics, we can ask nonetheless if a morally coherent constellation of cultural conditions informs the choice to leave church *and* deem oneself a "none." Do these conditions underlie both continuity and contrasts in social circumstances, even if no one cause determines this choice, no one motive inspires it, and no one reason justifies it?[12]

More than two-thirds of those who leave church agree they "just gradually drifted away" from organized religion, rather than breaking away all at once from a strong but conflicted institutional attachment. Many report spotty church attendance and weak religious upbringing in their families of origin, and they note thinning religious commitment in their teens. Most of those who decided to leave their childhood faith say they did so before reaching age twenty-four. Most who returned or switched to another denomination or faith tradition did so before reaching age thirty-six, often while marrying and raising children of their own.[13]

This jibes with overall declines in church attendance since the 1970s in step with more young adults postponing marriage and parenting, as women advance their education, careers, and income to support themselves and dual-earner households. Fewer are marrying in their twenties, and fewer still are bearing children early on. Millennials are having fewer children, and having them later, as they face greater challenges to finish school, start careers, afford housing, and achieve financial independence in a riskier economy with fewer good jobs at living wages in hollowed-out middle-class labor markets.[14]

Fewer millennial parents return to the fold than parents in earlier cohorts of church dropouts, fewer single parents return than married parents, and fewer parents raised without religion join up now than before. But religious participation remains significantly higher among parents with young children than individuals or couples without children. This proves true in the overall population, among those who continue to claim a religious preference, and those who belong to a congregation. You are only half as likely to identify as a "none" if you are married with children than if you are unmarried without children. You are just as likely to be a "none" if you are a woman or a man without children, twice as likely as the one "none" among every five mothers.[15]

About half of American adults had left their childhood community of faith by 2010, if you count those who switch faiths or switch denominations within a faith tradition, those who return to their original faith community, and those who join a faith community after an unchurched upbringing. Their reasons vary widely, depending on where they come from and go to. Those who switched are the most likely to say they did so because of changed circumstances or family reasons. They married someone from a different religious background, moved to a new community, or had children reaching school age or leaving home for college. Most report that their "spiritual needs were not being met" beforehand and that afterward they had "found a religion they liked more," especially its services and style of worship.[16]

By contrast, less than half of those who left church cite unmet spiritual needs sharply spurring them to leave, and few report finding a better congregation. Most say they "stopped believing in the religion's teaching," even though they continue to believe in God, albeit more often as a nonpersonal "Higher Power of some sort" than a personal Lord and Savior, biblical Creator and Redeemer, or moral Lawgiver and Judge. They drifted away from common prayer, though many continue to pray on their own, albeit less often than churchgoers. They still believe in an afterlife, though less firmly than churchgoers.[17]

In belief and practice, the unchurched prove to be much more heterogenous and individualized than steady churchgoers. They are less likely to profess the same creed, recite the same prayers, or rehearse the same rites, and more likely to find God in the woods than in the pews. Conversely, those who identify with "nothing in particular" prove more diverse than self-identified atheists and agnostics by race, gender, education, and politics. They feel more open toward organized religion, and less set in rejecting it. They are more likely to attend church at least a few times yearly, and to share "new age" spiritual beliefs such as reincarnation with many mainline churchgoers. They prove likelier over time to switch their identification to a faith tradition, with one in six choosing to identify as a Christian between 2010 and 2014 and one in twelve choosing another faith.[18]

Three in four "nones" criticize the "religious institutions, practices, and people" they left behind, especially those they found morally "hypocritical/judgmental/insincere." But few single out any one negative experience or incident in church as the reason they left. Instead they found religious organizations "too focused on rules, not spirituality," with leaders who "want money/power, not truth/spirituality." They reject churchly claims to binding moral authority or fully revealed truth, holding instead that "many religions are partly true, none completely true."[19]

CHANGING GENERATIONS IN A CHANGING PUBLIC SQUARE

"Religiosity" has declined among individuals in the United States over the past two generations. But it's measured not so much by lost belief in God or surging secularism as indexes of lower doctrinal adherence, congregational membership, weekly worship attendance, and denominational affiliation rooted in the biblical scripturalism, Reformed congregationalism, and evangelical revivalism of dissenting Protestant traditions and institutions that ground America's history as the first new nation without an "established" state church or rule by divine right. The ranks of "nones" have grown since 1990 and grown more widely since 2007. But net declines in US churchgoing have continued to concentrate among White Catholics and Protestants, both evangelical and mainline, signaled by aging denominations and advancing in step with demographic changes led by mainliners yet eventually followed by evangelicals, too, marrying later and bearing fewer children.[20]

During the 1970s more than half of baby boomers in their twenties dropped out of church in unprecedented numbers, but many of these dropouts returned in middle age, especially those married with children. By contrast, members of Gen X and millennials prove much likelier to stay out of church and stay childless, while older Americans across cohorts prove only somewhat more likely to identify as "nones" since 1990. In an aging society this yields a modal age of thirty years old among "nones" today instead of tweny-three years old in the 1970s, compared to a modal age of fifty-eight years old for evangelical Protestants and sixty-seven years old for mainline Protestants today. Church growth and decline, in sum, reflect larger demographic changes in the composition of the US population brought by generational replacement and successive waves of immigration since 1970.[21]

Church growth and decline also reflect structural changes in American public life. A more densely crowded, formally organized, and fiercely contested public square commingles more politicized churches and parachurch advocacy groups with more religiously charged parties and paraparty political-action groups. This crowding and polarization blur bright lines of church-state separation, and they cloud the coherence of religious authority tied more tightly to political power. The partisan public presence of institutional religion on the rise triggers its decline in personal identification among those caught in the middle, as changes in religious and political institutions combine to spark more ideological strife and moral conflict.[22]

Racial, religious, and ideological identities have grown more aligned with Democratic and Republican partisan identities, especially among White "conservative evangelicals" in the GOP. They comprise nearly half of GOP voters, while "nones" make up almost a third of Democratic voters. In 1972, half of all weekly churchgoers were Democrats. Now only a quarter are. In the 1970s conservative White Protestants leaned Republican more than did religious "nones" by about 10 percentage points. Forty years later they did so by more than 60 points. Four in five White evangelicals voted for Donald Trump in 2016, and three in four religious "nones" voted against him. Partisan identities in turn have grown stronger and more sharply negative toward the opposing party, along with rising racial resentment among White Republican voters. In 1986 both parties shared equally in White racial resentment. Today it proves 40 percent more widespread in the GOP, as Blacks since 1992 doubled their share of the electorate from one to two of every seven voters, largely in the Democratic Party, while working-class Whites continued to move to the GOP, most notably in the South and the Midwest.[23]

Particularly among younger, more educated, and more moderate or liberal-leaning Americans raised in culturally conservative churches, the rise of the Religious Right and more polarized party politics have unleashed a backlash against religious institutions and an exodus from them.[24] By 2018 half of religious "nones" reported they left church because "I don't like the positions churches take on social/political issues." Up sharply since 2010, the numbers of these defectors rival those who "question a lot of religious teachings" among "nones" identified as "nothing in particular." Half of "nones" call themselves "liberal," compared to a quarter of churchgoers. Their self-identification is broadly cultural, not just partisan political. Generational turnover has widened the ranks of unchurched Americans marching under the banner of personal autonomy and individual responsibility, not only in the spheres of sex and drugs or courtship and marriage, but in advancing spiritual freedom of choice and self-expression over binding duties to keep the faith and go to church.[25]

SPIRITUAL AND/OR RELIGIOUS

Moral shifts in personal values and attitudes imply deeper cultural changes in shared visions of virtue and exemplary ways of life in a free and fair society. These changes underlie claims professed by many unaffiliated adults raised in both mainline and conservative churches to be "spiritual but not religious" in belief and practice that reach beyond the pews. In this light they think of themselves as "religious persons," even if they do not show up on church rolls or in worship services. Unaffiliated *believers* outnumber unaffiliated *unbelievers* by two or three to one among the quarter of all US adults who identify as "nones," much as self-identified "agnostics" outnumber "atheists" among them. Rather than championing unbelief in the streets of the secular city, the unchurched typically seek spiritual meaning and moral commitment in a home of their own freed from tutelary religious authority and dutiful creedal orthodoxy.[26]

At the same time, most of the "spiritual but not religious" quarter of all Americans in fact identify with a religious group, a third of them Protestant and a sixth Catholic. Their numbers include some recruits from the ranks of those who call themselves "*both* spiritual *and* religious" and still comprise half of all Americans. At comparably rising rates over the past decade, however, Americans both in and out of church report feeling "a deep sense of spiritual peace and well-being" and a "deep sense of wonder about the universe." This shift in sensibility suggests an openness to spiritual experience and insight spreading among Americans in and out of the pews, led by more educated and culturally liberal cohorts since the 1960s but now widely diffused across the middle of US society. This marks a more experiential, expressive, and individualized inflection of religiosity rather than a repudiation of religion. It shows up in positive correlation between standard measures of religiosity and self-identification as a "spiritual person" rather than a negative correlation between religious faith and spirituality. More than two-thirds of all Americans say they are "very spiritual" or "moderately spiritual," compared to only four in ten of all "nones" but seven in ten unaffiliated believers.[27]

The spiritually awakened, in and out of church, can thus criticize organized religion for its spiritual failures, even as most churchgoers profess themselves *both* spiritual *and* religious in their faith, and many of the unchurched affirm their own personal spirituality but withhold their institutional loyalty from organized religion. Among "spiritual but not religious" Americans out of church, "spiritual" serves as a contrast term to organized religion per se, opposing authentic selfhood to hypocritical institutions. Among churchgoers, however, it serves to underscore their personal commitment, above and beyond the low threshold of merely routine religious observance, to uplifting practices of prayer, contemplation, study, service, and witness. These range from charismatic tongue-speaking in the Spirit or evangelical devotion to Jesus as personal Lord and Savior to daily mindfulness meditation practiced intently by mainline Protestants, Ignatian exercises by Catholics, or kabbalah by Jews.[28]

Among spreading circles of healthcare professionals attuned to popular usage, spirituality is "the way individuals seek ultimate meaning, purpose, connection, value, or transcendence," including organized religion but extending "well beyond to include ways of finding ultimate meaning by connecting, for example, to family, community, or nature." As spiritual awareness spreads across the spectrum of American religiosity, it inflects the meaning of religious beliefs and practices in substance by multiplying and dividing the varieties of spiritual experience and the ways individuals seek "ultimate meaning," transcendent or not.[29]

Almost all "Sunday stalwart" traditional Christians say they are *both* spiritual *and* religious, but only a quarter hold new age beliefs, compared to six in ten US adults overall. At the same time nearly all "diversely devout" adults say they are both spiritual and religious, and they hold new age beliefs, yet they rarely attend church. By contrast, two in three "religion resisters" say they are spiritual but not religious, yet almost all hold new age beliefs and almost never attend church. Only one in five "solidly secular" adults identify as spiritual, and almost none say they are religious or hold new age beliefs or ever attend church.[30]

However advocated, enacted, or betrayed, such claims to spiritual autonomy and authenticity frame more specific criticism by "nones" of religious institutions: They "focus too much on rules," act "too concerned with money and power," and get "too involved with politics," while failing to "meet the spiritual needs" of their people. So charge two-thirds of "nones." Yet nearly half of churchgoers agree! They have kept pace with religious "nones" in more often reporting their own spiritual experiences of a deep sense of wonder about the universe, while outpacing the "nones" in personal feelings of spiritual peace and well-being.[31]

On the other hand, three in four "nones" agree with churchgoers that bodies of worship also bring people together, strengthen community bonds, and play a key role in helping the poor and needy. But relatively few "nones," compared to Americans overall and churchgoers in particular, think it very important to belong to such a "community with shared values and beliefs." Why not? Don't churches serve to "protect and strengthen morality"? Only half of "nones" agree, compared to four in five churchgoers and three in four of all Americans. Do individuals need communities of worship to feel connected to God, nature, or spiritual energy? Most "nones" say they feel so connected on their own, and they often think on their own about life's meaning and purpose. Do we need to believe in God to be moral and have good values? No, say most US adults today, including five in six "nones." Two in three mainline Protestants concur on no such need to believe, but only one in three White evangelicals and one in two Catholics agrees.[32]

CHURCHES PRO AND CON

Most Americans say churches and other religious organizations have a positive impact on the way things are going in the country. But only one in three "nones" agree, along with four in ten of those who remain affiliated but seldom if ever attend services, by contrast to three in four weekly attenders. Liberal Democrats prove likelier to say the impact of churches is negative than it's positive. By contrast, conservative and moderate Democrats favor churches by two to one, and three in four conservative Republicans agree. Are political and cultural liberals simply emptying out the pews? Hardly. Most Americans who now call themselves "nones" seldom attended when they still identified with a church, and few of them identified strongly then.[33]

Americans who claim a "strong" religious identification attend services as often today as forty years ago. Regular attenders persist, while those who once attended occasionally now attend rarely if at all. One in four American adults never attends church now, compared to one in nine a generation ago. But nearly one in two still attends occasionally, every month or so, down only a bit from 1986 to 2016. Amid demographic change and generational turnover, in short, some churches are emptying out and others are declining in numbers, particularly of young adults. But not all. Others are growing and holding their own.[34]

To many leaders of mainline churches, especially those committed to witnessing for peace and justice in accord with progressive causes, political backlash against the religious right seems paradoxical if not perverse as a reason for rejecting liberal Protestantism. What would you have us do that we are not already doing to reach out to our own children, raised in the church and now absent from it? So they ask in response to advice that they diversify their message to appeal to alienated liberals who still believe in God and still hunger for communities committed to the needy, the peacemakers, and the planet, as opposed to churches backing the religious right against abortion, gay marriage, and gun control. Should churches keep out of political matters? Two in three "nones" think so, and six in ten White mainline Protestants and Catholics agree. By contrast, six in ten White evangelicals believe instead that churches should "express their views" in the public square, even if they should not endorse political candidates or crown the president as King Cyrus.[35]

Few "nones" see themselves as fervently atheistic or anticlerical. But neither were they very active church members when they still claimed church affiliation. Most say they still pray and commune with God on their own, and they trust their spiritual awareness or personal faith can thrive beyond church pews, among heartfelt friends and like-minded fellow travelers in the wider world. Will that prove true? Will their awareness grow without participation in spiritual community? Will their personal faith flourish without congregational practice and formation? According to surveys since 2000, belief in God and the afterlife has declined among the unchurched, although their frequency of personal prayer has held steady. Meanwhile churchgoers have come to pray more often, believe in God no less surely, and trust in the afterlife more firmly. Even more reason, argue mainline church leaders, to widen outreach to the unchurched, especially those who identify as "nothing in particular," and to strengthen religious formation and education for marginal church members and their children in particular. These leaders urge vigorous congregational action now to hold onto their own, and to build on hopes that youthful church dropouts will drop back in when they mature and settle down, even if they do not get married with children.[36]

LOST AND FOUND

Will those who have left church return to the fold? Some do now, but certainly not all. One in six of those who identify as "nothing in particular" returns to claim Christian affiliation over time, but barely four in a hundred agnostics and atheists do so. Will more return as the ranks of the unaffiliated expand? That's possible, as Americans continue to move in and out of church, but it's unlikely without a great revival or reversal, judge analysts from familiar facts. Nearly four in ten young adults today identify as "none," four times more than a generation ago, at rates rising with each new cohort, albeit holding steady so far between younger millennials and members of Generation Z (born since 1996). Millennials are two times more likely to leave church than baby boomers, and less likely to drop back into church in middle age even if they marry and raise children. Nine in ten "nones" grew up in families that they report as not so strong in church membership or active in church participation. These young adults are half-again likelier to leave church if their parents divorce or do not share the same faith, two growing trends over the past generation. Meanwhile two in three Americans raised in unchurched households remain unaffiliated today, compared to one in three in the 1970s, as unchurched young adults increase in number and grow likelier to marry each other instead of a faithful spouse who leads them back to the fold.[37]

Why return to church? To grow closer to God, answer the faithful, particularly a personal God in whom we can love and be loved. To live a good life in the light of God's grace, word, and will, within a community of moral formation and coherence we can share with our children and our parents. Such answers to this question prove apt among churchgoers and arguable among "nones," insofar as they differ over premises in principle and outcomes in practice. Only one in three "nones" agrees that it is important for children to be brought up in a religion so they can learn good values, by contrast to eight in ten mainline Protestants and Catholics, and nine in ten evangelical Protestants. Only one in five "nones" agrees that it is necessary to believe in God to be moral and have good values, compared to six in ten White evangelical Protestants and Catholics, and eight in ten Black Protestants, albeit only four in ten White mainline Protestants. Only one in four "nones" believes in a personal God, while three in eight believe in an impersonal force in the universe, and one in three does not believe in God at all.[38]

Most unchurched Americans answer "no" to polls that ask if religion is personally important in their lives and whether it does more good than harm in society. This leaves less than a quarter of the unaffiliated as "apatheists," who feel personally apathetic or indifferent to organized religion but recognize its social benefits. It leaves less than a fifth among them as "unattached believers" who affirm that religion is personally important to them. Like those who identify as "nothing in particular," instead of atheists or agnostics, most of these unattached believers attend worship at least a few times a year, believe in a personal God, and often "think about God."[39]

Although only one in five unattached believers says she is currently seeking to join a religious community or congregation, seven in ten agree that children should be brought up with religion so they can learn good values, and half agree that it's necessary to believe in God to be moral and have good values. Compared to half of "nones" overall, three in four unattached believers say they still feel a personal connection to religion as part of their family history, ethnic background, or cultural heritage, even if they no longer identify with a given denomination or feel any need to return to their childhood church to reconcile with their past.[40]

Will the mainline churches reach out further to their unaffiliated alums to try to bring them back to the fold, itself remade by actively embracing their return? However exceptional in their circumstances or striking in their success, some exemplary congregations can be found doing just that. They reach out to embrace culturally liberal young adults living and believing on their own.They draw them back to the fold as singles in search of friendship and community, not only as couples on the way to marry and raise children. Exemplary congregations also embrace more intently and attentively their youthful members as they enter adulthood and weigh their spiritual choices. They engage the unaffiliated who identify as "nothing in particular" with more feel for those in need of social support, communal involvement, or help at home with childcare or eldercare.

At the same time, church leaders need to keep in mind the rising ranks of the unchurched and their intramarriage, the widening range of spiritual practices and their social settings beyond the pews, and declining conversion among Americans raised without religion when they come of age and form families of their own. These trends promise to make it even more challenging for many churches to reach the unchurched in the future than they find it is today.[41]

ON THE THRESHOLD

Americans in and out of church both agree and disagree on what is good and bad in organized religion. They take distinct moral stances that nonetheless overlap on key issues. They share underlying logics of argument and modes of discourse, for example, in counterposing congregations that impose extrinsic "rules" to those that meet intrinsic "spiritual needs." Churched and unchurched Americans do not turn out to be mutually exclusive, homogenous social groups holding internally consistent moral views that contradict each other. Many members of each group switch back and forth, particularly in their twenties and thirties. One in four of those who identified as "nothing in particular" in 2010 claimed a religious affiliation by 2014. A "liminal" fifth of each group switch from year to year between identifying themselves as religious or nonreligious, churched or unchurched, while they straddle the threshold of a given religious tradition or denomination. At the same time, four in ten Americans who think of themselves as "spiritual but not religious" turn out to be church-affiliated, two in five of them Protestant and one in five of them Catholic. In fact, almost half of "SBNR" survey respondents say they pray every day, including one in five of the unchurched along with two in three churchgoers.[42]

What are we to make of such ambivalent attitudes, inconsistent views, and mixed behaviors? They belie conventional either-or distinctions made between being religious or not, based on definition of an individual's religious "identity" in terms of their choosing to identify with this or that denomination or tradition—Protestant, Catholic, Jewish, or something else?—with “no religion” or “none” typically offered as the residual alternative in a choice forced by standard survey questions. So “liminals” emerge only across successive surveys, confirming gradual changes in American religiosity by contrast to the seven in ten Americans who more consistently call themselves religious. But liminals also reveal that those who move back and forth to count themselves either in or out of church account for much of the statistical “rise of the nones,” along with the one in ten Americans who more consistently chooses “no religion.”[43]

Religious identification has indeed been falling over the past generation. But this decline is not unilinear or unilateral. Liminals remain more likely than not to identify with a religion. They make up a third of those brought up with no religion, and they account for a quarter of those from nonreligious families who identify as religious once they reach adulthood.[44] Liminals sit “in between” consistently nonreligious Americans, who typically identify as atheists or agnostics, and their consistently religious counterparts, who typically score high on conventional (and conventionally evangelical) indicators of religiosity. They believe in God without doubt, believe in the Bible as the literal word of God, and regularly attend weekly worship services.[45]

Liminals raised in mainline Protestant denominations are *less* likely than conservative Protestants or Catholics to consistently claim a religious identity. This suggests links between liminality and the decline of denominationalism, particularly among mainline Protestants more often intermarried across denominational lines and less often catechized within any given confession. While conventionally marginal members of religious organizations continue to claim a religious identity with minimal participation, liminals typically continue minimal participation while giving up such self-identification. They move in step with a normative cultural shift over the past generation away from denominational loyalty and doctrinal orthodoxy toward personal autonomy in choosing one’s own religious outlook and spiritual path.[46] They overlap in belief and belonging with those who identify as “nothing in particular,” including the one in four who shifts or returns over time to a faith tradition, and the one in six who comes to identify as a newborn or reborn Christian. They neither embrace conventionally organized religion nor reject religion itself.[47]

WHAT LIES AHEAD

Can we find deeper cultural dynamics and thicker moral narratives within families across generations to make more sense of these modal changes in spiritual and religious self-understanding without ignoring their social variation and complication? To that task we now turn. We will look first at intergenerational narratives of religious formation and upbringing, spiritual awakening and exploration, which span stories of conversion and breakthrough, doubt and drift, return and rebirth. Then we will probe further to interpret the moral meaning and arc of these changes.

We will focus on most but not all the unchurched, by concentrating on those not so far from church doors. They remain friends of the church if no longer family members of a congregation. They are believers if not belongers, spiritually open and attuned if not actively seeking an organized body of worship. They are church visitors and occasional attenders, prayerful and faithful in their own diverse ways, however selective or relaxed in outlook and practice, rather than coolly indifferent, fervently atheistic, or strictly agnostic. Almost none of them attend weekly worship or take an active part in church groups. But many say they pray daily. Most believe in God, heaven, and hell, even if they doubt you need to believe in God to be moral. Three in four say they are spiritual, and one in two say they are religious.[48]

They are not necessarily those most likely to turn around and turn into staunch members of a congregation or come right back to the churches of their childhood. But they can tell us more fully how and why they came to leave church, where they stand now, and what kind of life in spiritual community they look for and yearn for along the way ahead.

NOTES

1. On the definition and usage of "leaving church" and "unchurched" here and below to refer to varieties of religious disaffiliation and non-affiliation specified by shifting categories of classification in different surveys over decades—including "no religion, nones, nothing in particular, agnostics, atheists, liminals, marginals, nominals, spirituals, unattached believers, secularists, and rejectionists," by contrast to terms of "religious affiliation, attendance, participation, membership, preference, identification, orientation, and belief." See the preface, and the endnotes below detailing the categories used in each survey cited, particularly notes 2–7, 9–21, 24–25, 36–39, 42–48.

2. In 2021 some 29 percent of US adults identified with "no religion," up from 16 percent in 2007, 19 percent in 2011, and 23 percent in 2016, reports Gregory A. Smith, "About Three-in-Ten U.S. Adults are Now Religiously Unaffiliated," Pew Research Center, December 14, 2021, 4–10. Between 1990 and 2000, the proportion of all Americans reporting they preferred "no religion" doubled from 7 percent, its level for about 20 years, to a record 14 percent in the General Social Survey (GSS); and from 1987 to 2012, it tripled from 7 to 20 percent at an average rate of increase of one-half of one percentage point per year, sustained over 25 years, while the percentage in each cohort rose 4.1 percentage points, implying generational succession at the root of two-thirds of the increased tendency to claim no religion, based on

cohort differences rather than a period trend, according to Michael Hout and Claude S. Fischer, "Explaining Why More Americans Have No Religious Preference: Political Backlash and Generational Succession, 1987–2012," *Sociological Science* 1, 2014: 423–47, especially 423–28 and 442–44. Among those born in the 1980s with a religious upbringing 22 percent claimed "no religion" in 2012, compared to 14 percent of those born twenty years earlier, and only 4 percent of those born fifty years earlier in the 1930s. Correlations between political and religious self-identification strengthen from 1987 to 2012, with "nones" rising from 18 percent to 36 percent among "liberals," from 6 to 18 percent among "moderates," and from 4 to 7 percent among "conservatives," according to Hout and Fischer 2014, 424–27, 442. GSS data show the ranks of "nones" exceeding 10 percent of all US adults by 1996, 15 percent by 2006, and 20 percent by 2014 to rival the ranks of Catholics and evangelicals alike by 2018, reports Ryan P. Burge, *The Nones: Where They Came From, Who They Are, and Where They Are Going* (Minneapolis: Fortress Press, 2021), 2, 28–31, while noting that GSS calculation of "nones" as 23.7 percent of the US population in 2018, by contrast to 31.3 percent calculated by the Cooperative Congressional Election Study (CCES) and 26 percent calculated by Pew Research Center, stems from broadening the unaffiliated category from "no religion" as the sole GSS response to "nothing in particular" or "agnostic" or "atheist," as do CCES and Pew surveys.

3. Religious "nones" among Democrats and Democratic-leaning voters rise from 20 percent to 34 percent between 2009 and 2019, while the share attending services a few times a year or less rises from 52 percent to 61 percent, compared to Republican "nones" up from only 10 percent to 16 percent, and infrequent attenders up from only 38 percent to 45 percent; while 62 percent of all self-reported Christians continue to attend at least monthly in 2019 as in 2009, but 64 percent of millennials attend less often, reversing the majority of monthly attenders (52 to 47 percent) in 2009, according to Gregory A. Smith et al., "In U.S., Decline of Christianity Continues at Rapid Pace," Pew Research Center, October 2019, 6–16, 20–21. But monthly church attendance on average reported by all Americans drops by only 14 percent from 1972 to 2018, and by just 7.8 percent among all churched Americans, while religious "nones" rise 18 percent, according to GSS data analyzed by Burge, *The Nones*, 57, 113–14, showing gradual declines in church attendance lagging and only loosely linked to more sharply declining religious affiliation, although 93 percent of agnostics and 96 percent of atheists "never/seldom" attend church, while half of "nothing in particulars" never attend, a quarter seldom attend, a tenth attend yearly, and another tenth attend monthly or more often.

4. US church membership held steady at 70 percent of adults or higher from 1937 through 1976, dipping to 68 percent on average through the 1990s, then dropping by a fifth, with most of that decline occurring since 2008 in step with declining religious identification, although religious identifiers are now less likely congregational "belongers" than before (led by millennials at 57 percent vs. Generation X and boomers at 65 percent or more), and belongers are now slightly less likely to attend, according to Jeffrey M. Jones, "U.S. Church Membership Down Sharply in Past Two Decades," Gallup Poll, April 18, 2018, 2–7.

5. Gregory A. Smith, "About Three-In-Ten U.S. Adults," Pew, 2021, reports indicators of personal religious belief, practice, and attitude showing relatively little falloff compared to sharp declines in religious preference, particularly among those who identify as "nothing in particular," since most come from families already marginal to organized religion, and inactive if not indifferent to congregational participation. Yet now they feel freer to declare themselves as "nones," according to Claude S. Fischer, "Declaring You're a 'None'" August 19, 2013, 1–5, at http://madeinamericathebook.com; and Claude S. Fischer, "Latest News on 'No Religion,'" October 13, 2014, 1–6, at http://madeinamericathebook.com. Both the ambiguous status of "nones" and the variety of survey questions posed to ascertain it underlie its inexact measurement: Gallup counted 21 percent of Americans as "nones" in 2021 and GSS counted 23.7 percent in 2018, based on their agreement with the sole response option of "no religion," while Pew counted 26 percent and CCES counted 31.3 percent in 2018 based on a broader choice of multiple response options, including "nothing in particular" or "atheist" or "agnostic," as noted by Ryan P. Burge and Perry Bacon Jr., "It's Not Just Young White Liberals Who Are Leaving Religion," April 16, 2021, at https://fivethirtyeight.com.

6. On the causal interplay of religious and political identity, see Michael Hout and Claude Fischer, "Explaining Why More Americans Have No Religious Preference," 2014. Cf. Michele Margolis, *From Politics to the Pews: How Partisanship and the Political Environment Shape Religious Identity* (Chicago: University of Chicago Press, 2018); and Aaron Gullickson, "The Diverging Beliefs and Practices of the Religiously Affiliated and Unaffiliated in the United States," *Sociological Science*, 5 (2018): 361–79. Also see Michael Hout, "American Religion, All or Nothing at All," *Contexts* 16 (2017): 78–80; Hout and Fischer, "Why More Americans Have No Religious Preference: Politics and Generations," *American Sociological Review*, 67 (2002): 165–90; and Fischer, "Declaring You're a 'None,'" and "Latest News on 'No Religion," stressing that most "nones" remain unaffiliated believers, and citing 2006–2012 biannual GSS panel data to show liberal cultural-political shifts rising in favor of personal autonomy and freer "lifestyle morality" (premarital sex, homosexuality, marijuana) *prior* to cohort declines in religious affiliation, and making these declines much more likely. For evidence that self-identification as a "none" and as "spiritual but not religious" result partly but not only or entirely from political backlash against the Religious Right, see Ruth Braunstein, "A Theory of Political Backlash: Assessing the Religious Right's Effect on the Religious Field," *Sociology of Religion* (November 2021): 1–31.

7. Generational survey data and studies of socialization agree that the spread of higher education, professional problem-solving, and white-collar work rewards critical thinking and interpersonal initiative over following orders and factory-floor routines in blue-collar labor. On related postwar value shifts from obeying authority toward personal autonomy and "thinking for yourself," see Melvin Kohn, "Social Class and Parental Values: Another Confirmation of a Relationship," *American Sociological* Review 41, 1976: 538–45; and Daniel R. Miller and Guy E. Swanson, *The Changing American Parent* (Wiley, 1958); as elaborated by Duane Alwin, "Cohort Replacement and Changes in Parental Socialization Values," *Journal of Marriage and*

Family, 52 (1990): 347–60; and as applied by Hout and Fischer 2014, 433–37, 443, to interpret some 70 percent of each cohort born after 1950 valuing personal autonomy over obedience, compared to 60 percent accepting recreational sex and drugs on countercultural grounds, and only 10–20 percent rejecting God and the Bible, thereby favoring changing norms and lifestyle ideals of autonomy over secularization as root causes of declining religious affiliation in response to political polarization over the past generation. Also see Jeffrey Arnett and Lene Arnett, "A Congregation of One: Individualized Religious Beliefs among Emerging Adults," *Journal of Adolescent Research* 17, no. 5 (September 2002): 451–67. Seventy percent of White evangelical parents say it's extremely important or very important to them that their children share their religious beliefs, compared to only 8 percent of unchurched parents, 29 percent of White non-evangelical Protestants, 35 percent of Catholics, and 53 percent of Black Protestant parents; with only one in six of all parents stressing shared religious beliefs as extremely important, while two in three stressed their children growing up to be "honest and ethical" adults, according to Pew Research Center, "Parenting in America Today," January 24, 2023, 9–10.

8. On more Americans convinced that individuals should form their own religious beliefs independently of religious institutions, parents, or other influences, see George Gallup Jr., and James Castelli, *The People's Religion: American Faith in the 90's* (Macmillan, 1989). Since the 1960s more ideologically polarized parties have called conservatives to respect authority, defend "law and order," and stand by "traditional values," while urging liberals to embrace "pluralism, diversity, and choice" for the sake of mutual tolerance and social inclusion with personal autonomy and equal rights for all. See Marc J. Hetherington and Jonathan D. Weiler, *Authoritarianism and Polarization in American Politics* (Cambridge, UK: Cambridge University Press, 2009); and Thomas B. Edsall, "The Contract with Authoritarianism," *New York Times*, April 5, 2018.

9. "Nones" who "believe in God or a higher power" tripled from 4 percent to 12 percent of adults between 1988 and 2012, according to GSS data analyzed by Hout and Fischer, "Explaining Why," 2014, 428–38, while "nones" who do *not* believe in God increased from only 2 percent to 6 percent. Since the 14-point increase in "no religious preference" is offset by an 11 percent drop in "not-strong" and "somewhat-strong" religious preferences, but only a 3 percent drop in "strong" preferences, "nones" emerge mainly from those with weak religious attachments to begin with, leaving the strongly attached relatively untouched, implying cultural and institutional polarization between churched and unchurched American believers, coincident with their liberal-conservative political polarization, rather than forces of secularization multiplying unbelievers across US society as a whole. On millennials mistrusting a wider range of public institutions more deeply and earlier in their lives than their parents, see Michael Hout, "Why millennials are less religious than older Americans," Pew Research Center, January 2016, citing GSS data. On lower levels of education, income, civic involvement, and political activity among "nothing in particulars" than atheists, agnostics, and churchgoers see Burge, *The Nones*, 101–13.

10. See Gregory A. Smith et al., "Decline Continues," 2019, 7–8, 16–18, on broader-based declines between 2009 and 2019 in churchgoing by race, gender,

education, region, and party identification as well as generation. "Nones" in 2021 still proved younger, more educated, and more liberal than most US adults, but they averaged forty-three years of age, seven in ten held no college degree, one in four voted for Donald Trump in 2020, and one in three was a person of color, report Burge and Bacon, "Not Just Young White Liberals," 4. "Nothing in particulars" grew from 14.3 percent of all adults sampled in the 2008 CCES survey to 19.9 percent in 2018, compared to White evangelicals up from 16.4 percent to 17.5 percent, mainline Protestants down from 13.5 percent to 11.9 percent, and White Catholics down from 14.6 percent to 11.9 percent, according to Burge, *The Nones*, 101–13, noting that "nothing in particulars" rank higher in age than atheists and agnostics and lower in education, income, political activity, and partisanship.

11. See Besheer Mohamed et al., "Faith among Black Americans," Pew Research Center, February 2021, 9, 14–18, 71–76; Jeff Diamant and Besheer Mohamed, "Black Millennials Are More Religious than Other Millennials," Pew, July 2018, 1–3. Cf. Burge, *The Nones*, 90–92, using 2008–2018 CCES survey data to show consistent trends at higher levels, as 17.7 percent Black disaffiliation in 2008 nearly doubles to 33.4 percent in 2018, marking a steeper rise of "nones" among Blacks during this decade than in any other racial group.

12. Gregory A. Smith et al., "Decline Continues," 7–8, 16–18.

13. Luis Lugo et al., "Faith in Flux: Changes in Religious Affiliation in the U.S.," Pew Research Center, April 27, 2009, 4–5, Q4a-Q4s; Cary Funk and Gregory A. Smith, "Nones on the Rise," Pew, 2012, 33ff. On the weak religious upbringing of "nones" in their families of origin, see Hout and Fischer, "Explaining Why," 2014; Claude Fischer, "Declaring You're a 'None'"; and PRRI, "Religion and Congregations," 7–8.

14. On postponed marriage and parenting in step with declining church attendance, see Robert Wuthnow, *After the Baby Boomers* (Princeton, 2007), 51–70; and Pew, "'Nones' on the Rise," p. 30. In 1950, the median age of first marriage was 22.8 years for men and 20.3 years for women; by 2002 it had risen to 26.9 years for men and 25.3 years for women, halving the share of married men in their twenties. The babyboom peak of 3.77 children per mother on average in 1957 fell to 2.1 by the mid-1970s.

15. Among unmarried Americans in their twenties without children only 13 percent of men and 20 percent of women attend religious services nearly every week, rising only slightly as they enter their thirties and forties, by contrast to 30 percent or more married men with children in their thirties and forties attending, and 40 percent or more married women in their thirties and forties with children, according to Wuthnow, *Boomers*, 21–23, 62–65. In 2018 some 35 percent of unmarried US adults without children identified as "nones," compared to 30 percent of spouses without children, 23 percent of all adults, 20 percent of single parents, and only 16 percent of married couples with children, according to Burge, *The Nones*, 62–67, 86–89, noting the causal interdependence of changes in marital and parental status with political backlash and higher education, as Republicans have grown 10 percent more likely to be married than Democrats, liberals have grown more educated, and White evangelical Protestants have grown more politically conservative and more Republican since

1990, while "nones" continue to grow in numbers, including 38.5 percent of women without children, 40 percent of childless men, 28 percent of men with children, and 19.8 percent of women with children.

16. Two-thirds of "nones" raised Catholic and half raised Protestant report they "stopped believing in the religion's teaching," compared to only half of Catholics who switched to Protestant churches and only one in six Protestants who switched denominations; but 71 percent of unchurched Catholics and Protestants alike report they "just gradually drifted away from the religion," while 43 percent of Catholic "nones" and 39 percent of Protestant "nones" report their "spiritual needs not being met," compared to 71 percent of Catholics turned Protestant and 51 percent of Protestants who switched denominations. Some 48 percent of Catholics and 40 percent of Protestants left church mainly due to "religious and moral beliefs," while 36 percent of Catholic "nones" and 20 percent of Protestant "nones" mainly faulted "religious institutions, practices, and people," according to Pew, "Faith in Flux," 2009, 1–8, 12–16, 21–34.

17. Pew, "Faith in Flux," 2009, 1–8, 12–16, 21–34. Cf. Gullickson, "Diverging Beliefs and Practices," 2018, 361–65, 376–77, on belief in God and the afterlife declining among "nones" since 2000 but prayer frequency holding steady, compared to churchgoers. Reasons given by "nones" for leaving church remained consistent from 2016 to 2022, with 78 percent who "stopped believing in the religion's teaching," 43 percent opposed to anti-LGBTQ doctrine, 32 percent put off by scandalous church leaders, 20 percent by "a traumatic event in your life," 20 percent by a church or congregation that "became too focused on politics," and 34 percent citing a family of origin "never that religious growing up," according to PRRI, "Religion and Congregations," 2022, 7–8.

18. Some 47 percent of all "nones" believe "spiritual energy can be located in physical things" and 38 percent believe in reincarnation, including 61 percent and 51 percent, respectively, of those who self-identify with "nothing in particular." But so do 43 percent and 33 percent respectively of all mainline Protestants, double the percentage of White evangelicals and comparable to historically Black Protestants, according to Claire Gecewicz, "'New Age' beliefs common among both religious and nonreligious Americans," Pew Research Center, October 2018, 1–4. About a quarter of those self-identified as "nothing in particular" in 2010 joined or rejoined a religious denomination or switched identification to a faith tradition by 2014, while only an eighth became agnostic or atheist, according to Burge and Bacon, "Not Just Young White Liberals," 5. Cf. Ryan Burge, "Plenty of 'Nones' Actually Head Back to Church," *Christianity Today*, February 6, 2018; and Burge, *The Nones*, 117–22.

19. See Pew, "Faith in Flux," 2009, 21–34. Nonbelief among "nones" concentrated in the quarter of them self-identified as "atheist" (82 percent) or "agnostic" (63 percent), with only 37 percent of those identified as "nothing in particular" offering nonbelief as a key reason to leave church, while more often reporting they "dislike organized religion," and declaring themselves "religiously unsure/undecided," according to Lipka, "Why?" 2016, 2–4, while only one in five of "nones" deemed their last congregational visit "mostly negative," and few attributed their leaving church to any such bad experience.

20. Sweeping secularization and supply-side theories fail to account for specific evidence of religious disaffiliation and switching reported in GSS surveys since 1972, according to Darren Sherkat, *Changing Faith*, 36–55ff. Some 25 percent of college-educated Americans identify as "nones" in 2018 compared to 20 percent of high-school graduates and dropouts, reports Burge, *The Nones*, 81–85, but more and less educated adults alike doubled their likelihood of identifying as "nones" since 1990, contrary to secularization theories opposing religious belief to the "disenchantment" of higher education and scientific reason, even if college-educated baby boomers born in the late 1940s were two times likelier than their less educated counterparts to leave church before 1990. Contrary to supply-side claims in favor of evangelicalism, higher fertility and earlier childbearing among women from conservative denominations explain 76 percent of their membership growth for cohorts born between 1903 and 1973, according to Michael Hout, Andrew Greeley, and Melissa J. Wilde, "The Demographic Imperative in Religious Change in the United States," *American Journal of Sociology* 107, no. 2 (September 2001): 468–500. Between 2007 and 2012 White evangelical and White mainline Protestants declined comparably by 2 percent and 3 percent respectively to 19 percent and 15 percent of US adults, while the unaffiliated rose by 4.3 percent from 15.3 to 19.6 percent of all adults, report Hout and Fischer, "Explaining Why," 2014. On varieties of secularism in American politics consistent with distinctive patterns of membership, participation, and innovation in mainline churches and beyond their boundaries, see David E. Campbell, Geoffrey C. Layman and John C. Green, *Secular Surge: A New Fault Line in American Politics* (Cambridge, UK: Cambridge University Press, 2021).

21. Michael Lipka, "Which U.S. religious groups are oldest and youngest," July 2016, 2–3. For survey evidence that some 58 percent of baby boomers dropped out of organized religion for at least two years during youth or young adulthood, of whom one-third or so stayed out while more dropped back in, see Wade Clark Roof, *A Generation of Seekers* (Harper San Francisco, 1994). Cf. Burge, *The Nones*, 70–81, using GSS data to show the religiously unaffiliated share of boomers (born 1946–1964) dipping from 13 percent in 1972 to less than 10 percent in 1988, then rising to 16 percent in 2018, by contrast to unaffiliated members of Gen X (born 1965–1976) rising steadily to 20 percent in 2018 and millennials (born 1977–1995) to 33 percent in 2018, while the Silent Generation (born 1925–1944) rises from 5 percent in 1972 to 11 percent in 2018, and the Greatest Generation (born 1901–1924) rises from 3 percent to 7 percent, thereby aging all "nones."

22. On religious implications of structural change in the U.S. polity see Tipton, *Public Pulpits* (University of Chicago Press, 2008), ch. 2; Lilliana Mason and Julie Wronski, "One Tribe to Bind Them All: How Our Social Group Attachments Strengthen Partisanship," *Political Psychology* 39, issue supplement S1, February 2018: 257–77; and Alan I. Abramowitz and Steven W. Webster, "Negative Partisanship: Why Americans Dislike Parties but Behave Like Rabid Partisans," *Political Psychology* 39, no. 1 (2018): 119–35. Cf. evidence of greater ideological division due to a "recent secular surge in American politics," according to Campbell, Layman and Green, *Secular Surge*, 3–44.

23. Pew Research Center, "Religiously Unaffiliated People More Likely to Identify with the Ideological Left," September 25, 2020; and Pew Research Center, "In Changing U.S. Electorate, Race and Education Remain Stark Dividing Lines," June 2020, 26–28. See Darren W. Davis and David C. Wilson, *Racial Resentment in the Political Mind* (Chicago: University of Chicago Press, 2022), ch. 4; Thomas B. Edsall, "Trump's Cult of Animosity Shows No Sign of Letting Up," *New York Times,* May 7, 2021; Lillian Mason, Julie Wronski, and John V. Kane, "Activating Animus," *American Political Science Review* (2021): 1–9; and Joseph E. Uscinski et al., "American Politics in Two Dimensions: Partisan and Ideological Identities versus Anti-Establishment Orientations," *American Journal of Political Science* 65, no. 4 (July 2021): 877–95. On conservative White Protestants and White "nones" diverging in political identification since 1970, see Claude S. Fischer, "The Politics-Religion Vortex Spins," September 17, 2018, at http://madeinamericathebook.com. On the rising partisanship of White weekly churchgoers since 1972 see Burge, *The Nones*, 131.

24. Hout and Fischer, "Why More Americans Have No Religious Preference: Politics and Generations," 2002; Hout and Fischer, "Explaining Why More Americans Have No Religious Preference," 2014. Cf. Fischer, "The Politics-Religion Vortex Spins," 2018, noting church defectors politically alienated from their fellow congregants in evangelical churches swinging to the religious right, according to Paul A. Djupe, Jacob R. Heiheisel, and Anand E. Sokhey, "Reconsidering the Role of Politics in Leaving Religion: The Importance of Affiliation," *American Journal of Political Science* 62, no. 1 (January 2018): 161–75; and Ruth Braunstein, "A Theory of Political Backlash," 11–23, arguing that such radical politicization spurs more religious disaffiliation and "spiritual but not religious" self-identification, more countermobilization on the religious left and more intense "counter backlash" on the religious right supported by pro-Trump "secular conservatives," while it depoliticizes cross-pressured "liberal religion" and discredits "moderate" religious groups within organized religion in general more than it bolsters them against radical religious groups in particular.

25. See Lipka, "Why America's 'nones' left religion behind," Pew, August 2016; and Pew, "Why America's 'nones' don't identify with a religion," August 2018, 2, showing that 60 percent of all "nones" by 2018 cite questioning religious teachings as "very important" vs. 49 percent who cite political alienation, a margin narrowing to 51 percent citing doctrine vs. 47 percent citing politics among respondents identified as "nothing in particular," once atheists and agnostics are removed from the sample

26. Cary Funk and Gregory A. Smith, "'Nones' on the Rise," 44, reports 18 percent of "nones" self-identifying as a "religious person," compared to 65 percent of the US general public and 75 percent of churchgoers, with 37 percent of "nones" self-identifying as "spiritual but not religious," compared to 42 percent as "neither spiritual nor religious"; and 68 percent of "nones" affirming that they "believe in God or universal spirit," 21 percent that they pray daily, and another 20 percent that they pray weekly or at least monthly. Only 36 percent those who say their religion is "nothing in particular" think of themselves as neither a religious nor spiritual person, by contrast to 57 percent of those self-identified as "atheist/agnostic," but a third of these atheists and agnostics nonetheless call themselves "spiritual but not religious."

Michael Hout, "American Religion," 2017, 80, estimates just 14 percent of "nones" to be atheists in 2016, equal to 4 percent of the adult US population, with agnostics equaling another 7 percent, based on GSS data. On individual spiritual autonomy freed from the tutelary authority of organized religion in the modern West, see Bellah, "Religious Evolution," 39–45.

27. By 2017 some 27 percent of all US adults identified themselves as "spiritual *but not* religious," up 8 percentage points since 2012, while those self-identified as "spiritual *and* religious" dropped from 59 to 48 percent, led by college-educated, politically liberal Americans aged between 30 and 65 but broadly based by gender and race/ethnicity, according to Michael Lipka and Claire Gecewicz, "More Americans Now Say They're Spiritual But Not Religious," Pew Research Center, September 2016, 1–7. On correlating religiosity and spirituality, see Rich Morin et al., "The Religious Typology," Pew Research Center, August 29, 2018, 14–18, 22–24, 29, 35, showing that 46 percent of the full sample self-identified as *both* spiritual *and* religious, 25 percent as *neither* spiritual *nor* religious, 24 percent as spiritual *but not* religious, but only 4 percent as religious *but not* spiritual.

28. See Morin et al., "The Religious Typology," 14–18, 22–24, 29, 35. On the spiritually awakened choosing to leave church to seek a new spiritual community, switch congregations, or stay and dwell more deeply in their home church, see Robert Wuthnow, *After Heaven: Spirituality in America since the 1950s* (University of California Press, 1998), ch. 1.

29. On medical-therapeutic definition of "spirituality," according to the International Consensus Conference on Spiritual Care in Health Care, see Tyler VanderWeele, Tracy Balboni, and Howard Koh, "Health and Spirituality," *Journal of the American Medical Association* 318, no. 6 (August 2017): 519–20, with its functional stress on "spiritual community participation" associated with "healthier lives, including greater longevity, less depression and suicide, and less substance abuse."

30. See Claire Gecewicz, "'New Age' Beliefs Common among both Religious and Nonreligious Americans," Pew Research Center, October 1, 2018, 1–3; and Morin et al., "The Religious Typology," Pew, 8–14, 29, specifying belief in reincarnation, astrology, psychics, and "the presence of spiritual energy in physical objects like mountains or trees," and reporting 62 percent of all US adults hold at least one such belief, including 67 percent of mainline Protestants, 47 percent of White evangelicals, 70 percent of Catholics; and 62 percent of "nones," including 78 percent of those identifying with "nothing in particular" but only 22 percent of self-identified "atheists."

31. Cary Funk and Gregory A. Smith, "Nones on the Rise," Pew, 2012, 22–24, reports two in three "nones" criticizing religious organizations as too focused on rules, politics, money and power, while 47 percent of churchgoers agree, along with 51 percent of all Americans. From 2007 to 2014 the percentage of "nones" feeling "a deep sense of spiritual peace and well-being" rose from 35 to 40 percent, compared to a rise from 58 to 64 percent among all churchgoers; and the percentage of "nones" feeling a "deep sense of wonder about the universe" rose from 39 to 47 percent, compared to a rise from 39 to 45 percent among churchgoers, report David Masci and

Michael Lipka, "Americans may be getting less religious, but feelings of spirituality are on the rise," Pew, January 2016, 1–3.

32. See Funk and Smith, "Nones on the Rise," 22–24. Since 2007 more Americans in and out of church have reported experiencing "regular feelings of spiritual peace, well-being; wonder about the universe," according to Gregory Smith et al., "U.S. Public Becoming Less Religious," 2015, 22–27, 92–96. When asked to describe "a moral person," religious "nones" referred most often to "honesty" and "gratitude" as essential traits, with 23 percent citing the Golden Rule or kindness to others and 12 percent citing tolerance and respect for others; compared to self-identified Christians most often citing "believing in God" (86 percent), "being grateful for what you have" (71 percent), "forgiving those who have wronged you" (69 percent), "being honest" (67 percent), and "working to help the poor" (52 percent), according to Pew Research Center, "Religion in Everyday Life," April 2016, 1–6. Cf. Wilhelm Hofmann, "Morality in Everyday Life," http://science.sciencemag.org, 11 May 2015, showing self-identified "liberals" more often referred to Fairness/Unfairness, Liberty/Oppression, and Honesty/Dishonesty than did "conservatives," who focused more often on Loyalty/Disloyalty, Authority/Subversion, and Sanctity/Degradation, with these differences persisting when controlled for religiosity.

33. Pew Research Center, "Sharp Partisan Divisions in Views of National Institutions," July 2017, 1–2, 4, 11. Cf. Hout, "American Religion," 2017, 78–80, citing 1986–2016 GSS data; and Burge and Bacon, "It's Not Just Young White Liberals," 2021.

34. See notes 2–4 for survey data on declining religious attendance.

35. Funk and Smith, "Nones on the Rise," 73–74; Daniel Block, "Is Trump Our Cyrus? The Old Testament Case for Yes and No," *Christianity Today*, October 29, 2018. On culturally conservative White "God and Country Believers," who rarely attend church or condemn abortion but embrace Trump as a savior sent by God, see Ruth Graham and Charles Homans, "Trump Is Connecting with a Different Type of Evangelical Voter," *New York Times*, January 8, 2024.

36. Cf. Aaron Gullickson, "Diverging Beliefs and Practices," 2018; Hout, "American Religion," 2017; Hout and Fischer 2002; Hout and Fischer 2014. On reaching out to unchurched believers and embracing marginal church members, see C. Kirk Hadaway and Penny Long Marler, "All in the Family: Religious Mobility in America," *Review of Religious Research* 35, no. 2 (1993): 97–116; and Burge, *The Nones*, 117–36.

37. See Robert Jones et al., "Exodus," 3–9, on Generation Z (born since 1996) compared to millennials (born 1981–1996); Pew Research Center, "U.S. Teens Take after Their Parents Religiously, Attend Services Together, and Enjoy Family Rituals," September 2020, 2–18; and Melissa Deckman, "Generation Z and Religion: What New Data Show," *Religion in Public*, February 10, 2020, at https://religioninpublic.blog. Americans raised by a religiously unaffiliated single parent or two unaffiliated parents are likeliest (62 percent) to identify as "nones" in adulthood, along with 38 percent of those raised by one affiliated and one unaffiliated parent, compared to 25 percent of those raised by one Catholic and one Protestant parent, 20 percent of those raised by two Catholics, and 14 percent of those raised by two Protestants.

Millennials are much less likely than baby boomers to be raised by two parents with the same religious background (56 percent versus 69 percent), according to Pew Research Center, "One-in-Five U.S. Adults Were Raised in Interfaith Homes," October 2016, 2–6. Between 1991 and 1998, Americans aged 18 to 35 identifying as "nones" jumped from 8 percent to 20 percent in GSS surveys and went on to raise their children accordingly, yielding nearly half of those children self-identified as "nones," concludes Ryan Burge, "How America's Youth Lost its Religion in 1990s," Religion News Service, April 13, 2022, 3–5.

38. Cf. Robert Jones, "Exodus," PRRI, 10–12; and Morin et al., "The Religious Typology," Pew, 46, 64–67.

39. Cf. Robert Jones, "Exodus," PRRI, 12–17; and Pew polls in 2012–2014, cited in notes 2 and 5, that define most of the unaffiliated as "unchurched believers," with 61 percent saying they believe in God, 37 percent reporting they prayed at least once a week, and a third affirming that religion is at least somewhat important in their lives. See Burge, *The Nones*, ch. 4, on "nothing in particular" as an intermediate category and "transfer station" for "nones" in transit, by contrast to atheists and agnostics more stably settled further from religion.

40. Jones, "Exodus," PRRI, 12–17, 22–23.

41. Cf. Hout and Fischer, "Explaining Why," 2014, 444; and Burge, *The Nones*, 123–36.

42. Funk and Smith, "Nones on the Rise," Pew, 45–52, reports four in ten adults raised without religious affiliation identifying themselves as affiliated in 2012; and four in ten "spiritual but not religious" Americans counting as affiliated, 39 percent of them Protestant and 18 percent Catholic, with 44 percent of "SBNR" adults saying they pray every day, including 21 percent of "nones" and 66 percent of the affiliated. Roughly one in ten members of each religious tradition counts as "liminal," with ongoing shifts in nominal affiliation, while their self-reported religious beliefs and practices remained largely constant, according to Putnam and Campbell, *American Grace*, 135–36. With no significant change in religious belief or practice, some 30 percent of "nones" in the first wave of GSS panel studies from 2006 to 2014 claimed religious affiliation a year later, with a comparable number of "liminals" moving from religiously affiliated to unaffiliated self-identification, according to Chaeyoon Lim, Carol Ann MacGregor, and Robert D. Putnam, "Secular and Liminal: Discovering Heterogeneity among Religious Nones," *Journal for the Scientific Study of Religion* 49, no. 4 (2010): 596–618. Cf. Hout, "American Religion," 2017, estimating 20 percent of U.S. adults proved likewise liminal from 2006 to 2014, according to GSS panel data.

43. Michael Hout, "Religious Ambivalence, Liminality, and the Increase of No Religious Preference in the United States, 2006–2014," *Journal for the Scientific Study of Religion* 56, no. 1 (2017): 52–53, 58–62. Committed "nones" and "liminals" each made up about 10 percent of the US population in the mid-2000s, yielding 16 percent of adults stating no religious preference in biennial surveys, with the sum of "nones" and "liminals" exceeding 16 percent because in any given survey, some of the "liminals" will choose a religious preference and the rest will not. GSS panel data confirm that from 2006 to 2014 more and more Americans preferred "no

religion"—14 percent in 2006, 16 percent in 2008, 17 percent in 2010, 19 percent in 2012, 21 percent in 2014—and an even larger percentage preferred "no religion" at least once in three interviews. This confirms the existence of "liminals" but not their prevalence, nor their increased likelihood to choose "no religion" in more recent years, compared to more Americans overall consistently choosing "no religion." Reanalysis of GSS data from 2006 to 2014 shows that the proportion of US adults choosing a religious identity fell from 72 percent to 67 percent, in step with a rise of 5 percent in Americans choosing "no religion" during the same period. Declining attachment to organized religion is evident in a rise in the proportion of "liminals" by 2 percentage points, and a rise in the proportion of consistent "nones" by 3 percentage points, along with a rising likelihood of 10 percent among "liminals" (from .33 to .43) to choose "no religion."

44. Hout, "Religious Ambivalence," 52–53, 58–62.

45. Hout, "Religious Ambivalence," 52, 58, 60, 62. Liminals emerge equally among those raised mainline Protestant, conservative Protestant, or Catholic. But liminals raised as conservative Protestants are significantly less likely to choose "no religion" ($p\tau \approx .33$) than those raised as mainline Protestants ($p\tau \approx .38$), who are slightly less likely to choose no religion than those raised as Catholics ($p\tau \approx .40$).

46. Penny Long Marler and C. Kirk Hadaway, "Toward a Typology of Protestant 'Marginal Members,'" *Review of Religious Research* 35, no. 1 (1993): 34–54. See Darren Sherkat, *Changing Faith*, 48–72, contrasting the importance of religious-ethnic identity for recent waves of immigrants loyal to non-Christian and "other Christian" traditions, and its weakening salience for younger generations of culturally assimilated Protestants, Catholics, and Jews from "dominant ethnicities."

47. See Burge, *The Nones*, ch. 4; and notes 5–7, 9–10, and 16 above.

48. Cf. categories used to distinguish between religiously affiliated and unaffiliated American adults based on congregational attendance, participation, and formal membership in a congregation or denomination; self-reported religious "preference" or "identification" by denomination or faith tradition; "no religion" or "none" with or without further self-identification as "nothing in particular" or "agnostic" or "atheist," as featured in surveys such as the General Social Survey and Pew Research Center polls. These categories of classification include typological distinctions and estimated percentages of all US adults, for example, in "The Religious Typology" summarized by Becka Alper, "From the Solidly Secular to Sunday Stalwarts," Pew Research Center, August 29, 2018: Sunday Stalwarts (17 percent) + God-and-Country Believers (12 percent) + Diversely Devout (10 percent) = the "Highly Religious" 39 percent of all US adults; Relaxed Religious (17 percent) + Spiritually Awake (15 percent) = the "Somewhat Religious" 32 percent of all US adults; Religious Resisters (12 percent) + Solidly Secular (17 percent) = the "Non-Religious" 29 percent of all US adults. Also see typological categories of classification and percentages drawn from surveys and interviews of specific populations, for example, young adults aged eighteen to twenty-three, in Christian Smith, *Souls in Transition*, chapter 6: Committed Traditionalists (15 percent); Selective Adherents (30 percent); Spiritually Open (15 percent); Religiously Indifferent (25 percent); Religiously Disconnected (5 percent); Irreligious (10 percent).

Chapter 2

Along the Way

Let's turn from numbers to voices, from survey data to firsthand stories of young adults in and out of church, told in tandem with their babyboom parents. These are parents who taught their children to pray or find their own way, who brought them to worship every week or now and then, who tried to keep them in the fold or opened the doors of spiritual perception into a wider world beyond church walls. We will not hear from everyone identified as "unchurched" or "nones" in polls. But we will listen to a range of those raised mainline or evangelical Protestant, Catholic or Jewish, devout or doubtful. We will hear their diverse voices in conversations inflected across generations, deeply indebted to parents their children follow or bypass on the way to worship, echoing or editing the scriptures they hold sacred, rehearsing or restaging the rites they live out. Through these differences run underlying visions and virtues we hold arguably true enough to contest and revise. Through these changes run the dramatic dialogues that hold us together.

I. SPIRITUAL SEEKERS AND PERENNIAL VISITORS

Nearing seventy and long committed to practicing her faith within mainline Protestant churches, an educated, artistic woman reflects on her upbringing in a devout Presbyterian family, her continuing quest for spiritual depth of experience and meaning, and its resonance for her daughter and grandchildren. "I've always been driven by a hopeful, yearning kind of spiritual curiosity," Natalie says carefully. "It's basically good, but it's challenging, too, especially in looking for a kind of perfection that goes beyond ordinary life." How so? "If you only immerse yourself deeply enough, you can become one with God, one with nature," she answers. "Nature can reveal itself intimately to us in a single picture that goes way beyond us. Drawn by the hand of God! It mirrors God. It manifests the All in its minute grandeur," she sums up in terms that draw classical ideals of natural law and Calvin on nature as divine into Romantic promises of authentic self-fulfillment and mystical union.

"You can capture the secret of the cosmos, and make it your own," Natalie affirms with the keen aesthetic sense of a graphic designer attuned to artistic self-expression and religious communion alike. "That's not just a good story. But experiencing it can be dangerous if you don't ground it and share it," she warns. "It needs the grace of praying together in the body of a church with Christ crucified at its heart. Jesus doesn't escape the world as it is. That's what enables us to love God and our neighbor. That's the wonder of it," she nods, "the immanence of it."[1]

Does Natalie's spiritual curiosity go back to her upbringing? To some extent, she agrees, but it seems inbred, too, "like being more naturally drawn to art than my brothers and sisters. My mother taught us little prayers, starting when we were two or three years old, and she took us to church all the time. My father would come, too, from time to time." He had his own faith, she felt, but it was more personal, more private, even though he belonged to the church. "You had to find your own way to faith, as he saw it. You had to make up your own mind. The church couldn't do it for you. Or do it *to* you," she reflects. "I wanted to get confirmed in the church when I was around twelve or thirteen, and he said 'No, later. This is too important a decision for you to be making at this age. Wait until you're old enough to really choose for yourself.' I was disappointed at the time, and kind of mad at him," Natalie recalls. "I couldn't understand why I couldn't go through it with all my friends." What about now? "He was stressing my own personal responsibility as an adult to commit myself fully, to follow my own conscience," she answers, along lines linked to historically Protestant emphasis on the need for adult baptism, or adult profession of faith to seal the covenant created in baptism, in order to signify a personal "regeneration" or internal conversion and so attain full membership in the church that no sacrament of itself can confer.[2]

Does this contrast still ring true to Natalie's religious experience and conviction today? Nodding to theological distinctions between Word and Sacrament, and arguments that we need both, Natalie replies, "It's not either-or. Sacraments don't magically turn you into a saint or a really good person. But just hearing the Word and thinking about it won't do it either."[3] It's worth asking, "How will I survive as an individual, or an individual person of faith?" Natalie allows. "But you can't answer that question without wondering, 'How do we live in community, and witness to its truth?' Do you have to be a martyr to do that?" she asks. "In the Greek 'martyr' means 'witness.' But for us it usually means someone who gets killed for some great cause or belief, and who wants to do that?" she frowns. "We want to be free and thrive."

Do individuals have to take part in communities of worship to be faithful? "You can't do it alone. That's the truth," Natalie answers forcefully. "So it's always time for the Last Supper, for two or three gathered in his name, and 'Do this in remembrance of me,'" she attests.[4]

> We become one body in breaking bread together. You can't make sense of the mystery of "I am going away, but I will be with you always," without worshipping together and living out the story, from creation to crucifixion and resurrection. You can't make sense of the love that runs through the story from beginning to end without taking part in the life of the liturgy. That's the only way to get outside yourself and thrive. It's the only way to get outside the church in order to let its light shine in the world. Maybe it's the only way to accept that the church is always dying in some particular worldly form, but it's living and changing, too, in the real presence of Christ.

For Natalie, the interplay of these convictions and her deepening participation in the liturgy of ecclesiastical Protestantism define a trajectory drawn over decades of adulthood living in the San Francisco Bay Area. It led from her small-town Presbyterian upbringing through artistic and "mystical" exploration as a college student, into taking her children weekly to a local Lutheran church where she taught Sunday school until they reached adolescence, then finally joining an Episcopal congregation at age sixty.

Led by a brilliant preacher adept at interweaving moral insight and social awareness with gospel stories, for Natalie this congregation centers nonetheless on the liturgical drama and spiritual intimacy of the Christian story. "Our pastor always talks about the actual world, and he always talks about the Jesus who knows us and loves us," Natalie explains. "It's unerringly 'prophetic' in naming the world's brokenness. But it's not just about social justice, or blaming someone else," she says. "It's immediate and personal. It's about how to live here and now, in prayerful communion with Jesus. It comes from the heart of worship, and leads back into it." The Eucharist is not just a commemoration, Natalie affirms. "Yes, it's just bread, it's just wine—and it's the actual body and blood of Christ we're experiencing together at the communion rail."[5]

This religious enactment and experience inflect Natalie's ongoing dialogue with her own children, particularly her daughter Jill, a lawyer in her thirties with an analytical edge, strong commitments to progressive social causes, and sustained civic involvement. "Most Sundays she'll ask me if the pastor is preaching, and she'll come if she can. If it's a fill-in, she'll give it a miss," Natalie smiles, recalling such an exchange in the presence of her school-age granddaughter as they headed to church together one Sunday. "Mommy! You're supposed to go!" responded the precocious eight-year-old. Her mother began to explain that going to church is a choice made in good conscience, not a duty commanded by God. "The story of Jesus is a metaphor," Natalie recalls Jill saying. "It's a story we interpret."

"I can agree with that," Natalie nods. "It's not just a set of facts or rules. But going to church is not just going to hear a lecture. It's praying and singing together. It's incarnation and communion!" Natalie shakes her head, "I can't impose that on anyone, certainly not my daughter, and I don't try. She has to experience that for herself, or not. And she has to be the one most responsible for raising *her* daughter. Thank goodness!" Natalie laughs. "All I have to do is be present and take part in this communion as much as I can, and recognize just how much we already share. When it comes to volunteering for the church's homeless ministries and service projects, my daughter is right there. And I'm right there with her, too, as a kind of *perennial visitor*. I'm still on the way to church. I'm not all the way there yet."

Born Again and Again

For that convergence Natalie's husband Jim gives thanks, and both his wife and children are grateful to him in turn for all he has done to make it possible. It hasn't always been easy, beginning with his own strict upbringing in a "fundamentalist Baptist church" in rural Texas and winding up a high school English teacher in the Bay Area of northern California. "That church was important to me growing up as a boy," he recalls, at once a sanctuary and school, a source of stability and order where he came to shine and stand out as both bright and devout. "My parents were loyal to the church. They were tithers. We went to church on Sunday morning and Sunday night, Wednesday night to prayer meeting, Thursday to Bible study, Friday to choir practice. Plus all kinds of special meetings for missions and discipleship. So we had a lot of church." At the age of twelve, Jim recalls vividly, he got saved:

> Morning, noon, and night you hear the call to conversion. You feel it hit, and you see your friends looking you in the eye, and getting all worked up to walk down there, to weep and cry and get hugged.
>
> Is this the day—the afternoon, the evening, the weather, the season—to be saved? Yes! So, I raised my hand and came forward, and gave my life to Jesus. Behind the pulpit we had a baptismal pool that was transparent and filled with water. I got all dressed up, and I went up and got dunked in front of everyone.
>
> Whatever it was, it worked for a while. I was wiped clean. I went for it absolutely and wholeheartedly. I was the one who narrated the Christmas pageant when I was fourteen. But it wasn't magic. I hoped it was magic. I hoped it was real. I invested myself in it. But I invested myself in other things, too, mostly in school once I got to high school, and that became my savior.

Entering a large consolidated high school in a small city an hour away from his home, Jim entered a wider world of learning and social experience that he had the ability and inspiration to make his own.

"I had to learn a new language, a lot of languages, in order to navigate," Jim explains. "But I found teachers who nurtured me, despite all my mistakes." Jim began arguing with his parents about "ultimate things," then withdrawing into strategic silence when they pushed back vehemently. "Gradually I began to triangulate, and put some inner distance between myself, my parents, and what was happening in church, again and again, through all six choruses of 'Just as I Am.' I had to protect myself, my soul, my individuality. I kept going to church and 'believing in Jesus.' But I began thinking for myself, my deeper spiritual self."

Once Jim left home on a scholarship to an elite college in California, he left church as well. He "never looked back," until he met Natalie. She took him with her to the local Lutheran church she had joined. "We walked in, and the hair stood up on the back of my neck," Jim marvels. "It was visceral, just my lizard brain reacting against all the closed-minded self-righteousness I had fought so hard to escape." Yet when their children arrived, and Natalie took them to church, Jim steeled himself and did his best to go along.

"Natalie was able to give them a Christian upbringing, and I agreed to it," Jim sums up. "I would only go to church with them occasionally, but I didn't oppose it." When Jill, their first child, took enthusiastically to Sunday school, Jim recalls, "She put up a big banner with the Lamb of God on her bedroom wall, proclaiming, 'I have called you, and you are mine.'" Jim pauses with feeling and shakes his head in wonderment. "How can I accept this?" he asked himself. "By knowing that I really want my kids to have a sense of something higher, an experiential belief in something that's bigger than themselves," he answers. "And they do. They have a sense of cultural connection to the whole, through the church."

Does Jim have an ongoing role in this process? "I try to open up little back doors, as gracefully as I can," he replies, "to give them room to maneuver and find their own way, as they mature. Who's to say they can't go to church? Not me. I'll help them any way I can to make up their own mind," he pledges. "And I'll keep seeking every day to affirm my own sense of something higher."

Is that something recognizably Christian or biblical? "I'm not swimming in the Christian sea," Jim replies firmly. "But I can't be righteous or judgmental about declaring it out of bounds." Is there another sea to swim in? "It's art itself that expresses the truth we live in and live out," Jim answers. "That's the sea I swim in." Is Jim religious about art then? In a way, he acknowledges, "Art saved me. It helped heal my childhood wounds from fighting against the false authority of received wisdom." Like the inevitability and the freedom of a well-written character, he reflects, "Literature helped me find my own story and calling, not just to make art, but to raise a good family and have a good marriage. So I give thanks for being married to someone who shares that calling," Jim smiles. "She goes to church. She knows that at a certain point God-talk turns into babble for me. And still somehow she has the serenity to trust her own experience with the reigning religious metaphors to make sense of life, and she's enabled our kids to do that, too."

That's much harder for Jim to do, he confesses, although he continues to mull the sacred stories he hears running through diverse religious traditions. "Call it nonattachment, if you like, but there's a certain way of enclosing hurt or pain in the story of Buddhism, as I read it, and treading the eightfold path beyond it. Then you look at the wounded hands and feet of the risen Jesus. See all that he suffers for us and with us. There's an aesthetic difference in how human suffering is rendered, and that carries over into how we experience it and what we do to save ourselves. Those stories mean a whole lot more to me than all the doctrines that follow and supposedly sum them up," Jim judges. "Go back into the stories, see how they're put together, move them around, let a little light in. Make them new," he urges with the modernist enthusiasm of a creative writer. "But if the doctrines tickle the keys of your piano, then go into the House of the Lord, and play away," he allows. "The mystery of existence and the human spirit is so awesome and so engaging, you can find your way to it one way or the other, if you get out of yourself and into the world."[6]

Is Jim missing something by not joining a congregation or community of faith? "I am missing something," he answers directly if drolly. What is it? Well, he pauses, "I wish I were also active in town politics and council meetings. And I would like to be in a book club. And singing in the men's chorus. I do! I would really like to play in the softball game on Friday nights with the guys at the tavern, shoot a round of golf in a foursome on Sunday afternoons, and get to alumni reunions." Communities are many, Jim makes clear, and none of us can give our all to all of them. Like a literary character at once constrained and free, we must make choices in life, and so he has chosen, focusing on family and friends, along with the arts and his work as an English teacher. "I can drop in and drop out, and still find my place," Jim sums up. "I can recite the Creed on Easter Sunday, even if I feel differently about it. Maybe I'm lying. But I don't want to fight about it, and I don't want to have to do it all the time either. 'Live and let live.' That's part of 'Do unto others.'"

Real Church in the Real World

"We're together on what's most important about church," agrees Jill, Natalie's daughter, "even if we come to it differently. My mother loves the liturgy, and it bores me," she smiles. "I sort of sleep through it mostly, even though I find it calming sometimes. Then I wake up for the sermon. That really gets me going. That's where the real church is for me, the church that's in the world and gets you doing something about it," she stresses. "So I'm not so worried about getting to church every Sunday, or always getting there at the beginning. Sometimes I'll just go for the sermon, or skip it if somebody else is filling in, and I'm too busy."

If that's where Jill stands now, how did she get there? "My mother taught my brother and me to pray when we were little," she recalls. "Pillow prayers, she called them, just before we went to bed. We grew up going to church almost every Sunday, the local Lutheran church. It was a really tight community. I had friends there my own age, and I can remember really wanting to go there," she notes. "I went to Sunday school. I was in a youth group. We did service projects. We went to Mexico with Habitat for Humanity when I was thirteen. It was all my mom. My dad never set foot there."

Yet her father stayed true to a personal faith grounded in good conscience, Jill reflects. "He wasn't against us going as kids, as long as we wanted to. He just wasn't part of it. When we were old enough, we could decide on our own to keep going or not." Did this difference between her parents influence Jill? "I was aware of it growing up: You're not a baby anymore, so you can choose. And I did choose when I was around seven or eight," she recalls, in counterpoint to her mother's story of confirmation delayed. "I wanted to be baptized. There were these classes to go through. I remember reading this pamphlet in the class, and it said babies went to purgatory or limbo or wherever, if they weren't baptized. I was offended, and I said in the class, 'I don't believe this! Do I have to believe this to be baptized?'" What happened? "The teacher was really good, and she said it was okay not to," she smiles, "so I could get baptized."

What did Jill make of this epiphany on the path to baptism? "Now I see it as a kind of healthy skepticism I had that goes all the way back to the difference between my parents. But it's also something they agreed on, and I found out my church agreed, too: You can believe what you want, and not believe what you don't want." Is that simply a matter of wanting? Does conscience come into choosing what and how to believe? Is it a choice lit by reason, made in coming to the use of your own understanding? Of course, Jill agrees now, but then it was mostly the reassurance that she would not be forced or threatened to accept the unacceptable if she wanted to belong.

"We grew up feeling you could be spiritual *and* you could be religious," Jill affirms, "and you didn't have to believe all this stuff about purgatory and limbo, or else you couldn't go to church. You can go to church, and live it out your own way," Jill holds, by contrast to "the stereotype that *either* you're religious and you go to church and you believe all the dogma—*or* you're spiritual, you don't go to church, and you reject it all. It's not either-or, at least not for me." Likewise for her mother, Jill recognizes, and for the "liberal" Protestant churches in which she was raised. For this church Jill gives thanks, even if she remains off the parish rolls, by contrast to the "fundamentalist" churches she criticizes in the name of freedom of conscience and religious exercise alike.

Sacred Rites and Moral Practices

Does Jill's aversion to dogmatic authority asserted from the pulpit extend to uniform rites of worship rehearsed at the altar? By contrast to loving the liturgy like her mother, she admits, "I can take it or leave it. But I can see there's something important there." What's that? "It's like a meditative practice. You're saying the same things, you're doing the same motions, even if you don't exactly believe it. It gets you feeling open and alive to something bigger. That's not a bad thing, especially when you have to be in control of so much of the rest of your life," as she must in order to balance a professional career and family and meet the daily demands of both.

Shared liturgical experience in bodies of worship, Jill allows, can nurture a vital kind of moral coherence and commitment that other institutions need help in fostering. "You can't just tell everybody what to think, even if you're in the right, like 'Do no evil. Love your neighbor.' How do you actually get people to feel it and do it?" she asks. "Can your family take care of that all by itself? Can you find a great school to help out?" Jill asks doubtfully of the institutional frameworks and practices of moral inspiration and formation that good character and commitment require.

"Ideally, we should be able to come up with a bunch of moral values we all agree on, but we don't!" Jill thinks back to the early days of her marriage to her undergraduate boyfriend, "a fully lapsed Catholic" whose high ideals and deep commitments she continues to share. "When we first got married, we decided we're not gonna go to church. We're going to do something by ourselves, just family and friends. We're all gonna get together, and it's gonna be great! But, of course, we didn't," she admits. "Almost no one does. So what happens when you take the church out of the moral equation? I don't know."

If religious practice and community prove vital for moral formation and commitment, then doesn't Jill's dedication to social action and witness call for shared practices of worship and prayer, not only moral teaching and social action, in order to shape a better world? Yes, she agrees, but that presumes no prior acceptance of church orthodoxy or authority. Instead, she holds, it invites ongoing discussion of their meaning among those who seek truth no less than justice. "If you believe 'Jesus is the Son of God,' as a matter of fact, or 'Oh, my God, no, he's not,'" Jill posits, "then that ends the conversation.

But maybe that should begin the conversation," Jill proposes. "What does that mean?" she asks. "That language, that imagery?"[7]

What do ideas of God mean for understanding human nature and social responsibility among different sorts of believers and nonbelievers, Jill wonders, and for living out our ideals? "Let's talk about that!" she urges. "That's what the pastor does, and that's why I come to hear him, to get at a bigger truth." What has she learned? "Whether you believe in heaven or hell after this life, we can talk about creating heaven or hell on earth by doing right or wrong," she replies. "We can get at the mysteries of human existence by talking about Jesus and the Bible. We have to use words and images to do that. That's part of who we are, and these stories are part of our world." Conversely, can biblical stories be misunderstood or traditions misdirected to inspire moral contradictions and misdeeds? "To whom much is given, much is expected," Jill answers with a sardonic smile, "and if you look at churches abusing children, ruling out birth control, and accepting AIDS epidemics, you have to ask how they could be doing good instead. If you want to get angry at churches, get angry at them for abusing their power in the world."

For goodness' sake, then, Jill acknowledges the need for shared religious practices that draw on prayer to open moral dialogue, guide deliberation over disagreements, and inspire social action in concert. At the same time, when it comes to doctrine, she allows that each individual should "take what you can and use it for good, and don't take the other stuff." That said, she insists nonetheless on moral practices that define the community of the congregation as a whole: "We focus on social justice. That's embedded in what the church is. We serve the least of these. We minister to the poor. That is how we create our spiritual community. That's the Good Samaritan and the gospel truth: 'Do this in remembrance of me.'"

Thus Jill binds together Word and Sacrament in a spiritual community committed to Christlike social action for love and justice in the world. No one knows if Jesus is actually the Son of God as a matter of historical fact, Jill argues. But as a matter of moral conviction, she testifies, "I do know if everybody on earth took him as an example and actually loved their neighbor, we'd be a helluva lot better off!"

If living out this social gospel can be seen as sacramental, Jill reflects, then so can the sacrament of the Eucharist in turn reveal the church itself as the fundamental sacrament in its all-encompassing embrace of a world hungry for communion. At the early Sunday service Jill sometimes attends with her mother, she observes, "Everyone can fit up there at the communion rail at the same time. It's quiet, intimate. There are only a few of us." On one such occasion, she recalls, an apparently homeless man suddenly entered the church and joined the circle of communicants. "He knew exactly what he was doing. He folds his arms as the priest comes up to him. He receives the blessing, and he waits with us at the altar until everyone is done. And then he leaves, without saying a word," Jill pauses. "Amazing!" she exclaims:

> There is something about being up there all together, whether or not you believe it's the Body of Christ. My children love it! They get to have a cracker, yes, but there's something about how solemn it is, when the priest touches their head and they're with me. It feels important, even if they don't know why, and it feels special. It's bread you want to save and take away with you.

In her children's experience of the Eucharist, so celebrated in an intimate congregation, Jill spells out her own literal sense of "holy communion" in breaking bread together within the church as an encircling body of worship that knits its members together with one another and a world in need.

Can Jill imagine a congregation that embodies these moral and spiritual goods yet couples them with other virtues that would widen her participation if not deepen her commitment to it? "Sure," she replies, thinking back to her experience as a college student working with African American youngsters in a service project based in a local Black Baptist church. "You have to come to church with us, they said, and I did. It was revolutionary to me. People are singing so joyfully. Whoa! Get that joy together with this quiet. Get all those kids in there with their parents and grandparents," she urges. "Let the Spirit come down, and lift the people up! Don't save all the glad tidings for Christmas. Make a joyful noise every Sunday!"

Learning to Re-Center

Would Jill go to church more often if her congregational dreams came true right around the corner? "I'd go more often, if I had more time," she answers candidly. "That always comes up first when I ask myself that question," in light of the daily demands she faces of caring for small children, running a household, and sustaining a business career. "But I do think it's harder when you don't do it as a family," she reflects, given her husband's principled resistance to churchgoing, much like her father's stance, by striking contrast to a close friend's devoutly Catholic family. "They're all about church. Her husband teaches Sunday school. They take their kids to Mass on Saturday evening. They do all the bake sales, rummage sales, church dinners," she marvels. "I don't know if I could ever go that far."

Why not? Does such congregational activity extend too far from the church's spiritual center, or fall short of its moral aim in serving the larger community? Both, answers Jill, "because for me it's all connected through social justice. Volunteering in the schools and serving on community boards, working in the community are all spiritual practices." How so?

> If you remove yourself from the center of the universe, and you put something else there, then everything changes. All of us know this from moments in our lives, as the pastor says, if we have ever tended to loved ones in sickness or stayed up all night with a child with a fever. Doing this as much and as fully as you can, that's how you find heaven. And that's exactly where I am morally and spiritually, with no separation.
>
> Step out of the center of your own universe. Every Sunday when I'm able to go, that's why I go. It resets! That's what the pastor talks about—getting over yourself, giving over yourself—and it's a blessing. You have to do your own part, but just sitting at rest for a moment and letting it come to you. It's such a blessing!

Can such spiritual re-centering transcend ego and "reset" reality without churchgoing or Christ-centered conviction? Jill thinks so in principle, hopes so for the sake of others, and sees herself somewhere in between orthodoxy and unbelief. "The pastor knows I'm really gun-shy about Jesus. One time he sees me in church before the service, and his eyes get all wide. He comes over and says, 'I just need to warn you, there's going to be a lot of Jesus in the sermon today.' I say that's cool, I'll be all right."

Jill is wary of stage-and-sequence accounts of religious faith, but she finds the experience of her two daughters compelling by comparison to her own childhood. "When we go to church they want to sit with me, not go to Sunday school, so I can see them going through things. Like my younger daughter at age four with all these people coming over to her at the Peace and hugging her. She's shy and doesn't like talking to strangers. It scared her at first, but she faced it and worked to conquer it. Now she has. 'Mommy, I shook hands and smiled, I did it!'" Jill recounts. "That's part of creating community, and now it's part of her experience, too." So is the story and imagery of Jesus. "She's obsessed with Jesus!" Jill exclaims. She's thinking about heaven, too, in light of the recent deaths of a great-grandmother and infant cousin. "We passed a little chapel in an airport coming back from a trip," Jill recalls, "and my daughter looked in and saw some older women kneeling before a crucifix. 'They're with Jesus, like Grandma,' she told me, 'and they're taking care of the baby.'" Astounded at first, Jill began talking with her daughter about "where people go when they die."

Is this cause for concern or thanksgiving, debunking correction or faithful interpretation? It's cause for conversation, Jill replies, and she welcomes it with her children as they age. "It's so big for young kids, going to church, all the songs we sing, all the images everywhere. And Jesus *is* connected to dying and rising again. Kids can't get it conceptually, just like that," Jill says, "but they can love Jesus, and they can wonder about the mystery of it."

Jill recalls answering questions posed by her older daughter pondering this mystery at age eight. "Some people believe you go to heaven when you die, and some people don't," Jill explained. "Do *you* believe that?" persisted her daughter. "No, I don't really believe that. I don't know," Jill admitted. "Well, I believe people go to heaven," her daughter declared in turn. Was Jill taken aback? "No, I thought it was great. It's a wonderful thing to believe, and she wants to believe it, so let's talk about it." If such talk begins at a point like this, where does it end? "I'm not sure it does end anywhere, once and for all," Jill replies. But she is sure about rejecting as a false dichotomy that "either Jesus was a real historical figure—where's the evidence?—or this is all a myth, a fraud."

Instead, Jill finds herself as well as her children engaging "a story of how to live, a metaphor of life" we must take to heart and interpret in order to understand and live it out. Or we must somehow work through it and create an alternative vision of what's real and how to live in accord with it. "You can say that you'll leave it up to your kids to discover the meaning of life, so don't push anything on them. They get to choose," Jill grants. "But even if you try to leave that open, you're effectively choosing for them. You don't wake up at twenty with a perfectly open mind, and then you decide to see what this church thing is about," Jill argues. "So I love that I go to church and take the kids with me, and my husband doesn't go. That's the way I grew up," Jill acknowledges. "The kids can see two choices that are each valid in their own way, but they overlap, too, in what we say and do," about being a good person and making the world a better place. "We don't judge each other. We both try to answer whatever big questions the kids want to ask us."

Within this binocular vision of religious upbringing focused on the integrity of moral formation for her children, Jill expresses a fluid yet fluent view of their churchgoing. "Even though we don't come all the time, they have this experience, this example. As you get older, you may come more, if you get curious, or you may grow away from it." Churchgoing now provides an experiential threshold and practical baseline for the freedom of choice and conscientious responsibility Jill hopes her children will exercise to chart their religious future as they come of age.

"Finding this church has eliminated a lot of stress in thinking about how to give my kids a good start," Jill admits thankfully. "I've been taking my older daughter to volunteer with me since the third grade, to try to weave this into the fabric of her life. She helps serve dinner to homeless people who sleep at the church for a month each year, and she talks with them." That makes a deep impression, Jill believes, and it sparks moral questions and convictions in her daughter at the heart of faith, hope, and charity. "That's really there," Jill affirms, "so I think it's irrelevant exactly how much or how often we go to church."

What about Sunday school? "That's a next step. Should I make the time, and start taking them?" Jill pauses. "They're curious, they could really eat it up. But I don't think it's something you can dip in and out of, and the kids are so busy in school already. Sunday, too? I think we probably won't do it, but we'll see," Jill pauses. "Maybe that means they're missing something, maybe not." Her older daughter often reads a book during the sermon, Jill notes, but "last week for the first time she said she listened to the sermon, and it was 'kind of cool.' So she's already started on her own."

Did going to Sunday school as a child give Jill a head start on her daughter or dull her curiosity with rote learning? "Who can say?" she frowns. Then she recalls an eye-opening moment at Sunday school when she was five. "Can you draw a picture of God?" the teacher asked. "So I, very dutifully, drew a picture of a man with a big beard and long hair," Jill admits, "and the other kids all did something like that. When we were done, we all held up our pictures. Then the teacher held up her picture. She had drawn a sunburst!" Jill smiles. "Everyone said that's not God! And she said, 'Why? We don't know what God looks like. Nobody does.' That amazed me!"

Jill shakes her head. "That stuck with me as a kid, and I still remember it. This revolution that God isn't just a man. Oops! That's a really positive thing to learn in Sunday school. I hope my kids are getting some of that from me," she says, for example, in correcting stereotypically Anglo-American depictions of Jesus, to the disbelief of her four-year-old daughter, with the revelation that Jesus almost certainly shared the darker-skinned appearance of natives of ancient Israel. "On the other hand, maybe it's good to get that kind of truth from church," Jill allows, "from somebody who's not your mom."

The Bible is no fairytale, Jill believes. It's a story whose true mysteries of life will prove compelling whenever we engage them. "It will happen when it should," she hopes. "They're on the path," guided by their own developing conscience, curiosity, and sense of self. That path can be lit by their experience of going to church, Jill trusts, without obliging them to do something more as a religious duty imposed out of her own sense of self-centered conviction or fear.[8]

Jill bristles at the selfishness of religious proselytizers utterly convinced of their own orthodoxy and righteousness. "What right do they have to impose that on me?" At the same time, like her mother, she remains wary of her own literary and aesthetic pursuits serving as substitutes for loving your neighbor and working for justice. Playing music or writing poetry "can get you out of your own little life and connect you with something bigger," Jill allows, "but it's not entirely selfless." Is there something selfish about carving out the time you need? "I struggle with that," Jill admits. "It's not enough, if there's not something communal at the center of it," to lead creative self-expression toward changing society for the better. "There's still that vacuum, even if we're each making our own art or doing our own yoga exercises," she says. "We're still separate. There's some larger empathy we lose, if we're not coming together."

Public institutions depend on our not opting out, Jill reflects, especially if we think we can afford to do so. "Churches are imperfect, and they're not the whole story" of public life and social interdependence. "But they can be a vital part of it," Jill concludes, in enabling and inspiring their members to care for one another, and to embrace the larger society as a moral community. We don't need a perfect church, she says, "but we do need to own the institutions that are here. Shape them, change them, enable them to do what we need to do," Jill urges. "Bring different people together, even if it gets messy, instead of just preaching to the choir," composed of like-minded groups defined by one race, class, gender, generation, and their shared sense of moral superiority.

Sacrament and Word

Natalie's continuing quest for spiritual depth of experience and meaning at one with an immanent God underlies her journey from a Presbyterian upbringing through artistic exploration in college, then parenting as a Lutheran before becoming a "perennial visitor" drawn by the Eucharistic communion of an Episcopal parish at age sixty. For all its shifts in social setting and stage of life, Natalie sees her journey as continuous and coherent in its quest for harmony and wholeness. Her husband Jim tells a more conflicted before-and-after story of breaking away from the strict, fundamentalist Baptist church of his childhood. Yet in his own way Jim shares Natalie's commitment to autonomy in religious understanding and participation. You must find your own way to faith, as her father put it, and make up your own mind. So, Natalie hopes and prays her daughter Jill will experience for herself the congregational incarnation and communion of the Christian story. But she cannot impose it on Jill or demand it of her.

Genuine religious faith can be critical and dialogical, Jill is convinced, and thus reducible to neither a fixed either-or decision between believing everything or nothing, nor a fluid pick-and-choose stream of options to believe whatever you please. Religious practice can likewise illuminate gospel stories, spark spiritual conviction, and inspire moral virtue without requiring orthodox belief. Spiritual practices can reach far beyond church pews to a wide range of social service and community care through civic, political, educational, and other institutions that share with organized religion a core dimension of moral depth, compassion, and justice.[9]

II. GOD BEYOND THE PEWS

Joshua Linden would never call himself "spiritual but not religious," he says with a quizzical smile at the distinction. "'Unchurched' is an ugly word," he adds, although he doesn't see himself as "churched" instead. "I'm a theist, but it's taken me most of my life to realize it," he confesses by reference to decades of personal religious inquiry and spiritual practice while conscientiously pursuing a business career and raising a family. At the same time, it's been years since he has joined his wife Sharon every Sunday at a small Methodist congregation near their home in Atlanta. They began attending there when the oldest of their three children reached middle school, and they stayed with it together until the youngest graduated from high school and left home for college.

Did they go to church simply because they thought it would be good for their children? "Not exactly," Joshua replies. "But we thought they needed something at that point." Sharon had grown up in a committed Methodist family in the Midwest, and part of his family were Methodists by history. "The church we joined was near us here, with just a hundred members, and they welcomed us," Joshua recalls. "The kids fit in with the other kids their age. We started teaching Sunday school. The kids liked it, and it was good for us, too. I even agreed with the Sunday school teacher!" he laughs.

What the children needed most in church, Joshua reflects, was "learning and belonging, with a sense of connectedness to the local community." What sort of lessons did he teach them in Sunday school? Did he follow a church curriculum? "Oh, God no!" Joshua protests. For example, he recalls, "We told them the story of David and Goliath, and its message of courage. We made it into a hands-on project, with all these pieces of colored construction paper you could tear with your hands and put together in a collage to show David and Goliath fighting. Picture for yourself what that was like!" Dramatic and vivid, this morality tale came to life, says Joshua, as a war story shot through with fear, loyalty, and love in the heart-stopping struggle between a Philistine giant armed with a huge sword and spear and an Israelite boy armed only with a sling and stone but guided by the hand of God (1 Sam. 17: 1–58).

This religious learning and belonging did not lead the children to lifelong churchgoing. "It was important for them growing up," Joshua judges. "But it wasn't too long before they got to high school and began asking what's with this religion stuff and these Bible stories," he adds. "They began comparing the kids at Sunday school with the kids you get to know in high school. And, guess what, there are way cooler kids at high school. So they began to drift away as teenagers."

Was this internal drift a cause for concern or blame? "Kids pick up what you really believe in," Joshua replies deliberately. "They watch what you do. They feel how you feel. They could see I wasn't exactly a true believer right at the heart of things in the church. I didn't know anything about John Wesley or the Methodist way of doing things. My wife did, but I didn't, and she has her own complex kind of faith, too. Maybe I began to drift before the kids did," he allows, "and they just followed along." Before the children graduated from high school and left home for college, they no longer wanted to go to church every week, and their parents did not try to force them. "We never told them you have to go," Joshua says.

No simple logic of cause and effect drives this dynamic process, as Joshua sees it, and parents should impose no authority on the freedom of conscience of adolescents old enough to decide responsibly on their own to leave church or stay in church. At the same time, differences between parents in religious background, outlook, and commitment can alter their children's sense of the possible, Joshua acknowledges, and make their outlook binocular in choosing to follow this or that exemplary path. Why has Sharon stayed in the local Methodist church, long after her children left home? "I'm part of St. Paul's," she answers directly, before turning to news of its members and her work there, including the joys of teaching a new generation of children in its Sunday school, many of them recently arrived from the Caribbean. Why did Joshua leave church, along with his children, although his wife has stayed? "That's a longer story," he answers.

By contrast to Sharon's devoted religious upbringing, with both parents taking the family to church every Sunday, and her lively participation in church camps in the summer and the Methodist Youth Fellowship in her teens, Joshua's father grew up in an unchurched family, already a generation removed from its Protestant roots. His mother was a dutiful Methodist churchgoer, and she made sure the children went with her every week. "But my mother was an independent thinker, too," Josh recalls, bred by youthful resistance to born-again proselytizing and summer Bible camps she endured in the devout Baptist company of her country cousins. "That brushed off on me," Josh thinks back, particularly when he reached "the age of reason and began thinking through Sunday school for myself. It wasn't just the doctrine. It was the feeling of it, too." He recalls one telling event in particular:

> One Christmas when I was seven, we had a big piñata full of candy. We took turns hitting it with a bat until it broke apart. All the candy came pouring out, a mountain of it on the floor. We all started grabbing handfuls and handfuls—candy greed!—and then I looked up and saw it was just us boys.

> The girls were all standing back, being good, but kind of intimidated, too. I stopped and turned around, then I went and handed out some of my candy to the girls. You know, like being a good little boy, even though I kept plenty for myself and took it home stuffed in my pockets. Actually, I felt kind of ashamed. The whole thing felt kind of shameful and out of kilter.

Afterward, Josh recounts, "I went and told my mother about it. I said I didn't want to go back, and I asked if I had to. She said no, and I didn't." So began, he attests, "a long, winding journey from faith to doubt and back again to something that's not so easy to name. It's not about church. I'm not against church, but I don't feel like I really belong there either. It's about freedom of religion. Not freedom from it, but in it," he pauses. "Call it religious liberty or free exercise, if you like," he smiles, "although I may be more a religious libertarian than a deist."

Joshua's parable of the piñata is "terribly unfair" to the local church of his childhood, he notes now, revealing only "the haplessness of Sunday school teachers" unable to manage rambunctious kids, not the Hobbesian selfishness of human nature. But its depiction of congregational community as a greedy if boyish battle of all against all reflects Josh's own point of view as an individual beginning to think for himself. He does so in terms that anticipate charges of hypocrisy leveled at churches by the unchurched in recent surveys, even if they echo little of Jefferson's enlightened arguments for religious freedom in eighteenth-century Virginia.[10]

Joshua's journey from faith to doubt and back, as he sees it now, springs from his quest to find his own true calling in moral and spiritual terms. It began in a family that stressed good character over churchgoing, and it led to sweeping vistas of skeptical reason when he discovered Bertrand Russell in high school and existentialism in college. "I was proud of being an irreligious liberal in high school, like Spencer Tracy playing Clarence Darrow in *Inherit the Wind*," he recalls with a smile.

> But later on I got such a dose of the bitterness of intellectualized nonbelief that I started struggling with it. I took it seriously. It was absolutely real for me, not just a set of ideas you study in philosophy class, then you walk out the door into real life. Do we want to believe something that's false for the sake of comfort, or do we want to face the freedom of the truth? That led me to take God seriously, and I do, even though I've never run into a doctrine that doesn't raise more theoretical questions than it answers for me.

In the course of comparative religious studies later in college and "countercultural seeking" in the long 1960s after graduating, Joshua experimented with different forms of religious practice, including meditation across Buddhist traditions. "I kept bumping up against my philosophical skepticism when it came to reading the doctrine and hearing the promises of enlightenment beyond words" and beyond belief. "But the practical part of it made sense to me," Joshua affirms. "That you could follow some discipline to actually clarify your own feelings. Find some balance in your experience, and come closer to the way things are." How has that worked out over the years? "Who knows?" he asks in turn. "I've made my peace with it, as best I can, even if I don't want to try to explain it or defend it. I've tried to live it out and do some good in the world."

Getting In and Out of Church

"I didn't go to church when I was little, but I really wanted to, sort of," remembers Sally, Josh and Sharon's oldest daughter, now nearing forty with two young children of her own, a master's degree in public administration, and a full-time career as the director of a local environmental organization. "I wanted to, once I got to kindergarten and I found out other kids went to church," she explains. "Before that, almost all our family friends and their kids were like us. They didn't go to church, and they went to lots of other kinds of weird spiritual things," she reflects. "I didn't know it was weird then. But I did know my grandparents really didn't like it, because they were devout Methodists on one side, and skeptics about all this spiritual stuff on the other." Once she began grammar school, Sally realized, "Weird is the enemy, and I just wanted to be normal. I wanted our family to go to church, because church seemed normal. I knew that my mother had Christian faith, and she grew up going to church. So if we could just be a nice churchgoing family, I felt like we would be a nice normal family."

When the family finally began attending the local Methodist church after Sally turned eleven, she felt more than a little relieved. "Relieved doesn't even begin to describe it," she recalls. "We could tell people we go to St. Paul's Methodist Church. We didn't have to explain why," she smiles, "even though, as churches go, this was a really liberal church. My father had definitely not found Jesus Christ as his personal Lord and Savior, like my grandmother told herself. I knew my father was not on board with all that. But he was going ahead with it for our sake, even if he didn't say so, and I was really grateful because now we could just be normal and accepted." That sense of grateful relief continued through her adolescence, Sally says, "even though I had my own sort of teenage rebellion. I got confirmed and I still wanted to be *culturally* Christian, you know, someone who goes to a normal church with pews on Christmas and Easter, and have that be part of who I was. It just wasn't, but I wanted that very badly."

How did Sally work through this conundrum? Much to her parents' surprise, and a little to her own, she decided to attend a Catholic university in the Northeast noteworthy for its commitment to character formation as well as academic excellence. "It's like I was doubling down on religious tradition and rules." Did it all work out? Sally answers carefully:

> Well, I got a good Catholic education, but it didn't exactly make me a good Catholic. It was this thing I was doing, and I came to feel a real understanding and affection for people who are deep into it. In college I actually went through Catholic confirmation. At the end of it I realized, "This isn't me." It's not who I am, even though I can get along great with Catholics and evangelical Bible believers, too. I can talk the talk with them, but I'm not one of them. I'm not.
>
> I don't know if I'm a Christian, but I know I'm not that kind of Christian. I came back to who I am. I believe a lot of things about God and Spirit and the Universe that don't fit neatly into a church construct, and I've come to a point in life where I'm okay with that. I don't need to be "normal" any more. I'm kind of cool and quirky and different, and I'm comfortable with my understanding of Christianity and the good things I take from it.
>
> *Q: For example?*
>
> I love the story of the nativity. I love it! I think it's a beautiful, wonderful, hopeful story. "Star of wonder, star of night, westward leading, still proceeding . . . Guide us to thy perfect Light." That sings in my heart. But I don't believe, "For God so loved the world that he gave his only begotten Son, that whosoever believes in him should not perish, but have everlasting life." I know John 3:16, but I don't believe, "No one comes to the Father except through me." (John 14:6) I don't believe that as humans we can possibly understand God, and that we can know it all because we wrote it down in the Bible. That's arrogant!
>
> There are mysteries in the universe beyond my comprehension. There is a great beyond, which I know nothing about, and I'm not going to be so arrogant as to say I can tell you what that is. So I accept different human ways of pointing toward the mystery beyond, without claiming that I've seen it and know exactly what it is. I feel like I understand doctrinaire Christians, but I don't agree with them. I don't really care about angels dancing on the head of a pin, or justification by works or faith alone. What I care about is whether you're trying to be a good and decent person, and actually make the world better. Where is your heart in all this?

Doesn't this conclusion bring her close to her parents' sense of spiritual vision and moral calling, even if she is not exactly following in their footsteps? To some extent, Sally grants, "but my mother still goes to church every single Sunday, and that gives me the heebie-jeebies!"

On the other hand, Sally argued long and hard with her husband-to-be, raised without religious affiliation or participation, to persuade him to recognize that his professed atheism was, in fact, an agnosticism open and ethical enough for her to accept. "In order to really be an atheist, you have to *believe* in the nonexistence of God, as if you can prove that negative," Sally reasons with a scholastic nod to her Catholic education. "Where's the actual proof of that?"

Doesn't Sally's acceptance of God's existence and the mystery of the universe beyond the bounds of traditional religious doctrine or revelation fit with commonsense views many Americans now hold? Most believe in many paths to one infinite truth, which almost all religions approach in part but none possesses in full. Most now think you need not believe in God in order to be a good person. "I would agree with all that," Sally says slowly, "except that now we have kids."[11]

As their daughter enters first grade, and her younger brother follows just two years behind, Sally and her husband David continue to go back and forth on whether to take the children to church. "I've mellowed, and I'm more open now, but I'm still not sure about it," David acknowledges. "A few years ago I was against it. We never went in my own family, growing up, and I always thought of religious people as holier than thou. The holier they claimed to be, the worse they turned out, the more intolerant and hypocritical. So watch out!" Sally feels less wary. But she agrees wholeheartedly that "by their fruits you shall know them," and she feels profoundly grateful for her unchurched husband's exemplary goodness, compassion, and tender loving care.

Will taking the children to church help in their moral formation and guidance, or will it confuse them in light of their parents' ambivalence? Is their innocence in matters religious nothing to worry about, at least for now, or is it a kind of ignorance that requires remedy? "I'm not sure," Sally reflects. "We drive past my mother's church, and the kids ask what she does there. I say she prays and sings, she listens to stories and talks to God. 'Who's God?' they ask. 'Is that like Santa Claus?'"

Sally frowns, "I don't know whether to laugh or cry. For all the weirdness in my religious upbringing, I always believed in God. That informed my growing up. It gave me comfort. It helped me through trials and tribulation later in life. I don't feel like it's all explainable, but I don't feel like it's all just random either," she pauses. "What I worry about for my kids at this point is if we were to layer on God, instead of it just being something they've known forever, then they're gonna feel confused."

If any clear alternative emerges, it will come down to "just doing it ourselves," Sally suspects. "But they're starting to ask questions that are hard to answer honestly in ways a four-year-old can understand. 'Mommy, is there a God? Is God real? Where do people go when they die?' Should we just say,

'Mommy believes this, and Daddy believes that?' That's a terrible answer to give a little kid, that different people have different points of view, when she's asking what's true, what's real and what's not."

Can't a child's understanding of truth evolve as the child grows up, and can't such questions and answers evolve accordingly? Yes, Sally grants, "but I don't want them to end up without any sense of wonder at the endlessness of the universe and the endless mystery of it. Whatever you call it, we need to realize how small we are in relation to this mystery. Yet we're part of it, too. We don't have all the answers, and we're not here all by ourselves. The hubris of thinking you have all the facts and all the answers puts you on the path to becoming selfish and prideful, whether you go to church or not," she charges. "I want my kids to feel small, and full of wonder, when they stand next to the ocean, and look out forever," she vows with feeling. "I want to tell them how, when I was carrying each of them inside me, I could feel this little soul wanting to be here, to be part of this wondrous world. I want them to be able to hear me, and know what I mean, and not just think it's mumbojumbo."

Thus, Sally mistrusts scientific fundamentalism no less than religious fundamentalism. She harks back to the hubris of classical tragedy no less than the original sin of Genesis, as she denounces arrogance for leading us astray from a graceful sense of wonder at our place on the sublime shore of an infinite Universe, if not for getting us expelled from Eden. She trusts she can "carry on nuanced conversations about the meaning of life with my kids," when they get older. But she fears that "it may be too late by then." How so?

> Because right now is when they're wondering about all this. There's a language of faith that makes sense to kids at this age: "God is Our Father. He has a naughty-and-nice list like Santa Claus. You can pray to God like writing Santa Claus a letter saying you want a bike." Kids can get their head around this! So why can't we use these stories and pictures now, before they become jaded and cynical teenagers later on?

What kind of faith would such learning serve? "I want to embed that wonder—that feeling of silent night, holy night, and following that star," says Sally, "that I've had since I was four years old, when my mother and I made a nativity scene with a little tinfoil star. You don't have to explain it. You do it, and it's there inside you," she sums up. "Like there really is One God. Both my parents were in sync with each other spiritually on that, and I'm really grateful to them for it."

Loving Things in Particular

A serious student of philosophy as an undergraduate in a leading Midwestern university, Joshua actively opposed the Vietnam War, and decided against going on to graduate school. He married Sharon, his longtime college girlfriend, and went to work instead in a local bank to support their rapidly growing family and give Sharon the chance to parent full-time when their children were young. They raised three children, born only a few years apart, in a snug suburban house just large enough to give each child a bed and a desk of their own. There they stayed, in a house much smaller than they could afford on Josh's gradually rising salary, and much smaller than the childhood homes they knew growing up in households headed by an industrial engineer and a business executive.

After ten years of making home loans and mortgages at the bank without ever feeling at home there, Joshua left to become a mortgage broker on his own with a small office at home. Staying in Atlanta, where the bank had transferred him, and then riding the wave of its real estate expansion through the 1990s, he and Sharon lived below their means, prepaying the mortgage on their first and only house, and saving to put their children through college debt-free with the help of scholarships and student jobs.

Volunteering in the classrooms of her own children in grammar school led Sharon back to school for a MSW when the children grew older, and eventually she moved into full-time social work once they reached college. That in turn opened the door for Joshua to leave his career as a mortgage broker to seek his calling, while they continued to pinch their pennies, pay tuition bills, and save for the future. "It's not easy to find the right thing to do, at least it wasn't easy for me," Joshua admits:

> You get Oprah and Dr. Phil on TV saying, "Just think positive and you can do it." But it's just not that easy. When I quit the mortgage business, first I looked at counseling degree programs, and I took classes for a semester. What I learned there was that I didn't believe in therapy. It does good for some people in certain circumstances. But for me it seemed like a bog to get caught in, fussing about yourself and your own story.

Analytical, incisive, and well versed in running his own business, Joshua found himself failing to fit neatly into the niche of a novice counselor or volunteer tutor. He then set about reading systematically across a range of social problems—educational, environmental, world hunger, and public health—and programs designed to engage these problems. "I know it sounds impractical, like a terrible luxury, but it turned out to be very practical," he says of this year of research, while his wife's work enabled them to make ends meet. "I settled on global poverty," he explains, "and then I started looking for the right niche, something specific and real that I could do about it." Turning from research on global poverty programs to exploring social networks of their sponsors and backers, Joshua found a church-related fundraiser for Caribbean relief agencies willing to let him tag along on a trip to Haiti and the Dominican Republic.

In Port au Prince, Joshua discovered a struggling orphanage begun by a conscientious, dedicated man who had grown up in the city's slums and made his way through church schools to a college on the island. "He knows who he is and what he's doing," Joshua discovered. "I saw the place and met him, and I felt, 'This is it!' I admired him, and I loved the kids," Joshua smiles. "So did Sharon when she came, and we decided this was something we wanted to do together. We'll know when we see it, we had decided, and we did." Joshua brought his business background to bear in helping to raise funds and organize budgets for the orphanage, while Sharon focused on the classrooms and curriculum of its nascent school.

In this compelling journey has Joshua Linden found his true calling or undergone something like a religious conversion? "We'll see about that," he answers with care. "I can look back and say it feels closer to a calling than what I was doing in the mortgage business," he acknowledges. "But I'm conscious of the original sin of pride, let's say, when it comes to proclaiming a true calling or doing something good in the world. How do you act in the world, and act without ego or pride? I'm not sure I'll ever resolve that."

Now his vision of doing good seems less grand than fighting global poverty, Joshua allows. It's more like "just loving these kids, and trying to help them a little bit," without knowing where it will lead. "Unintended positive consequences, that's the faith I go by," he attests, lit by Wendell Berry's insight that "the only way that things of value in this world are preserved is by those who love them in particular."[12]

Faith for the Future

At this point in seeking to fulfill his calling, does Joshua think of himself praying or engaging in spiritual practice, even if he no longer goes to church? "I try to be quiet and still for a while every day, to practice awareness, even though I wouldn't call it a 'spiritual practice,' let alone 'worship.'" Does this make him an agnostic, then, or a homegrown Buddhist? Or, if not, then a Christian in all but formal self-identification? "None of the above," he replies. "But I'm closer to the Crucifixion than going up the Buddha scale of enlightenment." Why so? "It feels more trustworthy, given my own experience," Joshua judges. Conversely, "Biblical ways of imagining my experience are actually the best ways I can make sense of life and try to be true to it. I'm indebted to the whole tradition, from Genesis to Augustine, Aquinas, even

Luther!" he confesses. In that sense, he grants, "I'm a religious person," so claiming to be "spiritual but not religious sounds soft and self-indulgent," as if we can live outside cultural traditions, social institutions, and history itself.

Does this embeddedness hold true for his children as well? "Yes, I think so, in their own way. None of them goes to church now," he acknowledges, and none of them takes their school-age children to church, at least not yet. "But all of them are good kids. They're leading good lives, they're doing good in the world. Sally works for a nonprofit environmental group. One's a teacher, one's a social worker."

Do the children believe in God? "You'd have to ask them," Josh replies. "The biggest optimist of the bunch calls herself 'a happy atheist,'" he smiles, "but she's probably the biggest do-gooder, too." Joshua and Sharon have faith in their children, he affirms, and they give thanks for the lifelong friends their children have grown up with and still see "all the time, almost like church." This network includes one extended family of "warm, funny, good kids" with whom they continue to share weekly childcare, holiday dinners, and close communion.

Does this profile of faith and freedom beyond the pews of organized religion fit the future we foresee? Do we need congregational bodies of common prayer in worship, creedal instruction, moral formation, and care of souls to animate our faith and shape our future face-to-face? Or can we do without congregational community, at least if we are blessed by exemplary parents, warm friends, good teachers and civic leaders, caring coaches, and mentors? "That's a good question," Joshua allows. "You can get together with really close friends and feel the social solidarity, even when you notice they're your privileged, educated, upper-middle class neighbors," he smiles. "But it doesn't have the solidarity of that bass-note feeling deep down inside you, of being part of the Body of Christ or taking refuge in the Buddha, dharma, and sangha. It doesn't have that deeper sense of security."

"We're kind of living off the moral capital of our past," Joshua reflects, "mainly the Jewish and Christian tradition. We haven't discovered something new and better." Instead, he suspects we have turned these traditions, including other world religions, into "therapeutic strategies" of how to feel better, do better, and grow more successful. Families and friendships, schools, teams, artistic and civic groups may serve as schools for virtue, Joshua hopes, and we can't do it all by ourselves, he judges, without some underlying moral vision and conviction to inspire our efforts in common. "Otherwise in the end it all comes down to struggling for power," he fears, even if we try to engineer prudent social cooperation to make for mutual benefit if not maximize prosperity and progress. "The victors write history, and the victorious end justifies the means," however unjust, corrupt, or cruelly indifferent to those who lose out.

Can't the same be said of religion itself, for example, in the Augsburg formula of *cujus regio, ejus religio* establishing the ruler's religion as the religion of the state.[13] That was then, and this is now, Joshua counters. "I see high tech and big business and finance taking over to buy the best government they can afford," instead of Protestant princes and Catholic kings fighting over state churches. "Maybe we don't need organized religion," he concedes. "But we do need organized *something* to push back against the universal genius of tech utopia and corporate consolidation we see all around us. These masters of the universe don't know it all, and it can't go on forever like this." Like what? A world where only the rich can afford to buy a house or send their kids to college, Joshua replies, count on a career or save for retirement. Can't government and the rule of law, schools and the light of learning, make such a moral difference? "Maybe so," he allows in the time of Trump. "But right now it's hard to look around and see government doing its part," and we cannot simply assume that individuals can pick up all the slack on their own.

Is there an alternative future we can build to do justly, love mercy, and provide for the general welfare, too? "We need to pay taxes and provide for everyone," Joshua answers. "Not just because it's in our best interests. Or because otherwise we'll blow the place apart and pollute the planet." That's all too true, he holds, but it's not real enough or urgent enough to inspire selfish, shortsighted social actors in the present to do what's right. "We need to pay attention to something bigger than our small selves to survive in the long run, and live decent lives in the short run," Joshua concludes. "We need to love our neighbors," not just give them a chance to get ahead. "Can we do that?" he asks. "Can we even mean it when we say it?"

Is there anything each of us can do, here and now, in or out of the pews? "I have no grand prescriptions," Joshua admits, "But I feel like my job is to pray and meditate every day to make my own motives as good as I can. I know they're not that great," he grants. What do you do about that? "You open up, you see what's in there, and let go of it. You give it to God. Then you look around and see what needs to be done. Do what's next, and something surprising can happen."

Like what? "Like grandparents taking care of the kids once a week," Joshua answers with a smile. "When they come to our house, it's precious. I realize that now. This is going to be for a very, very short time, and then it's going to be gone. If we do this lovingly and mindfully and faithfully, with a good heart, then this loving care is going to be in them until the day they die."

Joshua pauses for emphasis, then reflects, "When I look back to what has meant the most to me, it's alive in apparently insignificant moments where something wonderful happened. So I'm a big believer in insignificant, unimportant people and insignificant, unimportant moments," he concludes. "That's where my faith is kindled, and where I feel it most deeply. So, I've always been a little allergic to self-importance," he laughs, "other than my own." As parents and members of many different communities, we can "plant small seeds and do all we can to enable them to grow," Joshua affirms, even if we cannot control the weather or the world we pass on to our children. Human beings can be wondrous as well as wicked, born free and dependent, so "we need one another to become human," and our interdependence gives rise to hope.

A binocular vision of religious understanding and practice unfolds across generations from the parents of Joshua and Sharon to their children and grandchildren. It takes in unchurched family members from Joshua's father to Sally's husband. It reaches beyond the poles of liberal and conservative Protestantism that frame the religious upbringing of Natalie and Jim. Yet the intergenerational dramas of both these families combine distinctive cultural themes and moral stances drawn from one parent or the other—including philosophical skepticism and aesthetic inspiration—not simply either-or decisions to go to church or leave it.

Sally shares her father's insistence on individual freedom of religious belief and practice within the broad landscape of biblical theism, and she shares her mother's inspiring sense of wonder and hope in the Christian story of creation and redemption. She affirms for herself and her children the conscientious, caring ideals of moral character her parents exemplify, and the circles of moral community they embrace. Her commitment to the ethical individualism of an interconnected sense of spiritual selfhood and social responsibility in a wondrous yet wounded world comes through currents of parental example with and without Christian churchgoing. These crosscurrents in turn challenge her to find her own way, in or out of church, to fulfill the faith her family shares.

III. GOD FOR GOODNESS SAKE

Today most Americans agree that it is *not* necessary to believe in God to "be moral and have good values." This view has spread in step with the growing ranks of those who claim no religious affiliation, but almost half of all churchgoing adults now agree. They include two-thirds of mainline Protestants, one-third of White evangelicals, and a fourth of Black Protestants, along with nearly six in ten White Catholics and four in ten Hispanic Catholics.[14]

More Americans today likewise judge participation in organized religion as unnecessary to form good persons or good citizens. Instead, they see it as an option for individuals to choose freely in light of their own experience in trying out alternatives within and beyond church walls for the sake of personal learning and enjoyment, social connection, and cultural enrichment.

These alternatives can be found in pews or classrooms, in circles of scripture study or yoga exercise, through charismatic testimony or therapeutic self-expression, spiritual discipline or athletic training. You can become one with the body of Christ in worship, or one with nature in hiking the wilderness. You can merge with the music in dance or with the game in play.[15]

So, for example, "Our parents took us to church, once we were old enough to know what we were doing," recalls Paul Weiss, a bright, serious young executive working as an analyst of corporate strategy. "Then they stopped taking us," he adds, once he and his younger brother came through adolescence and went off to college. His father and mother, an engineer and a public health administrator respectively raised in Reform Jewish and Catholic families, married in a civil ceremony they composed themselves. They wrote their own vows to express their commitment to love each other, help their neighbor, and work for social justice.

The family had not been going to church or temple before Paul and his brother reached school age, he notes, "But they thought we needed to go. Not to be indoctrinated, but to join a community and learn what this was about. It was cultural enrichment, learning the stories and teachings" from the Bible and Christian tradition. "Moses and the Ten Commandments, Jesus and the Sermon on the Mount," he nods. "You'll be better off for informing yourself about this, and I've found that to be true."

Were moral education and formation part of the process, too? "It wasn't just cultural history," Paul agrees. "It was a way into a conversation with your own spirituality, wherever that lies and leads you."

> You have to find your own path. You don't have to agree with this or that dogma. I didn't go to church to receive moral instruction from some authority. My parents are humanists. You form your moral universe through conversations and examples of being a good, kind person, being oriented to others instead of being selfish. It was more like the Enlightenment. Be responsible and fair because you should, not because God commands you or threatens you with hell.

What did Paul Weiss discover in going to church? "Church is different," he answers, thinking bactk to the "liberal, musical" congregation of the United Church of Christ (UCC) where his parents ended up after trying out Unitarian and other mainline Protestant congregations near their hillside suburban home in the San Francisco Bay Area. "That's the first thing you notice, the different way people talk and move around. Chanting. Kneeling and standing together. The music, the feeling of it. The space." He pauses, "My mother used to joke that she went to church mainly for the choir. I found a lot of truth in that. I felt it in the music and singing together."

Later in adolescence, Paul recalls, "I could feel something profound there, something spiritual, something deeper or higher that connected each of us and our family with everyone else." If you strip away all the evil done in the name of God through history, Paul says, "You can actually appreciate all the good that people have done, or at least tried to do, by listening to stories of Jesus and trying to follow his example."

Whether these stories are literally true, Paul reflects, as with stories of Moses or Buddha, "they've inspired millions of people to make lives we can learn from and cultures we can share in. That connects us. That's real." By contrast, Paul's younger brother reacted against churchgoing early in adolescence. "He thought the rituals were creepy, and saying the Creed was like a cult recitation," Paul laughs. "He said he didn't believe this stuff, so he shouldn't have to say it." Agreed? "I didn't exactly believe all this stuff, Christ sitting at the right hand of the Father in Heaven, and the one holy Church. But chanting it together every week with good people you know, there's something in that you can get with."

Moreover, conscientious religious belief can be no less selective than sincere religious practice. "It's not all or nothing. It's not 'In for an ounce, in for a pound,'" Paul reflects, like Jill rejecting belief in unbaptized babies left in limbo. "Maybe I'm an agnostic, but I'm not an atheist. What's the point of that? Trying to *prove* God doesn't exist? You're claiming a kind of authority for reason that makes you a true believer, too," Paul judges, much like Sally. "Is that authority real? I don't know. Most of my generation, or at least the people I hang out with, don't know either, and we don't see it as something worth getting into," he pauses. "It's not socially or culturally relevant to what I'm doing every day."

If Paul is agnostic toward religious doctrine presented as scientific data, historical fact, or logical proposition, he is more open to moral guidance and inspiration arising from faith lived out in exemplary fashion. He recognizes the living experience of religious rites and practices in shaping moral visions, moods, and motives. For example, the traditional Buddhist funeral rites he attended for the father of a close college friend from an assimilated Asian American family proved eye-opening and heart-touching. "You could see it expressing the family's care and respect for one another, their filial piety, the way they raised their children. All of that was coming through this tradition of mourning. It was wonderful," he affirms. "The monks in the temple took in the family and took care of them, and you felt like the body and soul of your father were going to the right place. You're facing death and casting around for something to do. You can see why humans have been doing this for thousands of years. This is powerful stuff!"[16]

Faith in Public

In the local UCC church he attended through high school with his parents, Paul admired the pastor he heard preaching love and justice without pontificating or scolding. "He wasn't preachy. He wasn't trying to make you believe something you didn't. He was thoughtful and kind." What was his message? "Do good works, be a good person," Paul sums up. The pastor engaged the world in ways that lined up with Paul's own progressive moral and political intuitions. "I admired him, and I had a really good relationship with him," Paul acknowledges warmly. That relationship continued as Paul joined his mother week by week in the church choir for several years, then tapered off before he left for college at eighteen. There he attended "rarely if ever" on his own. But he continued to go to church occasionally with his parents when he was home for the holidays and summers.

"I can't say I missed church after I started college," Paul Weiss recalls as a newly minted MBA hard at work in a demanding corporate job. "But now I realize that what I miss a lot from college was a little like church. Having friends you live and study with, you play with, you get to know and get close to. You run track together, you push each other. You put out for the team, you sacrifice for it. Do that, and you feel part of something bigger than yourself. It's an unspoken bond. It's almost like you would go to war with them, even if you might disagree with them about other things, or you wouldn't even be friends if you weren't teammates." Paul pauses, "I miss that intensity. Especially now, when you're working all the time, and you're casting around for the meaning of it all. What's it about?" he wonders. "Besides making money and paying the bills? Just hit the bars after work, then go home and watch TV?"

Aims of advancing a professional career and succeeding in business can be compelling, Paul reflects, but they fall short of creating a community of shared commitment and responsibility. "You want to make money and make your way," he acknowledges, "but it's not always clear that you're making things better for anyone besides the shareholders. My individual rights and liberties are important, but not to the exclusion of everyone else's well-being. That's troubling," he confesses. "It makes you angry, especially tax cuts that give to the rich and take from everyone else. It makes you wish you could be part of another country, but you can't, so where do you look?" Paul asks deliberately.

Would Paul consider ever going back to church or synagogue for the sake of such communion and community? "I've been in a serious relationship since college with someone from a mixed religious and secular background even broader than my own, and we're engaged to get married," he answers. Neither of them has attended church or temple since leaving home, Paul notes, but "we want to have kids, and we're thinking about how we want to raise them. So we've checked out some places, especially some Unitarian churches near here."[17]

Are they following in the footsteps of Paul's parents? "Not exactly," he replies, in terms of congregational choices centered on liberal Protestant possibilities. But he would take the same angle of approach to religious institutions and beliefs in general, he says, because his parents "gave us a lot of autonomy when we were old enough to use it. They took us to church as kids and exposed us to it up close. They didn't pretend you can just choose in a vacuum later on."

Paul's childhood experience of church informs his search for a congregation to attend as a married adult to find help in raising children. How so? "To engage with the real world and do good works," he answers, to sum up the moral message and example he seeks to follow. Engage practical social issues such as hunger and homelessness, but "don't reduce sermons to political speeches or turn the church into a political faction." Conversely, "don't just pass out the same old platitudes," he urges by reference to a powerful sermon he heard preached in a UCC church he and his fiancée visited. "It was awesome. He talked about George Floyd, and racial injustice on the ground, and what we all have to do about it, if we're not just going to keep being complicit."

If they can find and join such a congregation, Paul pledges, then "we're open to institutional religion. If it can help us in our spiritual self-development and help the community without playing politics. Institutions have power. Religious institutions aren't the most powerful," he concedes, "but maybe they can help us make things better in business and government." That calls for a caring community, Paul stresses, "not just a transactional political party that's operating in terms of 'more for us.' That's a lot of the political problem right now, and we need to mobilize against it," he argues, through "good works and collective action instead of highhanded moralizing. You don't need to reinvent the wheel or figure out how to do it all by yourself. You can just join in."

"The arc of the moral universe is long, but it bends toward justice," Paul quotes Martin Luther King Jr.[18] "That's what I thought earlier in my life. It's not all steady progress, but the arc gets more inclusive and progressive from the New Deal and the Great Society on. We're going to look out for one another, and not let anyone fall through the cracks. We're going to be responsible and take care of one another. Now I'm not so sure of that," Paul admits. "It looks like a lot of Americans don't feel that way, and they're willing to let things go off the rails. That's a pretty dark, depressing prospect," Paul confesses. "It makes you want to find another path and get with people in communities headed in a different direction."[19]

Would Paul feel more directly drawn to a particular church or synagogue if only that congregation were more appealing in some specific way? "Or maybe if *I* were coming from someplace different?" he asks in turn, thinking of friends in college from more traditional Catholic, evangelical Protestant, and Jewish backgrounds. "Some of my good friends from college keep kosher and separate sets of silverware. They're normal people, *and* that's part of who they are, even if that seems to me more cultural than religious per se," he observes. "That's just how it is for them, and I realize it's not my kind of family background or the town where I grew up," a cosmopolitan Bay Area suburb of educated professionals. His own background and religious upbringing seem inseparable from his aims in looking for a congregation now, he reflects, where "I can search for my own soul. Where what I say and do and believe can be in concert," in practical ways his children can see and come to do likewise as they come of age.

"There's a balance you have to find between trying to direct your children's good behavior and beliefs to fit with your own views and the good of society," Paul judges, "while accepting that they should grow into autonomous persons" who will choose to believe and act responsibly for themselves. "Choose life," he urges (Deut. 30: 19). "You can tell them that, but you can't exercise too much control and try to just mold people into a certain image, even if you think you know best." But what if you do know best, or at least you know better than your children before they come of age? Yes, Paul allows with a laugh, "It's easier to plan this out before you actually start having kids and having problems with them. Then you do what you can, and what you need to," he concludes. "You want them to follow their own better angels, but you can't force them."

From Church to Spiritual Search

Paul's mother Diane agrees, "They've both turned out to be really good kids. We tried to set a good example, but give them all the credit. Them and everyone else along the way—teachers, coaches, family, and friends." As parents, she allows, "We didn't have a master plan for going to church or temple. We had to feel our way, and we got a late start." How so? "Paul's brother came home from kindergarten one day and asked me, 'What's the difference between a fairy and an angel?" That really caught me off-guard!" she exclaims. "By that age I would never have asked that question, because I already knew all about real angels in heaven and make-believe fairies in fairy tales. I knew from church and Catholic school and my family. I'm raising a religious idiot, I thought, and I need to do something about it," she nods. That began the family's search for a congregation to fill this void.

How did this search compare with her own religious upbringing? “I can’t remember ever not going to church from the time I was a baby,” Diane replies. “We went every Sunday, all of us. Why? “Because you do. Because it’s real, and you should. You don’t have to figure it out.” Why not? “Because you’re immersed in it,” she explains. “Family, friends, school, nuns. We went to Catholic schools from kindergarten all the way through high school.”

Religious and moral matters were not simply given and taken for granted, “but it all fit together in one system,” Diane reflects. “It’s all structured, and it gives you a blueprint for how to live your life. You follow all these rules, and you try to be perfect. Deviate and you’re damned,” she smiles. “When I finally did begin to question it in college, I found out I couldn’t believe it all intellectually. But also the blueprint didn’t work for me anymore. It was still logically consistent in its own way, but it didn’t feel internally coherent to me,” Diane thinks back. “I tried my best to be good and follow all the rules. But I began to struggle with the false authority of it, the contradictions and hypocrisy I felt,” she frowns. “It started coming apart, and I couldn’t do it anymore. I wanted to live life as it was meant to be. But what do I do, given who I am?” she asks. To face that question, “I had to get out of the box, and look beyond the blueprint.”

What did Diane do instead? “I looked at what was good and not so good in what I was doing in my life, and how I was feeling about it,” she answers. Did she leave organized religion behind? “Not really,” she grants. “I stopped going to church. But growing up Catholic was a major part of what formed me as a child, and I carry a lot of that with me. As a child that dovetailed with thinking about God and Satan, heaven and hell, and feeling fear and anxiety about it. How does someone become a saint? How does someone lose their soul? How do these things happen?” she wondered. During her college years, Diane reflects, “Gradually the ethical piece became clear in all this.”

> You need to be a good person. Each of us needs to be strong in order to sacrifice for others. If you have more than others, then you should share it with them. I think that was at the root of the faith I grew up in. Maybe not for everyone else, but that’s what was most important for me in my family: How can you be a really good person, because that’s what life is about. That is what God wants, and God *is* good. That’s why we’re here, to make more good in the world. I still feel that way!

Along this dimension of moral depth Diane sees the continuity of her own religious upbringing with that of her children, despite her parents’ dismay when she stopped going to church in her twenties and their relief when she returned in her thirties with children of her own. “I never felt ostracized.”

Yet Diane's underlying moral conviction of God's goodness and human flourishing provides no panacea in practice. "You realize how hard it is to do," she grants, "given our human wants and needs, and the way we live. You see someone in need, and you think, 'I should help.' But you don't. You're in a hurry, you're busy. You'll do it next time," she says with a skeptical sideways glance. "You look around and see a lot of falling short, or maybe not even trying to be good. Wouldn't it be wonderful if we tried harder?" she shakes her head. "But we don't."

Why is that? "It's possible there is no why," Diane grants in reply. "The big bang just happened, and it's all random. I accept that conceptual possibility. But since we really don't know, and we have some real choices to make, why not 'choose life,' and let striving for what's good give real meaning and purpose to our life?" she asks in turn. "Or would you rather say we're just here for as long as we can manage to tread water and survive. Then we die, and it's oblivion? Not me!"

Is choosing to do good simply an existential or functional choice? Don't reciprocity and interdependence in human society put the lie to individual survival in a state of nature?[20] "Whether we're hard-wired or socialized that way, we feel good when we do good," Diane replies. "We feel bad when we do something bad, or we do nothing when we can help someone in need." Altruism and egoism are entangled in daily life, she allows, but "caring for someone gives you a bigger dopamine hit than getting stuff." Human beings "naturally" feel for one another, Diane is convinced, with a nod to natural law. That is one reason, she says, that "so many Americans feel disturbed and depressed" by the economic hardship and political strife now scarring the country.

What can and should we do about such social suffering and injustice, especially when political policy, public provision, and economic strategy seem to fall so far short? "Dear God, help me to be the person I want to be," Diane replies. "Help me to be courageous. Help me figure out what I can do to make things better, and do it. Let me be the person others need me to be." She pauses, then adds, "I say that a lot." Is that a prayer? "Yes, it is," Diane acknowledges. "It's a prayer to a greater good, some energy or entity for good in how humans treat each other in the world. 'God is *love*' captures that, if you put the stress on 'love,' and you love others for their own sake, not because you're going to get a payoff in eternity."

Diane has come to this view from her religious upbringing as a child, she thinks, partly through her own education and experience in coming of age. But it also stems from her marriage to Nat, who grew up in a nonobservant, culturally fluent, and morally committed Jewish family. "Do unto others, do your mitzvah," she sums up. "That's what Jewish tradition teaches, without holding out the carrot and stick of an afterlife in heaven or hell. I agree with that!"

"And even if it seems like we're going backward in the short run, I'm still looking for that big arc of history that ultimately bends to the good," Diane vows, invoking Martin Luther King with more trust perhaps than her son. Still hopeful? "I am," she affirms. "I can't predict the politics. But your spirit lives on in the people who love you, who carry on your love and sacrifice. They are grateful for your struggle to be good, and they try to carry it on."

Practice What You Preach

Diane's focus on moral example, inspiration, and intuition at the heart of religious faith has shaped the religious upbringing of her children, as she sees it now. "First of all, I want them to have a real sense of right and wrong, and to know why it is important to be an honorable and decent person," Diane recalls saying to Nat when they began to discuss childrearing and religion as the children neared school age. "Second, I don't want them to be ignorant of the Western canon. I want them to know about the lives of the saints and the parables of Jesus and the voices of the prophets." How did this translate into practice? "I'm willing to raise the kids as Reform Jewish," Diane told Nat. "But he said he'd rather just take them out hiking in the temple of nature."

Diane agreed, but she held out to join some religious congregation that suited them both, if only they could find one. That proved problematic at first. "Call me a secular humanist, because that's who I am," Nat avers, after growing up in a nonobservant family, then vigorously but vainly "seeking intellectual answers to ultimate questions" in college and being disappointed by Hillel as well as Campus Crusade for Christ in seeking a spiritual home. "In Hebrew *or* English," he sums up, "listening to the Word of God just wasn't my cup of tea." Yet Nat agreed to "go hunting for a House of God" for the children's sake. "I do believe our children study us to see if we practice what we preach," he explains. "That's what they learn, for better or worse, and that's what we agreed on."

Once the family began looking for a fitting congregational home, Diane recalls, "we found "encounter groups, faith healing, new age touchy-feely" in varied denominational guises, before winding up in a UCC congregation noteworthy for its liturgical worship and music. "The music was beautiful, the service was peaceful, and they weren't pounding on us" for doctrinal allegiance or personal testimony, Diane reports. "This could work, I thought, and we really did it. I joined the choir, my husband became an usher, and we went just about every Sunday while the kids were in school."

Their family grew close to the pastor, who in turn embraced them. "We went with the program," Nat explains. "But he enabled us to stay with it," by finding a middle path through what would otherwise have been "either-or, inside-outside decisions" about membership and identity, particularly whether to baptize the children. "We could belong to this community and affirm it," Diane sums up, "without having to deny who we were" and the diverse communities of faith that formed them, including their Jewish and Catholic families of origin.

How did their children take to churchgoing? "I think they kind of took everything at face value," Diane muses. "I can't remember them ever quizzing us about beliefs or prayers, at least not until high school. Paul seemed to take it all in as good stories, and he grew immersed in the music," Diane observes, much as she herself did. "The choir wasn't all that good, but the music was great. It was a total-body experience, once you got into it, where you become part of a larger organism. You join in something beautiful that connects you to all the goodness of life and all these people you sing with. You feel it, even if you also understand it as a neurological phenomenon. It transports you. It's so exquisite!"[21]

Meanwhile, Paul's brother "got adamant at fifteen or sixteen about not believing things, and not having to go along with the program," Diane recalls. "Not hostile but clear about it. He was doing fine at school, in sports, with other kids. So we said okay, you don't have to pretend. But come to church with us anyway." When Paul went East to college, he met several observant Jewish students who became close friends and housemates. "He really learned about Judaism from them," his mother says gratefully. "He read about it. He went to synagogue with them, even if he never really considered converting," his mother notes. "He was more interested in how it tied into their commitments and values. He wants to do good, and do well, and he's trying to figure out if that's possible," Diane nods in affirmation.

Granting this continuity between Diane's moral aims and the course of her children's religious upbringing, does she have any second thoughts on the process? "You have to set a good example, you can't just talk a good game," she answers forcefully. "I think we tried to do that in our own lives, even if we didn't go all out with it. We took them to the food bank, for example, but we didn't volunteer there every week. Our kids are both aware that they grew up in an upper-middle class, mostly White, privileged suburb," she reflects. "They're aware of the privileges they have had and still have" that "are not, in fact, granted to many, many people who deserve them just as much or more. And they're responsible for changing that." Both children have expressed how much they appreciate their parents for "modeling service," Diane acknowledges. "But raising kids this way puts a lot of responsibility on you for that modeling, and for really talking through things as they come up in real-life situations," she adds. "Is what you did in this or that situation really okay? Is what the other kid did okay? Why or why not?"

Such moral engagement not only takes time and attention, Diane cautions, when parents are often short on both. It can also press against parents' abiding concerns to keep their children safe and sheltered from moral conflict and confusion. "If you're not ready to give your children a structured moral blueprint like I had growing up Catholic," Diane judges, then "you need to get into their thinking as they get older. You have to tell them 'No!' when they're young." But "you can't just preach at them," she warns, "as if you have all the answers, lock, stock, and barrel. You have to recognize they are persons with minds of their own, and you can't just lay down the law."

When it comes to moral education and formation, including Sunday school or parochial school, Diane argues, "You cannot assume it's being done by somebody else, and you cannot trust anybody else to do it without getting involved yourself," until each child comes of age as a young adult. Then "you have to work through it for yourself, and integrate it into who you are." By that point, as a parent, "You hope your kids are good people with good friends, working hard, and finding their own path," Diane smiles. "And I do, thank God."

Goodness for God's Sake

The moral good of religion comes to the fore in this account, along with a stress on conscientious autonomy in living out this good in searching for one's own soul and finding one's own path. Threaded through generations, these "do unto others" ideals bridge differences between Diane's devout Catholic upbringing and her husband Nat's nonobservant Jewish family of origin. They frame their son's understanding of going to church for the sake of cultural enrichment and moral development in terms evident if less emphatic in our two prior cases. Moral formation, as Paul puts it, becomes "a way into a conversation with your own spirituality," by contrast to dogmatic inculcation and commanding moral authority.

In college Diane stopped going to Mass and apparently broke with the Catholic catechism of her childhood as decisively as Jim broke with his born-again Baptist revivalism. Yet Diane's upbringing carries over into her individualized examination of conscience, and her discovery of "the ethical piece" that redeems a good God and resolves the fearful predicament of losing or saving one's soul into the moral aim to become a good person who will sacrifice and share with others to make more good in the world. Her son may resist religious dogma, as he puts it in terms akin to Sally. But he appreciates the moral moods and motives bred by keeping kosher no less than singing Christian hymns. He links the moral promise of congregational life to the communion of college friends and teammates he misses now that he is yoked to a corporate career. He hopes for a moral counter-community in which to raise his children and sustain his own commitments to a more just and caring society. Thus the inherent good of religious participation in tune with faith in what's really real grounds the moral good of religion in forming virtuous persons, families, and citizens as a matter of principle, however challenging it proves to realize in practice.

IV. CONTINUITY IN CHANGE ACROSS GENERATIONS

Why not follow in your father's footsteps? That's an apt question for William Winters, the son of a devoted Methodist minister and the father of a conscientious daughter who left church after she left home in Atlanta for college in New England. Raised in a devout family, sitting in church every Sunday, and listening intently to his father preach, Will remains deeply faithful in his own way, although he attends services irregularly. He is mindful of the distance that his daughter, Marie, has traveled away from his churchgoing childhood, and he weighs his own role in this drama of continuity and change across generations.

"My father wanted me to love the church and follow him into the parish ministry," Will recalls. "He couldn't understand why I went to graduate school instead of seminary," to become a professor of philosophy instead of becoming a pastor. The roots of that choice of calling run wide and deep, Will believes, connecting family, church, and schooling to shape his commitment to finding his own way in the world as he came of age, not just following in his father's footsteps. "I was pretty much unconscious of it at the time I was growing up, but I felt some resistance to just following along in the church, and I think that made a difference in my own religious practice. I was observant, but I was holding back, too, and I think my daughter picked up on that."

For example? "I remember making a point to my daughter near the end of high school, and her reminding me of it later on," Will replies. "That once you go off to college on your own, you make whatever decision about church you think is appropriate for you. I stuck by that," he nods. "I never tried to get Marie to see things my way. I always felt that she respected my Christian angle of vision, even though she didn't share it. And I respected the integrity of her decision."

Will recognizes that he and his wife, no less faithfully raised by devout parents and no less well-educated in the liberal arts college where they met, concentrated their parental attention on the moral character and conduct of their daughter:

> "That was kind," we'd tell her, when she was caring. Or, "Always try not to be cruel," when she saw cruelty in others. As she got older, it became more about

> moral dispositions than moral rules or commands. By that standard she is really in line with our values. She really does embody the virtues of caring for others, fairness, and honesty. She tries not to harm anyone or hurt anyone.
>
> She was clear about becoming a good person, and what that meant to us. But she was not so sure church was all that important to us. She's said that, and I've thought about it, sometimes with some regret. I've asked myself how we gave her that message, and what we could have done differently.
>
> *Q: How so?*
>
> We would often miss going to church when she was growing up. And when we would go, I would often evaluate the sermon, and it usually came up short.
>
> *Q: So pick your spots, and judge for yourself? How does that compare with your own childhood in church?*
>
> I was always there. I can remember liking the music, when I was five or six years old, listening to the sound of my mother's voice singing hymns sitting next to me, and feeling it was beautiful. Of course, I didn't understand what my father was saying in the sermon, but I was aware of the tone and lilt of his voice, the rhythm of it, the emotion he could convey from the pulpit.

Will later came to realize more of the meaning of worship and appreciate its articulate energy as well as its emotional power. "You're inside the experience of it as a kid, in the flow of it. At what point do you begin to step outside and see it from the outside in?" he asks. By the time he was in high school, Will answers, "I began to read my father's books. They were mainly by old Protestant liberals. I was taken by their notion of a finite God, mostly running along the lines of Boston Personalism, headed toward process theology but not there yet." Such study in turn pointed Will toward teaching philosophy as a profession to pursue instead of preaching and pastoral ministry as a calling to follow.[22]

"We're born into a web of meaning and experience," Will observes. "Part of the allure of academic life is that we can climb outside it, look at the whole of it, and try to understand it. But we're still tangled up in it, and it's tangled up inside us, especially in the unbroken continuity of family, in one way or another, for all the change and conflict."

Will recalls conversations with his faithful mother, in his twenties and beyond, about life and life everlasting. "She wanted me to believe what she believed, for example, about heaven and the afterlife. 'You don't believe that this is the end of it, do you, that this is all there is?' She would ask me that, and I would say something like, 'Mother, these are things we just don't have knowledge of. We simply trust that God embraces us within God's life, which is an eternal life.'"

Will pauses, then adds, "Doing philosophy can be a little like psychotherapy, I'll sometimes tell undergraduates to lure them in. You can find out at least a little of what formed you, the traditions and other forces that shaped your world." You cannot absolutize your own tradition, he cautions, because it's one of many. But neither can you ignore it or dismiss it "without throwing away a part of who you are."

In fact, Will now sees much of the distance between his religious faith and his daughter's unchurched stance through the lens of their distinctive habits of mind, education, and professional work. A clinical researcher with an advanced degree in life sciences, Will's daughter has "a mathematical, statistical mind, with a real empirical bent," he says. "That has served her well in her work. I always gravitated more toward philosophy. So now we learn from each other," Will notes with a smile. Disciplinary differences do not tell the whole story, of course. Thinking back to his own adolescence, punctuated by church summer camps lit by blazing bonfires and hortatory preaching, Will recalls his daughter's more modest immersion as a teenager trying out the local church youth group, but gradually losing interest in its easygoing activities without finding fast friends or compelling ministry. "That was probably more an issue of belonging than believing," Will judges, "and the group not getting far enough beyond just hanging out to make it worth sticking around."

Existential struggles over God's goodness and human suffering challenged Marie's faith as a young adult, Will recognizes, in tandem with courtship and marriage across religious lines. Her husband remains politely yet firmly resistant to organized religion, after growing up unchurched since childhood, when his parents parted ways with their church over rigid pastoral authority exercised without personal concern or care.

The religious drama of Will's family extends across generations to his granddaughter, now in the third grade. "She's very bright!" he exclaims with a warm smile. "At times I've thought it would be nice if she could someday find herself in a church, in a Sunday school class or youth group, where she could talk with other kids her age about what's important, what's really important in her life." She and her parents now spend Sunday mornings doing things as a family, he knows, and he sees good in that. Yet he spots signs of religious curiosity and interest in his granddaughter, for example, in response to his rehearsing, much to her delight, the first song he can recall singing as a child: "Jesus loves me! This I know, / For the Bible tells me so; / Little ones to Him belong; / They are weak, but He is strong."[23]

However skeptical Will's daughter and son-in-law seem about organized religion, he asks himself, just how far away from him do they actually stand on religious belief? He wonders:

> Are their fundamental convictions about the world all that different from mine? We certainly differ, I wouldn't deny that. But I can also see continuities across the differences. Are the continuities deeper, more substantial, than the differences? Maybe. I think we share a sense of awe and wonder at the mystery beyond our propositions, although for me Christian faith offers a distinctive view of the mystery that doesn't resonate for them.

When it comes to congregational practice and denominational membership, there's a clear contrast between his daughter and himself, Will acknowledges, but it begins to blur when he opens the window wider to "moral and spiritual practices" that include supporting peace and justice, aiding the poor, and taking care of the environment through diligent recycling and energy conservation. "They're for all of that, not so different from us, even if they don't call it the stewardship of God's Creation."

Will accepts his daughter's decision to become unchurched as a matter of conscience and choice made as a morally responsible adult, even if he wishes that he himself had been more attentive to her early religious upbringing. At the same time, he hopes the upbringing of his granddaughter, Alison, will give her the same sort of freedom that he gave his daughter to choose from firsthand experience of congregational life, while he abides by his decision not to intervene with her parents to take Alison to church.

What could happen as Alison comes of age? Not quite anything, but perhaps something surprising, Will allows, as he considers several culturally cosmopolitan colleagues whose adolescent children became born again and joined spirit-filled "bible churches," much to their parents' dismay. "If Alison moves in that direction, will my daughter be able to say to her, as I said to my daughter, 'You make your own decisions and live with them, and I'll respect them.' I think so."

Rites, Rules, and Core Values

Will's daughter agrees. Marie and her husband, Jack, are committed to enabling their daughter, now nine years old, to decide for herself, freely and responsibly, whether to go to church when she comes of age. "Living out the core moral values she's been raised with, that's what's essential," Marie stresses. Alison now goes to church occasionally with her grandparents, and she joins her parents at church with her extended family on Christmas and Easter. She is interested in religion, and curious about it, and both her parents respond as honestly as they can to her questions about religious belief and practice. "Sometimes she'll say she does believe in God, or she's thinking about it, and I'll ask her what she's thinking," Marie smiles. "If she asks me about God, I tell her about God in the Bible and Christianity. Sometimes she'll ask if I believe in God, and I tell her the truth: I don't know, I'm not sure."

Marie explains, "There are parts of me that like the idea of an all-powerful Being in the world. And parts of me that don't, because then it doesn't make sense that there's so much suffering in the world." There are good people who believe in God, Marie tells her daughter, and good people who do not. Bible stories of what God does and says are true in their own way, and people understand God in their own way in different faiths and churches.[24]

This conversation will continue to unfold and deepen, Marie expects, even if it doesn't become entirely clear or conclusive until Alison comes to her own understanding of faith as an adult. In nurturing this open-ended dialogue and responding honestly to her daughter, Marie sees herself holding true to the respectful, responsible stance of her parents in her own religious upbringing, although she recognizes how different her own childhood seems from her daughter's. She reflects,

> I grew up steeped in church through my parents and grandparents. It was always very, very present, not something separate. I don't recall learning to pray by explicit instruction. "Now I lay me down to sleep" was in there with nursery rhymes and songs from the time I was very small.[25]
>
> So was going to church. It was a big, high sanctuary, and I vividly remember the feeling of that space. I liked the majesty of it. As I got older, my best friend and I would skip services and explore the old church school building next door. We had the run of the place from basement to attic—the nooks, crannies, and closets, the art studio and backstage dressing rooms.

"That became a kind of sacred space," Marie recalls, linked to her feeling for the "ceremony" of worship services. "I liked the music. I liked memorizing things and repeating them rhythmically, the Lord's Prayer, the Apostles Creed. I liked the ritual, the repetition and poetry of it. We used to recite lines we'd memorized, swinging back and forth on the swings out in the church playground."

By contrast, Marie recalls, "I zoned out during the sermons. They didn't interest me as a little kid. From pretty early on, third or fourth grade, the notion of some kind of bigger presence presiding over all of this never quite sat right with me, even if it sounded nice." Was she a skeptic at the age of eight or ten? "Well, more an empiricist, I'd say now. From very early on, the empirical data I saw didn't align with this big idea." What was missing? Didn't she ever talk to God in prayer? Didn't God ever talk back? "I really don't think so," Marie pauses, then reflects:

> What God and religion and spirituality all hinge on, for me, are values. The good of a life driven by moral values is what I took most strongly from church and my family from the beginning. It's hard to separate the two, because they are so intertwined. But church feels like one medium for defining and reinforcing those values. Over the course of my life since then I feel like I've encountered others that have had an equivalent or even stronger impact on me.

Does this ethical hinge separate Marie from Christian faith, or connect her to liberal Protestantism and its stress on a social gospel of doing justice and loving mercy between Sundays? She grants this intellectual and moral connection. But she underscores her stronger aversion "to obedience to some greater, invisible power telling me what to do, and following arbitrary rules laid down long ago. Following archaic rules that don't align with my own values feels wrong," she attests. "To the extent these rules align with my values, these rules make sense to me, and I feel like I don't need a religious structure to reinforce me in following them."

For example, biblical commandments not to kill, steal, covet, or lie make moral sense, Marie affirms, and so does loving your neighbor. But arbitrary rules of pious speaking and feeling do not, she objects,

> Sitting in Sunday school classes, you find out you have to talk in a certain way, with a preciousness of language I could never quite understand. You have to express a kind of piety I didn't feel, and get into an emotional posture I couldn't fit. It seemed like a pretense.
>
> When you step into this special space of the church, you become magnanimous. You speak in a special language that's very big and all-encompassing. It didn't seem right to me, that you had to put this part of yourself first in church, put it forward, when you didn't have to do that in other spaces. If that's really who you are, then you should always be that way. That's how you should act wherever you are. Why do you need the language of the church to express it or support it? To validate it?
>
> *Q: Did people at church seem hypocritical, then, or did church itself?*
>
> Not everyone. There were people who genuinely believed what they believed. They spoke about it honestly, even if I wouldn't use that language, and I felt like they weren't trying to impose it on me. With others it felt like they were reading a script, and if you didn't adhere to it, you were suspect and you would be judged. That always troubled me.[26]

As Marie entered adolescence, "church got more social," and ideals of fellowship and community came to the fore. As an unchurched adult, she allows, "that idea of community is the one thing I really long for and miss. But I didn't feel like I had that as a teenager," in but not of a youth group largely drawn from other neighborhoods and high schools. "I didn't really feel like I belonged, and that's where I started to pull back. I went for a while, but more and more intermittently," as the interpersonal reality of teenage cliques overtook high ideals of caring community.

Yet Marie continued to serve as an acolyte through high school, until she left home for college. Why so? "I loved the ritual order of it, walking down the aisle, lighting the candles, sitting up front surrounded by the sound of the organ and the choir. I was playing a special role, and I liked that, too. Being responsible and helpful, filling in when someone else couldn't make it at the last minute." Sermons sounded no less artificial and dull as Marie grew older, however, and her moral convictions and curiosity moved further afield. She recalls:

> I played a lot of tic-tac-toe on church bulletins during the sermons, but I began to get more annoyed about core values having to be cloaked in this very elaborate imaginary structure. Why can't we just hold these values, and live them out? I could see the good of the church as a place for people to gather in a community that provides support and service. But everything else seemed like something imaginary that I couldn't really buy, and I felt a lot of pressure at least to say that I did.

If sermonic theologizing seemed like such a fiction to a critical, conscientious adolescent, what sort of moral alternative did Marie discern in the shape of core values to which she could commit herself? "Honesty in saying what you believe and living it out," she answers. "A nonjudgmental stance toward others," especially if they look and sound different from you.

Marie pauses for a moment, then smiles, "If I had a religion, I think it would be more like Carl Rogers than Calvin." Perhaps unconditional positive regard could give rise to universal neighbor-love. If not, Marie urges, "Let's hope you can be truly authentic, truly nonjudgmental, and hold people with a truly warm and forgiving nature." These values align with traditional Christian virtues, she allows with a nod to her own upbringing as an Arminian Methodist. "But they seem clearer to me, coming without all the stories surrounding them and supporting them, and tying them to a single perfect person."[27]

Marie recognizes the resonance of this humanistic moral alternative with enlightened ideals of reason and conscientious autonomy enshrined in the American republic. She respects the actual psychological "support and structure" that organized religion can offer those in need. But she cautions against carrying over the impulse of this positive moral support in one's own experience into adverse moral judgment of others. "If I need this, you must need it, too, whether you know it or not. Is that really true?" she asks. She objects to true believers telling unbelievers that they have a soul in need of saving grace, and sins in need of confession and repentance.

On the other hand, Marie wonders, do the unchurched in turn respond to such self-righteous sectarian faith with no less judgmental indignation of their own? Sworn to liberal ideals of diversity and tolerance of all believers and unbelievers alike, too often they prove tolerant of all but the intolerant, she suspects. Why can't the unchurched be truly attentive and caring to everyone? If so, they will act in the exemplary image of the Good Samaritan, which most Americans claim to know and love better than any other bible parable. We can certainly agree in principle and "paint that picture of universal love of neighbor," Marie acknowledges. But we may still belie it in practice, especially among professionals who "give at the office" and get paid for doing good in the course of pursuing careers of public service or academic instruction. Let unchurched humanists practice what they preach no less honestly than faithful churchgoers, Marie urges in terms that echo Diane. Let both "look at all the times we fail to take the opportunity to help others, or fail to make the opportunity, not because we're so sinful, but just because we're too tired or too lazy."[28]

Character and Community

Marie appreciates the paradox of her holding humanistic views at odds with churchgoing yet "living in many ways consistent with very Christian values." But, she explains, "I hold them as human values. When I think of my Muslim or Jewish friends who hold the same values, I feel like they are no different from me." Whether construed as universal ethics or common human decency, Marie senses a common denominator of "core values" that span differences between the churched and unchurched as well as differences between one religion and another. She credits this recognition in good part to her parents' influence and initiative. She is grateful to them for "taking us around to visit different places of worship"—Catholic, Greek Orthodox, Pentecostal—when she and her brother were finishing high school and starting to pull back from the Methodist church of their childhood. She recalls,

> That really stuck with me: all these distinct sets of rituals aimed at the same idea of being good, even if each group criticizes the other ones for not saying or doing things as well. Each one is all for unity and love, while they set themselves apart from all the other ones. I love celebrating Rosh Hashanah and other holy days outside my own tradition. But I never want to feel tied to one prescribed way of holding core values that denies the others.[29]

We need to see the unity of our values, and unite behind them, Marie argues, because they're not written in stone, once and for all, like the biblical Decalogue or Stoic natural law. "They're more like lines drawn in the sand to hold back the waves of impulse that threaten us," she says. "I don't believe in Freud's id-driven psyche, but there is a kind of social id, and we're constantly choosing between holding the community together and using it to serve ourselves," or dividing it against itself in the sectarian name of jealous gods.[30]

Alongside her undergraduate major in biology, Marie minored in comparative literature and "fell in love with stories that revealed characters tied to ideas. I felt free to dive into them, because we were talking about works of art instead of 'holy scripture.' Who decreed that this one set of writings, even though it contains some great stories and ideas, is the Word of God?" Marie asks, joining Jim in opposing artistic freedom to religious compulsion. Sometimes she feels tempted to surmise that "authorities concocted these myths once upon a time to keep people in line," in terms of a moral and social functionalism that reaches from Plato through Jefferson to latter-day skeptics. At other times Marie leans more toward cultural and literary conceptions of humans as inherently meaning-making animals who sustain their "moral values and commitments to community" through symbolic constellations of myths and rites to inspire their moods and motives as well as charter their institutions.[31]

How does Marie compare her own outlook to the two in three Americans who believe in a biblical God, and the nine in ten who believe in God as "some higher power," if not a personal being? "That's a kind of naivete I would like to be able to share," she admits. "But it's hard for me to avoid looking at the world more scientifically, and seeing a lot of chance and chaos, unfair and unpredictable flows of experience that defy any organizing power." Does she see herself as "spiritual but not religious" in terms familiar from surveys of young adults in and out of church today? "I respond viscerally to that," she objects. "It sounds self-deceptive to me, and New Age silly, too. I find the natural world moving and restorative, but not full of spirits." Marie rejects such animism, as do most self-identified agnostics in surveys, even if she can recognize recent medical definition of spirituality as "the way individuals seek ultimate meaning" and value.[32]

Marie follows an exercise regimen that includes elements drawn from yoga, she notes, and she certainly gained interpersonal awareness through therapy and counseling in her twenties. But she thinks of such activities not as "spiritual practices," but rather as ways of "taking care of myself and others," particularly by "slowing my stream of thought to stay present in the moment, not getting lost in the future or the past, acting more in line with who I want to be."

As a path to moral integrity of intention and action such practices seem to Marie less consonant with spirituality or churchgoing than with her chosen profession as a clinical medical researcher who draws on social sciences devoted to human cognition, behavior, and emotion. "Going to work is sort of like going to church for me," she acknowledges, with an eye to the moral depth of her calling, and its continuity with her religious upbringing. "Helping people live better, healthier lives is part of what got me into this line of work," not just doing science. She sees her abiding concern to "act fairly and kindly" also carrying her into administrative roles that require "soothing hurt feelings and helping right small injustices" as well as keeping up with all the paperwork of a research laboratory. "I try to be trustworthy," Marie sums up. "I try to keep my word, and not make promises I can't keep."

Are there other activities or relationships in Marie's life that seem to her more or less religious, such as dwelling among friends and sharing their moral concerns along with enjoying their good company? That's important, she replies, "although that gets harder to sustain with kids and increasingly busy professional schedules, with both of us working full-time. We've let that slide, much more than my parents' generation. They were much more woven into a fabric of friends in church, neighbors, and colleagues. I worry about that for myself sometimes," she confesses, "even though I know it's not just us."

"It's the world that's changed," Marie judges, increasing the demands of work and the costs of household formation to squeeze middle-class life. "I would love to be part of a nonprofessional community centered around supporting each other and the larger community," Marie vows, "without some judgmental kind of piety, where you can belong *and* hold it lightly, where you can be committed without being serious all the time. You can be playful."

That could be more like a civic group or a sports club than a church, Marie grants. "I have friends who have found that in sports groups," she notes, "where there are the rules of the game, and the tight engagement of teamwork. But it's not a revelation from on high," even though teams can compete fiercely, athletes can judge each other critically, and fans can follow them fervently. "I see that with my daughter, who's on a little, low-key soccer team at school," she observes. "But those girls are tight, they work hard. Some are better than others, but they're so eager to hold each other up and excited to cheer for each other. Team spirit!"

Reading, studying, and talking together in a small monthly book group that Marie has recently joined also strikes her as similar to a religious congregation. "That's meaningful for me, and it's focused on making meaning," she stresses, even though the group has read no explicitly religious literature. "It's an interesting group, full of people I wouldn't have met otherwise," college-educated friends of friends from across metro Atlanta, mixed by background, race, and occupation. "The group is still emerging," Marie says, "but I can see the potential for care and connection among us, and that makes me feel closer to what I'm looking for."

Does such experience tug Marie toward church, or promise a fulfilling alternative to it? "It's not either-or," she replies, and as yet she and Jack have felt no need to go church-hunting for their daughter's sake. "We've been really happy with the ethos of her school," Marie reports gratefully. "It's diverse, it's a public school in the neighborhood, but it's an extraordinarily kind place that works to instill good values. Alison really feels held by that care, and we marvel at it."

What would it take to bring Marie and her family back to church? "Be open to ideas," she answers. "Connect people, serve the community. That's what appeals to me." What puts her off? "Solicitously pious intensity! Proclaiming that this is the kindest, most progressive, inclusive place," she grimaces, even if those virtues ideally define what she wants in a church, no less than a school or book group. "Just don't overdo it!" she stresses. And, as a practical matter, an ideal congregation shouldn't demand too much time or motion as a measure of commitment. "Just in terms of time I need to be flexible," she concedes. "I can't take on one more big commitment," with fixed demands for attendance and participation to satisfy in order to cross the threshold of membership in a strongly bounded congregation.

Likewise, Marie adds, "I want a group that is constantly open to questioning. Where there's not an absolute in setting the bounds of what we believe to be true," and rejecting everything beyond that boundary line as falsehood and error. "Let's be open to learning something new, and listening to people with different perspectives," Marie urges. "Let's do things together that help us become better, without setting a high bar you have to clear to be deemed good enough. Can we engage people in a way that draws them in without trying to co-opt them?" she asks with feeling.

Caring yet thoughtful, ritually embracing yet morally purposeful, socially practical yet not merely functional, where does this striking ideal of congregational community fit in the landscape of Marie's own life at present? Maybe it shouldn't simply fit in, she replies, at least not too neatly into the highly disciplined, rulebound, and meritocratic striving endemic to professional schooling and careers among the educated middle class. "We need a community constructed in another way, where the means don't turn into an end in itself, like climbing a ladder to nowhere," Marie concludes. "Eventually you get tired of doing that, and feeling compelled to do it," even though we are truly called to serve humankind and improve the world we share, however faithfully we conceive its creation and seek its redemption.

✤

What are we to make of these four stories spanning generations, their recurring themes and variations, their major and minor chords, their counterpoint and interplay? How do they trace faith in flux and compose community, unraveling old rules and reasons, reimagining meaning, and reweaving rites in practice? Let's explore their central themes of spiritual experience and insight shifting religious self-awareness and self-expression. Are these changes profound enough to spark inner vision and guide everyday life, yet pervasive enough to reknit community and inspire a better world? What are the axial assumptions of selfhood and society essential to frame these accounts of spiritual needs and gifts? How do they redefine faith's unfolding, chart its trajectory, and charter its institutions? To these questions we now turn.

NOTES

1. Cf. Colin Campbell, *The Romantic Ethic and the Spirit of Consumerism* (Basil Blackwell, 1987); Charles Taylor, *Sources of the Self* (Harvard University Press, 1984), Pts. IV–V; Taylor, *A Secular Age* (Harvard, 2007), Pts. III–V; and Taylor, "Religion, the Spiritual, and Art," Art Gallery of Ontario, November 30, 2016, accessible at ago.ca/events.

2. See, for example, Perry Miller, *The New England Mind* (Belknap Press, 1983) volumes 1–2; H. Richard Niebuhr, *The Kingdom of God in America* (1938; Wesleyan, 1988), chs. 2–3; E. Brooks Holifield, *Theology in America* (Yale University Press, 2005), chs. 2–6, 17–18; and Burkhard Neunheuser, *Baptism and Confirmation* (Herder/Palm Publishers, 1964).

3. Paul Tillich, *Systematic Theology*, 3 vols. (University of Chicago Press, 1951–1963), 3: 27–38; Tillich, "The Permanent Significance of the Catholic Church for Protestantism" (Protestant Digest, Incorporated, 1941), 31 pages; and Robert N. Bellah, "Paul Tillich and the Challenge of Modernity," in Richard Madsen et al., eds., *Challenging Modernity* (Columbia University Press, 2024), ch. 8.

4. Cf. Gregory A. Smith, "A Growing Share of Americans Say It's Not Necessary to Believe in God to Be Moral," Pew Research Center, October 16, 2017, 1–3; H. R. Niebuhr, *The Social Sources of Denominationalism* (Henry Holt, 1929), 3–25, on "the ethical failure of the divided church"; and Ernst Troeltsch, *The Social Teaching of the Christian Churches* (Harper & Row, 1960), 51–64, 993, on worship at the root of all church formation.

5. See Wayne Meeks, *The Origins of Christian Morality* (Yale, 1993), ch. 6; and John Howard Yoder, *Body Politics* (Herald Press, 1992), ch. 2, on Eucharistic rites of Christian communion.

6. Michael North, "The Making of 'Make It New,'" in his *Novelty: A History of the New* (University of Chicago Press, 2013).

7. Cf. Richard Rorty, "Religion as Conversation Stopper," *Common Knowledge* 3, 1 (1994): 1–6.

8. Some 58 percent of Americans believe "the holy scripture is the Word of God," including 31 percent who believe it "should be taken literally," and 27 percent who hold that "not everything should be taken literally," compared to 33 percent convinced it is "not the Word of God," with literalists making up 55 percent of evangelical Protestants, 24 percent of mainline Protestants, 26 percent of Catholics, and 10 percent of religious "nones," according to Pew Research Center, "Interpreting Scripture," Religious Landscape Study, 2015.

9. See Robert N. Bellah, "Religious Evolution," 39–45, on "modern" religious beliefs and practices diffused beyond church walls; and Robert Wuthnow, *Acts of Compassion* (Princeton University Press, 1991), ch. 6, on popular moral construal of the Good Samaritan parable.

10. Cf. Gregory A. Smith et al., "Faith in Flux," Pew Research Center, April 2009, 10–20; Thomas Jefferson, "Virginia Statute for Religious Freedom" in Edwin S. Gaustad, ed., *A Documentary History of Religion In America* (Eerdmans, 1982), 259–61.

11. Pew Research Center, "Many Americans Say Other Faiths Can Lead to Eternal Life," December, 2008, 1–7.

12. Wendell Berry, "Poetry and Place," *Standing by Words* (Counterpoint, 2011).

13. Stephen Ozment, *The Age of Reform 1250–1550* (Yale University Press, 1981), 259ff.

14. Gregory A. Smith, "A Growing Share of Americans," 1–3; Pew Research Center, "The Partisan Divide on Political Values Grows Even Wider," October 5, 2017, ch. 5.

15. See Charles Taylor, *A Secular Age*, 1–4, 12–15, 18–21ff, on the changing cultural "context of understanding" secularity as "a move from a society where belief in God is unchallenged, and indeed unproblematic, to one in which it is understood to be one option among others, and frequently not the easiest to embrace," compared to a self-sufficing humanism.

16. Cf. Clifford Geertz, "Ethos, World View, and the Analysis of Sacred Symbols," in *The Interpretation of Cultures* (Basic, 1983), 126–41, on religion as moral drama enacted in rites and storied in myths.

17. Carlyle Murphy, "Interfaith marriage is common in U.S., particularly among the recently wed," Pew Research Center, June 2, 2015, reports only 61 percent of Americans married a spouse of the same religion in 2010–2014, compared to 81 percent married before 1960, with 15 percent marrying a spouse from "a different Christian tradition" (mainline, evangelical, or Black Protestant, Catholic, or Orthodox); 18 percent marrying an unchurched spouse; and 6 percent now in an "other mixed marriage," including non-Abrahamic faiths.

18. Martin Luther King Jr., quoted in "Out of the Night," *The Gospel Messenger* (Elgin, IL, February 8, 1958), 14; King, "Wesleyan University Baccalaureate Address," June 8, 1964; and Theodore Parker, *Ten Sermons of Religion* (Crosby, Nichols and Company, Boston, 1853), 84–85.

19. See Alexis de Tocqueville, *Democracy in America,* ed. J. P. Mayer (Doubleday, Anchor Books, 1969), 513–24, contrasting "moral associations" dedicated to doing

good to "industrial associations" to advance economic interests and political associations to check tyranny.

20. See, for example, Susan Moller Okin, *Justice, Gender, and the Family* (Basic Books, 1991), on the family as the first school of justice and injustice; and Erik H. Erikson, "Life Cycle," *International Encyclopedia of the Social Sciences*, ed. David L. Sills (Macmillan, 1968), vol. 4, 244–48, on virtues formed through stage-specific social practices and relations.

21. Cf. Ann M. Graybiel, "Habits, Rituals, and the Evaluative Brain," *Annual Review of Neuroscience* 31 (July 2008): 359–87; and Emile Durkheim, *The Elementary Forms of the Religious* Life, trans. Karen E. Fields (The Free Press, 1995), 216–41, on the collective effervescence of ritual enacted in rhythmic movement and music.

22. Borden Parker Bowne, *Personalism* [1908] (Kessinger Publishing, 2007) upholds the absolute value of each person and the personhood of God against materialism, positivism, and social Darwinism.

23. "Jesus Loves Me," lyrics by Anna Bartlett Warner 1859, published in Susan Warner, *Say and Seal* (Lippincott, 1860); hymn by William Batchelder Bradbury, 1862.

24. See Pew, "Faith in Flux," 2009, 1–34, on no religion seen as completely true; and Gregory A. Smith, "A Growing Share of Americans," 1–3, on no belief in God needed to be moral.

25. "Now I lay me down to sleep,/I pray the Lord my Soul to keep/If I should die before I 'wake,/I pray the Lord my soul to take," in *The New England Primer* (1750 edition), 23, wedding the absolute will of a Calvinist God and the loving embrace of an Arminian Jesus.

26. Cf. Lionel Trilling, *Sincerity and Authenticity* (Harvard, 1971); and Charles Taylor, *The Ethics of Authenticity* (Harvard, 2018).

27. Cf. Carl Rogers, "A Therapist's View of the Good Life: The Fully Functioning Person," (1961), 409–19, in *The Carl Rogers Reader* (Houghton Mifflin, 1989), Howard Kirschenbaum and Valerie Henderson, eds.; and John Calvin, *Institutes of the Christian Religion* (Westminster Press, 1960), John T. McNeill, ed., vol. 1, bk. 3, ch. 7, section 6, 696–97, on universal love of neighbor, however undeserving some seem, given the image of God in all humans.

28. On psychologizing the Good Samaritan story see Wuthnow, *Acts of Compassion*, ch. 6.

29. See Alexis de Tocqueville, *Democracy in America*, 290, on innumerable sects in the United States: "Each sect worships God in its own fashion, but all preach the same morality in the name of God."

30. Cf. Thomas Hobbes, *Leviathan*, The First Part, chapters 1, 12, 13 (1651; Macmillan, 1962); Sigmund Freud, *Group Psychology and the Analysis of the Ego* (1921; Norton, 1990); and Frank Sulloway, *Freud, Biologist of the Mind* (Harvard, 1992), on Freud's psychic "drives" derived via nineteenth-century biology from Hobbesian sensations that generate the physics of an inner "war of all against all" as the natural condition of humankind.

31. Cf. Geertz, "Ethos, World View, and the Analysis of Sacred Symbols"; *The Laws of Plato* (University of Chicago Press, 1988), books 10, 12; Sigmund Freud, *The*

Future of an Illusion (Anchor Books, 1964); and Max Weber, "Science as a Vocation," in Hans Gerth and C. Wright Mills, eds., *From Max Weber* (Oxford, 1946), 129–56.

32. See endnotes 18, 30, chapter 1.

Chapter 3

Religious Individualism and Congregational Community

Let's compare these firsthand stories of leaving church to map their common themes, trace their cultural context, and explore their moral meaning. The opinions and attitudes of individuals come from their personal experience, to be sure. But they come through the social practices and relationships of the institutions all of us inhabit, and they come together in the symbols and traditions of the culture all of us share.[1] Our experience as particular persons situated in social space and historical time is shaped by birth and generation as well as interaction and choice. We come to know what we feel by thinking about it in institutionally arranged and culturally symbolized ways. These include contrasting traditions in modern American culture that constitute distinctive moral images and visions wed to moral languages as modes of discourse, logics of argument, and forms of reasoning. Moral imagination inspires our character no less significantly than moral reasoning justifies our conduct.[2]

To make moral sense of religious and spiritual change in our society today we need to interpret it in terms of key traditions in our culture and their contrasting styles of ethical evaluation. These styles ring true to our experience of distinctive activities, practices, and relationships structurally arranged within the different institutional sectors of social life. In turn these styles define that experience and justify the arrangement of these institutions as well as our conduct within them.[3]

Seen in this light, four traditions in American culture, each marked by distinctive forms of ethical evaluation and institutional salience, contest the practical meaning of modern selfhood in America across its differentiated yet interrelated social spheres. This quartet consists of the "biblical" tradition and the "republican" tradition, and two forms of modern individualism, one "utilitarian" and bourgeois, the other "expressive" and bohemian.[4] Each features its own cultural conception of the self with its own cardinal virtues—a faithful, just, productive or sensitive self. Each situates this self socially in a characteristic vision of who "we" are in relation to one another, and what it means, for example, to be free and responsible. Free from what and for what? Responsible to whom and for whom? Thus each tradition construes central social "values" in its own practical terms as the virtues of persons and institutions alike or at odds. If Athens and Jerusalem historically come first, it is only as traditions passed on to us from Socrates and Moses through such all-American hands as Thomas Jefferson and John Winthrop.

In the revealed tradition of biblical religion, the self is God's creation, and who we are is constituted in relation to God. That relation consists in a covenant of reciprocal duties and virtues based on divine commandment, first of all, to love God, and then to love our neighbor as our self. It is a covenant, too, to heed and seek God. As such it makes of life a pilgrimage, a venturing forth or journey like that of the people of Israel to the Promised Land given to God's chosen people. In this tradition each person is a "child of God," and all persons are ultimately equal and infinitely valuable, because we are all God's children. As such we are members of a people, a People of the Book, and the law and love of God it reveals. For the New England Puritans, for example, life was a pilgrimage of the soul to God. The self was a *microchristus*, "a small Christ," the conscientious application of Christ's example in this world, like "the Image of the Seal in the Wax."[5] Human community was essentially religious, binding persons together as members of one body: the church as the Pauline body of Christ, its members bound by love; the society as a shining city upon a hill, its laws subject to a higher authority, its beacon aimed at the Kingdom of God to come.

In the republican tradition of classical civic humanism, by contrast, human community is essentially the civic body of a republic governed by principled laws grounded in human reason. The self is part of nature conceived as a cosmos, as having an ultimate regularity and purpose to its order. The self is a *microcosmus*, then, not a *microchristus*. It belongs to the natural order in its essence, as Thomas Jefferson declares when he says that "the laws of nature and of nature's God" entitle a people to be independent, and all persons are "endowed by their Creator with certain inalienable rights."[6] Reason is the faculty by which we see the structure of this natural order, and it informs the practical wisdom by which we live in accord with nature's laws. In its covenantal framework of testimony, advocacy, and cross-examination between a lawful, graceful God and a sinful, faithful people, biblical religion also includes a reasoned dimension consonant with classical civic humanism, and it likewise resists reductive reconstrual into modern terms of rational legal rules predicated on functional grounds of mutual benefit or formal grounds of procedure, consistency, and generalizability.

Both biblical and republican traditions stand at a distance from the instrumental and utilitarian form of individualism we meet when we leave Jerusalem and Athens and arrive in the early modern city, say, Adam Smith's Glasgow, with its gentlemen merchants, or Ben Franklin's Philadelphia, with its industrious young clerks who know that time is money.[7] For them the self is defined by its progress, not as a pilgrim on the way to God or a philosopher-citizen on the ascent to truth, but as an entrepreneur on the way to wealth. Its steps are measured by the ever-expanding use of its power, time, and capital in productive activity. The self is not so much inspired by faith or enlightened by reason as driven by desire—for self-preservation and gain, to be sure, but also for social standing, attention, and love. Wants are taken as given to describe such goods, and right acts are those that produce the most good consequences as reckoned by calculating the costs and benefits to arrive at the "bottom line" to decide what to do. Classical reason seeks to know an objective natural order and moral truth, and both obliges and inspires the self to live by their measure. In this new idea of reason, self-defining subjects align strategic means to subjectively given ends. A good society, then, is more like a productive machine, a fair contract, and a thriving market than the corporate body of a church or republic. It protects individuals against injury and coordinates their interests to assure the greatest freedom to each to pursue their own ends and thereby bring about the general prosperity.

The Romantic tradition of expressive individualism scorns the city's offices and factories for the vibrant streets or grassy countryside of poets like Walt Whitman or the white-sand beaches of our own leisure-time dreams.[8] It begins with the individual not as an actor efficiently pursuing her own self-interest but as a personality which experiences, feels, and simply is. Self-expression and intimacy with others are the touchstones of identity, not self-preservation and gain. Inner feelings and empathic experiences are what define the self. Acts are right because they "feel right." They express the self and respond to the situation most appropriately. Persons are good because they are "sensitive," in touch with themselves and the moment. Expressive community is more like the "lifestyle enclave" of a hip commune, country club, or bedroom community than a church, a republic, or a marketplace. It is a circle of friends and lovers who share attitudes and tastes. They experience a flowing together of feelings and wills unmediated by God's authority, nature's laws, or the bottom line's calculated consequences.

FREE TO BELIEVE AND BELONG

Framed in terms of contrasting cultural traditions of moral language and vision, these stories of leaving church feature freedom of religious choice, exercise, and expression as a universal right that each individual enacts in manifold ways. Individual autonomy is enacted as the freedom *to* define religious practice, belief, and identity for yourself. It is the freedom to make faith your own, if not to make your own faith, but clearly to make up your own mind in finding your own way to faith. It is the freedom to follow your own spiritual path, pursue your own spiritual quest or journey, and fulfill your own spiritual needs, not simply to pick and choose items of orthodox belief and practice on the à la carte model of a cafeteria menu, or select services to attend on the general admission model of a theater schedule.

This autonomy implies a self freely committed to a congregation as a voluntary association, to be sure, but not bound by it as a body of members one of another, each constituted by the community of character and practice they share. Instead rights-bearing individuals treat one another with mutual respect for the integrity of decisions each makes to come to church or leave, to stay or go, to visit often or only now and then. As individuals we can seek and share spiritual experience without becoming fully converted, forever reborn, or essentially transformed by it into members of one social body.[9]

We are a nation of joiners, not loners. We're volunteers who go out and get involved, not isolated people who hide at home. If we must shelter in place through a pandemic, we gather online and talk by phone. Freely chosen groups span our autonomy and community with warm fellowship and welcome familiarity, if not intimate friendship and lifelong loyalty. All-American individualism and voluntarism go hand in hand. They free each of us to join with anyone we like, to leave at will, and ignore busybodies who don't know better than trying to boss us around with fake rules and reasons. "You can't make me." Besides we're all in this together on our own, so I'd be a fool not to decide for myself, along with everyone else. We have long stood against constraints imposed by big government in particular, however much we depend on its vital services and spotty safety net, and now we feel more mistrust of big business, big banks, and "big religion," too.[10]

Defining yourself as "spiritual but not religious," both or neither, implies autonomous selfhood in turn. Here freedom *of* religious exercise shifts and expands into freedom *from* membership and participation in the congregations, denominations, and related organizations that make up "organized religion." You need not belong to believe or practice your faith, and you may belong in your own way even within church walls. Freedom of religion means freedom *in* religion, as Joshua Linden affirms, in or out of church. Your religious belief and practice alike can be both critically responsible and sincerely selective. "It's not all or nothing," Paul Weiss sums up. You are certainly free to believe or question specific church tenets, as a young Jill Anderson judged in her Sunday-school case of unbaptized babies bound for limbo, without being forced to accept morally unacceptable dogma in congregations that try to divorce teaching and formation from moral difficulty and dialogue.

By contrast, "religious nones" like Joshua's daughter Sally more sharply declare themselves spiritually free *from* organized religion, particularly its tutelary, magisterial authority to define doctrine and compel conduct. "This isn't me," she declares after her Catholic catechesis and sacramental confirmation at college, affirming instead her own "cool and quirky and different" spirituality that doesn't "fit neatly into a church construct." Marie Winters even more directly opposes her core values of "truly authentic, truly non-judgmental" mutual care and forgiveness to the scripted piety and pretence of organized religion.

Nearly half of American adults report they pray daily, and they are at least somewhat spiritual *and* religious. Yet only one in eight of this prayerful plurality attends services weekly and fewer still take part in church groups. Only one in six US adults self-identifies as a "Sunday stalwart," at once spiritual and religious, a prayerful weekly attender and active volunteer in church groups. Those who identify themselves as "spiritual but not religious," and choose "nothing in particular" in the way of religious preference, typically affirm a world of spiritual meaning and activity that stretches beyond organized religion and unfolds alongside it. They oppose confessional orthodoxy, commanding moral authority, and compulsory discipline as sectarian obstacles to finding and following one's own spiritual path. Most of them agree that churches do more good than harm, affirming a diffuse ecumenical sympathy. But one in four disagrees and rejects organized religion as a whole.[11]

Some of the unchurched such as Marie Winters mistrust "spirituality" per se as a self-deceptive new age category that blurs the moral and therapeutic value of practices of self-care such as yoga or mindfulness meditation. Others like Joshua dismiss the "spiritual-religious" distinction itself in popular usage as masking dimensions of depth that reveal the unity of all religion, within and beyond the pews, while reducing it to parochial details that distinguish denominations and congregations from one another instead of embracing them as many paths to one truth.

Religious "faith" itself shifts meaning along the path each person chooses and charts, away from orthodox belief and practice in terms of full assent to official creeds and full observance of official rites or participation in weekly worship, daily prayer or scripture reading, keeping kosher, or holy living. Grant that half of American adults pray daily, including many of the "spiritual but not religious." Yet two in three Americans who pray say they "talk to God, God does not talk to them." Only one in three says God talks back, including just one in four mainline Protestants and Catholics, and one in two evangelical Protestants. Why do such striking differences prevail between Americans who hear back from God and those who do not? Evangelical

Protestant background and tradition underlie this dramatic difference in outcome, bred by distinctive practices of learning to pray to a personal God who answers back.[12]

It's "more like learning to *do* something different than *think* something different," notes an insightful ethnographer, with an eye to the unconditionally loving, forgiving, and intimate God of neo-evangelicals, in close step with middle-class suburban life today and far off from the commanding God of fiery Fundamentalism, Calvinist sovereignty, or Judaic covenant.[13] Such practical experience inspires and expresses trustworthy conviction in God's caring, conversational presence rather than following from prior belief in a personal God given as a logical proposition or orthodox tenet. It likewise inspires and expresses trust in oneself as open to God's intimate touch, worthy of God's absolute love, and led by God's encouraging, comforting voice through the bustling but lonely crowd of the larger society.

At the same time, more than half of all Americans say they "believe in God as described in the Bible," including three in four mainline churchgoers and one in four of the unchurched who identify with "nothing in particular" in terms of a religious denomination or tradition. Yet we can ask how deep or detailed such biblical belief proves to be, if two in three prayerful Americans say God does not talk to them; and those who do hear from God often report just how difficult it proves in practice to learn to focus their attention and distinguish God's voice from their own thoughts in the hubbub of a multimedia world. This may seem commonsensical or reassuring in a modern society of separate, sensible sovereign selves, normally buffered against hearing voices or being possessed by spirits, however open they are to embracing romantic intimacy and spiritual energy.[14]

But the Hebrew Bible reveals God as "I am who I am," a first-person speaker with a personal proper name (Exodus 3:14). The Christian Bible elaborates God's kinship name in triune terms of Father, Son, and Holy Spirit. God is also named by common nouns that extend from the "God, Word, and Breath" of creation in Genesis to "the Alpha and Omega" of the Almighty in Revelation. What does it mean to be "made in the image and likeness of God," if not created by such a biblical God, who gives each of us a personal proper name of our own, a name in kinship with the human family, and names to share in common with the whole of creation and the cosmos? Imagine being "One with the All," in tune with universal being or charged by divine energy, typically answers the one in three Americans who believes in "some higher power/spiritual force," but not in God as described in the Bible. These ranks include half of the unchurched and a quarter of all mainline Protestants and Catholics, and their voices are broadcast everywhere.[15]

A Sunday stalwart reciting the Lord's Prayer may sound far from an unchurched young adult "sort of talking to myself" while imploring,

"Universe, please work with me." But many of the "diversely devout, relaxed religious, and spiritually awakened" Americans classified by surveys as "somewhat religious," actually span the distance between traditional churchgoers and those explicitly resistant or indifferent to religion. Here "spiritual curiosity" spurs a quest for oneness with God and nature, as Natalie Anderson attests, and "spiritual yearning" leads Paul Weiss to "search for my own soul."[16]

This journey typically turns away from a search for salvation seen as life everlasting in another world to come after suffering and struggling against evil in this world. It sidesteps a pilgrim's progress through a worldly slough of despond and release from the prison of vanity. Instead, it turns toward a modern quest for spiritual integration seen as immersion and unity with an immanent God, a sublime Nature, or a divine radiance that reveals "the All in its minute grandeur." So Natalie suggests, with a nod to Romantic ideals of artistic self-expression and mystical self-realization spreading from educated elites to modern mass media and popular culture. Such religious individualism can turn perilous, she cautions, at once indulgently self-centered and impossibly perfectionist, unless it is grounded in Christian tradition through congregational practices of Sacrament and Word.[17]

But others are not so sure of such peril or so insistent on such remedy. For example, when it comes to attending weekly church services or starting Sunday school, how much official doctrine and devotion do her young children need, asks Natalie's daughter Jill, in order to sustain their radiant curiosity about Jesus and the Eucharist? Does Joshua's daughter Sally need to take her preschool children to church at all, she asks, in order to "embed wonder," to instill in them a sense of spiritual gratitude and awe at the mystery of the universe shimmering along the ocean's shore? Diane concentrates on the need for religious learning through congregational participation to deepen conscientious moral insight as well as cultivate cultural literacy, and her son Paul attests to the value of such formation in his upbringing.

Most of the spiritual but not religious among the unchurched think you need not believe in God to be moral, however, and you can find spiritual meaning and energy beyond church pews and practices, for example, in communing with nature. Moreover, you can find in all religions the same core principles of transcendent truth and moral goodness, the same basic beliefs and values, without needing to study distinctive doctrines or practice devotional rites peripheral to this common core of truth. Such incidental "nit-picky details" prove distracting at best, and at worst divisive in sparking fights over irreconcilable differences in church dogma and custom.[18]

Many religions are partly true, none completely true, agree most unchurched Americans, even if many churches see themselves as unique and uniquely true. So Marie argues for uncoupling "core moral values" of doing justice and loving mercy from blindly following archaic moral rules and obeying commands from an all-powerful God on high, heedless of human suffering here below. From the Good Samaritan to the compassionate Buddha, she invites us to compare exemplary moral characters across mythic literatures and world religions, to discover the unity of human values we can embrace in action. Art expresses the actual truth that all humans live in and live out, Jim likewise affirms, and literature helps us find our own life story and calling set free from the parochial authority of *sola scriptura*.

SOFTENING UP THE SELF, CONNECTING WITH OTHERS

By contrast to distinguishing denominations, doctrines, and services of worship, a personal quest for spiritual immersion and unity with God, Nature, and the All cuts through such distinctions. It seeks to soften up the autonomous self and open up its buffered boundaries, to discover its authentic essence and full potential, deepen self-awareness, and embrace cosmic consciousness. How so? By "spiritual practices" reaching across a range no longer bound by any single congregation, denomination, or tradition of worship and prayer, according to many of these intergenerational accounts, even those centered on Christian liturgy and gospel stories.

Meditation and mantras, for example, can come from many sources to serve the soul, improve psychic health, or inspire moral virtue. You need not be Christian or Jewish, let alone Hindu, to practice yoga in a class at work, a fitness studio, community center, or even an ashram. You can do so for hours daily at home with video instruction or an occasional fifteen-minute "stretch-and-chill" session at the office, whether you seek simply to relax from stressful work, feel calmer and more resilient, or process pain and trauma in spiritual healing. You may prioritize self-care to "integrate body and mind in a compartmentalized world," counsels a workplace yoga program, or learn to "be kind to the entire being, all the time, so you can, in turn, be kind to others." In sum, "Self-care is important because it enables us to replenish our energy in order to be of service to others. We listen better, empathize more, and focus."[19]

Opening up and integrating the self in such terms also implies opening oneself to others and "connecting" with them, particularly in congregations that bring persons into communion. For Natalie, for example, this means praying side by side in the pews, sharing the eucharist at the altar, and embracing one another face-to-face in loving God and neighbor. The priority of personal spiritual practice and experience to official religious doctrine and creed proves no less clear in such a quest than the priority of congregational communion and care to ecclesial authority and duty in defining membership.

But from the outset there arise questions of transformative ties that bind and social responsibilities that inhere in congregational practices and relationships. These questions clearly persist for "perennial visitors" like Natalie, who attend irregularly every month, put an offering in the passing plate, and volunteer to serve meals for the homeless, even if they do not show up on the membership rolls or at worship every week, pledge to contribute every month, or serve for a year on a church committee.

In fact, half of all Americans attend church less than monthly, and few irregular attenders make close friends there. Although most of the unchurched acknowledge that churches "bring people together and strengthen community bonds," unchurched young adults in particular say they find closer companions and a deeper sense of belonging in other kinds of community, including circles of friends at school or work, in romance or play, in partying or just hanging out. For some, like Paul Weiss, the promise of such companionship spurs the search for a congregation truly worth joining, if only they can find one.[20]

Personal relationships among members of a congregation may express their awareness of belonging to the Body of Christ, the People of God, or the whole of humankind revealed in the light of common prayer, worship, preaching, meditation, or confession—and analogous rites drawn from disciplines that range from yoga through psychotherapy, in groups that stretch from Alcoholics Anonymous to Habitat for Humanity. Thus Natalie celebrates the Episcopal liturgy and Eucharist, which her daughter Jill accepts but downplays in favor of social gospel preaching. Her father Jim lifts up literature and art as practical alternatives to the myths and rites of evangelical revivalism he rejected at age twenty. He wryly sets out an abundance of communities more congenial than the church of his childhood, if only he had time to join them all, even as he grants the ongoing role of religion in charting the wider spiritual seas he shares with his spouse and children.

Sally thinks back to the hopeful, loving "Silent Night" sense of life she shared with her mother Sharon in nativity stories and hymns, and she wonders how she can carry on this intimate spiritual connection with her own children without feigning faith in "a church construct" she does not feel. Diane appreciates the transcendent experience of singing classical liturgical music together in a church choir and sharing it with her son. Joshua finds in playing the piano on his own a form of meditation that joins him in concert with the graceful whole of sacred music. Marie looks back on a childhood steeped in the rhythmic enchantment of reciting prayers and singing hymns together, before coming of age as an "empiricist" bored by pious sermons and put off by a God hidden from humankind.

CHURCH AND SOCIETY: FOR AND AGAINST

Congregational community shines as a moral example of mutual love, peace, and justice to the larger society, in the eyes of Natalie, Jill, and Sharon, enacted in ministries to aid the hungry and homeless, immigrants and exiles. For them it is a moral counterexample, too, a witness community critical of the larger society for its indifference to the gospel truth of neighbor-love, and its failure to fulfill the country's promise of liberty and justice for all. Such a "prophetic" congregation that practices what it preaches without political partisanship is exactly what Paul and his fiancée are looking for. For his mother Diane the church proves a more equivocal moral advocate and critic, well intentioned but comfortable enough in its suburban pews to sponsor food banks and homeless shelters that serve the suffering, yet to hold back from tackling the "systemic problems" of the poor, homeless, and jobless.

Sharper criticism of congregational leaders and followers as hypocrites serves to justify Jim's decision to leave the fundamentalist fold, and John's wariness in weighing with his wife Sally whether to join even the most liberal church for the sake of their children. It informs Marie's ambivalence toward a church proclaiming universal neighbor-love and forgiveness yet practicing cliquish exclusion and sectarian self-righteousness. Instead, she upholds ideals of mutual care and connection in a genuine community of friends no less open to free inquiry and meaning-making than committed to the common good.

Such criticism rings true to surveys of religious "nones" blaming churches for failing to practice what they preach, for imposing too many rules, and pursuing money and power instead of serving to meet authentic spiritual needs. They question the moral authority of churches to insist on the theological and ethical integrity of their doctrine as a whole, instead of letting individuals pick and choose the beliefs they think most sensible and the norms they find most helpful. Each person has a spiritual need and a moral right to choose beliefs that ring true to their experience and fit their situation, by this account, whether it be belief in a personal God or a higher power, a right to birth control or marriage equality, commitment to capital punishment or economic justice.[21]

Where should churches stand in relation to society at large and its public square in particular? We hear a range of views about the shape and stance of religious institutions in response to this question. Churches should stay out of politics, Jim remains convinced from his own fundamentalist upbringing, and they should keep their revealed truth, dogmatic authority, and self-righteous moral commands to themselves. They should not try to legislate their faith by force of votes or lobbies, his daughter Jill agrees, and they should not try to impose their creeds on other persons by proselytizing. Yes, they are free to shelter their own members, express their faith in public, and seek to persuade others by their good example and good arguments, but not to pressure or mislead them. Tempted by "holier than thou" hypocrisy, church members should certainly not exclude or discriminate against nonbelievers as second-class citizens, Sally and her husband John stress, let alone close ranks and fight as true believers to create "a Christian America."[22]

Conversely, churches should not simply stand above or apart from the larger society, by these accounts, or fit into it all too easily, without discerning its injustices or questioning its moral flaws. Marie asks for a caring, thoughtful, playful community of equals to nurture peace of mind and generosity of spirit among friends, by contrast to the meritocratic striving and stressful demands of professional life "climbing a ladder to nowhere." Natalie lifts up the congregation as a shining example of a beloved community of mutual care and responsibility, inspired to "let its light shine in the world" of a competitive marketplace and a conflicted political arena. Her daughter Jill stresses active ministries of neighbor-love and justice in "the real church." They reach out to the hungry and homeless, the neediest members of the larger society and local community, not only to offer them meals and beds for the night, but to transform the structural causes of their plight by enabling them to find jobs, afford housing, and care for their families. Josh and Sharon exemplify such efforts in helping to build an orphanage and school in Haiti, working outside any one congregation but in tandem with interdenominational agencies at home and overseas.

Diane and her son Paul both underscore the good of a congregation in critical and constructive dialogue with the polity of the larger society as an exemplary "caring community, not just a transactional political party." They seek a church willing and able to act as a moral witness, advocate, and activist without "playing politics" or passing out "the same old platitudes." Religious communities should pursue a truer, wider path toward the common good than political partisans or powerful interests seeking their own advantage. They should inspire and guide "people in communities headed in a different direction," following Martin Luther King Jr.'s "arc of the moral universe," instead of falling for partisan promises to make America great again by excluding the needy and ignoring the least of these.

Sacred stories and traditions, understood conscientiously and critically, can start conversations in the public square among different sorts of believers and nonbelievers who seek truth and justice, Jill stresses, instead of foreclosing such conversation in favor of "just preaching to the choir" or asserting the gospel truth as revelation that requires no reasoning. Public conversation that embraces inspiring moral intuition and reasoned moral argument can in turn spur both social reform and ongoing religious reformation, Diane and Paul agree, making government more just and caring, and making churches more democratic in their own deliberation and decision-making.[23]

Diane and her husband Nat found an admirable church to connect their children to the local community and help with their moral guidance and cultural instruction. So did Joshua and Sharon. When the children left home for college, however, all but Sharon left church. Such selective participation may stem from a kind of moral and social functionalism in conceiving membership and participation in organized religion as useful means to this or that good end, but not necessarily as a good in itself. Thus Nat still communes and prays in "the temple of nature," and he remains committed to social justice and progressive politics as a "secular humanist" in solidarity with Diane and their children. Marie left church behind, but she still shares her parents' sense of "awe and wonder at the mystery beyond our propositions," as her philosopher father puts it; and she likewise supports movements for peace and justice to aid the poor and protect the environment.[24]

Joshua drifted away from the Methodist congregation that his wife Sharon continues to embrace. But he has pursued his own daily spiritual study and practice beyond "therapeutic strategies" of self-care to span meditation, sacred music, and scripture. At the same time, he recognizes the need for the depth of communal inspiration that common prayer and conviction sustain. He affirms churches for carrying personal concern for the common good into social action needed to counter corporate interests and partisan politics. He worries about "living off the moral capital of our past" without renewing religious traditions by practicing them together in the present. He and Sharon have stayed true to their calling to work for a Haitian orphanage, carrying out the Good Samaritan ideals they see their unchurched children carrying on by leading good lives and doing good in the world through the helping professions, civic activism, and charitable volunteering.

Forced to choose, most of our "spiritual but not religious" respondents identify themselves as cultural and political "liberals" rather than "conservatives," in line with survey data reviewed in chapter 1. Granted that such liberals are much likelier than conservatives to leave church. But those like Jim who leave stricter, more fundamentalist, or more sect-like congregations of origin seem likelier than those adrift from mainline churches to reject religious belief and practice outright, akin to self-declared atheists or agnostics raised in families with scant congregational participation or religious practice at home. They reject conservative faiths made in the Protestant image of biblical literalism, commanding moral authority, and revivalist emotional orchestration, for example; or marked by distinctive traits of conservative Catholic, Jewish, or other traditions such as the nagging guilt of secret sin and fear of divine punishment persisting from Diane's childhood catechesis as a cradle Catholic.

By contrast, "spiritual but not religious" liberals adrift from mainline churches seem likelier to pick and choose their beliefs and practices by reference to their congregations of origin. They chart their own spiritual course more or less distant from congregational commitment in the present by reference to how fully they took part in the practice of their childhood churches and how deeply they experienced its meaning, for example, whether they heard God talking back in prayer or felt the Holy Spirit filling their hearts and working in their lives.[25]

Listening to these stories of parents and children rehearsing their own religious upbringing and parenting underscores the continuity of religious change across generations. "We're born into a web of meaning and experience," as Will Winters notes. "We're still tangled up in it, and it's tangled up inside of us," in familiar ways. These entangled narratives confirm and clarify survey evidence of greater movement away from committed churchgoing and creedal faith between baby boomers and their parents than between boomers and their millennial children. They reveal that such change usually occurs more subtly than some simple breakdown and reversal from faithful certainty and institutional loyalty to rejecting religion outright and leaving church entirely behind.

Changes in religious belief and practice unfold as back-and-forth cultural conversation and moral drama, rather than running along univocal or unilinear tracks toward more spiritual and less religious outcomes. These intergenerational accounts likewise frame and extend evidence from surveys and interviews of young adults that show relative continuity and stability in levels of religious commitment and practice, or liminal lack thereof, in their individual lives between adolescence and young adulthood for most Americans today, whether they were raised in churchgoing or unchurched families.[26]

Notwithstanding a few fervent converts coming to God at age twenty from unchurched families of origin, and a few rebels fleeing the faithful fold like Jim, most Americans who drift away from church in early adulthood come from families less than fully committed to their faith, neither active at the center of a congregation nor utterly indifferent or opposed to churchgoing. Conversely, most teenagers take after their parents, including four of five raised as evangelical Protestants or Catholics, more than half of mainline Protestants, and five of six teens with unchurched parents, even as most who leave church do so after they leave home.[27]

Granted, for example, that Diane's parents were both committed Catholics and she was raised going to Mass every Sunday and attending parochial schools until college; that Jim was brought up by devout Baptists on weekly worship, fellowship, Bible study, and choir practice; and Sharon likewise by loyal Methodists. But they married partners raised in families more binocular in their vision of faithful belief and practice.

Natalie's Presbyterian father insisted on her taking the long path to adult confirmation to "decide for yourself" on matters of personal faith, and Joshua's mother freed him from dutiful Methodist churchgoing as a skeptical schoolboy. Nat's parents were relaxed in Jewish religious observance and humanistic in their "do unto others" ethic. Marie's ecumenical Protestant parents stressed moral character and conduct over pious devotion and theological assent. Their offspring carry on this binocularity, and they extend it. None resist religion or shrug it off as self-declared atheists. All are morally concerned, and almost all are spiritually attuned and interested, if not actively engaged in daily spiritual practices or exploring alternative spiritual movements.

One or two Sundays a month, Jill brings her daughter to the Episcopal church her mother visits more often, follows the sermon closely, and volunteers to help the homeless. She marvels at her mother's sacramental devotion, and she cherishes her daughter's embrace of life everlasting with Jesus in heaven to make sense of a death in the family. Yet she hangs back from sending her daughter to weekly Sunday school. Sally brings her children to church on Christmas and Easter to share in their spirit of joy and wonder. Yet she stops short of the regular attendance and deeper commitment she admires in her mother but can't quite share. Paul Weiss appreciates the cultural literacy, ethical learning, moral community, and musical harmony provided by his childhood churchgoing with both parents. He looks forward to passing on this legacy to his own children when the time comes. Yet he remains intellectually open-minded and epistemologically agnostic on doctrinal matters of belief in God and life everlasting.

These spiritually attuned, morally concerned young adults see themselves linked to congregations as visitors or alumni, but not bound up in them as members. Each remains free to choose when and where to attend, how and how far to get involved in a congregational community, and how often to take part in its practices. Why so? One place to trace the cultural and moral origins of such freedom to choose one's own faith in America today lies in our historic commitment to freedom of conscience.

FROM FREEDOM OF CONSCIENCE TO FREEDOM OF CHOICE

Freedom of conscience runs deep in the American grain of religious practice and belief all the way back to its Reformation roots. Dissenting Protestants oppose priestly rule and magisterial church authority imposed by prelates and princes. They celebrate a priesthood of all biblical believers, conscience-bound by faith alone to know God's will and love directly through congregational worship, personal prayer, and scriptural study of God's Word, exemplified by New England Puritans as God's people gathered in prayer around the Book.

In the city set upon a hill that John Winthrop lays out in "A Model of Christian Charity," this cardinal virtue is at once moral and civic, embracing Christian conscience and community alike in biblical "bonds of affection." For in order to "follow the counsel of Micah, to do justly, to love mercy, to walk humbly with our God," Winthrop preaches, "we must be knit together in this work as one man, we must entertain each other in brotherly affection . . . we must delight in each other, make others' conditions our own, rejoice together, mourn together, labor and suffer together, always having before our eyes our commission and community in the work, our community as members of the same body." Conscience is sovereign but bound by covenant with God and membership in the body of the church and the body politic.[28]

The sovereignty of conscience in republican terms likewise celebrates the self-government of all democratic citizens enlightened by reason to recognize the laws of Nature and Nature's God, as Jefferson declares. These laws endow us with inalienable natural rights to free exercise of religion as well as life, liberty, and the pursuit of happiness. Because "Almighty God hath created the mind free and manifested his supreme will that free it shall remain by making it altogether insusceptible of restraint," Jefferson argued to the Virginia House of Delegates, all attempts at religious establishment "are a departure from the plan of the holy author of our religion, who being lord both of body and mind, yet chose not to propagate it by coercion on either, as was in his Almighty power to do, but to extend it by its influence on reason alone."[29]

Religion enlightened by reason in turn maintains morality, and together "these firmest props of the duties of Men and citizens" support political prosperity, George Washington promises. Moral duties and sentiments rooted in religion and bred by communities of faith in tandem with families, form conscientious citizens and help regulate self-government by Americans without intervening in it, making religion "the first of their political institutions," Tocqueville concludes. Good government requires morality, and morality rests on religion.[30]

Free exercise of religion in American law responds to the social fact of varied religious creeds and communities spread across the colonies. So do cultural conceptions of the moral unity of all religion rooted in eighteenth-century ideals of its universal ethics and core principles, at one with human reason and civic virtue. "There is an innumerable multitude of sects in the United States," noted Tocqueville. "They are all different in the worship they offer to the Creator, but all agree concerning the duties of men to one another."[31]

The one and the many meet in the "voluntary and individual profession of faith" made by democratic citizens such as Thomas Paine, "with all that sincerity and frankness with which the mind of man communicates with itself." He swears,

> I believe in one God, and no more; and I hope for happiness beyond this life. I believe in the equality of man; and I believe that religious duties consist in doing justice, loving mercy, and endeavoring to make our fellow-creatures happy.[32]

Mindful of Micah and the Rights of Man alike, Paine does not believe in the creed professed by any church—Jewish, Roman, Greek, Turkish, or Protestant. Instead he declares, "My own mind is my own church." All national establishment of churches seems to him "no other than human institutions, set up to terrify and enslave mankind, and monopolize power and profit." Paine respects those who believe otherwise, since "they have the same right to their belief as I have to mine." But he condemns the infidelity and "mental lying" of professing to believe what one does not. For this hypocrisy causes incalculable moral mischief and political corruption, excused by claims to divine revelation, "as if the way to God was not open to every man alike," and divine commands could convey good moral precepts beyond the ken of able lawmakers to discern without "recourse to supernatural intervention."[33]

Rights precede responsibilities for us, and no one is dutybound to practice any religion if they do not choose to do so. We may readily agree with Madison's "Remonstrance" that it is the right of every person to exercise their own reason in matters of religion, following the dictates of their own "conviction and conscience" and free from the dictates of others enforced by law or violence. Yet we may well pause at his deist definition of religion as "the duty which we owe to our Creator," and his reasoning that it is "the duty of every man to render to the Creator such homage and such only as he believes to be acceptable to him." This duty comes before civic duties in time and "degree of obligation," Madison argues, since before "any man can be considered as a member of Civil Society, he must be considered as a subject of the Governour of the Universe."[34]

Freedom of choice in religious matters today has come to mean both more and less than these explicitly biblical and classical conceptions of conscience in eighteenth-century America. This conceptual shift has occurred through a complex process of cultural change inseparable from changes in arranging our social institutions and pursuing our way of life in practice.

The democratization of Christianity after the Revolution, for example, coupled evangelical revivalist enthusiasm and republican popular sovereignty to free individual conscience and spiritual impulse further still from aristocratic clerical and political authority alike. It pushed aside the learned wisdom of the past and the doctrinal din of sectarian confusion, along with scholars and squires set above the common people. Invoking the principle of *sola scriptura,* it inspired every believer to engage the holy word of God directly, to open the Bible and think for oneself. Heeding the laws of Nature and of Nature's God, it enabled every citizen to grasp universal truths self-evident to human reason at the root of commonsense, and to envision a *novus ordo seclorem* of liberty and equality lit by the promise of a millennial kingdom to come.[35]

In affirming our right to religious freedom as contemporary commonsense, we echo our constitutional right to free exercise of religion. But we typically assert it as a moral right of each individual to choose her own faith or none at all, a right of personal judgment to join or leave a congregation or denomination as you will, not the freedom of a people to exercise their religion responsibly in diverse forms as equal citizens unbound by an established church. Three in four American adults believe there are many religious paths to one universal truth, not just one true path to God and heaven. But today this conviction seems more a matter of spiritual intuition of the All, and practical experience of the moral need for good values at the common core of all religions, than it does a matter of enlightened reasoning on natural law and natural rights.[36]

Such contemporary commonsense aims to meet apt demands for tolerance and mutual acceptance of growing religious diversity in a more multicultural society that spans a wider range of traditions than Protestant, Catholic, and Jewish. It also reflects cultural assimilation and social convergence across denominational lines, particularly but not only among Protestants, spread by higher education and greater intermarriage among successive cohorts with less distinctive confessional and catechetical formation in their childhood churches and families of origin.

Personal beliefs in God and goodness remain important by this account, but individuals should assent to such religious beliefs without accepting or asserting any authority to impose their beliefs on others. Each person gets to decide for herself what is true, right, and good in the realm of religion. Indeed, one's own intuition and decision authorize the truth and goodness of these beliefs. Individuals should live out their personal beliefs, to be sure. But such religious beliefs can prove so sweeping yet subjective that they need not oblige one to follow them out in any moral calling to take part in a given congregational community, field of study, line of work, network of friends, or rites of courtship.[37]

On the contrary, circles of social relationship set in school, work, sports, art, leisure, or romance often generate stronger moral motives and reasons for one's way of life than does congregational membership. This holds particularly true for young adults such as Paul Weiss, who extols the moral bonds and goals he shared with his college housemates and teammates as exemplary traits of a church worth joining if he can find it. Not only do these moral ideals and social relationships feel more appealing and engaging among friends than church members. They prove more compelling and binding, less a matter of personal discretion to pick and choose doctrines and prayers than a matter of discovering what one needs to learn and love in order to do well and do good, to live a good life by finding fulfillment at work and at home in adulthood.

The freedom to choose your own religion, as invoked by many unchurched Americans today, turns on institutional metaphors and logics of argument drawn from modern markets, schools, families, and leisure rather than religious practice and congregational life per se, let alone deist ideals of dutiful subjection to the divine governor of a naturally lawful universe. Each of us should therefore choose a religion, or a "worldview and ethos," because we find it useful, fitting, or appropriate. It should meet the "spiritual needs" only I can discover and define for myself. It should fit my own personal feelings and intuitions of what sort of spirituality suits me and works for me. It should ring true to my own authentic experience. However personally appropriate it thereby proves, it need not and indeed cannot prove consistent with collective ideas and judgments of some universal truth and common good self-evident to human reason in accord with natural law, contrary to Jefferson's key premise that "the opinions and belief of men depend not on their own will but follow involuntarily the evidence proposed to their minds" by Nature's laws and Nature's God.[38]

Seen in this light, choosing religious beliefs, practices, and communities implies a market-like transaction on the model of a consumer choosing an apt personal service or useful product that helps you do better. It may be a practical program of guidance, treatment, or training such as health care or psychological counselling, yoga classes or gym membership, to enhance your health, "wellness," or self-esteem. Such a transaction also takes in the self-expressive, fun-filled, and emotionally fulfilling dimensions of buying something that fits you and helps you feel better, for example, fashionable apparel, beautiful art, or lively entertainment such as a movie or a massage, a vacation trip or season tickets to the opera or ballpark. It's no sin to feel good and look good in style, to enjoy seeing and being seen at church, not just at play.[39]

Whether religion proves instrumentally useful or emotionally fulfilling, it should be good *for* you in the functionalist formulation of many young adults in and out of church today. It need not inhere in human existence as good in itself or come first as the hypergood of "the one thing needful" for salvation. Religion should help you to be good as well as feel good, insofar as such functionalism is both moral and cultural, not just psychological. Religion can be good for you, if only you choose the right kind of religion, whatever it may be, as long as it fits you and works for you. You should feel comfortable with its beliefs, fluent in its practices, and at home in its community. Although Americans are now pretty evenly divided over whether "believing in God is necessary in order to be moral," according to recent surveys, five in six religious "nones" agree you can be a good person without taking part in organized religion.[40]

Because morality is something that religious participation can help you learn, on the model of elementary schooling in reading, writing, and arithmetic, you may further this moral and cultural learning with religious tutoring in a congregation. You learn moral rules, principles, and commandments in Sunday schools and sermons, for example, to "Love your neighbor" and "Do unto others." In congregational fellowship, church groups, and Sabbath meals you find inspiring moral examples, internalize positive attitudes, and practice virtues such as fairness as well as faith, hope, and charity.

Then these good moral values and attitudes can gradually grow from their doctrinal roots and devotional rites in a process of personal development that echoes Enlightenment ideals of coming to the use of one's own understanding in grasping Nature's laws, and classical ideals of learning to heed reasoned dialogue in public life. Once students attain cultural literacy and complete a basic moral curriculum, they can "graduate" from church on the model of primary or secondary school. They can go on to higher education, and then out into the modern world of professional training and work, friendship and marriage, as autonomous moral agents and social actors on their own. Raised as a Methodist, Quaker, Catholic, or Jew, they remain alums of sorts, equipped with the good values needed to make good choices on their own, yet freed from the tutelary authority of parochial doctrines and pious practices no longer needed to sustain these values.[41]

This modern ideal of moral maturation also charts the course of individuation in growing up and out from dependence on a nuclear family of origin. Through parental love and examples that supersede commanding moral authority, this nuclear family forms and guides children to grow up and stand on their own two feet, to become independent and self-reliant. Children leave home and church alike to find their way in the world of higher education and work, courtship and marriage. Then they form a family of their own and find a church of their own.[42]

Since the 1970s, this middle-class model of congregational help with child-rearing has grown more problematic, as younger cohorts postpone marriage and parenthood. More young adults, especially those without college degrees, "fail to launch" smoothly into careers and homes of their own. One-third of Americans in their late twenties now live with their parents or grandparents, triple their proportion in 1970, and young adults aged eighteen to thirty-four are now likelier to live with their parents than otherwise for the first time in more than a century. Only half of US adults aged twenty-five to fifty-four are now married, compared to two-thirds in 1990. Even among those married with children, spiritual journeys less often begin in the congregations of their childhood, and less often end with little children leading their parents back to the fold.[43]

SELFHOOD AND SOCIETY

What are we to make of the mixed and manifold responses of unchurched young adults to questions of religious meaning, spiritual aspiration, and moral commitment? How far can we generalize from their particularity? Too far, many of these accounts suggest, if we assume one category can define or label them all in substance, for example, as post-Christian pagans or therapeutic deists. Even narrow if noteworthy social slices of those raised in mainline churches and now unaffiliated—White by race, suburban by social setting, and upper-middle-class by education and occupation—resist such sweeping classification, however suggestive or misleading.[44]

Instead let's heed common denominators that underlie the very diversity of these stories of each person finding her own path to an encompassing spiritual truth. First, count this as evidence of individualizing religious practice, outlook, and way of life. Second, note that this path leads individuals through *this* world as the only world there is, not as a brief and broken prologue to the next, be it a perfect paradise, heavenly homecoming, or life everlasting at one with God in the hereafter. Instead of rejecting this world, we should accept it. These stories affirm it as ultimately true and good, if only we come to experience its inner reality and inherent possibility. Third, identify at the sacred axis of this world-acceptance a dynamic, multidimensional self, capable of realizing its own potential and remaking the world itself. Instead of a biblical creator-redeemer God ruling the Kingdom of Heaven and creating each soul in His image, the divine dwells within us and permeates the whole of existence as universal spirit and cosmic consciousness, immanent presence and "higher power." It is the One and the All we can each reach and encounter in our own way, given so many paths leading to one spiritual truth.[45]

Visions of a multidimensional self at the center of a multiplex monist world run through a wide web of empirical and interpretive studies of American religion over the past generation. They highlight the growing individualism and voluntarism of younger Americans since the baby boom, their experiential focus in spiritual seeking and do-it-yourself rites, their "pick and choose" participation in faith traditions, their creedal bricolage and worldview "tinkering." These traits mark not only the vanguard of educated middle-class youth in or outside the mainline churches. They take in the increasingly educated and culturally assimilated ranks of born-again evangelicals, spirit-filled Pentecostals, and believers born into other world religions who have come of age in the United States since 1970.[46]

The "immanent frame" of modern world-acceptance defines this key dimension of intergenerational cultural change evident in the narratives we saw in chapter 2 of religious upbringing and formation across generations. Neither paradise nor purgatory, this one and only world proves imperfect but full of possibility, goodness, and grace all its own. Its ethos features a "buffered self," disembedded from kith and kin to appear as an autonomous agent and the shining star of a fluid drama of many social roles and relationships, activities and associations that each self can choose to enter or leave, pursue or put off.[47]

This buffered self is neither constituted by the interdependence of its social relations nor directed by some higher authority on the covenantal model of the people of Israel heeding the God of Deuteronomy, or the classical model of the *polis* forming citizens in soulful accord with the natural law of the cosmos. This separate self can appeal to biblical convictions of free will inhering in humans made in the image of God. It can invoke Enlightenment faith in the Laws of Nature and Nature's God creating all men equal and endowing them with universal rights to life, liberty, and the pursuit of happiness. But it relies on individual interests and feelings to migrate from freedom of conscience to freedom of choice in a world of protean possibility without binding moral hierarchies to check its rise or ultimate ends to chart its course.[48]

In terms of the economic interests, social contracts, and strategic rules featured in cultural commonsense today, each autonomous individual freely chooses to enter into this or that exchange, relationship, or association. Each decides by calculating the comparative costs and benefits of every such choice. Each reckons the balance of utility gained and self-interest served in giving and getting, checked by individual rights, common laws, and rational rules of procedure.[49]

At the same time, a softer, more sensitive side of this separate self, at once bohemian and bourgeois, seeks wholeness and fulfillment in expressing inner feelings, enjoying the life of the senses, and embracing others in romantic love, erotic play, domestic intimacy, creative art, and spiritual exploration, if not merging with them in the shared experience of mystical union. "Get out of your head and into your body," urge Romantics intent on knowing what's really real by feeling it in the firsthand experience of emotion, intuition, and empathy instead of the detached reasoning of utilitarian cost-benefit analysis or universalizing logics of Kantian argument. The good life should feel good, and the emotional wisdom of the body should reveal moral truths beyond rational rules of right action based on narrow self-interest and mutual disinterest posing as prudence.[50]

"Be here now," instead of being dutybound by the past or distracted by investing in the future. Embrace life and drink it in, bohemians invite, instead of standing off and seeing it from a distance. Salvation from sin and divine punishment, sought by denying desire and following ascetic regimens to mortify the flesh, gives way to freeing the spirit from inhibition and inertia, depression and anxiety, and affirming the self's inner light and goodness as worthy of emotional acceptance and love. Here "spiritual but not religious" intuition and impulse come to the fore as free individuals practice their own faith in their own way, in touch with nature and each other, lit by divine immanence and inspired by their own inner truth at one with the universe in the moment.

How did such dual selves emerge in the modern world? A complex intellectual history charts the origins and interplay of their two sides, instrumental and expressive. Howsoever selfish and solipsistic Hobbes supposes human nature, Adam Smith uncovers sympathetic moral sentiments that individuals imagine and feel for each other in social exchange, especially among family and friends in softer circles of mutual love that shelter them from the hard competition of the marketplace and public arena. John Locke offers a consensual, cooperative social contract to protect the natural rights of every individual and make each person happy to do their moral duty.[51]

To guard against Montaigne's urbane skepticism, Pascal calls on heartfelt intuition to aid reason in finding truth. Rousseau turns it to free the self spiritually from bourgeois repression masked as commonsense rationality, then fulfill it politically in an organic republic that imprints the general will on each human heart, bound together like Emile and Sophie by love of wisdom to form living civic cells. Romantics protest poignantly against the instrumental reason of the Enlightenment's emotionally detached self in an empirically objective world governed by Newtonian laws. Instead of standing aloof and untouched by feelings of passion and experiences of beauty, sensitive selves embrace an enchanting world that sparks their spontaneity and creativity. Instead of being tied down to the bottom line of utility, they heed the heart of romantic love to harmonize human wholeness and freedom in the "evermore" moment of time regained after the fall.[52]

Selves in touch with the moment stop the clock and get out of the office to stroll along the boulevard and picnic in the park, to see and be seen like dandies depicted by Degas and reprised by Proust, at once ephemeral and immortal. In lifestylish leisure and artistic fervor they reincarnate classical distinctions between *intuitio* and *ratio* along lines drawn from Aristotle to Aquinas. They revive medieval mystics such as Meister Eckhardt distilling Plotinus and Augustine to lift hearts to God and reveal the "groundless reason" of the Godhead at the root of the soul as pure *being*, not *doing*. With Renaissance humanists they celebrate the intrinsic goodness and free will of human nature to lead seekers to moral perfection and spiritual fulfillment without the need for devotion to extrinsic religious rites or works.[53]

"We know truth when we see it," whatever skeptics and scoffers say, proclaims Ralph Waldo Emerson to spiritual seekers in mid-nineteenth-century America. The soul seeks the beauty of nature, which satisfies this desire as "one expression for the Universe," he affirms. "God is the all-fair. Truth, and goodness, and beauty, are but different faces of the same All." Standing amid such a sublime nature, Emerson testifies, we transcend ourselves: "I am nothing; I see all: the currents of the Universal Being circulate through me; I am party or particle of God."[54]

Not so fast, object latter-day saints and early modern rationalists to Romantics urging us to become One with the All. We are sinners who must repent, for heaven's sake, they insist. We are thinkers who must work hard to know anything through the rigorous activity of discursive reason. Reason must examine, compare, distinguish, analyze, deduce, demonstrate, abstract, and generalize to gain knowledge, since no human knowledge comes through perceiving without conceiving. "Reason cannot intuit anything," declares Kant, "and the law is that reason acquires its possessions through work." Thus, Kant dismisses the pure "intellectual contemplation" of classical antiquity upheld in the nondiscursive faculty of spiritual vision exercised as *simplex intuitis* in scholastic usage. He spurns the enthusiasm of Romantics who have "only to attend to the oracle in one's breast and enjoy it, and so possess that wisdom whole and entire" that the "herculean labor" of true philosophy must work without rest or daydreaming to attain.[55]

Nevertheless, from Thoreau walking through the woods of Walden Pond in the "direction of his dreams," and Whitman taking to the open road to "loaf and invite my soul" at one with the universe, Americans in love with love have gone on to seek authentic self-fulfillment in the arms of romance, relaxation, play, and ecstasy. Led by visionary guides from Emerson to Oprah, they have explored new spiritual paths and climbed metaphysical peaks in search of transcendent truth, goodness, and beauty. Who among us wants to miss out on the fun, to lose out in love, or never to have loved at all? Who wants to know the market price of everything and the infinite value of nothing? After meeting Americans "filled with an enthusiastic, almost fierce spirituality," Tocqueville reflects in 1840, "The soul has needs that must be satisfied." Since "it soon grows bored, restless, and anxious amid the pleasures of the senses," we should not be surprised "if, among a people uniquely preoccupied with prosperity, mysticism did not soon make progress."[56]

Popular usage today contrasts the technical knowledge of information gained and measured or data collected and calculated with the direct knowledge of existential meaning discovered by firsthand experience in all its sensory and intuitive immediacy. Profoundly felt personal experience and spiritual insight lead to authentic truth, not abstract reasoning and intellectual argument over universal concepts. Follow your breath and feel your heartbeat, empty your mind and fill your soul. Such learning by hand and in the flesh—on the model of carnal knowledge, learning to swim, or improvise jazz—extends to soulful experience of immanent spiritual truth in nature and consciousness, within or without explicitly religious rites.[57]

"Turn on and tune in" to the innate rhythms of consciousness, advise latter-day spiritual counselors, psychotherapists, and mindfulness instructors no less persuasively if more prudently than countercultural sages and psychedelic oracles of decades past, in order to realize "the way to do is to be" as timeless wisdom here and now, not just a Taoist maxim once upon a time, nor an altar call echoing old-time religion to come to Jesus and be filled by the Holy Spirit. Let us be human, not machines for thinking and doing. "Religion's essence is neither thinking nor acting, but intuition and feeling," the young Schleiermacher countered Kant two centuries ago. "It wishes to intuit the universe," and it "longs to be grasped and filled by the universe's immediate influences," he affirmed. "Religion wishes to see the infinite," and feel its imprint on humankind.[58]

Modern ethics of authenticity in the West reshape the aim of human fulfillment by reframing the moral ideal that underlies it, as Charles Taylor argues. Instead of heeding God's biblical covenant or discerning the Platonic Idea of the Good to be true to yourself, you must get in touch with what lies deepest within you. That no longer unfolds as Augustinian self-awareness on the ascent to God or Socratic self-understanding on the ascent to truth, or even the governance of Adam Smith's conscientious "impartial spectator" as God's sovereign viceroy in each breast. Rousseau's call to overcome egoistic pride and follow the intimate voice of nature within each person opens the door to full self-determination by putting you in touch with yourself and the moment to feel and act, free of external social influence and conformity. The political force of the general will to fuse this common freedom into an ideal organic democracy, or an actual totalitarian state, gives way in turn to more inward ideals of Romantic individualism. Each person has her own unique way of being human. So each must overcome social pressure and psychic alienation imposed by narrow self-interest or instrumental reason, in order to hear and heed their own original voice calling them to authentic self-realization and the good of "doing your own thing."[59]

REINTEGRATING RELIGION

How does the way we imagine the world tie into the way we live in it? Grant that few Americans today read Romantic poets praising noble savages or urging sublime return to Nature from a heartless marketplace of getting and spending. Nor do many of us drop out to earn our livelihood farming on back-to-the-land communes or creating art in tune with the laid-back lyrics of psychedelic rock or the utopian ideals of countercultural manifestos.[60]

But the imagery and ethos of a spiritual life serenely at one with nature and joyously joined with others in wholehearted love, play, and fruitful creativity pervade American life today. We hear and hum its refrain of having fun together. We move to its backbeat, whether plugged in to Spotify at home or out at a concert with friends. We see its videos on our screens and in our daydreams. It surrounds our daily round, saturates our senses, and stirs our imagination. Ubiquitous as consumer advertising and home entertainment, streaming music and social media, these images and stories declare our personal independence, project our pursuit of happiness, and urge us to become who we really are by living the life of our dreams with the ones we love.

Indeed modern private life echoes in aspiration "the collective effervescence" of communal rites of renewal found in small-scale "tribal" societies based on hunting and gathering, for all the differences in actual behavior and structural arrangement between our way of life and theirs. We hunger to be whole and to be loved within all-embracing communities of warm friends and family, kindred spirits, and like-minded colleagues, despite or indeed because of the fact that we lead lives divided across distinctive social spheres of economic, political, educational, religious, and domestic activity and relationship driven by the division of labor. However, divided by class and caste, gender and generation, we remain cultural animals, left unfinished by instinct and hungry for holism in shared rites and myths to dissolve our differences and embody our community, to dramatize and deepen the authentic meaning of everyday life, and enable us to affirm it without doubt or despair.[61]

Hunting and gathering disperse work in small-scale tribal societies and make it routine, monotonous, and dull, as Durkheim observes of Australian "aboriginal" societies. Men and women, young and old, each go their own way to do their own work each day, focused on the mundane means of finding food to survive. Periodically, however, clans and kin groups gather to concentrate their social action and energy in cyclical religious ceremonies that dissolve everyday differences and re-create communion. These rites elicit deep feeling and heighten consciousness, enacted in rhythmic movement and sound, and expressed in symbolic images of human coherence and dramas of social unity. Persons reunite in a single social body by joining together in space and time, face-to-face and side by side. They keep together in time through dance and chant, clapping and drumming. By so animating sound and sight they create a time out of time, bringing myth to life in the vivid, fluid dreamtime of everywhen, and storing its felt meaning in mythic symbols. Opposed yet complementary, these two movements of consciousness in the counterpoint of everyday labor and effervescent ritual make up the whole of social life in primordial societies, at once playful and practical, poetic and pragmatic, no less symbolic and logical in their own way of life than we are in ours.[62]

But do such small-scale societies prove much better balanced than our own at home and work in their communal complementarity of symbolic and conceptual modes of consciousness? It's a practical question worth weighing, however pervasive our embodied rites of everyday interaction from shaking hands to waving goodbyes, however powerful our privatized rites of modern intimacy and our polarized myths of modern political factions and tribal subcultures. For so it seems in light of the "spiritual needs" and yearning expressed by young Americans today, in and out of church, to open their hearts and minds, to experience heartfelt release from their separate selves, and realize unity of body and soul with the whole of nature and existence.

How are we to realize and symbolize such unitive consciousness? How can we even try? By coming together in new ways, answer spiritual critics of conventional religion, to become one with the music, spirit, and beloved community of worship along fully participatory paths of shared rites and myths. By finding such paths that run truer, they add, than the free-form fragility of be-ins, communes, and psychedelic trips of the countercultural past or the mundane monotony of "organized religion" in the present. Not by technical reason and bureaucratic organization alone, they warn, can we live fully, nor by sermonic lectures and half-hearted hymns. Not if we remain unsure of the moral goods and aims that make life worth living, and make money and power worth pursuing merely as means to these ends.

Conversely, if we can never get enough of what we don't really want in the light of ultimate ends, spiritual seekers wonder, don't we need to reach beyond effervescent experience alone? Don't we need to seek genuine moral goods if not transcendent truths? If so, they ask, what can we learn from the visions and virtues of historic salvation religions? Can we draw on their practical moral inquiry into what we must do to be saved from fear and anxiety if not sin and damnation? By this account, whatever we believe or disbelieve abstractly—for example, about the integrity of persons or the solidarity of humankind—we want to see and grasp reality in ways that ring true to our deepest experience and make sense of it in practice. We want our experience in turn to clarify and confirm our vision of what is real, and how we should live in accord with it. "Is" and "Ought," as enacted in our rites and expressed in our myths, should fit and flow together in our moods and motives. The phenomenology of what we feel most deeply should align with the ontology of what we know most truly and ground the ethics we aim to live out most fully.

This holds true, say spiritual seekers, whether we follow the Tao or the Middle Path, heed the Gospel Truth or Socratic reason, accept the will of Allah, or answer the covenantal call to become the Law, not just follow it. We seek to be true to tradition by living it out creatively in the ongoing flow of the present, not by trying in vain to return to an ideal past and make it great again on the dot of a punctual present. Nothing is ever lost in the unfolding of human consciousness and culture, we can affirm. But what of all the changes in the way we live and the way we pray that have brought us to this present moment of religious drift and spiritual urgency?[63]

Communal rites of renewal draw together the all-encompassing circles of small-scale societies based on hunting and gathering. But these give way to priestly rites of sacrifice and prayer to diverse gods—kind and cruel, chaste and erotic—as settled agriculture expands economic surplus and social scale in "archaic" peasant societies headed by military, political, and religious elites. Instead of everyone gathering face-to-face to take part in tribal rites, divine priest-kings command sacrificial rites and prayers to span divine and human hierarchies rising in archaic civilizations such as ancient Egypt, India, Mesopotamia, and Mesoamerica.

Gods, cults, and courts multiply and divide their taxing labors to rule empires made in the image of an archaic cosmopolis that articulates religious and political reality into one natural-divine continuum. Through organic myth and metaphor, it distinguishes devotees of diverse gods, and unifies them into members of a single social body celebrated in civic rites such as the Greek Panathenaea and Roman Saturnalia. They remain political subjects of twin kingdoms, human and divine, and they depend on the growing powers of dominance and nurturance exercised by their rulers in both realms. Set in higher and lower castes or orders, they make up one social body of diverse members ranked from head to foot, and they inhabit one cosmos composed of diverse layers from the stars above to the underworld below.[64]

Prophets of historic salvation religions reject "this world" as a vale of tears, a delusory dream, or a passing moment before the timeless reality of another world beyond in heaven, nirvana, or Jannah. "Awake!" they call and live in accord with the reality of this transcendent realm. By transforming mythic narratives in dialogue with theoretic argument and critical "thinking about thinking" put into writing, prophets renounce worldly powers and principalities, called into question as false, evil, or empty within the symbolic framework of cosmological dualism.[65]

Salvific prophets crystallize an otherworldly true self or Buddhist non-self, deeper than the flux of everyday experience and the particularity of manifold worldly goods, tribal totems, or archaic gods enmeshed in moral ambiguity. This universal self stands facing a reality over against itself, with a moral stance and aim unified by seeking salvation as the one and only good of infinite value, bridging this world and the next. "For what shall it profit a man, if he shall gain the whole world, and lose his own soul?" asks Mark 8:36. This hypergood tops and transcends a ladder of higher and lower human goods more or less in tune with the order and energy of a single, centered hierarchic cosmos that now opens up to higher truth from above and beyond and within.

Morally universal conceptions of human beings emerge around the first millennium BCE as essential selves or boundless souls made in the image of God, Dharma, or Tao. They transform the transient experience of ritual exaltation into symbols of timeless truth. One God transcends all earthly rulers to become the biblical king of kings, calling a covenant people bound by universal laws to heed God and care for one another. Biblical prophets call down God's lawful judgment on unjust kings and offer God's grace to all persons as infinitely valuable "children of God."

Asian exemplars of universal wisdom and compassion likewise open up paths to perfection for all to follow. Transcendent justice and mercy strain the organic moral particularism of peasant-based societies, now developing more differentiated elites of prophets and judges alongside warrior-kings and priests, and diversifying into broader middle strata of merchants and artisans. Prophets call the people to their covenantal responsibility and moral integrity. Turn your whole heart to God, they urge, or open your eyes to the "mind-only" unity of Buddha-nature. They reset the ritual balance of primordial societies by revealing universal ethics of salvation and inventing new forms of congregational community to enable their practice.[66]

Early modern visions of life's salvific purpose and aim refocus attention on our calling to labor, love, and govern in this world as vital to life everlasting in the next. On the Calvinist model of "the Protestant ethic," they discipline willful individuals to obey the will of an almighty God through prayerful work and pious family life decreed for all, and they justify state power to extend religious governance from self-control to social control for the good of all. They move political subjects to become citizens, as the Protestant priesthood of all believers prefigures the democratic self-government of all citizens. They inspire capitalism on the rise in the urban households and workshops, marketplaces and public squares of middle-class societies emerging in Europe.[67]

What must we do to be saved? Against the eudaemonism of feudal peasants, artisans, and merchants working just enough to get by and live comfortably, this ascetic ethic stresses continuous, lifelong labor as daily prayer for monks in the world. No longer cloistered in contemplation, they are now inspired to action in the world to glorify God in new social practices framed by free markets, free labor, and self-government. Early modern markets and republics rely in turn on the discipline and diligence of persons formed by strict congregations and conscientious families that forge a reliable if rigid core of character by the pressure of dutiful moral authority on the anvil of doctrinal orthodoxy.

Collective rites exemplified by the Catholic Mass give way to more individual rites of religious commitment and regeneration, devotion and instruction. From the examination of conscience and sacramental confession set by liturgical calendar and monastic regimen within a cosmos ordered by divine providence for the sake of salvation, rites of continuous moral self-scrutiny and self-development arise within a new kind of natural and social order centered on mind and machine. Providentially designed by Nature's God with the ingenuity of a universal clockmaker, this mechanism requires humans to keep its cogwheels running by the constructive action of their diligent work day by day. Time is uniformly measured and consistently marked off by accurate clock-reading in offices, workshops, and town squares, not rung by Sunday church bells or stretched from dawn to dusk through seasons in the fields. For the sake of progress, for our own good and the mutual benefit of society, we need to make the most of time, without a minute to waste.[68]

By contrast, modern administrative states more thoroughly order the procedures of public life into regulatory regimes by coordinating the grid of disciplinary schooling, professional training and credentialing, scientific technology put to work, and the bureaucratic organization of highly divided labor in complex societies within a global economy. Meanwhile, they leave middle-class private life freer for individuals to follow their dreams and desires in romantic love, lifestylish leisure, creative art, therapeutic encounter, and recreational play along shifting currents fed by the media and music of popular culture.[69]

The regulatory exoskeleton of the modern world rewards technical skill, trained talent, and strategic savvy as professional virtues. It prizes productivity and efficiency, innovative problem-solving and consistent progress, set out in its own corporate creeds, myths, and rites if not always followed out on its bottom line of performance and payoff. At the same time, it allows our inner selves to pursue protean possibilities of creative self-expression and authentic self-fulfillment without demanding a core of character to withstand the uninsured risks of a laissez-faire marketplace, meet the unselfish requirements of republican citizenship, or face the hour of our death before it's time to go.

Work hard and play hard, this ethos urges. Feeling flat, tired, or trapped? Take a break and take some time off. Go on vacation, have some fun, get some rest, then get back to work refreshed and ready to go. Or retire, relax, and get away from it all, it promises. Enjoy life with a feel for fun instead of an eye on utility. Don't always check the clock or count the hours. Instead enter the flow of the moment to "loaf and invite my soul," as Walt Whitman calls us to join in a "Song of Myself," at one with nature and all the universe in living leaves of grass and liquid trees, voluptuous earth and billowing sea beneath a dazzling sun.[70]

DIVIDED SELVES IN SEARCH OF MORAL COMMUNITY

However thoroughly coordinated and regulated proves the procedural administration of modern society as a whole, its differentiated institutions multiply and divide models of selfhood, relationship, and practical activity across distinctive social spheres—economic, political, educational, domestic, aesthetic, and religious, too. At once normal and normative, this process yields such all-American ideals as coolly efficient and productive workers yet warm and spontaneous lovers, caring and conscientious parents yet stylish consumers, critical and creative scholars yet law-abiding citizens and rule-bound bureaucrats.[71]

Each such stereotype of selfhood in action and relationship implies distinctive virtues and capacities in practice, with its senses and sensibility specifically situated in social space and time. Friends stay in touch with intimate feelings, for example, and families with fond memories. Farsighted investors look ahead to foresee profits, and aesthetes appear tastefully turned out in today's fashion. Spouses hold hands in marriage forever and a day, and Bible believers heed God's eternal Word in daily prayer.

Each such self implies a set of institutional structures and norms that frame their interactive roles, for example, as good teachers and students in schools, parents and children at home, or clergy and laity in churches. Each enacts a distinctive genre of moral drama staged within a particular set of social arrangements, norms, and cues, even if these essential elements don't always compose an explicit script with a predictable plot or repertoire of responses. On the model of rites and myths they nonetheless elicit and enable fitting moods and motives, gestures and attitudes in specific modes of interaction, for example between laborers and foremen on factory floors or professional colleagues on corporate committees; landlord and tenant or homeowners as next-door neighbors; romantic lovers or just friends.

Despite, or indeed because of these contrasting dramatic roles, scenes, and settings of modern social life, the multiplication and division of selfhood we experience across institutional spheres also yield a countervailing impulse and aim to feel and act as whole persons, each integrated and unified, genuine and true, and each in touch with others in concentric circles of community.

"Just be yourself." Whether spoken to reassure or reprove, that familiar phrase implies you should know who you *really* are, even if acting that way isn't always easy.

If such self-knowledge was once bred by the moral community of congregation and family, school and public square, on the idealized model of Pilgrims building "a City upon a Hill" as a beacon of hope for the world, many younger Americans today see self-realization lying in pieces of a puzzle that each individual must put together and solve for herself on a personal path to spiritual fulfillment. Each of us must find our own way, write our own story, share it with someone to love, and draw it together in a circle of friends. For some that path leads in and out of church or alongside it. For others it leads out and away to a wider world of sacred experience, symbols, and selves in communion all their own.[72]

Why leave church? Unchurched young adults often answer by citing "too many rules," too much focus on "money and power," and too little attention given to "meeting spiritual needs." In doing so, they are criticizing "organized religion" as an institution that fails them by rehearsing the regulatory regimes of modern schooling, work, and the marketplace as structured social arrangements, and as moral dramas, too. Seen in this light, churches seek paying customers, fee-for-service clients, diligent volunteers, reliable donors, and loyal constituents instead of genuinely embracing persons as spiritual seekers and fellow pilgrims, intimate friends and warm companions, if not beloved brothers and sisters. Churches reduce heartfelt virtues and gospel stories learned by example and lived out in neighbor-love to rules of action calculated to get results or conceived to follow abstract principles.

Conversely, spirituality as practiced beyond church pews can thrive freely in a range of social settings devoted to feeling the spirit, embodying its beauty, and enacting its goodness. These include, for example, therapy, counseling, and meditation groups; yoga, dance, art, and aerobics classes; sports leagues and drama troupes; neighborhood and community clubs; singles and seniors groups; and societies for civic improvement and charitable aid. As such, unchurched Americans can see "spirituality" outshining organized religion on moral and practical grounds alike.

Churches can seek in turn to grow more "spiritual" by incorporating such social activities and settings into their own profiles and programs. They may take new forms as user-friendly neo-evangelical megachurches or charismatic Christian communities beyond denominational bounds. They may turn into more soulful, sacramental, socially engaged, or seeker-style congregations sponsored by mainline denominations yet tuned to a new ethos and its cultural carriers.[73]

INDIVIDUAL AUTONOMY AND MODERN WORLD ACCEPTANCE

The individualized, world-accepting, meaning-seeking "spiritual" stance of modern religion offers a critical point of departure in distinguishing it from its historic antecedents among the world's salvation religions. The collapse of cosmological dualism and world-rejection marks modern modes of religious symbolization, action, and organization in all their social implications. The historic duplex structure of this world and the next, sin and salvation, the shadow play of illusion here below and the radiant truth of reason on high, give way to the multiplex monism of modern world acceptance.[74]

This monism accepts the protean possibility of this world, neither bound by original sin nor perfected by divine grace or providential progress. It enables a peculiarly proactive and expressive sense of quicksilver selfhood that inspires each of us to choose our own unique path and follow it freely. It affirms personal responsibility for critically self-conscious and conscientious participation in the process of religious symbolization itself, shared among a modern priesthood of all believers no longer bound by duties of doctrinal orthodoxy and ritual observance imposed by the tutelary authority of established churches.

Liberal Protestant theology from Schleiermacher through Tillich frames such ideals for Western intellectuals. But these ideals resonate with popular convictions deep in the American grain that each person must think and feel for herself in matters of faith. This commonsense conviction also draws on religious freedom as an individual right guaranteed to all citizens by the US Constitution. Through such Enlightenment visions of constitutional and natural law, tied to the voluntarist social contracts of Locke and Rousseau, ethical individualism sharpens the mind and disenchants the soul of educated Americans, even as it sacralizes selfhood.[75]

Such conviction declares individual rights universal. But it also asks what the right thing is to do as a matter of obligation specified by law or contract, procedural rule or regulation. It commingles with widening currents of Romantic, aesthetic, and sentimental feeling among middle-class Americans in the nineteenth century to re-enchant their spirits and soften their hearts, warmed in turn by the religious affections of evangelical revivalism, Methodist piety, Pentecostal enthusiasm, and sacramental devotion among Catholics, Anglicans, and Lutherans. "Who, what, and how should we love?" asks this softer self. What sort of good life will enable us to feel happy and fulfilled?

In the cultural establishment of revivalist and reformist American Protestantism by 1900, ideals of individual autonomy and freedom of conscience turn on the normative need for all religious liberties to lead to deeper self-understanding and greater social responsibility for the shared fate of humankind. The search for moral measures of action, personal maturity, and social relevance at the heart of the modern quest for salvation after heaven makes religious commitment and moral conduct more personally demanding than ever.[76]

It also grows more difficult to live out these ideals in the actual practices and institutional settings of complex societies governed by large-scale corporate bureaucracy and public administration, compared to the flexible, self-revising social systems of democratic polities and market economies in step with *early* modern religion in the West. These institutions relied for their moral balance and discipline on the rigidity of Protestant orthodoxy and Puritan personality fostered in rigorist congregations and families, no less than medieval hierarchies and monarchies relied on an ethos of devout dependence, reciprocal duties, and natural law within the Great Chain of Being blessed by a magisterial Catholic Church.

Can the freedom that modern society prizes in terms of culture and personality, including its moral ideals of free markets and democratic politics, be stably institutionalized beyond the bounds of private life and leisure, romantic love, and playful self-expression? Can it flourish without demanding altruism or indifference from too many, critics ask, and permitting a powerful few to serve themselves by investing in the best government money can buy? Built around the strategic constraint and disciplinary grid of (post)industrial economies, administrative bureaucracies, and regulatory regimes, can such societies keep their promises to liberate and integrate the self yet sustain solidarity? In seeking to do so, will American society strengthen or sap its democratic ideals of responsibly shared self-government and actively sustained social reform to serve liberty and justice for all? Will it endure as a coherent moral community if not as one nation under God with the soul of a church?[77]

Against the current of conventional secularization theories that declare dogmatic orthodoxy disenchanted and piety privatized or abandoned outright by rising ranks of the unchurched, this view of modernity leaves open the possibility of faith transformed through critical yet sacred self-awareness of human integrity and flourishing to bring forth new visions of justice and compassion, grace and peace of mind we can live out today. Can the spirit of modern religion be re-enchanted and reincarnated, re-storied and ritually reborn beyond the bounds of systematic theologies and denominational conventions to revive the heart of congregations? Can it keep its mind on faithful dialogue and practical wisdom, yet come to its senses by reincorporating the full range of effervescent rites of renewal and passage, spirit-filled and sacramentally embodied? Can it sing, chant, sway, and march to awaken bodies of worship from cerebral sermonic slumbers, and open its institutional arms to embrace the span of charismatic, contemplative, and evangelical callings, priestly and prophetic, pastoral and monastic? Can it lay on hands and speak in tongues, meditate in silence and go on pilgrimage, visit the sick and feed the hungry?

Conceive the collapse of cosmological dualism and world rejection, the rise of multiplex monism and world acceptance, as pivotal points between historic and modern modes of religion. Then the Protestant Reformation and its global correlates become opening phases of transition to the spiritual seeking and fluid communion of modern faiths, and they enable critical conversion and constructive change beyond the bounds of both. The early modern moment no longer marks a distinct development or fulfillment of religious tradition, particularly in the Anglo-American Christian forms of Puritan Calvinism, evangelical revivalism, or social-gospel liberalism. It no longer opposes salvific faith to modern secularization construed as a breakdown of religious meaning and a failure of moral order.[78]

Realizing that earlier modes or stages of religious imagination, understanding, and practice continue to coexist with and within later ones, reveals the peculiarly modern anti-modern nature of many "fundamentalist" or "traditional" religious movements. This includes modern nation-states and populist parties marching under "God and Country" banners against infidels at home or abroad. It features early modern faith in the rationalism of Newtonian laws and Baconian experiments that biblical literalists marshal to defend "absolute values" against the "relativism" of late-modern historicism and culturalism.[79]

Recognizing such coexistence, interaction, and conflict between modes of religion also helps interpret the demographic facts that the world has never numbered more not-so-modern members of the historic salvation religions than it does today. One-third of the world's population is now Christian, one-quarter Muslim, and one-sixth Hindu. One-third of all Christians live in former European colonies. They continue to live out their common faith in distinctive ways, and they continue to migrate to the United States and Western Europe.[80]

In this light, we can more clearly weigh empirical evidence that much of America's peculiar religious dynamism and change has developed through demographic processes in a nation of immigrants arriving in successive waves defined by ethnicity and religious difference rather than through shifts in freely chosen commitments made by individuals among Anglo-Saxon Protestant denominations sorted by social class. Religious membership and identification shape moral commitments and social relations in marriage, schooling, work, and politics in ways inseparable from ethnic nativity and status, assimilation and segmentation.[81]

Seen from this angle, changes in religious membership, identification, and non-affiliation stem mainly from changes in the composition of the American population brought by waves of immigration and generational replacement since 1970. These are changes, first, in the composition of new immigrant groups which now number one in five Americans; and, second, in the religious alignments of younger generations amplified by higher fertility rates among new immigrants. By this logic, as older cohorts die off, identification with liberal and moderate Protestant bodies of Western European origin predictably declines. But conservative Christian churches are not growing, as supply-side theorists and evangelical activists proclaim. Nor are Americans rapidly abandoning religious identification, as secularization theorists foresee. Buoyed by immigrants from Latin America in particular, one in four Americans continues to identify with Catholicism. Immigrants from Asia, Africa, the Middle East, and elsewhere have more than doubled identification with "other Protestant" groups and "other religion" since 1972.[82]

Empirical evidence of religious switching likewise fails to bear out theories of secularization invoked to explain the recent rise of religiously unaffiliated "nones," and supply-side theories used to declare conservative Christian churches as winners over liberal Protestant losers in the religious marketplace. Switching now realigns the religious identification of one in three Americans, but few go far when they switch, and most stay with religious identities formed in their families of origin. Grand theories ignore the complex interplay of localized patterns of switching that channel the circulation of the saints through a changing ethnic milieu created by waves of immigration and marked by life-course events such as marriage and parenthood, schooling and occupational mobility.[83]

On the other hand, rising rates of religious non-identification among younger cohorts and newer immigrant groups imply changes in religious belief and belonging that reveal how and why denominational membership and identification still matter. Higher birth rates have ensured that more culturally conservative Protestants and Mormons make up a growing share of Americans who continue to hold religious identities. Meanwhile more moderate and liberal Protestant groups make up a shrinking share, as their alums swell the ranks of religiously unaffiliated "nones," Hispanic immigrants shore up Catholics, and Asian immigrants boost "other" religious traditions.

The relative growth of more conservative branches of Protestantism, religious non-identification, and non-Christian religion promise to shape the future of religion in America, and influence family life, social stratification, and politics in problematic ways. Evidence of cultural and political polarization in American religion today certainly seems striking by contrast to religion in mid-twentieth-century America led by moderate and liberal Protestants at home in the White House, Congress, and corporate boardroom. They were less powerfully contested by sect-like conservatives, and more often joined by an ethnically diverse Catholic Church open to Anglo-assimilation, even if fundamentalists stridently decried modernist liberals and cold warriors fervently crusaded against mainline-church leaders as communists and fellow travelers.[84]

Today non-Christian and religiously unaffiliated Americans slightly outnumber conservative Protestants, with each group claiming a quarter of US adults, while Catholics and mainline Protestants make up most of the rest. Tomorrow the United States will be a "majority minority" society, the Census Bureau predicts, with non-Hispanic Whites composing only 43 percent of the population by 2060 instead of their 60 percent in 2020. Well beyond the growing impact of the unchurched, questions remain about how this burgeoning diversity will shift religious belief, practice, and identification in relation to American family life, social standing, economic earning, and political alignment in the future.[85]

To weigh such questions in detail let us turn to the actual practices and arrangements of two constellations of congregations engaged in welcoming unchurched young adults and holding onto their own across generations, one an innovative evangelical megachurch growing in Silicon Valley, and the other an ensemble of activist Methodist congregations thriving in Atlanta.

NOTES

1. Mary Douglas, *How Institutions Think* (Syracuse: Syracuse University Press, 1986), chs. 1, 5, 8; Clifford Geertz, "Ethos, Worldview, and the Analysis of Sacred Symbols," in *The Interpretation of Cultures* (New York: Basic Books, 1973), 126–41.
2. Charles Taylor, *Modern Social Imaginaries* (Durham, NC: Duke University Press, 2004), chs. 1, 2, 7, 12; Robert N. Bellah, Richard Madsen, William M. Sullivan, Ann Swidler, and Steven M. Tipton, *Habits of the Heart* (Berkeley: University of California Press, 2008), ch. 2; Steven M. Tipton, *Getting Saved from the Sixties* (Berkeley: University of California Press, 1982), chs. 1, 5.
3. Here and below, see Steven M. Tipton, "Social Differentiation and Moral Pluralism," in *Meaning and Modernity*, ed. Richard Madsen et al., (Berkeley: University of California Press, 2002), 15–40.
4. Bellah et al., *Habits of the Heart*, chs. 2–3, esp. 27–35, 44–48, and 71–84.
5. Bellah et al., *Habits of the Heart*, 28–29. Cf. Sacvan Bercovitch, *The Puritan Origins of the American Self* (New Haven, CT: Yale University Press, 1975).
6. *United States Declaration of Independence*, para. 1, 2; Bellah et al., *Habits of the Heart*, 30–31.
7. Bellah et al., *Habits of the Heart*, 32–33.
8. Bellah et al., *Habits of the Heart*, 34–35.
9. On religious freedom, Christian ecclesiology, and modern subjectivity, see Ernst Troeltsch, *The Social Teaching of the Christian Churches* (New York: Harper & Row, 1960), vol. 2, 993–1013; H. Richard Niebuhr, *The Social Sources of Denominationalism* (New York: Henry Holt, 1929), ch. 1; Bellah et al., *Habits of the Heart*, 243–49;

Andrew M. Greeley, *Chicago Catholics and the Struggles within Their Church* (Piscataway, NJ: Transaction Press, 2010); Charles Taylor, *A Secular Age* (Cambridge, MA: Harvard University Press, 2007), ch. 20.

10. On voluntary association, see Alexis de Tocqueville, *Democracy in America*, ed. J.P. Mayer (New York: Harper & Row, 1966), vol. 2, part II, chs. 1–9; Claude S. Fischer, *Made in America* (Chicago: University of Chicago Press, 2010), ch. 4; and Claude S. Fischer, "Covid-19: Exceptionalism with a Vengeance," August 21, 2020, at https://madeinamericathebook.wordpress.com/2020/08/21. Most Americans agree that "government is corrupt and rigged against me," including two in three Republican and Independent voters and one in two Democrats, according to Institute of Politics, "Our Precarious Democracy," University of Chicago, 2022, 2. In 2022, Americans' confidence in institutions ranged from highs of 68 percent for small business and 64 percent for the military to lows of 7 percent for Congress, 25 percent for the Presidency, 41 percent for big business, 28 percent for labor, 28 percent for public schools, and 31 percent for "the church or organized religion," according to Jeffrey M. Jones, "Confidence in U.S. Institutions Down: Average at New Low," Gallup News Service, June 1–20, 2022, at https://news.gallup.com/poll394283.

11. See Becka Alper, "From the Solidly Secular to Sunday Stalwarts," Pew Research Center, August 29, 2018, 2–4, distinguishing somewhat religious "Relaxed Religious" and "Spiritually Awake" groups from "Sunday Stalwarts" on one side and "Religion Resisters" and the "Solidly Secular" on the other; Michael Hout and Claude S. Fischer, "Explaining Why More Americans Have No Religious Preference: Political Backlash and Generational Succession, 1987–2012," *Sociological Science* 1 (October 13, 2014): 423–47; Christian Smith with Patricia Snell, *Souls in Transition: The Religious and Spiritual Lives of Emerging Adults* (New York: Oxford University Press, 2009), 166–68; and Charles Taylor, *A Secular Age*, 534–35.

12. Pew Research Center, "When Americans Say They Believe in God, What Do They Mean?," 4, 9–14, 23, 27; and Alper, "From the Solidly Secular," 2–3, here and below. On continuity of change across generations of Fundamentalists and Evangelicals, cf. Darren E. Sherkat, *Changing Faith: The Dynamics and Consequences of Americans' Shifting Religious Identities* (New York: NYU Press, 2014), ch. 2; and Christian Smith, American Evangelicalism: Embattled and Thriving (Chicago: University of Chicago Press, 1998), 49, Table 2.8.

13. Cf. T. M. Luhrmann, *When God Talks Back: Understanding the American Evangelical Relationship with God* (New York: Knopf, 2012), xxi as quoted, and xv–xxii on neo-evangelical prayer; Stephen Ellingson, *The Megachurch and the Mainline: Remaking Religious Tradition in the 21st Century* (Chicago: University of Chicago Press, 2007) comparing neo-evangelical and traditional Lutheran prayer and piety; and H. Richard Niebuhr, *The Kingdom of God in America* (Middletown, CT: Wesleyan University Press, 1988), chs. 2–4, comparing Calvinist, evangelical, and social-gospel theological ethics.

14. Pew Research Center, "The Religious Typology," August 29, 2018, 45–46, reports that 74 percent of all Americans say they ever talk to "God/higher power," but only 28 percent say God talks back, with 97 percent talking and 54 percent hearing back among churchgoing "Sunday Stalwarts," and 93 percent talking but only

24 percent hearing back among the less churchy "Spiritually Awake," by contrast to only 54 percent talking and 15 percent hearing back among the largely unchurched "Religious Resisters," and just 17 percent talking and 2 percent hearing back among the "Solidly Secular." Cf. Luhrmann, *When God Talks Back*, xvi–xxii; and Taylor, *A Secular Age*, 37–42, 134–42, 300–321, 488–90, 607 on buffered yet porous selves, modern ethics of authenticity, and Romantic holism.

15. R. Kendall Soulen, *The Divine Name(s) and the Holy Trinity* (Louisville: Westminster John Knox, 2011).

16. Alper, "From the Solidly Secular," 2–3; and Smith, *Souls in Transition*, 159–60.

17. On the shifting search for salvation see, for example, Peter Brown, *The World of Late Antiquity* (New York: Norton, 1971), 72ff; Wayne Meeks, *The Origins of Christian Morality* (New Haven, CT: Yale University Press, 1993); John Bunyan, *The Pilgrim's Progress* (New York: Oxford University Press, 1998); Colin Campbell, *The Romantic Ethic and the Spirit of Modern Consumerism* (Oxford: Blackwell, 1987); and Robert N. Bellah, "All Souls Day," in Robert N. Bellah and Steven M. Tipton, eds., *The Robert Bellah Reader* (Durham, NC: Duke University Press, 2006), 515–21.

18. Ninety-nine percent of the "relaxed religious" and "spiritually awake" agree that one need not believe in God to be moral, and most agree that one need not attend church regularly to be a believer, according to Alper, "From the Solidly Secular," 3, here and below; while most unaffiliated young adults agree that all religions share a few essential core principles, "belief in God and basic morals," by contrast to the "nit-picky details" of their peripheral particularities, according to Christian Smith, *Souls in Transition*, 145–47. Most Americans (55 percent) over age fifty see belief in God as necessary for a person to be moral and have good values, but only a quarter (27 percent) of those under thirty agree; most Americans with no college (52 percent) agree, but only 34 percent of more educated Americans; 63 percent of those on the ideological right agree, but only 24 percent of those on the left and 37 percent of those in the center; 56 percent of those with incomes below the median agree, but only 32 percent of those earning above the median, marking the largest difference of any country and twice the average difference of Western European nations, which likewise prove less convinced of the need to believe in God to be moral in step with younger age and more income, education, and liberal ideology, report Christine Tamir, et al., "The Global God Divide," Pew Research Center, 2020, 4–12.

19. Ari Isaacman Bevacqua, "Bringing Yoga into the Workplace," *New York Times*, January 1, 2019. Cf. Les Kaye and Teresa Bouza, *A Sense of Something Greater: Zen and the Search for Balance in Silicon Valley* (Berkeley, CA: Parallax Press, 2018); and Amanda Lucia, *White Utopias* (Berkeley: University of California Press, 2020) on the therapeutic and utopian appeal of yoga practice done in homogeneous groups of thin, affluent, educated, urban White women who identify as "spiritual but not religious."

20. Cf. Christian Smith, *Souls in Transition,* ch. 6, on "selective adherents" and "irregular attenders"; and Alper, "Solidly Secular" on the "diversely devout, relaxed religious, and spiritually awake." See Claude S. Fischer, *To Dwell among Friends* (Chicago: University of Chicago Press, 1982) on chosen and given social networks; Christian Smith, *Souls*, 152–53, on young adults' social belonging in and out of

churches; and Pew Research Center, "2014 Religious Landscape Study," ch.3, on religious "nones" affirming religious institutions for "bringing people together."

21. Pew Research Center, "'Nones' on the Rise," October 9, 2012, 10–11; Pew Research Center, "Why America's 'Nones' Left Religion Behind," August 24, 2016; and Smith, *Souls in Transition*, 156–60.

22. Gregory A. Smith, "Most Americans Oppose Churches Choosing Sides in Elections," Pew Research Center, February 3, 2016, reports that nearly half say churches should express views on politics, but two-thirds oppose churches favoring one candidate over another for election. Cf. Andrew L. Whitehead, Samuel L. Perry, and Joseph O. Baker, "Make America Christian Again: Christian Nationalism and Voting for Donald Trump in the 2016 Presidential Election," *Sociology of Religion* 79, no. 2 (January 2018): 147–71; Philip Gorski, "Why Evangelicals Voted for Donald Trump: A Critical Cultural Sociology," *American Journal of Cultural Sociology*, 5 (2017): 338–54; and Katherine Stewart, "Why Trump Reigns as King Cyrus," *New York Times*, January 1, 2019, on Christian nationalists hailing Donald Trump as a nonbeliever anointed by God to serve the faithful on the model of the first Persian emperor praised in Isaiah 45 for freeing Jewish captives in Babylon in the sixth century BCE.

23. On the role of religion in public witness and moral argument compare Martin Luther King Jr., "Letter from Birmingham Jail"; Barack Obama's 2006 Speech on "Faith and Politics," *New York Times*, June 28, 2006; and Richard Rorty, "Religion as Conversation-stopper," *Common Knowledge* 3, no. 1 (1994): 1–6. On more church-like and sect-like stances of religion in public life, cf. Troeltsch, *Social Teachings*; Bellah et al., *Habits of the Heart*, ch. 9; Robert N. Bellah, Richard Madsen, William M. Sullivan, Ann Swidler, and Steven M. Tipton, *The Good Society* (New York: Knopf, 1991), ch. 6; and H. R. Niebuhr, *Christ and Culture* (New York: Harper and Row, 1951), on related ethical stances of Christ in moral agreement with culture and social norms, standing against culture, transcending and standing above culture, balanced between two kingdoms in tension with culture, and transforming culture by converting souls and remaking society.

24. On selective participation in congregational life by age linked to marital status, parenthood, and household formation in particular, see Wuthnow, *After the Baby Boomers*, ch. 3; and Bernard Lazerwitz, et al., *Jewish Choices: American Jewish Denominationalism* (Albany: SUNY Press, 1998), chs. 1, 5.

25. Richard Madsen, "The Archipelago of Faith," *American Journal of Sociology* 114, no. 5 (March 2009): 1263–1301; and Luhrmann, *When God Talks Back*.

26. Hout and Fischer, "Explaining Why," 2014; Christian Smith, *Souls in Transition*, 282–86.

27. US teens attend religious services about as often as do their parents, 44 percent at least once a month (declining to 38 percent in eleventh or twelfth grade), and often at their parents' behest, with teens less personally devout, but no less likely than most of their mainline Protestant or Catholic parents to see truth in many faiths and hold that people can be moral without belief in God, by contrast to two in three evangelical teens convinced along with their parents that only one religion is true, and six

in ten that belief in God is needed to be moral, according to Pew Research Center, "U.S. Teens Take after Their Parents Religiously," September, 2020, 2ff.

28. John Winthrop, "A Model of Christian Charity," in *Winthrop Papers: Volume II, 1623–1630* (Massachusetts Historical Society, 1931); Matthew S. Holland, *Bonds of Affection: Civic Charity and the Making of America* (Washington, DC: Georgetown University Press, 2007); Perry Miller, "Errand into the Wilderness," *The William and Mary Quarterly* 10, no. 1 (1953): 7, 16, noting Winthrop's covenantal commitment to "a due forme of Government both civill and ecclesiastical" to nurture godliness and charity, protected by power to subdue heresy and dissent, and later undone by Independents yielding to heresies of toleration and liberty of conscience advanced by Roger Williams, Anne Hutchinson, and the Antinomians.

29. Thomas Jefferson, "82. A Bill for Establishing Religious Freedom," 18 June 1779, *The Papers of Thomas Jefferson*, vol. 2, ed. Julian P. Boyd (Princeton: Princeton University Press, 1950), 545–53, para. 1, lines 1–8, as stated in Jefferson's draft submitted to the Virginia General Assembly and deleted in its adoption of the "Virginia Statute for Religious Freedom."

30. George Washington, "Farewell Address," September 19, 1796, from *George Washington, A Collection*, ed. W. B. Allen (Indianapolis: Liberty Classics, 1989), 521–22; Tocqueville, *Democracy in America*, 292.

31. Tocqueville, *Democracy in America*, 290.

32. Thomas Paine, *Age of Reason* (Independence Hall Association, 1999), Part First, Section 1, here and below, https://www.ushistory.org/paine/reason. Cf. Micah 6:8 (KJV): "He hath shewed thee, O man, what is good; and what doth the Lord require of thee, but to do justly, and to love mercy, and to walk humbly with thy God?"

33. Paine, *Age of Reason*. Part 1, Section 1.

34. James Madison, "Memorial and Remonstrance," in *The Papers of James Madison,* vol. 8, ed. William T. Hutchinson and William Rachal (Chicago: University of Chicago Press, 1971), 299.

35. Nathan O. Hatch, *The Democratization of American Christianity* (New Haven, CT: Yale University Press, 1989), 6–11, 140–46, 179–89; and Nathan O. Hatch, "*Sola Scriptura* and *Novus Ordo Seclorum*," in *The Bible in America: Essays in Cultural History*, ed. Nathan O. Hatch and Mark A. Noll (New York: Oxford University Press, 1982), 59–78.

36. Nearly half of all Americans (45 percent) turn to "practical experience and common sense" in looking for answers to questions of right and wrong, 33 percent turn to "religious beliefs and teachings," 11 percent to "philosophy and reason," and 9 percent to "scientific information," with 57 percent of religious "nones" relying on commonsense, and 32 percent of self-identified "atheists" relying primarily on science, according to Pew Research Center, "Importance of Religion and Religious Beliefs," November 3, 2015, 18–20. Here and below cf. Christian Smith, *Souls*, 145–50, on the perceived good of common principles of religion; Sherkat, *Changing Faith,* chs. 1–3, on immigration, religious diversity, and multiculturalism; Robert Wuthnow, *The Restructuring of American Religion: Society and Faith since World War II* (Princeton: Princeton University Press, 1990), 153–72, on higher education and social

mobility across denominational lines; and Robert Wuthnow, *After the Baby Boomers* (Princeton: Princeton University Press, 2010), 152–55, 183–200, on education and interreligious marriage, immigration, and ethnic diversity.

37. See Madsen, "Archipelago of Faith," on the individual's own decision to join a congregation authorizing its meaning and value; and Smith, *Souls*, ch. 5, esp. 152–59, 163–64, on religious belief and belonging, assent, and authority among young adults.

38. Jefferson, "A Bill for Establishing Religious Freedom," 545–53. Clifford Geertz, "Ethos, World View, and the Analysis of Sacred Symbols," 126–41.

39. Cf. Colin Campbell, *The Romantic Ethic*, ch. 3; Peter L. Berger, *The Heretical Imperative: Contemporary Possibilities of Religious Affirmation* (New York: Doubleday, 1980); and Perry Miller, "Errand into the Wilderness," 10, on Puritan jeremiads by 1660 castigating "a shocking extravagance in attire, especially on the part of these of the meaner sort, who persisted in dressing beyond their means."

40. Becka Alper, "Why America's 'Nones' Don't Identify with a Religion," Pew Research Center, 8 August 2018, 1–3. In 2011, 49 percent of Americans agreed it is "not necessary to believe in God in order to be moral" and 48 percent disagreed that it is necessary, widening to 56 percent agreeing and 42 percent disagreeing by 2017, with 85 percent of religious "nones" agreed on there being no need to believe, according to Gregory A. Smith, "A Growing Share of Americans Say It's Not Necessary to Believe in God to Be Moral," Pew Research Center, October 16, 2017, 1–3. Cf. Charles Grandison Finney, "The One Thing Needful," *The Oberlin Evangelist*, February 2, 1859; and Charles Taylor, *Sources of the Self* (Cambridge, MA: Harvard University Press, 1989), 20–24, 63–73, 100–106, on hypergoods.

41. See Christian Smith, *Souls*, 46–53, 145–65, esp. 148–50, on moral individualism.

42. On shifting moral dynamics of American child-rearing from subjugating children to the Calvinist sovereignty of parental and divine authority to enlightening their Lockean interests and reasoning as democratic citizens-to-be, see Philip J. Greven, *The Protestant Temperament* (Chicago: University of Chicago Press, 1988); Daniel H. Calhoun, *The Intelligence of a People* (Princeton: Princeton University Press, 1973); and Bellah, et al., *Habits of the Heart*, chs. 3–4. Cf. the developmental moral psychologies of Erik Erikson, Lawrence Kohlberg, and Carol Gilligan in situating selves in distinct institutional spheres at each stage of the life cycle, with Kohlberg subordinating mutually responsible circles of kith and kin (central to Erikson and Gilligan) to larger social grids of utilitarian exchange, strategic rules of bureaucratic administration, and legal-political procedural principles governed by the Kantian contractarianism of justice as fairness, according to John Rawls, *A Theory of Justice* (Cambridge, MA: Harvard University Press, 1971).

43. In 1940, 32 percent of young adults aged 25 to 29 lived in multigenerational households, falling to 12 percent by 1970, then rebounding to 33 percent in 2016; one in five Americans overall lived in multigenerational households in 1950, falling to 12 percent in the 1970s, then rebounding to 20 percent in 2016, with college graduates more likely to be living as young adults with a spouse or partner in their own homes and those less educated more likely to be living with their parents, according to D'Vera Cohn, "A record 64 million Americans live in multi-generational households," Pew Research Center, April 5, 2018. Married US adults aged 25 to 54 fell

from 67 percent to 53 percent of the population from 1990 to 2019, and unpartnered adults grew from 29 percent to 38 percent, due to the rising numbers of those never married (from 17 percent to 33 percent), including a jump from 4 percent to 13 percent in those cohabiting, according to Richard Fry and Kim Parker, "Rising Share of U.S. Adults Are Living without a Spouse or Partner," Pew Research Center, October 2021, 2. Cf. Wuthnow, *After the Baby Boom*, ch. 3; and Christian Smith, *Souls*, 150–51.

44. Cf. Ross Douthat, "The Return of Paganism," *New York Times*, December 12, 2018; Christian Smith, *Souls*, 154–56.

45. Here and below see Robert N. Bellah, "Religious Evolution," *American Sociological Review* 29, no. 3 (1964): 358–74, reprinted in *Beyond Belief* (Berkeley: University of California Press, 1991), esp. 39–44, on the "modern" stage of religious evolution; and Bellah, et al., *Habits of the Heart*, chs. 2, 3, 9. Cf. Max Weber, "Religious Rejections of the World and Their Directions," in Hans H. Gerth and C. Wright Mills, eds., *From Max Weber* (New York: Oxford University Press, 1946), 323–59; and Alan Strathern, *Unearthly Powers: Religious and Political Change in World History* (Cambridge, UK: Cambridge University Press, 2019).

46. See, for example, Bellah et al., *Habits of the Heart*, ch. 9; Robert Wuthnow, *After the Baby Boomers*; Bernard Lazerwitz et al., *Jewish Choices*; Andrew Greeley, *Chicago Catholics*; Tipton, *Getting Saved from the Sixties*; Wade Clark Roof and William McKinney, *American Mainline Religion* (New Brunswick, NJ: Rutgers University Press, 1987).

47. Charles Taylor, *A Secular Age*, 27–42, 131–42, 542–57ff; Taylor, *Modern Social Imaginaries*, chs. 4, 7, 11; Max Weber, "Science as a Vocation," in Gerth and Mills, eds., *From Max Weber*, 129–56; Robert N. Bellah, "Religious Evolution," 22–24, 31–45.

48. Here and below, see Taylor, *A Secular Age*, chs. 13–16, on ethics of authenticity, expressive individualism, and Romanticism. On creation in the image of God to frame free will, universal rights, and religious liberty, see Paul Ricoeur, "The Image of God and The Epic of Man," *Cross Currents* 11, no. 1 (Winter 1961): 37–50; and William Haller, *Tracts on Liberty in the Puritan Revolution, 1638–1647* (New York: Columbia University Press, 1933), vol. 1, p. 111.

49. See John Rawls, *A Theory of Justice*; Lawrence Kohlberg, "Moral Development," in David L. Sills, ed., *International Encyclopedia of the Social Sciences* (New York: Macmillan Free Press, 1968), vol. 10, 483–94; Immanuel Kant, *Groundwork of the Metaphysics of Morals* (Cambridge, UK: Cambridge University Press, 2012); Jeremy Bentham, *An Introduction to the Principles of Morals and Legislation* (Mineola, NY: Dover, 2012); John Stuart Mill, *Utilitarianism* (New York: Oxford University Press, 1998). Cf. Michael Sandel, *Liberalism and the Limits of Justice* (Cambridge, UK: Cambridge University Press, 1982); Michael Walzer, *Spheres of Justice* (New York: Basic Books, 1983); and J.J.C. Smart and Bernard Williams, *Utilitarianism: For and Against* (Cambridge, UK: Cambridge University Press, 1973).

50. Tipton, *Getting Saved from the Sixties*, ch. 1; Bellah et al., *Habits of the Heart*, ch. 2; Taylor, *A Secular Age*, 609–17, on Romantics' Dionysian opposition to the

rationalized "excarnation" of religious practice by the Enlightenment and Reformed Christendom.

51. Thomas Hobbes, *Leviathan*, ed. Michael Oakeshott (Oxford: Blackwell, 1946), chs. 12–15; John Locke, *Two Treatises of Government*, ed. Peter Laslett (Cambridge, UK: Cambridge University Press, 1988), and Locke, "Ethica A" in Mark Goldie, ed., *Political Essays* (Cambridge, UK: Cambridge University Press, 1997), 318–19; Adam Smith, *The Theory of Moral Sentiments* (New York: Oxford University Press, 1976), Part I, Section I, ch. I and Section II, ch. IV.

52. Harvey Mitchell, "Reclaiming the Self: The Pascal-Rousseau Connection," *Journal of the History of Ideas* 54, no. 4 (October 1993): 637–58, esp. 641–47 by reference to the Port-Royal edition of Pascal's *Pensées*, and Rousseau's *Emile* and *Lettres Morale*. Cf. Colin Campbell, *The Romantic Ethic*; Cesar Grana, *Bohemian versus Bourgeois* (New York: Basic Books, 1964); and Taylor, *A Secular Age*, 720–27.

53. See Ronald Pickvance, "Degas and the Painting of Modern Life," *Journal of the Royal Society of Arts* 128, no. 5285 (1980): 250–63; and Jeanne S. M. Willette, "Baudelaire and 'The Painter of Modern Life,'" https://www.arthistoryunstuffed.com, August 2010, on the *flaneur* as the curious, attentive, instinctive "passionate spectator," by bohemian contrast to Smith's imaginative yet dispassionate, conscientious "Impartial Spectator." Cf. Aristotle, *Metaphysics*, Bk. IV, 1006a (Princeton: Princeton University Press, 1984), 1588ff; Thomas Aquinas, *Summa Theologica* (New York: Benziger Brothers, 1911) II., 123, 12, ad 2; 27, 8, ad 2; 108, 2; Christian Jung, *Meister Eckhardts philosophische Mystik* (Baden-Baden: Tectum, 2010), 13–53; Troeltsch, *Social Teaching*, vol. 2, 796–802, on Christian mysticism and modern spiritual idealism; and Erasmus, *In Praise of Folly* (New York: Penguin, 1994), para. 66. Against Luther, Erasmus defends the autonomous capacity of moral self-determination among the pious. Against Duns Scotus, Erasmus baptizes Platonist confidence in inherent human perfectibility through heeding reason and disciplining passion, instead of seeing humankind so corrupted by original sin that it can be saved only by recourse to divine revelation and authority extrinsic to human reason and aspiration.

54. Ralph Waldo Emerson, "The Over-Soul," para. 14, ch. 9, in *Essays: First Series* (Boston: James Munro, 1841); Emerson, *Nature* (Boston: James Munro, 1836), chs. 1, 6–8; and *The Essays of Ralph Waldo Emerson* (Cambridge, MA: Harvard University Press, 1987), edited by Alfred R. Ferguson and Jean Ferguson Carr.

55. Immanuel Kant, *Kritik der reinen Vernunft*, quoted in Josef Pieper, *Leisure: The Basis of Culture* (San Francisco: Ignatius Press, 2009), 26–27; Kant, *Von einem neuerdings Erhobenen vornehmen Ton in der Philosophie* (Hamburg: Meiner, 1920), 387–406. Romantic expressivism since Rousseau rises to challenge Lockean deism and Kantian rationalism in defining selfhood in the modern West alongside cultural currents of scientized naturalism and Judeo-Christian theism, argues Charles Taylor, *Sources of the Self*, 428ff.

56. Henry David Thoreau, *Walden* (London: Everyman's Library, 1993); Walt Whitman, *Leaves of Grass* (New York: Library of America, 2011); Oscar Wilde, *Lady Windermere's Fan* (New York: Penguin, 2011), Act III, defines a cynic as "a man who knows the price of everything, and the value of nothing," and a sentimentalist as one

"who sees an absurd value in everything and doesn't know the market price of any single thing." On modern American spirituality rooted deep in religious liberalism and layers of metaphysical religious mentality, see Leigh Schmidt, *Restless Souls: The Making of American Spirituality from Emerson to Oprah* (New York: HarperCollins, 2005), 10–23; Matthew S. Hedstrom, *The Rise of Liberal Religion: Book Culture and American Spirituality in the Twentieth Century* (New York: Oxford University Press, 2013), 71–79, 172–224; and Catherine L. Albanese, *A Republic of Mind and Spirit: A Cultural History of American Metaphysical Religion* (New Haven, CT: Yale University Press, 2006), 1–18, 496–516.

57. On condensed and elaborated cultural codes, see Mary Douglas, *Natural Symbols* (New York: Pantheon Books, 1982), 21–31ff; and Robert N. Bellah, "The History of Habit," in *Bellah Reader*, 211–17. Cf. Tipton, *Getting Saved from the Sixties*, ch. 1, on countercultural expressive individualism; and David Sudnow, *Ways of the Hand: The Organization of Improvised Conduct* (Harper and Row, 1978) on learning to improvise jazz piano, interpreted as a model for learning Zen meditation by David L. Preston, *The Social Organization of Zen Practice* (Cambridge, UK: Cambridge University Press, 1988), ch. 7.

58. Friedrich Schleiermacher, *On Religion: Speeches to Its Cultured Despisers*, ed., Richard Crouter (Cambridge, UK: Cambridge University Press, 1996), Second Speech, 22. Cf. Marx on *feeling* and *being* as opposed to *having* in "Economic and Philosophic Manuscripts of 1844," quoted in Lionel Trilling, *Sincerity and Authenticity* (Cambridge, MA: Harvard University Press, 1971), 122.

59. Charles Taylor, *The Ethics of Authenticity* (Cambridge, MA: Harvard University Press, 1991), 15–17, 25–29; Taylor, *Sources of the Self*, chs. 3, 15; and Taylor, *A Secular Age*, ch. 13. Cf. Trilling, *Sincerity and Authenticity*, 122ff.

60. Compare, for example, William Wordsworth, "The World Is Too Much with Us" (London: Longman, 1802); Alan Ginsberg, "Howl," from *Collected Poems: 1947–1995* (New York: HarperCollins, 2001); John Lennon and Paul McCartney, "All You Need Is Love," 1967 Sony/ ATV Music Publishing, 2009; *San Francisco Oracle*, 1966–1968, especially no. 7, "Houseboat Summit"; and Theodore Roszak, *The Making of a Counter Culture* (Berkeley: University of California Press, 1969).

61. Emile Durkheim, *The Elementary Forms of the Religious Life* (New York: Free Press, 1995), tr. Karen E. Fields, 216–21; Karl Marx, "The German Ideology," in ed. Robert C. Tucker, *The Marx-Engels Reader* (New York: Norton, 1978), 160; Clifford Geertz, "Religion as a Cultural System," in *The Interpretation of Cultures* (New York: Basic Books, 1973), 91–94; William H. McNeill, *Keeping Together in Time: Dance and Drill in Human History* (Cambridge, MA: Harvard University Press, 1997), ch. 4. Here and below, see Bellah, "Religious Evolution," 25–32; Bellah, "What is Axial about the Axial Age?" *European Journal of Sociology*, 46, no. 1 (2005): 69–89; and Bellah, "The Roots of Religious Consciousness I. Primitive Religion"; "II. Historic Religion"; and "III. The Contemporary Relevance of Religion," delivered as the Beatty Lectures at McGill University in March 1974, entitled, "Relevance of Man's Religious Experience," and delivered in elaborated form at the University of California, Santa Barbara in April 1974, and at Boston University in April 1975. Unpublished papers, University of California, Berkeley, 1975.

62. Durkheim, *Elementary Forms*, 217.

63. Bellah, "Roots of Religious Consciousness: I. Primitive Religion," 7–18; Geertz, "Ethos, Worldview, and the Analysis of Sacred Symbols"; Taylor, *A Secular Age*, 605–17, 744–55; Robert N. Bellah, "Introduction," *Bellah Reader*, 4.

64. Louis Dumont, *Homo Hierarchicus* (Chicago: University of Chicago Press, 1970); Bellah, "Religious Evolution," 29–32; Bellah, *Religion in Human Evolution*, chs. 4–5. Cf. Walter Burkert, *Homo Neccans: The Anthropology of Ancient Greek Sacrificial Ritual and Myth* (Berkeley: University of California Press, 1986); and Nancy Evans, *Civic Rites* (Berkeley: University of California Press, 2010).

65. Here and below see Bellah, "Religious Evolution," 32–36; Max Weber, "Religious Rejections," in *From Max Weber*, 323–59; Weber, "Science as a Vocation," 148; Charles Taylor, *Sources of the Self*, 20–24, 63–73, 100–106, 611–12; Taylor, "The Diversity of Goods," *Philosophy and the Human Sciences: Philosophical Papers* (Cambridge, UK: Cambridge University Press), vol. 2, 234–38; and Taylor, *A Secular Age*, 566.

66. Bellah, "Roots of Religious Consciousness: II. Historic Religion," 1–7. Cf. Louis Dumont, *Homo Hierarchicus* (Chicago: University of Chicago Press, 1970); and Dumont, *From Mandeville to Marx* (Chicago: University of Chicago Press, 1977). On selfhood conceived and transformed as mind, heart, body, and soul, compare Whalen Lai, "The Meaning of 'Mind-Only' (wei-hsin): An Analysis of a Sinitic Mahayana Phenomenon," *Philosophy East and West* 27, no. 1 (1977): 65–83; Taylor, *A Secular Age*, 605–17; and Peter Brown, *The Body and Society* (New York: Columbia University Press, 1988).

67. Max Weber, *The Protestant Ethic and the Spirit of Capitalism* (New York: Scribner's, 1958), ch. 5; Ernst Troeltsch, *The Social Teaching of the Christian Churches*, vol. 2, 461–515, 688–91, 807–20; Bellah, "Religious Evolution," 36–39, here and below. See Louis Dumont, "A Modified View of Our Origins: The Christian Beginnings of Modern Individualism," *Religion* 12, no. 3 (1982): 1–27; Michael Walzer, *The Revolution of the Saints* (Cambridge, MA: Harvard University Press, 1965); and Philip Gorski, *The Disciplinary Revolution: Calvinism and the Rise of the State in Early Modern Europe* (Chicago: University of Chicago Press, 2003).

68. Taylor, *A Secular Age*, 540–44; Adam Smith, *Theory of Moral Sentiments*, 58–66, 128–78ff, explains that Nature's All-Wise Author interposes between "the weak eye of human reason and the throne of his eternal justice, a degree of obscurity and darkness" to enable each individual to carry on "the business of society" undistracted by the immensity of infinite rewards and punishments, and to serve as "his viceregent upon earth to superintend the behavior of his brethren." On watching time and making the most of it, see E. P. Thompson, "Time, Work-Discipline, and Industrial Capitalism," *Past and Present* 38 (1967): 56–97, on changing from "time passed" to "time spent," from cocks crowing the dawn of rural labor and farm tasks dividing the day through rites set by abbey orlogge to hours and minutes measured by bourgeois house clock, pocket watch, and factory-floor time clock. Cf Benjamin Mays, "I have only just a minute, / Only sixty seconds in it. / Forced upon me, can't refuse it. / Didn't seek it, didn't choose it. / But it's up to me / to use it. / I must suffer if I lose it. / Give account if I abuse it. / Just a tiny little minute, / but eternity is in it."

Mays prized this anonymous poem, according to Randal M. Jelks, *Benjamin Elijah Mays: Schoolmaster of the Movement* (Chapel Hill: University of North Carolina Press, 2012), 189.

69. John W. Meyer, "Self and Life Course: Institutionalization and its Effects," in George M. Thomas et al., eds., *Institutional Structure* (Newbury Park: Sage, 1987), 242–60; John W. Meyer et al., "World Society and the Nation State," *American Journal of Sociology* 103 (1997): 144–81; and John W. Meyer, "World Society, Institutional Theories, and the Actor," *Annual Review of Sociology* 36 (2010): 1–20. Cf. Charles Taylor, *A Secular Age*, 546–47ff. on disciplined work and reform in an age of mobilization giving way to an age of authenticity and the immanent frame of modern social imaginaries.

70. Cf. Adam Smith, *Theory of Moral Sentiments*, Part II, Section III; Walt Whitman, "Song of Myself," sections 1, 22–25, of the 1892 edition of *Leaves of Grass* (New York: Norton, 1973), quoted in Bellah et al., *Habits of the Heart*, 34; Wallace Stevens, "Sunday Morning," in his *Collected Poems* (New York: Knopf, 1954), 66–70; and Albert Camus, *Summer in Algiers* (New York: Penguin, 2005) on lyrical unity with nature freed from divine demand or grace, from supernatural happiness beyond the sun and sea, and from eternity outside the sweep of days and ebb of evening.

71. Here and below cf. Meyer, "Self and Life Course"; Tipton, "Social Differentiation and Moral Pluralism"; Geertz, "Ethos, World View, and the Analysis of Sacred Symbols"; Ann Swidler, "Culture in Action: Symbols and Strategies," *American Sociological Review* 51, no. 2 (April, 1986): 273–86; Florence R. Kluckhohn and Fred L. Strodtbeck, *Variations in Value Orientations* (New York: Row, Peterson, 1961); and Tanya Marie Luhrmann, "Toward an Anthropological Theory of Mind," *Suomen Antropologi: Journal of the Finnish Anthropological Association*, 36, no. 4 (Winter 2011): 1–15, 19–21.

72. See Erik Erikson, "Life Cycle," in David L. Sills, ed., *International Encyclopedia of the Social Sciences* (New York: Macmillan/Free Press, 1968), vol. 4, 286–92; Bellah, "The Roots of Religious Consciousness: III. The Contemporary Relevance of Religion," 10–20; Taylor, *A Secular Age*, 609–11; Steven M. Tipton, "Moral Languages and the Good Society," in *Soundings* LXIX, no. 1–2 (1986): 165–80. Ideals of the entire political-religious community engaged in moral and civic education flourish in ancient Athens, Jerusalem, and early Christian congregations as well as antebellum America, according to Plato's *Laws*, bks. 1–3, 6–8, 11–12; Aristotle, *Nicomachean Ethics*, bk. 10, ch. 9; Wayne Meeks, *The Origins of Christian Morality* (New Haven, CT: Yale University Press, 1993); Tocqueville, *Democracy in America*, vol. 1, part. II, ch. 9; Lawrence A. Cremin, *American Education: The National Experience, 1783–1876* (New York: Harper & Row, 1982); and Bellah et al., *The Good Society*, ch. 5.

73. See chapter 4; Ellingson, *The Megachurch and the Mainline*; Richard L. Wood, *Faith in Action: Religion, Race, and Democratic Organizing in America* (Chicago: University of Chicago Press, 2002); Taylor, *A Secular Age*, 737–44, citing Ivan Illich, *The Rivers North of the Future*, as told to David Cayley (Toronto: Anansi, 2005).

74. Cf. John Meyer, "Self and Life Course"; Erik Erikson, "Life Cycle"; and Bellah, "Religious Evolution," 32–45.

75. See Bellah, "Religious Evolution," 40–42; Bellah "Religion and Belief: The Historical Background of 'Non-Belief,'" and "Between Religion and Social Science," in *Beyond Belief*, 216–29, 237–59; H. R. Niebuhr, *The Kingdom of God in America*; Talcott Parsons, "Christianity," in Sills, ed., *International Encyclopedia of Social Sciences*, vol. 1, 425–46; and Talcott Parsons, "Christianity and Modern Industrial Society," in Edward Tiryakian, ed., *Sociological Theory, Values, and Sociocultural Change* (New York: Free Press, 1963), ch. 3; and Taylor, *A Secular Age*, 589–615.

76. Bellah, "Religious Evolution," 42–44; Taylor, *Modern Social Imaginaries*, chs. 1, 7, 11, 13; Bellah et al., *Habits of the Heart*, chs. 2, 3, 6, 11; and Bellah et al., *The Good Society*, chs. 2, 7. Cf. Perry Miller, *The New England Mind* (Cambridge, MA: Harvard University Press, 1983); Bercovitch, *The Puritan Origins of the American Self*; Andrew Delbanco, *The Real American Dream* (Cambridge, MA: Harvard University Press, 2000); and Madsen, "Archipelago of Faith."

77. See Robert Bellah, "Religious Evolution," 44; Bellah, "Civil Religion in America," in *Beyond Belief*, ch. 9; Bellah, "Religion and the Legitimation of the American Republic," in Robert N. Bellah and Phillip E. Hammond, *Varieties of Civil Religion* (New York: Harper & Row, 1980), ch. 1; Bellah et al., *Habits of the Heart*, chs. 10–11, and *The Good Society*, 111–44, 255–87.

78. Cf. Bellah, "Religious Evolution," 37–45; H. Richard Niebuhr, *The Kingdom of God in America*; Erik Erikson, "Life Cycle"; John Meyer, "Self and Life Course"; and Taylor, *A Secular Age*, chs. 15–16.

79. George Marsden, *Fundamentalism and American Culture* (New York: Oxford University Press, 2006); and Marsden, "Preachers of Paradox," in Mary Douglas and Steven M. Tipton, eds., *Religion and America* (Boston: Beacon Press, 1983), 150–68.

80. Webb Keane, *Christian Moderns* (Berkeley: University of California Press, 2007), 43; Pippa Norris and Ronald Inglehardt, *Sacred and Secular* (Cambridge: Cambridge University Press, 2004); Darren Sherkat, *Changing Faith* (New York: NYU Press, 2014), 31–49, 174–92.

81. Sherkat, *Changing Faith*, 1–6, 14–17, 31.

82. Cf. Sherkat, 36–49; Michael Hout and Tom W. Smith, "Fewer Americans Affiliate with Organized Religions, Belief and Practice Unchanged: Key Findings from the 2014 General Social Survey," National Opinion Research Center (NORC), University of Chicago, March 2015, 10, based on GSS denominational categories for "Conservative Christian, Other Protestant, Catholic, Jewish, Other Religion, No Religion."

83. Cf. Sherkat, 88; and Christian Smith, *American Evangelicalism*, 49, Table 2.8, showing that 78 percent of self-identified "evangelicals" come from evangelical families of origin, for example, with only 9 percent coming from "Fundamentalist" families, 7 percent from mainline Protestant, 12 percent from liberal Protestant, and 0 percent from Catholic families; with most fundamentalists (57 percent), mainline Protestants (51 percent), liberal Protestants (57 percent), and Catholics (83 percent) likewise hailing from families of the same faith. From 2018 to 2019 total membership in the Southern Baptist Convention (SBC), for example, fell almost 2 percent, a decline of some 300,000 members, marking its largest annual drop in more than

a century after declining 1 percent per year for a dozen years previously; while the Episcopal Church (ECUSA) declined by 2.29 percent from 2018 to 2019, after declining 17.4 percent over the previous decade, with an average age of 59 compared to 53 in the SBC, given generational turnover and the rising exodus of young adults over the past generation. The rise of nondenominational congregations enabled "evangelicals" to continue composing some 22.5 percent of the US population (down from 25.4 percent in 2014), despite the 1–1.5 percent annual rise of "nones" to 23.1 percent in 2019, while it remains to be seen whether a 1.4 percent drop in evangelical affiliation and a 1.8 percent mainline rise in 2016–2018, attributable to Donald Trump, persists or passes. See Lifeway Christian Resources, *Southern Baptist Convention Annual Church Profile*, 2019; Aaron Earls, "Southern Baptists Experience Historic Drop in Membership," June 4, 2020, https://www.lifeway.com; ECUSA Office of the General Convention, "Table of Statistics of the Episcopal Church," September 2020, www.generalconvention.org; Ryan Burge, "Evangelicals Show No Decline, Despite Trump and Nones," *Christianity Today*, 21 March, 2019; General Social Survey, "Religious Affiliation and Behavior," 2018, www.gss.norc.org; Gregory Smith et al., *Religious Landscape Study*, Pew Research Center, 2014, www.pewforum.org; and C. Kirk Hadaway, "Is the Episcopal Church Growing (or Declining)?" *Domestic and Foreign Missionary Society*, 2004, esp. 11–18, www.episcopalchurch.org.

84. See Sherkat, *Changing Faith*, 188–92; Wuthnow, *The Restructuring of American Religion*, chs. 5–7; Paul Mojzes, ed., *North American Churches and the Cold War* (Grand Rapids, MI: Eerdmans, 2018).

85. Sherkat, *Changing Faith*, 172ff; the U.S. Census Bureau estimates 59.7 percent of the total US population in 2020 as non-Hispanic White, at https://www.census.gov/topics/population.html.

Chapter 4

Congregating across Generations

The Soul of Silicon Valley

Young Americans have been leaving church in rising waves since the 1960s, but not all at once and not all evenly spread out across social space and time between one cohort and the next. Mainline churches proved most vulnerable at first, particularly to the countercultural flood tide running along the baby boom's front edge.[1] Despite doing better at holding onto their own children coming of age, evangelical churches, too, have gradually followed suit and slowed in growth, as their millennial members have begun to marry later and bear fewer children.[2] Some congregations prove exceptions to these numerical trends, however, in holding their own and bringing young adults back to the fold. Predictably enough, many of these churches are situated in settings such as college towns and metropolitan suburbs rich in the sort of schooling, employment, and cultural advantages that attract young singles, couples, and families—and offer them attractive alternatives to church. Such settings alone hardly account for these exceptional congregations, no more than they determine the decline of others nearby, but they set the social stage for the moral drama these churches share.

How can the life of congregations respond to these rising waves of cohorts coming of age and leaving church, doubling in size over the 1990s and continuing to flow through altered institutional channels of schooling, work, play, and marriage? Can congregational life embrace the full range of their social difference, economic inequality, and cultural aspiration, stretching from agnostics to mystics, from the diversely devout to the spiritual but not religious? To find out, we need not try to compile a "how-to" list of plug-in programs and activities for young adults to pursue in and out of the pews. Instead let's explore a "why-so" landscape of insight and practice true to bodies of worship and care that actually respond to the hopes and fears of those at the threshold of adulthood and beyond. From what and for what do they seek to be saved? How do churches respond to what they want and discern what they need?[3]

We can ask leaders and members of exemplary congregations about what they think and what they do to keep good company with the next generation, and why this makes good sense. We can investigate the best practices of such congregations, in particular an innovative evangelical church growing from Presbyterian roots in Silicon Valley in this chapter, and then a trio of vibrant Methodist congregations in suburban Atlanta in the next. None is typical in the remarkable extent of their social service, outreach, and witness. But together they represent a range of such efforts, from food pantries to tutoring programs, evident in congregations of virtually every denomination and religious tradition in the United States.[4] They feature outstanding missions of community service and social witness in step with pioneering initiatives to engage and care for young families and singles. They pair up with particularly promising partners, such as immigrant settlement programs backed by government; overseas mission trips with global NGOs; food banks with corporate sponsors; teaching and mentoring programs with public schools and professional groups to match committed volunteers to needy students; and grief-counseling networks with caregivers trained to "just be there and listen, no matter what."

Across church aisles or across town, around the block or around the world, we can weigh moral maxims that "charity begins at home" and Good Samaritan convictions that "everyone is our neighbor." We can recognize shining examples of service and outreach set by congregations with relatively few material resources yet great generosity of spirit and love of neighbor in taking care of their own and their neighbors everywhere in need.[5] At the same time, much is expected of those to whom much is given, including insight and effort to engage the moral challenge of spiritual change moving young Americans in and out of church. So, we focus on these relatively well-educated and well-off congregations to see what they are making of their blessings, how they are engaging their members in this mission, and why they are so inspired.

MIXED MOTIVES TO CONNECT

The evangelical vision of Alto Church in Silicon Valley is framed in biblical terms of the Great Commission to "go and make disciples of all nations" (Matthew 28:19–20), to proclaim "the good news of the kingdom" (Matthew 4:23), and aspire to exemplary love of neighbor, for by this "everyone will know that you are my disciples, if you love one another" (John 13:35). At the same time, this vision of a church centered on Jesus with a life rooted in scripture takes particular form in Silicon Valley today. "Everybody's welcome," it proclaims. "Nobody's perfect," it grants. "Anything's possible," it promises. It opens its doors to everyone and celebrates its diversity across the lines of generation as well as color, class, and denominational background. Given its locale and core composition of educated professionals, predominantly White with a growing Asian minority, the church is particularly noteworthy for embracing older and younger members in telling ways.

Age-graded day care and Sunday school classes from toddlers to teens, along with parenting and couples classes common to many mainline Protestant churches, are joined here by exceptionally large and lively worship services, "life groups," seniors' classes, and retreats for "18–35 singles." There are also "50+ singles" groups, "divorce recovery and relationship rescue" groups, and dozens of groups based on age, neighborhood, and interests ranging from Bible study to bicycling, from "engaging extreme poverty" to playing tennis and sharing high-tech work. "It has to be the biggest singles group ever in a church, or anywhere else," marvels a nonmember who works nearby. "You see them every day and night of the week, you walk by and hear the music. Everyone around here knows about it." Alto Church welcomes families with young children as "vital to the future of the church," notes a minister, "but we know more than half of all households in the Bay Area are single persons living alone, and we want to embrace them, too."

In the striking picture that Alto Church paints of congregating across generations, what often catches the eye and ear of outsiders, significantly enough, are all the single young adults, since they seem so conspicuously absent from many mainline churches.[6] Not only do high school and college students come to singles services for people eighteen to thirty-five because "that's where the heavenly girls are singing in the choir" of a high-energy rock band, says a young-adult minister with a smile. They keep coming, even if they don't meet the prince or princess of their romantic dreams, she adds, because "there's real connection and community here, where people really care about you for who you are, not for who you pretend to be on Facebook or Twitter. We know about looking great online and feeling bad about your life, feeling alone and feeling like nobody really knows you or likes you."[7] That's an everyday reality for many young adults, she points out, driven to achieve in competitive schooling and careers in Silicon Valley, studying and working on the side to pay high rents, meeting and dating in a fluid world of singles who can hook up and move on with no strings attached, but with wounds and wondering left behind from years of iffy courtship.

"We're okay with mixed motives," adds another youth minister, "and we want to work with them. People go where people are. You come because someone you like invites you. You come back because there's a good crowd and a good vibe here. But you keep coming because there's something else, something you don't find in a club or a party: Loving one another like Jesus loves us." Conversely, "Just because you love your parents and grandparents doesn't mean you want to go to church with them every Sunday, and then go to a bar to find someone to love," reasons a youth minister in his early thirties. He continues,

> Birds of a feather flock together. I want to worship and hang out with other young professionals who are believers. We want a space of our own, with our own music and feeling to it. We want to be able to find our own way, to ask our own questions, and explore our own answers and doubts without threat. You can be biblical and Christian, without having to start with someone else telling you what you have to believe in order to belong.

Service projects and shared social activities also prove more accessible and engaging when they are generationally tuned. "School and careers here take almost all the time you have," says an unmarried tax lawyer in his early thirties, "so I want to plug into something worthwhile with people I know and like from church. I can sign up to do something like helping serve dinner at a night shelter once a month, but not be tied down by it, because there are lots of other people involved in it. It's well-organized, and it's scheduled online. Just go to the church website and click." Social scale and resources also make a difference, notes this lawyer: "I've gone to smaller churches, and you can certainly find commitment and companionship there. But you can be known and connected in a church like this that's riding the wave, with lots of action you can choose to get in on."[8]

BELONGING BEFORE BELIEVING AND BEHAVING

An older minister explains why he pioneered the church's "contemporary worship" services, tuned to young singles in a separate "café" setting stripped of "church trappings" and equipped with professionally designed theatrical lighting and staging, sound systems, and projection screens:

> Personally, I love stained glass windows and choirs singing hymns. But the church itself felt stuffy and staid a dozen years ago, like the kind of place young people want to get away from, not come into. We wanted to flex that, and loosen it up into a "casual, coffee, kids, come-late" kind of experience. We wanted to open it up. Give it a big, wide front door, and create space inside where you can get involved and share with people your own age.
>
> You can listen to music you like, sing along, tell people your story and listen to theirs, without worrying about having to agree with some set of beliefs

> first, before you can belong. We consciously switch that around. We're not fundamentalist.
>
> It used to be "Believe first." Align your thinking with the way we think, do things our way. Then you belong. Now it's flipped on its head. Now it's like everyone can belong, and be known just as they are, *before* they choose to conform.

That's been a big switch, "not just for churches, but for all sorts of community organizations," judges this minister. "Some churches have been able to make that switch, and others haven't."

This recent shift in popular culture runs deep in the American grain, this minister observes. It is rooted in revivalism's aim to awaken affections and save souls through personal experience of conversion in a Protestant priesthood of all believers that lifts up participatory practice as the first virtue of bodies politic, including the body of Christ.[9] It also springs from the Gospel truth, this minister reasons in theological terms informed by his early years as a corporate consultant:

> If God created every person and looks after them as His beloved children, then God pursues them, too. If Jesus died not to condemn the world but to save it, and the Holy Spirit acts in His People to be the People of God, the salt and light of the earth, then we shouldn't be afraid to welcome in everyone as they are. Just as Jesus did! Rich and poor, across all cultures, the obvious sinner and the invisible sinner. Jesus flowed freely across all those lines.
>
> So, we're being true to the Gospel, even if it's a scary change for churches that used to have themselves all lined up with a more linear culture. This is more art-form now. There is comfort, maybe even blessing in that more linear organization. But our culture won't accept that now.

Such construal of cultural change applies aptly to the counterpoint of educated middle-class work and play. It puts high-tech stress on problem-solving innovation and administrative efficiency bred by elite education and sustained effort at work in highly disciplined STEM fields, while relaxing its hold on personal life and leisure left free to flow along "art-form" currents of aesthetic appeal and individual taste channeled by popular media and music.

Some critics see such cultural change as enabling self-centered, mushy mystics to trump self-controlled, orthodox Puritans.[10] But this veteran minister in the vanguard of "a new evangelical revolution" sees such cultural change not only favoring his own church's stance, but lifting up the experiential truth of God's love and the unity of the true church across denominations:

Once you were supposed to come into church on belief in the Christian principles, because they're true. "Here's the Gospel message, and here's why you should believe it." Then you belong. Now it's more, "Come in and belong!"

Why? Because people need places to belong to be healthy. They know that from self-help culture, and they're looking for places to belong, especially millennials raised in broken homes with a lot of hurt, looking for all the love and structure they missed growing up.

"Everybody's welcome." We can mean that here only because as followers of Jesus we know the Gospel message is so compelling that by belonging in church it will come to touch your life and change it. God loves people and finds a way to slowly touch their hearts, and open them up to a relationship with Him. God made people wanting to be called out and come to Him.

God offers us the indwelling presence of the Holy Spirit to transform this weak flesh. You can't live out the message without the Spirit at work in you. You have to experience it, and you have to continue to cultivate it. Then you can relax and let this process take place.

You can trust God, and how much God respects the individual will of each person. It's not just anything goes. By their fruits ye shall know them, and we will be held accountable. But God will not impose His will on me, God will wait for me. That's a beautiful story! It's actually a love story.

Q: Does it always have a happy ending?

It's a story that includes some confusion and messiness. "Nobody's perfect," and we live in a world with your phone always on, full of distractions designed to addict us. Church is just one of a dozen "self-help options" that can enhance your life in some way—health, exercise, spiritual well-being.

Hard-core conservative churches can succeed by holding you in a tight-knit fellowship. But they fail by deciding on some kind of legalism or holy living that supposedly makes you more of a Christian than the next person. No alcohol, no divorce, no political correctness! Actually it just makes you more like some narrow parameter of a person picked up from the culture at a particular time and place. That makes people crazy, and it pushes them away from church.

We want to bring them into a really open place where you can ask tough questions about God and yourself and why things happen in your life. But we're a tight family, too. We will hold onto you and help you hold it together through your divorce, or the kid blowup, or your cancer. That's hard to walk away from.

> If the church stays true to the Gospel, it can hold all that tension and frailty. It can break through all that mistrust, all that marketing. Not many institutions can do that.
>
> *Q: Why is that?*
>
> It's hard for anybody to hold things openhandedly and offer them freely. It's hard to be patient. It doesn't compute to our systems and how we're judged. We're raised to produce and show results *now*. We need to measure those results in order to feel that our work is worthy of our efforts, and [to] satisfy our own need for accomplishment.
>
> It's like missionaries who used to go to faraway lands, work for decades to win souls, and see nothing. But they trusted God that they were planting seeds of the Gospel that would someday grow and bear fruit. You have to be very secure in your faith to do that. Don't be so worried about your own little church in a big sea of denominations.
>
> The Body of Christ is becoming a truly small-c "catholic" church, free from harsh distinctions between denominations. Those walls are having to come down. Face it, that needed to happen. Many of us grew up in a world where everyone in our own church has the Bible all right and we're on the highway to heaven, while everyone in the church down the block has it dead wrong, and they're on the road to hell. That just cannot be true!

"It's sad," he muses, frowning. "Why did we think they were our enemies, when there are so many real enemies out there" in a world of broken homes and hearts, torn by war, hunger, poverty, racial hatred, and ecological crisis, which the faithful need to face together?"

This approach appeals to a generation educated to question convention and find their own way, notes a youth minister. They prize freedom of choice as well as conscience, and they embrace interpersonal openness alongside familial closeness. They oppose sectarian boundaries, holier-than-thou hypocrisy, and a rigid sense of superiority among competing denominations no less than the magisterial authority of an established church. Disciplined by the demanding rules and measured results of higher education and high-performance work, they celebrate expressive feeling and emotional intimacy on the wide road to true friendship and spiritual communion instead of dogmatizing reason and revelation on the narrow path to orthodox faith. They concede that belonging to other kinds of community can fill the self-help role of religion and yield comparable social benefits. Yet they affirm coming to experience the Gospel truth of Christ's redemptive love and the Spirit's transformative presence by taking part in the living body of the church and flourishing in its practice.[11]

MORAL INTEGRITY IN A DIVIDED SOCIETY

This seeker-friendly approach can pose challenges of its own, allows an older minister, since it risks "the make-believe of discipleship without discipline, love freely given without obedience, and emotionally powerful worship experience without biblical authority." Facing these challenges, he vows, "We don't want to just spend more money to put on a better show with a bigger emotional bang for a bigger audience, and then wind up with a depersonalized kind of Christianity Lite.[12] So, we really call them to serve. Don't just sit there in the pew and watch the show. Stand up and pitch in. Become the hands and feet of Jesus! That's the 'why' of the Body of Christ," he stresses, by contrast to the "how-to" of a high-performance megachurch built mainly to serve its own expansion by attracting the unchurched.

How can churches do better for their members, the unchurched, and those straddling their doorstep? "We need to be more transparent," answers this older minister, "and we need to be less hurtful." That's easy to recognize in principle, he notes, but hard to spell out in practice and harder still to live out. Why so? "Churches preach honesty, but they get used to hiding things," such as sexual abuse and financial problems, behind a façade of false authority and fear of scandal now exposed to growing scrutiny and protest across a range of social institutions, for example, by the #MeToo movement.

"The church really needs to come clean right now, especially with young people," this veteran pastor explains, "so if someone really wants to check us out, they get to see our underwear drawer, and how we fold our underwear, or if we fold it. Or if we're hiding something underneath it," he smiles. "We're willing to show you we don't have anything to hide. If the church is set up [honestly] like that, then most of the people won't even bother about it," he allows. "But they deserve to see everything, and we need to make good on that when we invite them in and show them around."

How do churches hurt their members and drive them away? "Not intentionally," replies this minister. "But we do it and we have done it, and it doesn't matter if we didn't intend it. We still need to ask forgiveness." For what? "For falling short, for not living a wholehearted life. For not being integrated. For being compartmentalized in our faith and our life, our marriage and our job. Our society teaches us how to split things up. Our faith should show us how to pull them all together, if it's real. It should bring down those barriers that push us along on different tracks." Why doesn't that happen? "Well, it feels less comfortable and convenient," he replies. "It's more countercultural. It's hard to live out the integrity of our faith, even though our people are seeking God and looking to us to show them the way."

Here lies the inescapable challenge of exercising true authority in church, this minister reflects: "Parents have power over their children, but they don't always use it fairly or lovingly. For pastors, too, you have to hold this power in a very humble, holy way to even begin to deserve it. If we're not living in unity with what we're teaching and preaching, then God have mercy on us! You can't ignore this spiritual authority just because you don't want it or don't deserve it. It's there!" he exclaims. "It's a responsibility that you have to live into humbly, by asking for God's mercy to let you do it right, or for sure you will do it wrong and you will hurt people without knowing it."

Morally divided selves and compartmentalized social roles emerge from the modern institutions we inhabit, by this account, and they challenge religious communities and their leaders to respond with transparent honesty and faithful integrity in practice as wholehearted persons and mutually responsible members of God's people. "It's easier said than done," grants this minister. "But we have to keep trying. I haven't noticed many people getting healed by themselves. I know that doesn't always mean going to church for everyone. But church gives us a place to be healed, to be known, to belong and be safe, when it's done in the right spirit," he concludes. "And we need that. Just as we see how much our own kids need us to care for them, God feels the same way about the people who come through our doors."

STRATEGIC SUCCESS AND LIVING FAITH

In related terms, a longtime minister credits the strategic success of Alto Church's "evangelical revolution" in attracting young adults and holding onto its own children coming of age. But he weighs the limits of this strategy, and asks how it can be truly transformed, starting with recognition of the responsibility babyboom parents must share for their children leaving church:

> My generation, baby boomers, has to bear part of the responsibility for our children drifting away from church, because we played with spirituality. We played with religion. We know what's required of us, we know what faith is supposed to look like, and we've gone through the motions. But has that gone deep enough in our own spiritual lives to really make a difference?
>
> *Q: A difference in what?*
>
> In the way we live, and the way our children see us living. Everybody means well and wants to do the right thing, and many of us go to church more or less

> regularly. We want God around somewhere in our lives, and we want to be able to get hold of Him when we need Him in an emergency—a 911 God. But we don't really want Him messing with our stuff all the time and interfering with the way we actually live.

"Have we struggled enough with what living faithfully really means, emotionally and spiritually, to make a difference in the lives of our children?" Fred Heiden asks. "I'm not so sure about that," he answers. Then he explains:

> I look at my own kids, and I wonder what kind of model we have given them. Some of them are right there with me in trying to live faithfully every day. Some of them are more distant, a step or two away. Then I look at my grandchildren, and they're removed a step further away.
>
> Some of my kids have stayed deeply involved in church ever since childhood. They married in the church, they've raised their own kids in the church. When they moved away, they found churches like their own. They made real friends there. They became elders and deacons. They call on Sunday afternoons, and we talk about the sermon they heard that day and the sermon I preached.
>
> But some of them, their lives took a hard turn, and they left. They haven't been back, maybe for all the wrong reasons. But they have their reasons why, and I understand some of it, why they can be arguing with God.
>
> What I don't understand is how that squares with what they see in us, and how we depend on God. We rely on God to direct our lives. Maybe I wasn't clear enough or open enough about it in the years the kids were growing up. Maybe I was too busy.

"So I can question myself," Heiden admits. "But I'm not giving up hope for them. I know they can start fresh," he vows. "They can find a church, and they can find real friends there."

After working for decades with parents and children in the church, Heiden reflects on his own children and grandchildren. He weighs the diverging course of their religious and spiritual lives, without setting spirituality at odds with organized religion. Instead, he stresses the spiritual depth, integrity, and passion of living faithfully as *both* a spiritual *and* religious person, while he contrasts the "spiritual grounding" of genuine faith to the merely "social fabric" of routine churchgoing. He seeks to grasp the moral coherence of divergence in these ways of living rather than draw a single line of cause and effect through contrary trajectories of congregational commitment and deepening faith versus widening distance and drift from church, whether marked by arguing with God or following one's own sunny spiritual path.

Where adolescents and young adults find their friends, whom they date and mate, stresses Heiden, cannot be discounted or divorced from whether they continue to grow up within a congregational community or leave it behind at childhood's end:

> A lot of it is relationships. One of the kids married someone who didn't grow up in church, and he doesn't want to find out about it now. She will go now and then on her own, but she'll go to the beach or the movies instead if she feels like it, or that's what their family is doing.
>
> I look at my grandchildren, from college age down to kindergarten. I love them, and they love me. But the oldest one has all kinds of questions about God, and she's not buying any of this. The next one is away at college. He just shrugs and smiles when I ask him if he's going to church there. I look down the line, and it seems like they're less connected to a life of faith than my own kids. They're less worried about going to church or not, even though they're good kids. They wake up in the morning, they thank God for the sunshine and the trees, then they go do their own thing.

"Devotional life is crucial," stresses Fred Heiden in pointing out another factor essential to sustaining participation in Christian community within the church and family alike. It grows through a reciprocal process of spiritual and moral formation, he observes, grounded in congregational worship and personal prayer, nurtured by shared study and pastoral care of souls. In his most self-critical moments, Heiden confesses, "I feel like we have failed our kids," in exemplifying devotional life and teaching it by example. "Devotional life was scattered at our house when the kids were growing up, because of my hours at church, and all the time I was out taking care of people. So, we end up making excuses" for falling short with our own children in practicing what we preach, Heiden judges. "Has it been real for them?" he asks.

> Have they seen an impassioned spirit for God? Have they felt it in us? I can say it, and I mean it. But is that enough? I can't imagine getting up without God. I really can't. But does that translate into my life with others every day, especially my kids? I wish I could say, "Yes, it does." I consider myself a pretty devout, honest person. But there are a lot of cracks and fissures in there, gaps and absences, and some of those I think my kids have taken on. Does that make me the only one? No, in Silicon Valley we've got millions of absentee fathers!"

Many such parents, Heiden observes, are away at work, striving long and hard to hold the pace in Silicon Valley, and excel at demanding technical and professional jobs, after succeeding in highly competitive universities. In this milieu, going to church can all too easily become something secondary in importance if not incidental, Heiden notes, a matter of personal discretion in the binding course of supporting a family and advancing a career.

This hardly excuses individual parents from responsibility for the religious formation of their children. But it narrows sources of support for such formation across the social institutions and cultural norms of upper-middle-class life in Silicon Valley, Heiden argues:

> Once upon a time in this country, at least in small towns, the question was, "What church do you go to?" Now it's more, "Do you go to church? Oh, really?" Around here, it can just be, "What do you do? Where did you go to school? Were you an undergrad at Stanford? Where did you do your MBA or JD?"
>
> We do a lot with high school students in our church—youth services, Bible study, classes, music, trips. We have a "Senior Sunday" when they graduate, a whole weekend when they get to preach, plan worship, play music. But then, when they get to college, they disappear. They don't go to church there, and they only show up here at Christmas.
>
> All the energy and effort that lead up to that point, we have to ask how deep does it go? Isit really spiritual, or is it just social? It should be both. But if it's just social fabric, then it unravels. It's a social scene without any spiritual grounding.

Congregations and families need to do better when their children leave home for college as young adults, Heiden believes, and then leave college for the world of work. But friends and peer groups become even more crucial at this point, he acknowledges, in answering questions of freedom and commitment, autonomy and authority.

FREEDOM, AUTHORITY, AND RULES

These questions now come to the fore in social settings that put parents at arm's length and problematize *in loco parentis* authority across the board, observes Fred Heiden, including the tutelary authority of the church. In these new circumstances, he asks:

> Who do you latch onto and get involved with? Who gets you involved in church or pulls you away from it? Who are your friends? Who do you love?
>
> That's the key, especially when you go away to college. You're out from under your parents, you're experiencing freedom for the first time, and you're *going* to be free one way or the other, whether you grew up in a Christian home or not. You don't have your mom and dad telling you to go to church every Sunday, or

just dragging you there. You don't have a small-group leader or youth minister keeping track of you.

That's part of growing up and maturing. The kids discover life. They find out they can make their own decisions about how to live, without their parents' consent, without asking permission. Then church can seem like a place where you have no freedom. Someone else is always telling you what to do, and there are too many rules. So you think, "I'm not gonna get caught in that any more. I'm outta here!"

Church leaders and parents are not to blame for all this, Fred Heiden allows with a smile, but it's not all the fault of "the culture" or "the society" either. "Churches can put a bunch of rules and regulations on the kids that are not all that helpful," he judges, "without enabling them to find out for themselves what faith means." How so? "You show them what it means for you by living it out the best you can," he says. "Then you have to give them the space to ask that question themselves. Only then can you help them answer it through their own experience."

Fred Heiden weighs how heavily regulated the world of higher education and professional work turns out be in the experience of young adults coming of age in Silicon Valley, and how that spurs their search for freedom, intimacy, and community in the realm of spirituality as well as art, leisure, and romantic love:

There are rules everywhere, and smart people need to learn the rules to connect and contribute and make their way through life as adults. Around here, in Silicon Valley, almost everyone works hard. Kids see their parents working hard. They see their peers studying hard in school, most of them.

Do they see everyone coming to church, and church making a difference in their lives? No! At Stanford and other schools around here, it's a distinct minority who are actively and authentically involved in church, who take their faith seriously, who really want to sing those hymns they grew up with.

Talk with kids brought up going to church with their families and not going anymore once they leave home. You hear, "Well, I don't know, I wouldn't say that there is no God. Maybe there's a higher power, but I don't see any need for it in my life," even though they can tell you all about the spiritual side of yoga or something else they're into. That's pretty normal now for a lot of young people.

Go to a big church wedding for students with unchurched friends, Heiden notes by way of example, "and you find out a lot of them don't know what to do. They're talking and laughing in the middle of the service, shouting out to the bride and groom at the altar, cheering and hooting. It's like a crowd at a rock concert or a football game." Not knowing any better or feeling any different marks children raised in unchurched families, suspects Heiden, but closer to home lies the harder problem of churches imposing all-too-conventional rules instead of nurturing faithful freedom, care, and community on the path to self-discovery.

PUT ON LOVE IN A COMMUNITY OF CHARACTER

The challenges of this social and cultural milieu for "traditional churchgoing" lead Fred Heiden back to probing the heart of Christian community and the need for its radical renewal to revive the moral pulse of this generation:

> Christian community is not about rules. It's about "putting on compassion and kindness," and coming to "clothe yourself in mercy, humility, gentleness, and patience. Bear with each other; forgive each other as God forgives you. And above all these put on love, which binds all together in perfect unity." (Col. 3:12–17)
>
> Yes, the church has rules, and God gives commandments. But they come down to "Love God and love your neighbor." You can only do that in relationship. The church is not really about "Thou shalt not." It's about caring for each other, loving each other, as God loves each one of us.
>
> God calls us to *learn* to love each other, because we can't just do it right away. There are some people I don't like. God says that's okay, you can learn to love them, you don't have to like them.

By contrast to act-specific rules and commandments, Heiden describes the church as a community of character formed by its members practicing particular virtues such as mercy and kindness in forgiving and bearing with one another. Mutual aid, care, and neighbor-love go hand in hand with loving God, with each relationship illuminating and inspiring the other in practice.[13]

"What if you wake up every morning and talk with God about what you're gonna do today, and you go over it together?" Fred Heiden asks of learning to carry on an intimate, conscientious conversation with God in daily prayer. "Putting on love" of God and neighbor depends on learning how to act and feel in the shared practices that actually constitute the congregation by forming its members and embodying its vision. Without taking part in these practices, he stresses, believers cannot truly come to belong to the church, and they cannot truly come to know the nature of their own "spiritual needs" and their own selfhood in relationship.

This vision of Christian community in practice reframes conventional tensions between social rules demanding propriety and conformity, on one hand, and ideals of personal freedom and self-fulfillment, on the other. However far back cultural conflicts may reach between bohemian and bourgeois ideals of selfhood, Heiden believes, this moral conflict has grown socially stronger and personally sharper for more Americans over the past generation.[14]

This moral conflict has also grown more problematic for churches, Fred Heiden thinks, as they find themselves now caught in the wide-open realm of autonomous personal choice and enjoyable private life as a refuge from the constraining discipline of schooling, work, and public life bound by bureaucracy. Or they wind up rehearsing such discipline with parochial rules of their own. "It's a cliché, but it's also true that the culture has changed for kids growing up today," he notes:

> "Don't drink, don't get pregnant, don't wreck the car." That about covered it for kids in high school back in the 1950s. Now, everything is okay, as long as you can manage it, and not get off-track. Study hard, work hard, and play hard, too. Go out and have fun.
>
> That can sound like freedom. But it also puts pressure on kids—and on churches—to be fun and free. Don't look stuffy and staid. Try to be all things to all people. We can't be so narrow, we've got to be wide open. Isn't that what liberal education teaches us? So once I've gone to college and opened up my mind and gotten free, I'm not going to go back into a narrow church environment where they're always telling me what I can and can't do.

Don't church leaders understand what's going on the lives of young people today? "We think we do," replies Heiden. "We have strategies to target them. But we're almost always behind the curve. We're blasting them with Christian rock, instead of bringing them to prayer and praise with liturgical music and "Amazing Grace."[15]

Many mainline and evangelical churches target young adults, especially young families with children, but singles, too. They devote a great deal of resources, time, and ingenuity to this effort, as Heiden knows firsthand. But he fears they run underlying risks in pursuing this strategy of "giving them what they want," instead of what they need. "Can we go all out to bring them in without downplaying our biblical understanding and our theology?" he wonders. "Why not let go of seminary training and ordination for ministers, and just hire from within?" he asks. "Find really nice, personable, sincere kids who love the Lord and love reaching out to people like themselves. If your pop music is good enough, and your personal message is accessible enough, why do you need congregational prayer, pastoral prayer, or hymn-singing?"

BODIES OF WORSHIP

Why concentrate on worship if churches prize organizational growth and giving, congeniality and community service? Christians congregate to worship God, first of all, and they can learn to do so only by putting this practice first, answers Fred Heiden. "It's our responsibility to pray together in worship as God's people. We learn how to pray together by doing it," he stresses. "Worship is what we do together and experience together as a congregation. It isn't someone up in front entertaining everyone else in back in the audience. I'm not praying *at* you. We're praying together to God."

> In pastoral prayer you have a responsibility to the congregation. During the week you take time to think about what's actually going on in your congregation, and what's going on in your own life. You want to reflect on that reality, and then express it to God when we pray to Him. So, when we pray together, I'll watch people nodding or turning to their partners—however they're responding—because we're in this together. I don't understand how we can worship without that.
>
> Just watching someone performing up front is not worship. That's not church. That's not connecting with God. That's more like going to a theatre and being entertained by having people singing at me. Then I have people preaching at me and telling me what I'm supposed to do—I'm supposed to serve and sign up for stuff—so I've got an hour of being told what to do.

That isn't helping anybody to know God and grow in faith, Heiden objects. "We have to wrestle with what God says. But if we're not telling them what God says, and we're just telling them what I think, then what's the point?" he asks. "Do we actually read Scripture in our services? How can you not read Scripture and not pray in a service, and still find God?"

If churches cannot bring us closer to God, then they have nothing to offer that college, popular entertainment, and playful leisure can't do better. "If I'm a smart college student, and I'm looking for something worthwhile to rock my world and change my mind from what I'm getting all week," Heiden wonders, "then why should I come to church for a little second-run entertainment or a fifty-minute lecture? I can get a lecture at school. If I can't find God here, why should I bother to go to church?" he asks. "Why not just go to the beach or the movies, or take a walk in the woods?" By contrast to social clubs or service groups, he insists, bodies of worship can fulfill their purpose as communities of character and practice that form and guide their members only through "talking with God and listening to God."

"We have to listen to one another," Fred Heiden elaborates, "to uncover *our* spiritual needs in order for me to find out my own spiritual needs. I have to find out what people are going through before I can share God's word with them. In Colossians Paul says, '*Put on* mercy and kindness,' and '*clothe* yourselves' with goodness.' You have to do it every day, over and over again," Heiden stresses. "You're not gonna do it perfectly all at once, so we have to slow down and 'bear with each other.' It takes time to change from the outside in and *put away* anger and malice. It's not just getting born again and letting your light shine from the inside out." At the same time, Heiden urges, "Give it to God," and let God work in your life:

> "Clothe yourselves," Paul says, "since you have been chosen." God has already called us. So, if I wander into church for the first time in a while, as a college student or young person, is that really just my choice? Nah, I don't think so. I think God wants you here. You're here by divine appointment. You make a choice, but God has a hand in it. He doesn't turn away. He knows what's going on in our thinking, in our hearts and our minds, because he made us this way. He knows what our needs are. He knows what we're going through when life is hard, and He's here to walk us through it. *He* chooses us![16]
>
> *Q: For what?*
>
> For something we don't really know at the start. That's part of our journey, to figure that out together. Since God has brought us here, let's put on mercy and kindness, and let's see what happens. Let's be practical *and* liturgical. Let's move in and out of Scripture to try things out. You'll begin to find out how to feel and act with people in new ways, face-to-face in a new kind of family you really need. It's what we were created for, whether you realize it beforehand or not, if you're locked into your computer and your iPhone all day, trying to connect and getting more disconnected.

Seen in this light, the face-to-face community of a congregation in worship rehearses the covenantal community of Deuteronomy (6:4–6) in promising those who love God and heed God's word that becoming one with *thy* God will unify the whole of each person, just as becoming one with *our* God will unite the whole of God's people.

By contrast to either/or, zero-sum pictures of more or less connected individuals drawn by American commonsense, these biblical stories of covenantal relationships between God and the whole of a people, and between God and each person as a whole, are mutually generative and reinforcing.[17] As a body of worship, the congregation transcends a social network or voluntary association of individuals. The congregation likewise reaches beyond sociable "meeting and greeting" in weekly Bible class through pastoral prayer that leads to prayer chains of members praying for one another and others, too, from one Sunday to the next throughout the week. Fred Heiden explains:

> We spend time praying in Bible class before we turn to the lesson. That opens us up to one another. Over the years it's gone way beyond only talking about ourselves or someone else in church. Now we're praying for Aunt Sally's brother or second cousin. You watch and you see folks in the room writing down the name and relationship of this or that person to pray for through the week. What was their name again? That's family stuff![18]
>
> A lot of the young people who live in this area or go to school here, live on their own or without any family. They need that. And it's essential to the church. It turns you outward, so you're focused on others, you're not just thinking about yourself. Every family has issues and problems. We need to say it, and walk through it together, and not pretend we've got all the answers beforehand, because we're doing life together.
>
> Can it happen with 300 people in the room? Yes! But we have to be intentional. We have to create those spaces to pray together so it's personal *and* it's talking with God on a different scale. It's teaching us about God in a different way, like singing together in worship, when we really give ourselves to it instead of just mouthing the words, and letting the choir carry it from up front.

By this account everything in worship—prayer, preaching, scripture reading, music—reveals to members of a congregation "who God is and who we are together in relationship to God," Heiden concludes. "It has to make sense theologically to be real, not just sound good or feel good" as a growing enterprise or congenial club, in order to incarnate the church as the people of God and a family of unselfish love.[19]

Christian churches have taken many different social forms through history, Fred Heiden notes, and American churches today take shape along many different social dimensions. The congregation composes a kind of family you can be born into, but it's also a voluntary association that you can choose to join and leave. It incorporates an economy of offerings, expenses, and property and a polity of offices, laws, and elections. The treasure of faith is contained in earthen vessels (2 Cor. 4:7), Heiden agrees, but money and power can prove problematic in sustaining its integrity. That holds true especially for young adults who are alert to the economic competition and payoffs of mass-market evangelism no less than the partisan alliances and strife of religious lobbies that blur bright lines of church-state separation. Pastors' children in particular "hear too much church politics," fears Heiden, and they "get disenchanted with 'organized religion,' even if they still believe in God. Other kids hear it, too, and they ask, 'What's *that* all about?' when there's disagreement or confusion about what's going on in church, even when a church is growing and successful."

Is such institutional ambiguity and moral hypocrisy inevitable? Can church leaders allay the disillusionment many young adults report of churches too focused on money and power, and too little concerned with meeting the spiritual needs of their people?[20] "Okay, the church *is* partly economic and partly political," Heiden concedes. "But why does it exist? What's it for? Why am I coming to work in the morning?" he asks in turn.

> My goal is to love people, and by loving them to bring them into a closer relationship to God, and help them understand how God is working in their life. That's my calling. That's what I've always thought, because God loves us and cares for us. That's not a business goal or a political goal. It's not like making a million dollars or getting a million votes, or even "loving your customers" and building your brand. It's not a church-growth number you can count, or a metric you can chart.
>
> When a son or daughter calls me at home to say their mother is comatose and dying, why do I get up from dinner and get over there? It's to help comfort the family, whether they're just sitting there shell-shocked, or they're coming apart, sobbing and sobbing. It's taking the hand of a dying person, and asking the children to come to her bed, and pray together. It's about how much we're loved, how much God loves us. How He's here and taking care of us.
>
> Who's responsible for that? God's responsible. Not me. But how does God choose to do all this? Through the church. And we make up the church. Who else is there to do this? Almost nobody! Maybe your family, if you're blessed by a loving family that happens to live nearby, but almost nobody else.

Making God real, by loving one another as God loves us, fulfills Christian faith and human nature alike, Fred Heiden concludes: "What are people really looking for? True love! A love that will not die, that will not fade away. We can't know it until we experience it. It's a love from God, and everybody needs it. We just do. No matter what we're going through, we need a kind of community that can come around you and love you, no matter how hard and messy things are." God redeems an unjust world through love, Heiden testifies: "God doesn't make evil and suffering go away. It is a mystery, and sometimes it's a terrible one. But God shows up in the middle of it. He cries with me. He holds me when I can't stand up. He allows me to do with Him what I can't do by myself."

Particularly in places like Silicon Valley, Fred Heiden reflects, people are blessed by great prosperity and opportunity, especially privileged young adults who devote their gifts and resources to studying and working hard. "If they're healthy and whole, they don't think they need God. Things will work out. They'll get married and have kids, and bring them to church to get help raising them right."

But when disaster strikes or loss comes, Heiden fears, "If there's no deeper connection for them, then there's nowhere they can go. If they're lucky, they can feel terrible for a while, then try to put it behind them and bounce back. But there has to be more to it than that," Heiden trusts. "It's not just about having 'values.'[21] It's about the reality of life and death, and how we struggle with it to love God and each another. The church can show us that. If it doesn't, then people will look someplace else," after dismissing church as bad business, politics, or schooling.

GETTING INVOLVED

For all its seeker-friendly appeal to young adults, this "hybridized mainline almost megachurch," as a youth minister put it, includes more traditional "hymn and choir" services of worship, favored by many middle-aged families as well as seniors. It features a range of Bible study classes that include seniors in groups that have grown together for decades, carrying their leather-bound copies of the King James Bible well worn by page-turning and dense with margin notes. It urges worshippers to join small "life groups" to deepen their faith. It invites them to enact it in service to others in the church and the community through dozens of projects that range from teaching Sunday school through helping the homeless to sharing mission trips abroad.

Married couples in their sixties and seventies include spouses of several years or decades who have met and married in the church. Middle-aged divorcees and widowed seniors on their own have found new friends and companions, if not always new partners, in the church's large singles groups. They have found "a safe place to heal your heart" in "relationship rescue" groups.[22] "Pain is the great leveler," sums up a minister responsible for leading these groups. "It makes people move and want to change, even if it takes a while. Here we're mostly mid-thirties and up," he explains. "When you're younger you know it's the other person's fault, not yours, and you're bound to walk around the corner and find someone perfect the next time. Gradually you realize that it's you, too," he smiles slowly.

> You need to change, and you realize you can't just do it all by yourself. You need help, you need to do it with others, in the right kind of community where you can be accepted, and you can also be accountable.

> You can come here and not be judged. "Nobody's perfect." But you can become responsible, too, and if you keep coming, then you can come into relationship with Jesus in your life, and with other Christians who love one another.

"I've been coming to divorce recovery for a year, and nobody's pressured me to join the church," a woman in her thirties testifies gratefully. Such "healing groups" are open to those who are not church members, if they come in good faith and abide by rules of confidentiality and not dating others in the group.

No less open are other church classes and life groups as well as worship services. Indeed, the church lifts up such openness to outsiders in need as exemplary Christian charity and hospitality. It welcomes guests without obliging them to become formal church members, for all the personal encouragement and spiritual inspiration it devotes to embracing them in its community of worship, fellowship, and service. "You can come to worship here for months or even years," notes a minister, "and you don't have to do the 'starting point' classes to move toward membership. You already belong, you're already part of us, and we already accept you and love you."

Wanting to change, to do better and become better in life, marks one formative point of entry into this evangelical church set in a relatively educated and psychologically fluent social milieu. "Did you ever want to do something different, and you just jumped in and tried, and you couldn't do it?" asks one minister in a starting-point class for newcomers. "I thought I wanted to run a marathon," he says by way of example. "I went out to run for the first time since high school PE, and I got 100 yards, before I had to stop and rest, because I was out of breath and exhausted. So you have to train, you have to practice. The best way to do that is with other people, including people who know how to do it, who can show you how."

So, the church offers itself as a community of traditional Christian practices, including worship, prayer, scripture reading, and confession. But it also holds up "spiritual practices" and invites newcomers to try out "unplugging, solitude, silence; taking a walk in nature, taking the slow lane, taking a day of rest; caring for a friend, and serving the poor." Weekly starting-point classes invite newcomers to try out spiritual practices such as introducing themselves sincerely to say what they most hope for at the first class or recalling who was the most loving and accepting person in their childhood. What were their key experiences of faith and community, of spiritual gifts and callings?

Only after a month of such classes does a low-key altar call "invite people to come up for prayer, come over to join a life group, and take the next step to join the church," explains a minister. "But we don't press them. We don't *need* them to become members. In fact, we tell them, if you decide to become a member, this is a place where members serve, not where they get served first. Guests get the front seat, members take the back seat."

For guests on the way to becoming church members, it is friendship that usually comes first and leads them forward. It is bred in life-group networks devoted to common interests and activities, as informal as sharing a weekly walk in a local park or a bike ride in the nearby hills. They need to commit themselves to nothing more than a regular round of golf, indistinguishable in practice from any other except perhaps for a shared prayer and the absence of expletives, off-color jokes, and stiff drinks in the clubhouse.

Good friends and good causes often go hand in hand. The African American director of a large food bank just a few miles and a world away from the church looks out her window at a half-dozen electrical engineers smoothly swinging hammers and guiding skilsaws to build a new food-storage annex for the project. "They've known each other for years," she reflects. "Some came from the church, then they brought others over from Habitat for Humanity. They don't hang out much with everyone else, they don't wear their hearts on their sleeves. But they like each other. They're good workers, they know what they're doing. They're worth their weight in gold, and we love them."

Does anything mark off members of the church from other volunteers? "More of them actually show up than some of the others, even other church folks," replies the food bank director. "Not because they're better people or more Christian," she adds, "but because they get more hands-on encouragement, especially from a few ringleaders who come over a lot and bring them along. They don't just send a check, like some other churches, although we are grateful for that, too," she smiles, "and we couldn't get along without it."

Recalls one veteran volunteer, "I just happened to come the first time, because they asked at church for someone who could do electrical repairs. I did it, I saw they were meeting a real need for food and clothing, and they didn't turn anybody away. I met some of the people there. They were honest and organized. I liked them, so I kept coming back. I talked about it at singles meetings and Bible classes, and I brought other people back with me. Mostly word of mouth, even though after awhile we put it up on the online bulletin board for service projects."

The food bank relies on donations from local grocery stores, corporations, and chambers of commerce, along with civic and religious groups, to feed and clothe needy members of a majority-minority community pinched by low wages, high jobless rates, and skyrocketing housing prices in Silicon Valley. So, food-bank leaders appreciate volunteers committed to their cause without seeking to politicize it. "Our community needs political activists and organizers, but that's not our role here," says one. "We have to make that clear to some more 'progressive' church folks who want us to get into it, but not to these folks. They are mostly White and educated, but they're pretty diverse politically. They know how to get along, and they want to do good without making it left-wing or right-wing good."

Church members have also become immersed in a weekly teaching and mentoring program to share "fundamental financial paradigms, life and job skills" with a thousand "under-resourced" high school students at risk of being caught in multigenerational cycles of poverty in Silicon Valley's poorest neighborhoods. The program's focus on "how money works" ties together education and earning with practical insight for students in high schools where most fail to graduate, start college, or enter the skilled workforce. It aims to teach by example as well as information, and it hunts for exemplary volunteers.

"We partner with high-school principals and teachers in their own classrooms during regular school hours," explains Dick Rice, the program's director. "So we need professionals and executives who can free their time to take part. We go out to local churches, civic groups, corporate groups. We talk to them about what we can do person-to-person to break the chain of poverty and financial illiteracy by enabling teenagers to learn about budgeting, credit, loans, interest, and foreclosure. Not just how to balance your checkbook and avoid predatory lenders," Rice makes clear, "but how to balance your life and negotiate the American financial system. So these kids can start making good decisions about school and work, find a mentor, get on a career path, and self-determine."

Where does this "FutureProfits" program start with volunteers? "With a brainwave and a heartbeat," laughs Rice, a veteran community organizer with local roots and a seminary degree. "Actually, we're looking for people with a good heart, and a certain level of sophistication in how they see race and economics. Poor people don't just need to try harder," he stresses. "You need to get that to get into this. But you don't need to be liberal or conservative politically. We welcome capitalists!" he exclaims. "We want them to help these kids learn how to become good capitalists themselves in terms of being smart and responsible about money." Volunteers need a certain amount of skill to handle the material, and "the confidence to stand up in front of a bunch of terrifying high-school kids," smiles Rice. The program appeals to Rotarians as well as Unitarians, he notes, while pointing out,

> Church people are some of our best volunteers, because they also bring a feeling for justice and empowerment as caring for all God's children and answering God's call to be responsible for Creation and work for the Beloved Community. That's how I approach it, coming from Dr. King and Bonhoeffer, and not just with liberal churches. Most of the evangelical churches we work with recognize

> that now in their own way. They're not just about saving souls and letting the body of the world go its own way.
>
> Some church volunteers come to us after they've done things like short-term mission trips to Mexico or Central America, and they've become frustrated by drive-by do-gooding. We're practical, and we stick with it for a whole school year. That's an hour in class every week plus prep, and ten hours of training up front.
>
> That's a pretty big commitment. It engages you, if you're ready for it. If you're ready for a relationship with kids who don't really know any people like you. People who wear khakis and button-down shirts to work in an office or lab, who have advanced degrees and good jobs and investments.

"That relationship can make a difference in how these kids see the world and their chances in it going forward," Rice promises, "even if you don't wind up mentoring them to get into Stanford or get a job with Google by the end of the year."

What can churches do better or do differently in serving the community and the world? "Most churches put their own members first," answers Dick Rice. "They come to us in order to serve their members by serving the community. *We* do this, first of all, to serve kids in need and their community," he counters. "Then, second, to give volunteers good experiences." These two aims don't always line up, he finds, and community programs that depend on volunteers who are also donors feel the tug toward putting them first. Church leaders know this feeling firsthand, Rice adds, and they can draw on it to help keep these priorities straight and keep these partnerships focused on serving the needy instead of the wealthy.

Churches can also help community projects hedge against the temptation, typical among high tech firms and civic groups led by elite problem-solvers in Silicon Valley, to "look for the quick fix and the big tech breakthrough to solve community problems from above instead of working away on the ground," observes Dick Rice. "Yes, we need systemic solutions to come through legislation and investment. But you don't fix four hundred years of African American slavery and exclusion with a great app!" Churches, too, can find themselves forgoing the long view of history and the long hard work needed to remake the future, Rice warns, in favor of the "short-term mission flavor of the month," when they should instead sustain their commitments to social witness and service.

Churches centered on educated professionals, notes this community activist, also face the challenge, bred by their own success, of valuing their own experience and opinions above those of the community they seek to help. "People who live on this side of the freeway are smart and hardworking, too," Rice declares. "They have to be in order to survive. Wealthy folks who haven't carried the burdens of the poor need to recognize that if they really want to help them." Mutual recognition and learning inhere in biblical ideals of justice and love, by this account, and churches need to put them into programmatic practice.

For example, recounts Dick Rice, a good-sized, well-funded congregation in the heart of Silicon Valley came to him with an offer to send its junior pastors to train leaders of a local Hispanic Pentecostal church to help it become more effectively organized. "More effective how?" asked Rice in reply, since the local church in question numbered a thousand members, counted four of five adults in small groups and as many children in Sunday school. It organized scores of volunteers to feed four hundred hungry persons every week, shelter the homeless, and welcome new immigrants. "What do you have to give them?" queried Rice before suggesting an exchange program in which leaders of both congregations would participate in mutual learning and planning. "There's a lot to learn on both sides," he noted, "including the explosion of Pentecostal Christianity in the Global South that most mainline church folks know almost nothing about."[23]

Underlying the practical challenges of tutoring and mentoring needy high-school students, and related programs backed by Rice's community organizing, runs the riptide of larger social changes against efforts to enable the least of these to enter the middle-class mainstream of American society. "We're working to enable poor people and immigrants to rise up and contribute and thrive," he attests, "when middle-class opportunities and security are shrinking for everyone. So how do we preach redemption and liberation to the captives, when fewer and fewer folks are free?" (Isa. 61:1) Rice pauses, "The churches in America need to ask that question, and press forward with that conversation. Sometimes I wonder if they're ready to do that."

Why not start on the ground in key congregations in Silicon Valley, invites Dick Rice, particularly where some church members are worth $100 million and others lack $100 in net worth. "Commit to no hunger in the church, first of all, to food and clothing for all." Then work for jobs, housing, and schooling for everyone in the pews. "God made enough for the whole of Creation," he affirms, "so let's live that way in community, with peer accountability and responsibility in discipleship. No freeloading. You couldn't keep people out of the churches then, instead of straining to get them in!" We need to dig deeper to live out the unity of our faith in a more deeply divided society, Rice stresses. "That's why we want to get well-off, well-educated faithful people into the schools with kids in need. Because after a while it's not 'those brown kids.' It's these kids I've come to know and care about—Jamal, Luis, Eduardo. That's a start on building relationships across cultures and classes that depend on love instead of power," Rice lifts up his hands. "It's a step to bring the Kingdom closer, to follow Jesus washing the feet of the disciples."[24]

HEARTFELT HEALING TRANSLATES TRADITION

In her fifties but still a newcomer to Alto Church, Laura Ponti has a feel for young adults grounded in her own unfolding experience of love and work. After twenty years near the top of a thriving high tech corporation, she reports, "I had a good run, and the company was very good to me. But I was ready to do something different." Her father's death coinciding with the breakup of a long romantic relationship brought her to a crossroads that led to Alto Church and to a new kind of calling. After taking time off to help her widowed mother, then rest and travel on her own, she realized, "I actually love business, and I'm good at it, so why not find a pro bono business to get involved in?" She began volunteering in a community program to help single mothers find jobs, day care, and affordable housing. She started fundraising for it, then joined its board of directors, and eventually became its chief executive. "I took it step by step," she explains, "and I decided this is something I really care about. I love children, but I put my career first. Now here I am with no kids but enough money and freedom to do something to help mothers with kids, but no husbands and no money."

Working for a fraction of what she earned before, Laura reflects, is "a choice I was free to make, since I wanted to give something back, and not just give money. Lots of nonprofits need the kind of skill set I have, and I'd rather be helping to do this instead of making more money for people who already have plenty." In fact, leading a nonprofit organization with an annual budget of several million dollars has proven more complicated than managing units of a billion-dollar corporation. "Before all I had to do was keep things organized and make my numbers," she explains. "Here I have to inspire people to take part and contribute, since we're mostly volunteers and donated money. It's not just teamwork and the bottom line. It's really about who we are as a community."

Joining Alto Church also centered on community for this executive. "I always believed in God, but I stopped going to church years ago," Laura Ponti recounts. "Then I look up and, abruptly, I'm single again. I'm seeing a therapist, but I hit rock bottom, and I don't know how to get out of it. I'm really struggling with the breakup, and I want to go someplace where I'm not the only one. I start looking around online and asking friends, and I find out about the relationship-rescue groups here."

An exploratory first visit turned into a homecoming. "I was blown away," Laura recalls. "I knew I wanted a community connection, and I wanted God in on it, but I didn't know how to put the pieces together. So I go to the group on Monday night, and it was like twenty years of seeking all came together in the unity of spirituality, psychology, and Christianity. When it comes to boundaries and how people grow, being loving doesn't mean being a pushover."

Put off by traditional Christian language of sin and repentance, heaven and hell, Laura realized she "had been throwing out the baby with the bathwater."

> Words like "sin" and "kingdom" and "righteousness": when you take them at face value in today's world, they're incredibly off-putting. But that's not really what they mean. You have to translate them into something much more practical, and you have to have a community to do that in. That's where the big "Aha!" was for me.
>
> Being "saved" doesn't mean you're damned if you don't, or Christians are better than everyone else. It means that we're all walking around with pain in our heart, and that pain needs to be healed. It needs to be healed by a love that's greater than any one human being. Knowing that love, and trying to show up every day as the best person I was made to be, that's what it means to be saved.
>
> Being a "sinner" doesn't mean you're evil if you go and rob a bank. It's not good and bad like black and white. To sin means to miss the mark. If I'm in a bad mood and I snap at someone instead of really listening to them, I miss the mark, because I was taking out my frustration on someone else who didn't deserve it. We're all sinners because we're all human. "Nobody's perfect." We have good days and bad days. But God loves us, and we can do better.

Belonging before believing, given God's love lived out by Alto Church members for seekers in need of a caring community of character "made all the difference in the world," attests Laura.

So did capable church leaders "willing to show their vulnerability, and model that for the people around them. Wow! That really moved me," Laura testifies. "Practice what you preach. So, I said, 'This is where I want to be.'" The most important "life lessons," Laura has learned, turn on "letting others come into your heart, letting yourself feel their need and their goodness, so it's not just give and take. You give each person you love a piece of your heart. But it's not just one size. Your heart grows larger."

BUILDING COMMUNITY ACROSS GENERATIONS

Synergy and shared moral transformation among members in a body of common prayer, service, and fellowship also figure in discussions at Alto

Church on the limits of age-grading groups and activities and how to span generations. A clinical psychologist who belongs to the church and admires the ingenuity of its age-specific activities for enabling distinct generations to congregate with their peers and worship with the familiar feeling of traditional hymns or the surging heartbeat of Christian rock, nonetheless underscores the good of activities that bring young and old together. "Put a nursery in a nursing home, or a Christian preschool in a church hall," she urges, "and something wonderful can happen. People can reach across generations to care for each other, teach each other, and play with each other."

Service projects, day care, shared study, and social concerns can shape community across age cohorts, this psychologist affirms, "But people should have a good time together in church, and not just do good. It's important to play together, celebrate and enjoy one another, and have a good time in good company." This church does a much better job of play than most, she allows, but it can do better still, she is convinced. So she is eager to help in ways that span the arts, healing, listening one-on-one, and conversing in small groups within the chorus of common prayer and worship.

A founder of one such small group explains how it emerged from a network of singles just out of college, then spread from young adults to their school-age children and their parents over the course of two decades. "When we started we were all in our late twenties and early thirties, either single or married without kids. A lot of us had been in the big singles group together," recalls Joel, a technology manager and longtime volunteer church leader. "In fact, that's where I met my wife," he smiles. "Later on, people started bringing their own kids when they got older, instead of leaving them in Sunday school, and some invited their parents who lived nearby."

Children and teens now join their parents in "Bible-centered" discussion around tables of six to eight persons, and sometimes they join in the talks their parents give to the class as a whole. "We don't dumb it down for the kids, but we don't pitch it over them either," Joel notes. "It's real. People laugh and cry. They break down over a death in the family, cancer, trouble with teens. They get angry: 'I can't believe this shit!' You can hear people swear in front of somebody else's twelve-year-old. We're willing to deal with it, if it's for good reason, from deep pain," he confides. "Or say 'No, that's not okay,' and redirect them, either in real time or after class, to apologize and keep it respectful."

Such mutual response and responsibility exemplify the intergenerational interplay of feeling and judgment that span equality and difference, as Joel sees it, and mark Alto Church as a priesthood of all believers. "Give people their voice, listen to them, and friendships will go deeper," he promises. "Yes, we can pray for world peace and praise Jesus as the answer. But we can also hear people tell it like it is, pray with them, and go through conflict together.

We're not just here to pat you on the back and cheer you on. But life *is* better in community."[25]

At the same time, Joel grants, "making real community is hardest for people in their twenties and thirties, especially for singles with all the work pressure and the high cost of living around here. Bringing them into community is our biggest challenge, and my biggest passion," he says. So it turns out to be "really frustrating when you pour so much into these relationships, and people leave the church," even if it's only for a better job or a more affordable house elsewhere. Then group members need to console each other for their loss, give thanks for their continuing community, and renew their faithful efforts to reach out to young adults and embrace them.

Alto Church has worked hard to excel at "getting people in the door with welcoming worship and accessible sermons," Joel reports, then encouraging them to join small groups and volunteer for service projects. What comes next? "That's what we're working on now," he answers. "How do we get deeper Bible teaching and spiritual formation into these small groups? How do we get a critical mass of real teachers and pastors into every life-group? Do we need to build an in-house seminary or set up some kind of joint program for continuing education?" he asks. While he weighs these alternatives for adults in middle age, Joel stresses, "We want to wrap our kids in Christian community. We want them going to school with kids from church, and we want people looking out for them. Do we start a full-time school?" he shakes his head. "We're not there yet. We want them to be 'in the world but not of it,' too. So shouldn't we put them in public school and let them be the salt and the light? That's what we're working on."

A longtime member of Joel's group affirms this vision of sharing Christian community in practice, especially when it comes to deepening the understanding of youths old enough to question and doubt their childhood faith. "Let's go deeper, let's put everything on the table, and help them become authors of the next chapter in their own life of faith," urges this devout scientist, after seeing his own children drift away from church as they came of age. "Both of my kids are very decent people," he explains.

> They have good values, they will do good things in the world. So from a humanistic standpoint I feel like they're on a solid trajectory. I worry a lot, though, about whether they have the tools to connect to spiritual reality. Yes, they acknowledge God exists, they appreciate God in their own way. They used to chafe at biblical literalism and use that as an excuse to stay away from church when they were teenagers. Now it's more a kind of God-sized hole in their feeling that there's something else, that this world doesn't make sense all by itself.

Now in college and law school, both children are still single in their early twenties, and their father remains hopeful that they will return to church when they marry, raise children, and settle into careers and families of their own.

Nonetheless, recognizes this conscientious father, "like everything else, there is a practice of faith. I haven't provided them with much of that," he confesses. "So it will be harder for them to develop their faith. There will be more barriers, if they do it at all. And that I feel crummy about, I have to say." His children assure him in turn that "I did them a big favor by not dragging them to church as kids, and they'll have open minds to get with God when the time comes. Very clever!" he smiles. "But I'm still looking for ways to nudge them, very gently, toward living a life closer to God," he concludes, "like I'm trying to do myself."

A long-established family psychologist in Joel's group weighs the balance between trying to hold children in church as they come of age and letting them make their own choices and go their own way. "If you lose kids in junior high school and just let them go, it's hard to get them back. Young Life has a good model, but you can't just bring unchurched kids to church and plug them into a youth group. They're like fish out of water. They feel like they don't fit, and they're right." What can parents and church leaders learn from such failure to fit, and what should they do about it? She replies:

> The church has its own language and jargon, its own hymns and ways of doing things. We need to realize that. Some churches have done that, maybe some too well, and tried to make it much easier. Plug in the kids with Christian rock instead of hymns of the faith. It's "7–11 music," 7 words, 11 times!
>
> We live in a different day. But if you want kids to get plugged into church, they have to feel like they belong. They have to feel like a part of it. You have to be asking the same questions they're asking themselves.
>
> That goes for older singles, too. If all the programs and priorities go to families with young children, there's no place for you. That's a problem in a lot of churches, especially where it's all about the numbers, evangelizing and "reaching the world for Jesus."
>
> What about taking care of your own sheep? There's lots of talk about belonging. But if you're single, or older and single again, it's still easy to feel like you're not really seen or acknowledged. You don't fit, so you don't get much pastoral care or encouragement. You're on your own.

How should churches respond? "Listen to people, pay attention to them. Meet their needs, and people will come and stay," stresses this psychologist. It's a maxim that applies no less to singles seeking companionship and a caring community than to families with young children seeking Sunday schooling, childcare, parenting peers, and support in a world of demanding dual careers and few extended families nearby or longtime neighbors next door.

Is it really harder to keep kids in church today than a generation ago? "Answer yes, and then look for reasons why," replies this psychologist. "That's what we usually do, unless we start thinking about what *we* actually did and felt back when we were growing up," she smiles. What's different now? "Around here there's more sense of entitlement for a lot of young people growing up much better off than we did. Individuation starts earlier now in some ways, but later, too," she reflects. Adolescents in educated middle-class families are driven to achieve through high school and college, she notes, by families with more economic resources but less time for parenting while mother and father both pursue careers. Even warm, engaging congregations attentive to teenagers can "come off as telling the kids what to do" in this demanding milieu, "and they get sick of it. They want to try their own spiritual wings," she thinks, and they find plenty of encouragement to do so in flights of pop-culture fantasy, romance, and entertainment. "They want to get out from under, and not be bossed around. They still believe in God, maybe their own God, but they want to do it their way."

Charges of moral hypocrisy, false authority, and failure to meet spiritual needs aimed at religious leaders and followers by unchurched young adults strike this psychologist as significant but not decisive. "There's plenty of hypocrisy to go around, wherever you look," she points out, including government, business, and the media. "But hypocrisy begins at home," she stresses. "If your parents tell you to go to church, but they don't go themselves, both of them, then that's a real problem: 'How come I have to, but you don't?'"

For teenagers, adds this family psychologist, it becomes more of a problem "if you find no real friends your own age and no one you can relate to, even if it's a good church with good programs." She compares complaints from her own churchgoing children of "no cool kids at church" with her own experience of growing up in a tight-knit church youth group that included close friends in high school. "We had a Christian fellowship club," she recalls with a smile. "We had a young married couple who led it. They were beautiful together. They loved each other, and they really loved us. They inspired us."

Parents need to live out "good modeling" of religious commitment and participation, stresses this psychologist, and they need to attend closely to their children's changing religious experience and understanding as they grow up. "If you are not happy in church, we want to know, and we'll help you change that. Tell them that," she advises, even if it means switching congregations. "Don't ignore them, or put up with their indifference. Respond to them, and help them be responsible."

Charges of churchly hypocrisy from the unchurched can hit home, acknowledges this psychologist, particularly when they aim at user-friendly "seeker churches" high on performance values in attracting newcomers but low on genuine care and continuing concern for members. "Authenticity is at the heart of deciding to stay or leave church," judges this psychologist. "If you truly experience the pastor being the same person off-stage as you hear preaching onstage, then you can accept them. You don't need perfection. You need congruence," she explains. "You can be a great performer in the pulpit—smart, quick, funny. But you need to care and be available, too, and not just for ten minutes at the church door to shake hands after service. You need integrity, even if you're in a big church, and you can hire someone else to do the pastoral care, the singles ministry, and so on. You need to connect, and for that you need a heart for Jesus," she stresses.

"If Jesus grabs your heart as a kid," reflects this psychologist, "you can ask all the questions in the world. You can bang your head against doubt, and still not lose your way. Is this real? Are you really talking with God in prayer? You want some proof or miraculous sign, and that's not going to happen, at least not the way *you* want it." Emotional self-awareness and self-expression have come to the fore in generations since World War II, she observes, and that has challenged repressive forms of church authority both morally and spiritually in the light of conscience. "Many of us in my generation, especially women, grew up with a lot of nonsense about discounting emotions: crappy stuff happens to you, but you just smile and love Jesus, because everything is fine," she grimaces. "Well, it's not, and it's not right to lie about it! I could never make peace with that part, because you have to tell the truth to find forgiveness. But I always knew in my heart, from the time I was baptized at eight years old, that Jesus really does love me. It was the pastor, who loved us and would do absolutely anything for us, who drew us to God. He loved us, we knew that, and we loved him, and so we loved God."

By contrast, churchgoers and church leaders who profess their faith but fail to live it out by loving their own children give them the strongest possible reason to leave church, charges this psychologist: "You were talking a good game, and making your way in the world. But you weren't there for me, so why should I keep living your lie?" That compelling question can lead toward psychotherapy, she counsels, "because we need to make peace with our upbringing and the models that fail us." Faith betrayed and promises broken by those who fail to love and care for us push young adults out of church more directly than intellectual doubt, by this account. So do "models" of competing ways of life, callings, moral character, and community, whether bohemian or bourgeois, mystical or materialistic.

On the other hand, urges this psychologist, churches need to offer space and engaging dialogue for children coming of age to question creeds and weigh commitments. Churches cannot simply rehearse doctrine or ignore it, assert authority or deny it. "You can't just give kids all the answers, before they discover their own questions," she cautions. "You can't just call it God's will or free will or a mystery, when they ask why God would make a world where people have to suffer or go to hell. You don't always get the last word, just because you're the parent or the preacher. There has to be openness and discussion, and there has to be some kind of light shining into this, in our families and churches, for grace to come into it," she pauses. "You have to stand up for the gospel truth, too, not the letter of the law, whether you're a Democrat or a Republican. You have to love your neighbor as yourself, and not just stand by while they separate parents and children at the border."

At the heart of congregational communities no less than faithful families, by this account, lie teaching and learning by example to love God and be loved in turn. This binds generations together in practice. It shapes the integrity of their virtues in mutually attentive, responsible relationships that make their love and their justice both moral and social goods.

FROM BEGINNING TO END

Many older members of Alto Church center their week around an early Sunday service, featuring organ and choir music instead of Christian rock. Some younger families join them there, says one mother, "for hymns we love and want our kids to know, too." This service leads into a ninety-minute Bible study class, led by the seniors pastor, Fred Heiden. It begins and ends in coffee and conversation among several hundred core members, who make up "a kind of church within the church," as one puts it.[26] Birthday greetings and friendly banter at the outset segue into personally detailed requests for prayer. These elicit and update news of illness and recovery, medical diagnosis and treatment, changing states of mind and emotion as well as physical health, deaths in the family along with children wed and grandchildren newly born.

In response to a wife's report to this Bible class that her husband nearing eighty has just been diagnosed with a brain tumor, forcing them to cancel a long-planned anniversary vacation to await a prognosis, Fred Heiden asks, "Yes, and how is *he* feeling through all of this?" Disappointed and worried, she answers, and Fred reflects, "This is when family really kicks in. We really need each other, and we need Jesus in the middle of us, just like he promises, just like he really *is* here in our midst, even when we think he's not."

Doubt and despair can be voiced in sharing such news and prayers. "Cancer, what's that about?" Fred asks in the case of a woman faithfully undergoing round after painful round of chemotherapy. "Why does God permit pain, and let the world go on this way instead of fixing it?" God's in charge, the pastor affirms, and God will heal us, even when we cannot see how or why. "God disciplines us from love, and God heals us from love, even when we don't get it. We don't get it! We don't follow God's will—just like my forty-year-old children still won't do what I say!" protests Fred in not-so-mock exasperation to shared laughter. Then he turns serious, "So God comes down himself! He knows we don't get it. He knows we need Him."

Week by week in the Bible class, Fred Heiden tells the story of a longtime church member in her eighties, lingering at death's door, until at last she can no longer talk or eat. "Why is God waiting around when she is ready to go?" We can ask that question, he acknowledges. "But do we know the whole of it?" he wonders. On a visit to the family the day before, Fred finds the dying woman's "granddaughter holding her hand, stroking her hand and talking to her, quietly and lovingly," as the woman smiles in peace. "So God is doing something wondrous in this family, for this family, here and now," the pastor reflects.

> And God is giving us the wonder of faith that we are really going to be with Him. It's not just lights out, or going to some ER waiting room. It's the promise Jesus makes in John 14:3: "And if I go and prepare a place for you, I will come back and take you to be with me that you also may be where I am."
>
> God has already done it! So once we accept Christ, we are saved! We can stop whining and worrying. We don't need to add anything on. We can stop right here, and thank God.

"Let us pray," Fred Heiden concludes, with a prayer of thanksgiving that rehearses the lines of the hymn opening the class, "It is well with my soul, whatever worldly trials and sorrows surround me, since Jesus has shed His own blood for my soul."[27]

Instead of dismissing death or hiding it behind the curtain that separates actively pursuing "young again" retirement from "getting really old," Fred vows that the church can instead open eyes and hearts across generations in a community of mutual care and recognition of persons as they age, decline, fall ill, and die. It can give them a sure sense of shared continuity to stay in tender touch with one another across the years and generations, with hope for their children and their children's children in this world as well as the next.

"Though outwardly we are wasting away, yet inwardly we are being renewed day by day," Fred Heiden quotes Paul (2 Cor 4:16 NIV) on God's constant renewal of the spirit as a gift of grace that enables us to live our lives in community day by day. In the face of finitude and death we can feel fear and doubt and anger, he allows, but we can trust that God will abide with us. "Jesus will put his arm around us and take us home," he affirms. No one gets over death, but we get through it together in the communion of the church as one body and one family, risen once and for all yet born again and again. "We take nothing with us when we go. What do we leave behind? What lives on? How we love God and each other."[28]

NOTES

1. Steven M. Tipton, *Getting Saved from the Sixties* (Berkeley: University of California Press, 1982); Richard Madsen, "The Archipelago of Faith: Religious Individualism and Faith Community in America Today," *American Journal of Sociology* 114, no. 5 (2009): 1263–1301; Michael Hout and Claude S. Fischer, "Explaining Why More Americans Have No Religious Preference: Political Backlash and Generational Succession, 1987–2012," *Sociological Science* 1 (2014): 423–47; Michael Hout and Claude S. Fisher, "Why More Americans Have No Religious Preference: Politics and Generations," *American Sociological Review* 67 (2002): 165–90; Robert Wuthnow, *After the Baby Boomers* (Princeton: Princeton University Press, 2007), chs. 1–3.

2. Michael Hout, Andrew Greeley, and Melissa J. Wilde, "The Demographic Imperative in Religious Change in the United States," *American Journal of Sociology* 107, no. 2 (2001): 468–500; Darren E. Sherkat, *Changing Faith: The Dynamics and Consequences of Americans' Shifting Religious Identities* (New York: NYU Press, 2014), chs. 1–3.

3. Max Weber, "The Social Psychology of the World Religions," in Hans H. Gerth and C. Wright Mills, eds., *From Max Weber* (New York: Oxford University Press, 1946), 267–301; and Robert N. Bellah, "Religious Evolution," *American Sociological Review* 29, no. 3 (1964): 358–74. Between 1991 and 1998, religiously unaffiliated "nones" jump from 8 percent to 20 percent of all Americans aged 18 to 35 in GSS surveys. See note 39, chapter 1.

4. Mark Chaves, *Congregations in America* (Cambridge, MA: Harvard University Press, 2004); Mark Chaves and Shawna Anderson, "Changing American Congregations," *Journal for the Scientific Study of Religion* 53, no. 4 (2014): 676–86; Mark Chaves, Helen M. Giesel, and William Tsitsos, "Religious Variations in Public Presence," in Robert Wuthnow and John H. Evans, eds., *The Quiet Hand of God* (Berkeley: University of California Press, 2002), ch. 4; Omri Elisha, *Moral Ambition* (Berkeley: University of California Press, 2011).

5. See Marla Frederick, *Between Sundays: Black Women and Everyday Struggles of Faith* (Berkeley: University of California Press, 2003); Mary Pattillo-McCoy, *Black Picket Fences* (Chicago: University of Chicago Press, 2013); Richard L. Wood, *Faith in Action* (Chicago: University of Chicago Press, 2002); and Omar McRoberts, *Streets of Glory* (Chicago: University of Chicago Press, 2005).

6. Cf. Hout and Fischer, "Explaining Why More Americans Have No Religious Preference"; Cary Funk and Gregory A. Smith, "'Nones' on the Rise: One-In-Five Adults Have No Religious Affiliation," Pew Research Center, October 2012; and

Gregory A. Smith, Alan Cooperman et al., "U.S. Public Becoming Less Religious," Pew Research Center, November 2015.

7. Median house prices in this Silicon Valley suburb neared $2M by 2020, median rents rose above $2,300 per month, and median household income topped $160,000 per year, climbing over $235k for married families and dropping below $76k for nonfamily households. Most adults are married (55 percent), one in three never married, and one in nine divorced or separated, with a median age of thirty-eight years and 80 percent of adults under age sixty-five in a population 67 percent White, 15 percent Asian, 13 percent Hispanic, and 5 percent Black. Seventy percent of adults hold college degrees and 40 percent advanced degrees, with most working as educated professionals, executives, managers, scientists, and specialized technicians, according to U.S. Census Bureau data from its 2015–2019 American Community Survey 5-Year Estimates, https://worldpopulationreview.com/us-cities. Material quoted and paraphrased here and below is drawn from repeated rounds of participant-observation in this congregation in Silicon Valley in 2017 to 2022 and related research for Steven M. Tipton, *The Life to Come: Re-Creating Retirement* (Nashville: Wesley's Foundery Books, 2018), ch. 4; including interviews recorded with church members, leaders, and partners in selected service projects and congregations nearby. I am grateful for their generosity of attention, honesty, and insight.

8. Cf. Robert D. Putnam, *Bowling Alone: The Collapse and Revival of American Community* (New York: Simon & Schuster, 2000); Robert Wuthnow, *Loose Connections: Civic Involvement in America's Fragmented Communities* (Cambridge, MA: Harvard University Press, 1998); and Robert Wuthnow, "Reassembling the Civic Church: The Changing Role of Congregations in American Civil Society," in Richard Madsen et al., eds., *Meaning and Modernity* (Berkeley: University of California Press, 2002), ch. 10, on larger Protestant congregations with more diverse programs and activities attracting more mobile Americans with looser social networks and institutional ties in the course of their more varied "spiritual journeys."

9. See Perry Miller, *The Life of the Mind in America* (New York: Harcourt, Brace & World, 1965), Part 1; Timothy L. Smith, *Revivalism and Social Reform* (Nashville: Abingdon Press, 1957); George Marsden, *Fundamentalism and American Culture* (New York: Oxford University Press, 2006); John Howard Yoder, *Body Politics* (Independence, IN: Herald Press, 1992); and Rick Warren, *The Purpose-Driven Church* (Grand Rapids, MI: Zondervan, 1995).

10. Cf. James Davison Hunter, *American Evangelicalism* (New Brunswick, NJ: Rutgers University Press, 1983), ch. 3; Christian Smith, *American Evangelicalism: Embattled and Thriving* (Chicago: University of Chicago Press, 1998), chs. 1–4; George Marsden, "Preachers of Paradox," in Mary Douglas and Steven Tipton, eds., *Religion and America* (Boston: Beacon Press, 1983), 150–68; and Dan Merkur, "Mysticism," *Encyclopedia Britannica*, 2019, on psychologized counseling and pastoral care as rationalized forms of mysticism mushrooming in many world religions, www.britannica.com/topic/mysticism.

11. See chapter 6 for distinctions among "church-sect-mysticism" types of Christian institutions, as formulated by Ernst Troeltsch, *The Social Teaching of the Christian Churches* (New York: Harper & Row, 1960), vol. 2, 993–1013; and elaborated

in Robert N. Bellah, *Habits of the Heart* (Berkeley: University of California Press, 2008), 243–49; and Steven M. Tipton, *Public Pulpits* (Chicago: University of Chicago Press, 2008), 424–42.

12. Cf. Donald A. McGavran, *Understanding Church Growth*, 3rd ed. (Grand Rapids, MI: Eerdmans, 1990); Rick Warren, *The Purpose-Driven Church* (Grand Rapids, MI: Zondervan, 1995); Dick Staub, *The Culturally Savvy Christian* (Hoboken, NJ: Jossey-Bass, 2017); and Stephen Ellingson, *The Megachurch and the Mainline* (Chicago: University of Chicago Press, 2007) on church growth, seeker-friendly churches, and "Christianity Lite."

13. Cf. Christian Scharen, *Public Worship and Public Work: Character and Commitment in Local Congregational Life* (Collegeville, MN: Liturgical Press, 2004); H. Richard Niebuhr, *Christ and Culture* (New York: Harper & Row, 1951); Stanley Hauerwas, *A Community of Character: Toward a Constructive Christian Social Ethic* (Notre Dame, IN: University of Notre Dame Press, 1981), chapters 4–7; and Charles Taylor, *A Secular Age* (Cambridge, MA: Harvard University Press, 2007), chs. 14–20.

14. See chapter 3, 17–19, of this volume on the cultural interplay of bohemian and bourgeois ideals of selfhood and their institutional framing.

15. Contemporary music in worship proves most popular among those born at the end of the baby boom or beginning of Gen X, rather than millennials, with 22 percent of those aged forty to forty-five in a 1999 survey eager to hear contemporary music featured in a service of their congregation, compared to just 12 percent of those aged twenty-one to twenty-nine; although one-tenth to one-quarter of young adults, depending on denominational tradition, wanted to try "some experimentation" with popular music in worship, and 81 percent of self-identified evangelicals in their twenties liked pop/rock music in general, as did comparable majorities of mainline Protestants and Catholics, according to Wuthnow, *Beyond the Baby Boomers*, 129–31, 224–25. On the obligation to have fun, see Martha Wolfenstein, "The Emergence of Fun Morality," *Journal of Social Issues* 1, no. 4 (1951): 15–25; and Jean Baudrillard, *The Consumer Society: Myths and Structures* (Thousand Oaks, CA: Sage Publications, 1998).

16. Young adults typically see congregational participation and commitment arising from their own choice to seek or follow God instead of God choosing or calling them, reports Madsen, "The Archipelago of Faith," 2009, 1277–78.

17. Robert N. Bellah, *Religion in Human Evolution* (Cambridge, MA: Harvard University Press, 2011), 314–17; and Stephen A. Geller, "The God of the Covenant," in *One God or Many? Concepts of Divinity in the Ancient World*, ed. Barbara Nevling Porter, Transactions of the Casco Bay Assyriological Institute (2000), 286. Cf. Charles Taylor, *Modern Social Imaginaries* (Durham, NC: Duke University Press, 2004), 109–13, on "we the people" grounding the US Constitution in popular sovereignty, after the Declaration of Independence appeals to "the laws of nature and of nature's God" to invoke truths held to be "self-evident, that all men are created equal, that they are endowed by their Creator with certain unalienable rights."

18. See R. Stephen Warner, *New Wine in Old Wineskins: Evangelicals and Liberals in a Small-Town Church* (Berkeley: University of California Press, 1990), ch. 9, contrasting liberal ministers in the pulpit leading the laity in common prayers for

justice and peace among all humankind, and the "elective parochialism" of evangelical church members in face-to-face small groups praying for each other's personal needs and challenges.

19. Cf. Frederick, *Between Sundays*, 10–28.

20. See chapter 1, pages 1, 4, 6–7; Pew Research Center, "Faith in Flux," 2009, 1–8, 12–16, 21–34; and Funk and Smith, "Nones on the Rise," 2012, 22–24.

21. Gregory A. Smith, "A Growing Share of Americans Say It's Not Necessary to Believe in God to Be Moral," Pew Research Center, October 2017.

22. "Relationship Rescue" and "Divorce Recovery" weekly meetings feature small-group discussion after psychologists, therapists, attorneys, and other expert speakers set out "ways to heal and begin putting your life together," along with "Christian psychology video seminars," including a series based on Henry Cloud and John Townsend, *Boundaries* (Grand Rapids, MI: Zondervan, 1992) and *Safe People* (Grand Rapids, MI: Zondervan, 1995).

23. See David Martin, *Pentecostalism: The World Their Parish* (Hoboken, NJ: Wiley-Blackwell, 2001); and Allan Anderson et al., eds., *Studying Global Pentecostalism* (Berkeley: University of California Press, 2010).

24. The prevalence of high-SES friends among low-SES individuals predicts upward income mobility so strongly that if children with low-SES parents were to grow up in counties with economic connectedness comparable to that of the average child with high-SES parents, their incomes in adulthood would increase by 20 percent on average, given the impact on economic inequality of segregation by race and class, according to Raj Chetty et al., "Social Capital I: Measurement and Associations with Economic Mobility," National Bureau of Economic Research, Working Paper No. 30313, July 2022; and Raj Chetty et al., "Social Capital and Economic Mobility," *Opportunity Insights*, Harvard University, August 2022, 1–5.

25. See note 18 above, contrasting prayers for global peace and justice offered from mainline Protestant pulpits, and prayers for one another offered in evangelical small groups and church classes.

26. On the *ecclesiola in ecclesia*, "the small church within the church," spanning movements of church reform, separatist sects, monasticism, and religious orders, see John A. Coleman, "Church-Sect Typology and Organizational Precariousness," *Sociological Analysis* 29, no. 2 (Summer 1968): 56–66; Peter Berger, "A Sociological Study of Sectarianism," *Social Research* 21 (Winter 1954): 469; Harry Yeide Jr., *Studies in Classical Pietism: The Flowering of the Ecclesiola* (Lausanne: Peter Lang, 1997); and Troeltsch, *The Social Teaching of the Christian Churches*, 993–1013, on church and sect.

27. Horatio Spafford, Philip Bliss, "It Is Well with My Soul," in *Gospel Hymns No. 2* (New York: Biglow & Main, 1876), edited by Ira D. Sankey and Philip Bliss.

28. See, for example, Menlo Church, "Lessons from a Thousand Funerals," May 24, 2015, www.menlo.church/sermons; and New Community Church, "After Easter," April 7, 2021, www.anewcommunity.church/sermons.

Chapter 5

Congregating across Generations

Ages and Stages Transformed in Atlanta

Throughout the suburban swath of Silicon Valley, Alto Church aims to bring young adults into "a transforming relationship with Jesus, and authentic community with each other," spanning generations under the roof of an evangelical megachurch with Presbyterian roots, polycentric programs, and doors wide open to spiritual seekers as well as come-outers from mainline and conservative denominations alike. Age-graded services, classes, small groups, and community projects bridge doctrinal and liturgical differences across cohorts with plugged-in praise music and choral hymns, intimately uplifting sermons and diligent Bible study, homeless missions, and divorce-recovery peer counseling. In metro Atlanta, by contrast, a trio of Methodist congregations respond to related challenges by seeking to embrace young adults and flourish across generations in distinctive ways shaped by their diverse social histories in suburban and in-town neighborhoods.

I. SPANNING GENERATIONS

Pine Glen Methodist Church lifts up mutual care and recognition within "life changing communities," attentive to differences across generations that it seeks to honor and bridge. Large, resourceful, and carefully organized, the church welcomes all of God's children to "experience acceptance, affirmation, opportunity, and life transformation" through "ministries to all ages and stages," including adults and children, seniors and youth. Yet generational changes in this affluent postwar suburb of Atlanta have shifted these stages in practice.[1]

"Twenty years ago the seniors knew exactly who they were, and we knew exactly what to do with them," recalls a minister responsible for adults over fifty. "Get them all together in a bus to go to the art museum downtown, or take them to a retreat center on the coast for a few days. Let the ladies bake cookies and run the altar society, and let the businessmen lead the pastor-parish relations committee," she laughs. "But it's not that way anymore." Why not? She replies:

> Now we have seniors in their eighties and nineties, and we have baby boomers turning seventy, in their sixties and fifties, who don't think they're "seniors" at all, or even older adults. They don't feel "old," and they don't feel like they belong with people who do.
>
> They go to museums and concerts on their own, thank you. They drive their own cars to the beach, and they're not so big on church retreats. They want to explore new things, and get involved more actively out in the community, beyond the church. They want to *do* things, not just sit and watch.

In response to these generational changes among baby boomers in tandem with the spread of dual-career, college-educated young families, the church has opened up its programs and widened its partnerships with community centers, schools, and social agencies across metro Atlanta and beyond.

Pine Glen has plunged into helping resettle refugees in a small town nearby that has mushroomed into a remarkably diverse and crowded gateway city for first-generation immigrants. They come from the Horn of Africa, the Middle East, and Southeast Asia. They speak more than thirty languages. There you can stop behind a school bus, notes a church volunteer, "And you'll see twenty children get off the bus, every color of the rainbow, and not one White face. It's a different world, just fifteen minutes from the front door of this church, and it's our world. We can't be scared of it, even if some of us still are."

Besides providing volunteers and funds to these new partners, the church has gathered young adults more actively around core volunteer groups of its own, many led by "younger retirees," to start and sustain key ministries. "We pack two hundred meals and snacks into snack packs every Thursday evening for needy students to take home from school every Friday to help their families make it through the weekend," points out a young minister by way of example. "A dozen or so volunteers can get that done in an hour," she explains. "But only because of a committed core of five or six we count on to organize the packing, and do all the ordering and purchasing. They pick up everything beforehand from the food banks and markets, and they get it all out to the schools afterwards."

The church's mobile soup kitchen likewise relies on a large rotation of volunteers to serve the hungry and homeless in one of the city's neediest neighborhoods. But a core group of volunteers reliably provides expert food purchasing and preparation, which is essential to the program. "We partner with a church downtown to serve hundreds of meals every week on a just-in-time schedule," notes a minister. "Believe me, none of us on staff could make that happen by ourselves." Such concentric circles of church volunteers, young and old, work in tandem with local, metro, and regional partners in a wide range of service programs that Pine Glen cosponsors.

Pine Glen Methodist does not boast the extraordinary scale and budget of Alto Church in Silicon Valley. But its three thousand members, many of them well-educated, well-connected professionals and managers, make it one of Atlanta's largest and most resourceful mainline congregations. It lacks the high-profile "eighteen-to-thirty-five singles ministry" of Alto Church. But it draws three hundred members and visitors every Sunday to a "contemporary worship" service that sets Methodist liturgy to the beat of Christian rock music played by a band of church members led by professional musicians. The crowd swaying to the music here includes more married young adults with school-age children and teens in tow, and fewer singles than Alto Church, especially of college age and beyond. "We're more about young families here," reflects a youth minister, "not because we don't want singles in their twenties and thirties, but because of the neighborhood."

Pine Glen is a suburban enclave of single-family ranch homes built mainly in the 1950s and 1960s, many still occupied by their original owners with their children and grandchildren living nearby. Predominantly White by race and college-educated by class, it draws young families to its outstanding public schools, safe streets, and convenient commutes. Adjoining university neighborhoods offer apartments and congregations that attract more single young adults, including Methodist campus ministries, youth fellowships, and social groups. "Three-generation families anchor this church," notes a longtime member. "That may seem like a throwback, and I don't know how long it can continue, with more of the kids going away to work instead of coming back after college. But it gives us tremendous strength, if you can get everyone to agree on something."

When the church first faced the choice to sponsor refugee families more than a decade ago, they agreed to try it with just one family. That family turned out to be Muslims from Jordan. A month after they arrived and got settled, the family of five came to church with a translator, and "the mother got up and she spoke from the bottom of her heart," smiles a lay leader of the church initiative. "It brought tears to your eyes. By the time she got through, there wasn't a dry eye in the house, and there wasn't any more worrying about whether we were doing the right thing or not. We voted unanimously to go ahead and take families of any creed or color."

Why so? "Put a human face on suffering, and we respond," this layman answers. "It's not a million people at the border, or a thousand who want to come over the state line, and take our jobs and handouts," he frowns. "People here want to help others in need, person to person, just like they help each other. They don't want to 'change society,' or get into politics. They want to make the world a better place, one soul at a time." He pauses, then adds, "We have a big, active scout troop here, and a lot of us really are Boy Scouts, you know. We want to do our duty and help others, and we want them to do everything they can to help themselves. That's what the refugee families do, and that's why we've been able to double down and keep upping our support for them, without strings," he explains. "It makes you feel you're doing something good that will last, that will give people a new life for themselves and a future for their children."

Securing that future and building its long-term support in the church remain concerns for the founding organizers of the refugee program. "We want to hand it on to the next generation," vows one. These continuing commitments in turn lead members of the church to weigh its own trajectory across generations. "The older generation here is joined at the hip," observes this lay leader, now in his seventies. "We've known each other for years, our kids have gone to school and scouts together, married each other. It's almost like a small town in the middle of the city." Can that last? "I hope and pray it does," he answers. "But it has to change, too, and sometimes I worry that things are loosening up, you know, when I see the kids just sitting there listening to the rock band on Sunday morning, then heading out the door. Seven minutes, seven words, seven chords—and a dozen exits."

A youth pastor speaks to such concerns with reassurance. "Loosening up maybe, but not falling apart," she observes. "The Boy Scouts help move furniture upstairs into the apartments for refugees. We do a lot with the kids in classes and activities grouped by age. We're really intentional about keeping them engaged through junior high and high school, giving them room of their own, giving them new places and people to connect with. Like the mentors they can choose in confirmation class, someone older they can share things with like piano or painting, horses or computers. It's almost like having an extra grandmother you get to choose." In response this older lay leader allows, "Time will tell," with appreciation for such intergenerational efforts. "You have to give credit to the church for trying, and to all the mothers doing their all to keep their families on track."

Reaching Out and Holding On

Pine Glen devotes thought and effort to forming its children and holding on to them, particularly in their teens, as well as drawing in young families with children. It engages older members in all these efforts, for example, in low-key outreach to neighbors to share in concerts, BBQs, and local service projects. Retirees often take the lead in daycare and preschool programs. They connect with youngsters in confirmation classes by mutual choice and congenial interests. "More and more now we don't live near our parents. We're both working, and we can't send the kids over to Grandma's house after school," notes Mary Davis, a youth minister. "So it can be a godsend to find folks in church who love children and become like family to you."

Older members of the congregation no longer take for granted continued churchgoing by children of their own and others in the pews. Their willingness to step up in response encourages ministers at Pine Glen. "It's a wake-up call," nods Mary Davis. "They get that we all need to be involved to raise up and train these children, so that they'll be here when they're our age. They'll become who God wants them to be, because we've kept them here." She emphasizes:

> Older adults in the church feel an urgency today, more than ten years ago, to hold on to the children, teenagers and young adults, and keep them close. They're gonna fly away, if we don't really put our arms around them.
>
> That feeling in the older community of wanting to reach out to the kids, and plant roots in them, helps us reach across the age-groups in the church.
>
> For parents that starts at home. My seven-year-old said to me the other day, "When I grow up, I'm not gonna go to church on Sunday." Why not, I asked. "Because I can't think of anybody else in my class that goes to church on Sunday. I think I'm the only one."
>
> She said that, in the first grade! She just dropped it like a lead balloon right there at the dinner table, and my husband and I didn't know what to do. We sat there for a second in silence.
>
> *Q: Then what did you say?*
>
> "Yes, you will. That's what our family does. Because it's important to us. Because it *is* important." That's what my parents would have said to me, I realized. I saw the words coming straight out of my mother's mouth and into mine, coming right through me to my daughter.

This scene in an intergenerational drama suggests her own college years, Mary recalls, as she headed off to help with university worship every week. "I can still remember getting up early every Sunday and being the only person awake on my dark dorm hallway. 'Every week, really?' my roommates would wonder. They couldn't believe that I would do this!"

Echoing in her daughter's declaration, such wonderment underscores Mary's own sense of what is at stake for churches today. Look at in-town suburban neighborhoods built a century ago in Atlanta, she notes, "and you see a church on every corner, because that's what everyone did. Now we all struggle to get people to care enough to come for one hour, or maybe two. Now, when you can drive! You don't even need to walk like they did then."

In response to such social change and spiritual inertia, Mary Davis reflects, churches can and should attend to the goods inherent in congregating. "People do want to be known. In bigger churches it's even more important to pay attention to this, and help people get to know each other, because I can't know everyone." Look at service projects, she suggests, especially one-off projects like the church's annual Habitat for Humanity "build" or a weekend "super event" like the one that draws hundreds of people to Pine Glen once a year to pack thousands of meals for Africa.

"Do something together as a team, like picking up or delivering food, and you bring people together. It's not just men driving trucks," Mary smiles. "They look forward to doing something else together the next time. Maybe they start their own Bible study class on Saturday morning or Sunday after service. One group like that meets Saturday mornings at 7 am at Herb's house, men in their forties to seventies. He's retired, and they'll talk about work and retirement, he says, along with everything else."

Where does the church fall short when it comes to inspiring and caring for its members across generations? "Parents in their forties and fifties are on our rolls, but we don't know a lot of them, because they're not around," replies an associate pastor responsible for programs across age-groups at Pine Glen. "They're incredibly busy at work, and taking care of their kids, driving them everywhere in junior high, trying to keep track of them in high school. They want the church to help with their kids and fit into their schedules, but not make demands on them," he reflects, after fielding protests from a mother over required confirmation classes crowding her daughter's sports schedule. "I couldn't believe it," he marvels. "Church is just another extracurricular activity!"

Age-specific selective participation also shows up, finds this associate pastor, in cases where "the little children bring young parents back to the fold" of daycare, preschool, and Sunday school classes. Then parents of older children sometimes tune out and drift away. "Especially for midweek events, you see that gap between parents with young children and retirees. The ones in the middle are not there. That's a challenge for us," he recognizes. "We're working on it. But so far we haven't seen a flock of forty-year-olds fly back for dinner and fellowship on Wednesday nights."

One good sign for the future is a Sunday Bible class of some twenty-five couples in their early thirties with young children. "They're really tight," notes Mary Davis. "Every weekend they're over here with the kids together in the playground behind the church. They do birthday parties together, and retreats. They all come when we baptize their children." Their church life overlaps with their social life, she observes, even though most of the women work outside the home, and "we don't see so much of them during the week. Sometimes they skip worship, but they all come to Sunday Bible class, they volunteer, they contribute financially. So we're trying to rethink and respond to them while we stay the course," with an eye to better appreciating age-specific groups and activities for these young adults even when such appreciation seems to tug against common worship that aims to embrace and center the church as a whole.

Pine Glen has dramatically extended its outreach and service beyond its local community to missions that welcome refugees, feed the hungry across Atlanta, and support a school in Africa. At the same time, it wrestles with how to bring the wider world into the church. "That's a challenge for us," acknowledges a youth minister, "Can we learn about other religions? Can we learn from them, and partner with them? Can we face problems of social change and sexual identity, for example, in the debate over marriage equality? That's hard for us," he admits. Theological and moral, such disagreements in the church can cut across generations. "Some parents of teens really don't want us to talk about controversial stuff, even though it's all around the kids, and it's in the churches, too."

While Methodist pastors elsewhere struggle over performing same-sex marriages and ordaining gay clergy, and the denomination divides over related policies and principles set forth in the United Methodist *Book of Discipline*, some parents at Pine Glen prove all the more determined to protect their children by agreeing, "We should love the sinner, but don't be one of them," notes this youth minister, "and leave it at that."

> Go any further and [for them] it's as if you're saying, "It's okay to be gay," just like "It's okay to do whatever else you want to do." That's hard to take, when the beauty of the church comes from our freedom of conscience to wonder and keep learning about what God wants for us, and what God's love means for us.

"Protect your children, and trust your pastors, too," urges this minister. "We can trust one another and take care of one another. We can live with differences. Most older members of the church feel that way," he observes gratefully. "They are peacemakers. 'Come on,' they say, 'we love our grandchildren, straight or gay, and we love our church.'"

Thus questions of how congregations can better enable and inspire those entering youth or adulthood become matters of intergenerational relationship, dialogue, and participation in practice. Distinctions between "the church and the world," even in the most traditional or sect-like congregations, prove paradoxical. The larger society's difficulties and divisions enter into the church through its own members' socially situated experience, intuitions, and interests over generations, even as their common worship, convictions, and ideals of what makes life worth living go out with them to inspire their work in the world and inflect their way of life, if not to transform society.[2]

"Depart and Serve," urges a sign posted at the exit of the main parking lot at Pine Glen Methodist. "It may seem sappy or preachy at first," allows a longtime "snack pack" volunteer. "But it's actually a prayer that gets to you after a while, about what we can do and who we can be, by the grace of God." Liturgical music colors such prayer and carries this dialogue across generations, at once modulating the moods and motives of worship in church and amplifying the felt impact of prayer in the world of everyday life between Sundays.[3]

Worship in a New Key

"We're not playing for a house full of eighteen-year-olds," points out Pine Glen's director of contemporary worship, a deft guitarist in his mid-thirties who grew up sitting beside his mother on an organ bench in his father's church. "We're playing for who's here. That's a mix of teenagers, younger kids with their parents, and some older folks who just like the music," including baby boomers.

What sort of music? "Not just Christian rock," Andy Hall replies. "It's not just what we think people want to consume. We're not a cover band pumping out million-dollar commercial Christian music every week ad nauseam. It's more about what's authentic, what rings true. So I listen for the beautiful truth in scripture, the poetry in liturgy. I try to bring that together with what we're passionate about." By contrast, Andy says, more conventional evangelical seeker-churches tuned to young adults too often turn out "hollow, cheesy, cookie-cutter Jesus music" that deserves derision as the backbeat of "hypocritical, inauthentic religion."

At the same time, Andy suspects, too many local congregations find themselves tempted into "the comparison trap" of trying to mimic the high production values and shoulder the high costs of contemporary worship found in evangelical megachurches and TV programming. "It's hard work, especially if you don't have the budget," he confesses. "You need to feel a call, and you need to work your butt off," orchestrating services, rehearsing music, building sets, and programming lights and video. Moreover, if young adults raised on *American Idol* want worship designed to win a TV talent show, Andy concedes, they can find it nearby in metro Atlanta. "Go a few miles down the road to Passion City or Northpoint Church, and you can hear the people who wrote the songs on TV and won the Grammys. We can't compete with that."

What guides the making of contemporary worship at Pine Glen? "Don't shove things down people's throat," Andy urges. "If there is a spark of the divine in what we're doing, allow people to connect to that themselves. That's much more powerful than trying to argue them into it with all the reasons why this is true. That just turns people off." Likewise for high-pressure, emotionally manipulative altar calls, Andy judges, since they "distract you from hearing the real beauty of hymns like 'Just as I Am.'" True art overcomes sacred-secular divisions, as he sees it, which widen when worship gives way to entertainment for the sake of church growth. "Look at the comments under PreachersNSneakers," he notes, "and you see one person after another laughing at these hypocrites," for sporting thousand-dollar basketball shoes on the stage of televangelism and megachurch media streaming.[4]

On the other hand, pointing toward the mainline churches, Andy concedes, "There *is* a lot of legalism in the church today, a lot of rules. *And* there's also grace and a calling to be better than we were. That can make us uncomfortable," he thinks, and lead in turn to the unchurched dismissing real human possibility as churchy moral hypocrisy and cheap grace. "The power of positive thinking tells us we can be whoever we want to be. 'Just do it!' Well, maybe I don't want to be reminded I'm not really who I pretend to be on Facebook," he suspects. "So the church has its evils that it needs to work on. *And* we need to look at our own excuses and self-deception, too."

Young adults' skepticism toward organized religion today has deep roots, Andy believes, since "it goes back to the idea that churches try to control people. 'Do this, or God will punish you and send you to hell.' It's the old carrot-and-stick routine of following orders to get to heaven and stay out of hell. But it's much harder to scare kids today, because they don't really believe in that God anymore." On the other hand, instead of promising, "God will make you happy and successful if you come to church," Andy wants the church to speak the truth of God's love: "We have been given so much. In response to God's love, let's come together to thank God and follow God by the way we live."

> Get out of your bubble, and come into a community that goes beyond your selfish experience on earth. Come and take part in the Body of Christ, and you will be enriched by giving, not by getting more money. Wake up to your privilege. Share the gifts you have been given. Make the world better, especially where people bearing burdens need help, instead of holding up White Jesus and telling them to be more like us to make their life better.

Lift up the gospel truth in a new key that rings true to the experience of a new generation, Andy sums up of his sense of calling, as he prepares each Sunday's service, starting with scripture, then rearranging traditional hymns, and working through new releases of contemporary Christian music. "I listen to a lot of bad music that way," he laughs. "But I need to keep up to make good choices. I like to think we're pretty diverse in musical style, but style is less important than message," he explains. "We almost never play any hit-single fundamentalist fist-bumpers you'll hear on contemporary Christian radio. But you'll hear us play some of the deeper cuts coming out with really beautiful modern psalms. I'm looking for that gorgeous poetry wherever I can find it, because music sticks with us. People don't go home humming the sermon."

Many young adults today affirm their own personal religious beliefs, Andy recognizes, and they practice their own faith in their own way. "Pray on your own every day," he agrees, "take a walk in the woods, and thank God for creating this wonderful world. But praying and singing together in one voice in one space can be so much more powerful," he adds. "Nobody can do it all by themselves. 'Preach faith until you have it, and then when you have it, you will preach it,' like Wesley said.[5] Some Sundays I have a hard time singing these songs," he admits. "But there are three hundred people out there singing for me, until I can sing again. That kind of community is beautiful, and we need it. Go to the source, *then* go out and pray and commune with nature on your own. There's something in a body of believers that transcends your own body and voice."

Growing up with spotty church participation and scant religious formation underlies the conviction of many young adults today, Andy argues, that they need no congregation to practice their personal faith. "That's why we moved modern worship from the same time slot as Sunday school, so the little kids can go to children's church, then come back and join their parents for worship. Do it together, and the kids learn how to worship from their parents," he promises. "Singing hymns in your mother's arms, praying alongside your father. That sticks with you for the rest of your life, and you want your kids to have that feeling, too."[6]

Much of the responsibility for intergenerational worship rests with parents, Andy contends, but it rests with churches, too. Age-grading can go too far in congregational life, especially in large churches with plenty of resources and programming. "We need to break down the silos," he proposes in terms that resonate with the criticism of age-grading in Alto Church. "Parents and children need to go to church and worship together," he urges, even if congregations pursue distinctive classes, programs, and events for young and old from toddlers to seniors.

Congregations also need to break down their walls against the surrounding society, Andy Hall argues, insofar as church members see themselves set apart from the world and set above the unchurched. "*In but not of the world* doesn't mean it's damned and we're saved," he points out. "You can be a good person without going to church. But humanity is good because of God, because of the goodness of Creation, and some people seem to let that goodness shine through more than others." Taking part in a community of faith can inspire and enable us to do that, Andy stresses, if we let it. "We're all created in the image of God," he affirms, "and if that's good enough for you, go for it. But for me the community makes it possible to live that out, not just say it. How much better can I be if I'm consciously trying to follow the way of life Jesus leads, and trying to serve the people he loves? The church can support my effort and strengthen my awareness. Yes, we can be better, and most of us need help to do it."[7]

To the contrary, some "houses of worship can be echo-chambers of hate and self-righteous anger," Andy charges, and fugitives from such harmful sectarian intolerance "probably can do more good on their own. We're called to be holy and set apart," he allows, "but we're also called to go out into the world, not run away from it. Go out, speak truth in love, and let your light shine" (Eph 4:15). Young adults are open to that call, Andy senses, and they need to answer it. They also need a church community that enables them to grieve and mourn, he adds, instead of making them pretend to be relentlessly upbeat. "Songs of lament and the story of Job show us that God doesn't dwell just in the happy moments. There's real pain in the Cross, and there's no redemption without it."

Such pain and difficulty have sharpened for many young adults today, Andy Hall observes, faced with stiffer challenges in finishing school and starting careers, courting and marrying, settling down and bringing up children. "Onward and upward isn't working for everyone," he says. "That's where the church can be poised to connect with this next generation if it pays attention. Don't blame the kids for not showing up because they're selfish and lazy," he counsels. Instead of working to "make more stuff, get rich, or get to the weekend," many young adults today want to work to "make a better, fairer world for everyone," not just survive in this unfair and daunting economy.

"The church has to pull its head out of the sand," Andy urges, and discern the difficulties young adults face in living out the aspirations they hold dear. "A lot of them aren't making it in the job market or the big corporations. Most of the little startups fail, and you barely get by in the gig economy. How can we get with young people and help them do things together?" Churches need to stop worrying so much about themselves and ask better questions about who lives next door and what they are doing instead of coming to church.

"It's time to get nimble," Andy sums up. "Get up and get going. Let's show what we can do with a generation of world-changers."

Songs of love and loss, sunshine and stormy weather, cross back and forth over sacred-secular lines, Andy believes, in ways that express the spiritual dimensions of experience young adults share at a rock concert or symphony, at dinner with close friends, or camping out in the wilderness. "We're over the days of going to church out of obligation, because you're supposed to, and plenty of young people think they're okay without it." Instead of finding fault with this shrugged-off sense of churchly duty, Andy asks, why not respond by affirming and engaging their spirituality? "Say *yes and*, not *yes but*."

"Let God smile on this," prays Andy. "If we're really bearing light, then we can lean into the community we find around us. We can invite people around us to lean into their own spiritual experience and examine it. *Why* do you feel like you're in a holy place under the stars but not in church? Why? And what happens when that magic moment passes? Then what?" Even in Pine Glen's updated calendar of modern worship, Andy observes, they often include a full liturgy of confession and Communion to help spark these questions. "What are we saying when we confess? When we say the Creed, what do these words mean?"

This tack also offers a path through cultural-political polarization between self-declared liberals and conservatives. "I have die-hard socialist friends who hate the reactionaries who call all Muslims terrorists, but they feel like maybe all Christians *are* bigots and bullies," he laughs. "Are we getting punished because we deserve it?" For all their commitment to peace and justice, Andy thinks, mainline churches in particular must recognize, "We helped make the mess, and we need to take the lead to clean it up," by putting time, money, and service into making a more peaceful and just world, especially for the neediest across town, not only across the ocean.

"I can't fault people for being down on the church," Andy concedes, "as long as we do disgusting stuff in God's name, you know, hurting the little children, or backing tax cuts that rob the poor and give to the rich, as long as we get our little cut." He frowns, "Maybe we should just try to be nice to each other, and leave God out of it, instead of doing evil in God's name, and praising evildoers for being godly."

What should the mainline churches do instead? "It's on us in the church to work for good with our heads down. That's true for liberal Christians in particular," Andy Hall attests, "especially when the good lies in one direction and the denomination seems to be going the opposite way," for example, on issues of gender justice and marriage equality in United Methodism. "I talk with young people ready to leave the denomination, and I can't question their experience of betrayal. But I can tell them I believe that staying and struggling in love is the best way to work for change."

In their stance toward young adults in particular, Andy thinks mainline churches need to get back to their own roots to revive their worship and discipleship, not only their music. "We need to be true to who we are," he sums up, "not to some evangelical megachurch model, just because it seems to work better on young people.[8] Let's not sell our soul trying to pump up the body. We've co-opted some of that, and now we're reaping some of the not-so-hot rewards. We need to figure out who we are once again," with appreciation for the broad span of Wesleyan tradition across Anglican, conciliar, and connectional church currents as well as evangelical, pietist, and revivalist movements.

"Our greatest gift is our story, so let's tell our gospel story," urges Andy, "instead of trying to figure out some brand-new story we think everyone wants to hear," in order to sell a made-over church brand. "We need to tell *our* story, and let our passion and centeredness come through, because this is *the* story that connects us all. Let this be enough, and let people come to this story on their own path. Let them connect to it in their own way," Andy concludes. "For a tradition built so solidly on a mystery, we sure like to say it has all the answers," he smiles. "If we let people lean in to that mystery to find the answers for themselves, they will."

Sharing Church

"Sometimes going to church is just not worth it," acknowledges Ed Stevens, Andy's closest collaborator in planning contemporary worship at Pine Glen. "Kids can feel that way when we don't get worship right." What makes it right? "When it's balanced between participation and performance," sums up this youth minister, as Andy nods in agreement. "It's made by hand. It's personal, and it tells a story you can get into and share. It's doesn't have to be perfectly polished. Just be good enough so you're not distracted by hissing audio or blurry video."

Participation in common worship is an inherent good, by this account. Professional performance cannot replace but can imperil it by turning congregants into audience members. "Belonging brings together the gifts of the people," reasons Ed, "so you have to find out who's in the community, and what gifts and concerns they bring to church. It's a kind of potluck, where we get to ask ourselves, 'What can I bring that adds to the community and affirms who I am in community?'" That inviting question draws young adults and college students in particular, Ed points out, "because for years they've been told to wait until they graduate and get a real job, then they can really contribute and change things. It's not so different from what young ministers hear," he smiles. "Wait your turn, and we'll get to you. And by that time you'll be ready to do the same old thing!"

In fact, genuinely reviving rites of worship bridges both chronological and cultural generations, stresses Ed Stevens, for example, when young and old at Pine Glen join in to "sing songs and do things that challenge us to go out and live the gospel: 'God's part of this, grab my hand, and let's go!' That's not just for young people. A lot of grandmothers feel that way, too, and it goes for worship and mission," he attests. "That doesn't mean you have to do Bible study with your parents. But how about praying with your kids, or learning how to frame a house with a retired carpenter at Habitat for Humanity?"

Some older adults have more time and resources to devote to such shared service, Ed notes, and they can teach twentysomethings larger lessons. "Some seniors are needy in ways all of us should look at and think about. One in five Americans has a disability. Live long enough, and you'll probably be one of them," observes this youth minister. "But some seniors are living well below their means, and lots of younger people can learn from that." How so? "Because living more simply can give us back some time. It can free us from hurrying so much to get ahead, and worrying so much about making ends meet."

Pine Glen today looks affluent and well established to outsiders, allows Ed Stevens, and most of its young families are financially secure. But not all are affluent, he adds, and the church "has weathered financial storms to get here. People pledged their own mortgages as collateral to build this sanctuary" a generation ago, and that unselfish spirit remains a key part of the church's challenge today. Younger generations often feel cheated in facing a less promising economic future than their postwar parents, he notes. They need to open their eyes wider with help from the church, he urges, "to see how just how rich we are. We're in the richest one percent of people in the world if we're making $50,000 a year in the USA today. We're privileged, so let's share it to do for those who don't have what we do. Lift up their voices. Don't feel guilty, don't ignore them, don't blame them."

"Where's Jesus?" asks Ed Stevens. "With us, and with the neediest, so we need to get with them. That's the social gospel. But it's actually *the* Gospel," revealed as a true story of God's love and justice. This story can reach the unchurched and reveal its truth even to those with little religious upbringing, he believes, in a world where "cultural Christianity has lost its clout," and organized religion its mantle of social respectability and moral duty.

"The cultural trappings of American religion stand in the way of experiencing the gospel and loving your neighbor," Ed judges, "or even thinking clearly about Christian tradition, for example, if you're raised with the Prosperity Gospel and the power of positive thinking. Come to church and feel better! Everything happens for a reason, so don't feel sad. Just try harder and make the most of all God's grace."[9] That upbeat message denies sins of social injustice at the root of economic hardship, Ed argues, and it runs risks of cheap grace. It ignores the personal suffering that many young adults endure today, he knows firsthand as a minister called to counsel college students struggling with clinical depression and anxiety. "They feel up against it. You have to get to the top to be safe, and if you don't, it's on you. Be successful! You can worry about being faithful later on, but you don't have to."[10]

Seen in this light, rising waves of the unchurched and the ebb tide of religious upbringing in their families of origin can clear the ground for religious rebirth rather than spread spiritual drift or speed the rise of a secular city. "Don't just wait around for young people to decide to come back to church or not," warns Ed Stevens. "In our baptismal vows for infants, we promise to care for this child. We're promising as the whole body of Christ, not just this local church. There's no such thing as someone else's child. We're all God's children, made in God's image. So let's do all we can to enable people to come back to church when they want to," he urges, "by helping them find out what they *really* want."

Pine Glen has built a full array of programs tuned to young families: contemporary worship, children's ministries, parenting and Sunday school classes; day care and nursery care, midweek Communion service and fellowship dinners for families. "But it all comes down to relationships," this youth minister sums up, "with all the people who love you and are responsible for you in the church. You don't need to feel guilty to be responsible. You don't need to sign on for Bible class or a committee for a year in order to come to church this Sunday. We understand there are seasons in a person's life, and young adults are pressed and pulled in different directions," Ed pauses for emphasis. "We don't want you to come to church because you feel obligated. We want you to come because you *need to*. You need to pray and sing and worship, and you know you can't do it all by yourself. If you think you can, maybe you don't know yourself. How do you ever realize that?" he asks. "Good question! Especially if you want to live a meaningful life, and make a difference in the world. And we do."

Faith in human aspiration, the goodness of creation, and the need for redemption reach across class-bound, color-coded social differences, by this relational account, and they bridge cultural cohorts at odds over spiritual autonomy and religious authority.

II. GROWING YOUNGER BEYOND THE BELTWAY

Intergenerational efforts of church renewal stand out sharply for a minister long engaged in advancing them at Pine Glen and now seeking to do likewise in a smaller congregation farther out "beyond the beltway" in less affluent suburbs of metro Atlanta. At Hillside Methodist Church, she welcomes families with young children leading their parents back to the fold. She gives thanks to them, and she concentrates on responding to their needs. "It's harder than it looks," Karen Bennett notes, "especially when you don't have a big head start," like she enjoyed at Pine Glen. There, some two dozen young couples began coming to services with babies and toddlers a decade ago. "Once we noticed they were coming on Sundays, and not connecting anywhere else, we went around and got their names and emails, and got them all together for dinner. We started a group for them, and it took off. That led to expanding our daycare program for the toddlers, then reworking the contemporary worship service to include more young families."

"Out here I'd love to have lots of eighteen-to-twenty-five-year-olds living nearby," Karen reflects, "in college or out working on their own, and looking for somewhere to go to meet other young singles and couples for fellowship. That's not so hard to do," she says, given a congenial core eager to make new friends, "if you start with small groups, dinner, maybe a class on Sunday." Instead her church is swimming in a suburban sea of strip malls, grammar schools, and aging subdivisions with affordable first homes for working families raising young children.

"What we have here are twenty-five-to-thirty-five-year-olds who are married and both working, and having babies. School-age kids and their parents: that's our fastest-growing group," Karen reports. "They'd like to live closer in, but they can't afford to. They're buying houses near schools. They're looking for full-time day care for the toddlers and preschoolers." How will Karen's church respond? "We can do this, and we will," she vows. "It takes a lot of planning and organization—staff accreditation, state licensing—even to step up from the morning day care program we already have in place. But they're going to keep coming, and they have this need. It's an opportunity, and we're going to respond," she pledges. "You can get into the day care program without joining the church. But it will help bring us together, and we'll get to know each other." The little children will lead parents and church members closer together, even if they don't lead all the parents back to church.

What is Karen's congregation doing in the meantime? "Connecting young parents, and plugging them in to participation and leadership," she replies. "Come in now, and you see younger faces in the pews, and younger people leading things we haven't done before. People in their thirties are leading the planning and staffing committees, and we're out in the local community in new ways." These include a "snack pack" program that provides hundreds of weekend bag lunches to students from needy families. "It's modeled on what we did at Pine Glen," Karen explains. "But here it's for schools in the neighborhood, not way across town," since many local students qualify for low-income school-lunch programs.

Whites, Blacks, and Hispanics each make up a third of the area's residents, in distinct if overlapping neighborhoods. Most of the working poor, largely Hispanic and African American, live in unincorporated areas surrounding the predominantly White middle-class subdivisions closest to the church. "The church is almost entirely White," Karen recognizes, "but we're committed to serving the community as a whole, and that's already changing who we are." She explains,

> In this area there's no community center, because the interstate runs through it. You've got strip malls along the freeway exits, but no downtown shopping district. We're divided into three different school districts, and there's no local high school. It got consolidated into a bigger one miles away inside the beltway. There's no town swimming pool or rec center. We've got five neighborhood pools in five subdivisions, where the kids go to swim practice and hang out in the summer.
>
> So where is our community gathering place? We don't really have one, and we need one. The church can't do it all, but maybe we can help give this place a heart.
>
> All our missionary work is local. It's focused right here! You'll see our name in the local paper for snack packs. It's on posters in store windows for food banks, school supplies, and clothing drives.

Hillside Methodist started a co-op with other local churches for social ministry, Karen reports, "So you'll see our blue T-shirts on volunteers stocking shelves in the co-op food pantry, teaching a class on household debt-management, or answering phones for emergency help to pay your rent or utility bills."

In a congregation of college-educated young parents pursuing dual careers and raising small children, Karen Bennett finds it challenging to "practice what we preach about discipleship," particularly in the form of traditional Sunday school classes. So she is exploring alternatives, including "spiritual practices and exercises" of contemplative prayer and meditation aimed at both young adults and their children. In this effort she sees clear-cut statistical profiles of culturally conservative churchgoers and unchurched liberals beginning to blur on the ground.

> We've started to teach preschoolers to pray with mindfulness. It began with some parents talking with the children's minister. She's a mom who's also a therapist and has training in mindfulness and cognitive-behavioral therapy.

> It's very basic: learning little prayers, concentrating on praying the words, and learning to feel the difference between "still body" and "active body." Listen to music, and write or draw about how it sounds.

Parents have appreciated the children's class so much that they've organized a follow-up for parents together with their children. "We'll start in the fall, when school begins," Karen says. "It's spiritual practices we can learn and do together!"

This marks a good example for Karen of connecting church and local community across generations and conventional differences between cultural liberals and conservatives or secular and sacred spheres. "Don't be too defensive," she counsels. "See what's going on out there. See what young people are doing if they're not in church," she suggests. "You don't have to co-opt it, or resist it. You can learn from it."

Karen likewise considers the case of an old college friend, raised Methodist, who left church in his twenties and has not returned, "He started taking a yoga class last year. It meets every week, at the same time, and he won't miss it. He talks about what his teacher says, and what he's learning from it."

> I said, "Wow, that sounds a lot like what I do every week! Except I'm not stretching, and I wear a robe."
>
> He said, "Oh, it's not like church at all.' Then he thought about it for a minute, and says, "Yep, it is. Except I'm doing something physically, and the teacher will address me personally sometimes, if something comes up in the middle of an exercise. We talk about it then and later, too."
>
> It's a small group, so he can talk and explore his own life more, rather than just thinking about it while sitting in an uncomfortable pew for an hour, and having to recite the Creed and say things he may not believe.

Karen then reminded her old friend that worship includes not just sitting but standing and kneeling, singing and chanting, in ways that change bodies and minds, sometimes surprisingly, if not always miraculously. Small reflection groups in congregations like her own, she added, can nurture self-exploration, self-expression, and mindfulness, too.

Is there a ministerial moral to this story? Yes, Karen Bennett answers by posing a question of her own, "Is this worth my time?" That's a good thing for people to ask about going to church and taking part in a faith community, she judges.

> We should accept that, encourage it, and not feel threatened by it. We should encourage people who feel like they're on a spiritual journey, even if they're not sure where they're headed, or how to get there.
>
> They're working hard five or six days a week. They want to be engaged spiritually on some deeper level. If we're not serious about that, they don't want to waste their time here, just going through the motions. They can do better at yoga class, or sitting at Starbucks plugged into a motivational podcast.
>
> Everyone wants community, but finding it isn't so easy. More people now are brought up in cities and suburbs with their real families spread out across the country. They leave home, and their "family" becomes the people they find to surround themselves with at school and work.
>
> "Do you really want a relationship with me, or do you just want another person in the pew and another dollar in the plate?" I'm aware of that transactional default, and needing to connect instead. Most young adults aren't just looking for another casual friend like the ones they already have. They're coming to engage their minds and hearts, and share something deeper.
>
> If you're looking for a church to become part of, you want to know you'll be missed if you're not there. We don't want to grab onto them, and be oppressively welcoming. But we do want them to know we will hold them close, so we need to open our arms and our hearts to them. We need to make room to do that, and not be hurrying to get them signed up and onto a committee as quick as we can.[11]

"Full inclusion" has become a buzzword in Methodism now, Karen Bennett says with a half-smile, "but it's not just about the question of whether we will let gay people get married in church and ordain them as ministers. The larger question, especially for young adults, is whether we will be truly open to everybody. If we won't, we're denying the world we live in, *and* we're denying the goodness of God's Creation. If we do that, we'll drive people away from us."

If the Methodist church is forced to choose between good and bad rules over "full inclusion" and "marriage equality," Karen Bennett vows, "then I choose the good rules. But I'd rather not focus on fighting over rules, and most people in the church feel that way, too." They don't want to bargain for false compromise or forced unity, she is convinced. Instead, they want to share living prayers for a spirit of forgiveness and compassion in the face of human fault and finitude. For her, she pledges, "It's Romans (12:9–13): 'Let love be genuine, hold fast to what is good, turn away from what is evil. Outdo one another in showing love and care and affection.'" Genuine communities draw people through love and care for each other, Karen affirms, "not through having great rules, even though you need rules, and they need to be fair. If that love is genuine, I'm going to feel it and share it. I don't get that everywhere, so I'm going to take part in it, and take care of it."

How do visitors and newcomers to a local church come to feel such personal care and share such loving community? "How do they become part of it?" Karen Bennett asks. "It takes more than a meet-and-greet moment," she believes, "even if you're sincere. Most new people hate that 'peace be with you' moment when you turn around and strangers take you by the hand. They hate that! That's why newcomers will come in ten minutes late and leave ten minutes early, to miss that stuff."

What's the alternative? "Bring people together in Communion at the heart of worship," Karen stresses, "not just a little hug at the edge of it. Now we do Communion every week instead of once a month. We give it more time, more movement and feeling, instead of playing it down to lift up the sermon and, of course, the offering," she smiles. No less important, Karen adds, is nurturing relationship that reaches from worship to friendship within the body of the church. "Get to know people one-on-one, get them into small groups," she urges. "But don't force it. No compulsory chitchat or hugging. Let visitors come in and find a place to sit in peace, when they don't know anybody else there," she counsels. "Then create another place afterwards, where people can have a cup of coffee, say hello, and talk for a while. It can be about kids or school, that job interview last week, or your sick father feeling better. It doesn't have to be church talk."

Accept the fact that most twentysomething young adults don't want to go to "traditional" churches, counsels Karen Bennett. "Most of them don't want to do what sixty-year-olds like to do, or even forty-year-olds with children. Why waste time trying to get them to? That seems futile," she concludes. "Let's put our energy and resources into imagining something new, and creating it together with a new generation."

"How do you connect person to person with this or that twenty-year-old?" Karen asks. "Probably not by trying to get them to come to your traditional 11 o'clock service." What if you don't have a "contemporary worship" alternative? "Okay, then what about a small group with other singles in it," she suggests, "talking about what's going on in their lives? What are they already interested in, involved in?" she wonders. Arts, sports, books, service projects, spiritual connections in your everyday life? "Go out there and do the things you like, find other people who like doing those things, too, and make community with those people," she urges. "You're not reinventing the wheel, or doing things you don't like just to try to get people in the door. If you like to run, start a running club in the neighborhood, and see who wants to join you. Go running, and get to know each other. It's not aggressive, it's not oppressive. You can even run by the church!" She laughs, "Put out the word, and invite them in."

Generational differences run through neighborhoods and churches alike. "How do you do ministry in the suburbs," Karen Bennett asks, "when there are lots of different kinds of suburbs," by generation and stage of life as well as race, class, and ethnicity. "You have to ask, 'Who are we?' Especially if the area is not all one age or social background, and there's not much of a community center already established there."

The same holds true in the case of the Methodist denomination, Karen suspects, as it struggles with continuity and change across generations, not only across liberal-conservative divisions. "We've worked so hard to hold the church together that we've sort of straddled the middle for the past forty or fifty years. We've done that so well, promising all along that eventually we'll get it right. Now it turns out that we've gotten it wrong, particularly for younger folks who aren't so 'traditional' on gender issues," she acknowledges in the midst of divisive denominational struggles over gay rights, ordination, and marriage equality.

"Actually, we've done a lot right, but you can't just go around explaining that. You have to let your light shine in the local church," Karen concludes. "That's not so hard for us in this pretty progressive neighborhood with lots of young families. But it's not so easy for everyone," including congregations in in-town neighborhoods rich in same-sex households and rainbow flags, not only in culturally conservative exurbs fervently opposed to progressive peace and justice.

III. COMING HOME TO INTOWN CHURCH

Walk through the wide-open glass front doors of Intown Church on a Sunday morning, and you'll smell fresh-baked scones along with French roast coffee. You'll hear Van Morrison celebrating "Days Like This" on a sparkling sound system instead of Bach or Wesley on the pipe organ. "We like to start with radio music," explains Pastor Wendy with a smile, "not too noisy but warm and welcoming, like coming home."

In fact, the sanctuary combines the look of a homey living room and a folksy concert stage upfront, with a Persian rug on the floor under a low altar table, surrounded by a semicircle of musicians' chairs and flanked by two graceful floor lamps, turned on and off to mark the start of service and its end. Raised nearby and now in their mid-thirties, Wendy and Dan, her spouse and co-pastor, are both musicians and liturgists as well as preachers and community organizers. "Lots of hats," he laughs, "but we get to wear them all here," in an in-town neighborhood filled with educated young singles, couples, and families, straight and gay, replacing an older generation of middle-class families and "aging hippies" in modest 1920s bungalows now being remodeled and climbing in price. The church's five-hundred-seat sanctuary and extensive school building have been remodeled, too, after decades of declining attendance and deferred maintenance, by a denomination ready to invest in the church's rebirth and willing to give the new pastors room to find their own way. "They have done their part," says Wendy, "and now it's our turn."

Where did they start when they arrived two years ago? "We wanted to do a church where we could invite our friends," Wendy answers. "A church we'd like to be part of ourselves, if we weren't being paid to show up." Have they succeeded? "We've just begun," she replies, "but we're up to a hundred-plus on Sundays now, mostly local folks" in their mid-twenties to forties, singles and couples, families with young children, largely White by race with some college-educated African Americans and Asian Americans mixed in. Did these locals come from other churches nearby? "Just a few," she notes. "Most of the younger ones grew up in church, then they left on their own or got kicked out for being too liberal or too gay, or wanting to ask too many questions and think things through for themselves."

Former Methodists and mainline Protestants usually drifted away from their childhood churches, Dan observes, while those in more conservative evangelical or fundamentalist churches more often "broke out or were kicked out of churches where we don't ask questions, because the answers are all in the Bible." Many of these neighborhood locals moved to Atlanta after college, in fact, drawn by white-collar or professional jobs, and attracted to an "artsy" in-town suburb with shady streets, short commutes, and a noteworthy gay population.[12]

Mainline or evangelical Protestant by upbringing, many of the church's new neighbors were surprised by the warmth of its hospitality and "nondogmatic welcome" reaching across generations, cultural politics, and gender roles as well as the railroad tracks separating them from a Black suburb nearby. "There's a season of life where people are often out of church," Wendy acknowledges. "That's generational, too. It doesn't bother us that you haven't had a good reason to set foot in a church since you were a kid." Wendy weighs what makes Intown Church different and inviting:

> People who walk in here often say, "I'm not Christian, and I'm not looking for a church. I'm just looking for community." Or, "I'm only here because my friend or my neighbor invited me, and said you were different."
>
> Once you're out of school, out in the job market and working all the time, it's hard to find friends and make connections. It's easy to feel lonely or bored. Where do you go to find community? Aerobics class, a soccer league, a softball team? Maybe that's not enough.

Q: You're different how?

> A lot of our folks actually do think most churches are hypocritical and sexist. They're full of male God-language. They don't care about science or making a difference in the world, and they don't want to engage in questions and doubts. We do. We're a place where you can do good with other people.
>
> And lots of people here really do deeply love the ritual and the liturgy. We're "creative and casual," like we say, but we're also really liturgical. We know that refugees and exiles still long for the songs of their homeland. You still remember singing those hymns and holding your grandmother's hand in a Southern Baptist church, even if that church later cut you to the core.[13]

This double-edged relationship to the church of their childhood figures critically in how young adults join in shaping the congregational community of Intown Church. "It resonates sweetly, but it also hurts," Dan says. "It leaves you wrestling with the grief and pain."

In small discussion groups as well as pastoral care and counseling, church leaders and members are alert to "the PTSD dynamics" of those seeking a way back to church through a past that has left them feeling wounded and betrayed by organized religion. "Some of them sit in the back, near the door, so they can get up and take a break from worship when they need to," notes Wendy. "But at the same time there's something holy and healing in sharing the liturgy you love with your own children every week. We do Communion every week, and folks come back every week. The preaching doesn't have to be spectacular all the time. You can come to the table, and that's why they're here. We count on that!" Wendy laughs, "Because we're more about process and participation than perfection."

Liturgical Formation in a Culture of Consent

Liturgy embraces and shapes the congregational community of Intown Church with an accent on participation. "Our folks get that. Church is about them being together, their presence mattering," Wendy sums up. Coffee for a half hour or so before Sunday worship is "not just about gossiping, it's about meeting and connecting face-to-face." Once worship begins, congregants can go out to refill their cups and bring seconds of scones or biscuits back to the service with them. "We want to break down that boundary between the world and the church. Everything that's here is welcome in the sanctuary. Bring everything you have to worship. You can't upset us, and you can't upset God," she affirms.

"Make a mess, and we can mop it up," Wendy promises. "Bring your kids, because all of who they are is welcome here." That's particularly important at first for many of the church's young parents, she adds, because "they don't trust church enough yet to put their kids in the church nursery. We understand that, and eventually they will trust us. They'll take their kids out for the sermon, then bring them back for the Communion, because by then the kids love it. How great is that?" Wendy asks. "We're forming tiny little liturgical people!"

Blurring if not erasing a bright line between sacred and secular marks a key aim of Intown Church. "You can respect the difference between sacred and profane," Dan allows, "but if the Spirit is at work in the world, then we can share its wisdom and beauty in light of God's word and love for the world." The church's new doors are clear glass, he points out, and "we keep them open as much as we can because we want all the interplay we can create between the church and the community." They built a new wing linking the church with the school and fellowship building during the renovation to "tie the worshipping community into a larger community of care."

They replaced the pews with movable chairs to make the sanctuary a multipurpose space for the neighborhood as well as the congregation. They found a talented set designer to re-create the chancel's look every few months in tune with the liturgical calendar, strong on seasonal colors and light on explicitly Christian symbols. "We want to work with everyone, including people who aren't interested in Jesus," Dan attests, whether they are Jewish, Muslim, Hindu, or resolutely nonreligious. "We want to love our neighbor, and we believe you can do that even if you don't worship as a Christian," in concentric circles of mutual care, concern, and responsibility that ground social ideals of inclusion and diversity in Christian ethics of neighbor-love. Early on, recalls a core church member, "We did a bunch of service projects in the sanctuary, then we just had Communion. No sermon, no buildup. I wouldn't want to do that every week, but it felt like we were doing something different, and it mattered," in joining together to begin anew.

"Just showing up and being present in the world to love your neighbor brings together the worship community and the witness community with everyone else," Pastor Wendy affirms. It sheds the light of experience and reason on scripture and tradition, she explains in Methodist terms. "It brings down the spirit and lifts up the people."[14]

> The Spirit is still living and breathing in the world. So we start off service with something like Van Morrison doing "Days Like This." To say wherever you've been, whatever you've been up to, even if you've been out of church, God is still there in your life. God is still showing up with you. And you've been showing up with God, too—believe it or not—whether you've ever heard of "prevenient grace" or not.[15]

> God is using all these other ways to speak truth in the world. We open with a radio song to connect people's sense of outside-world and church-world. You may know this from somewhere else, but the holy shows up there, too. You are worthy of being here. We're affirming that. Come on in! Lightning isn't going to strike.

> God's wisdom shows up in the world in all kinds of ways. If we have just one image of God, we're putting God in a box. So every liturgical season we do a different representation of God's presence: purple panels lit up like stained-glass windows around the altar for Lent; big white paper flowers blooming for Easter.

More than one kind of music and more than one image of God have a place in Intown Church, affirms an older, married member of the church, and enable it to embrace the whole of God's People. "I love that, even if I wish sometimes for a little bit more prayerful, reverent music playing at Communion than, say, Lady Gaga doing 'Born This Way,'" she admits. "But that's like a theme song for gay rights, and I can accept why it's there." Just so, agrees Pastor Wendy, pointing out that such pop tunes often counterpoint a classical prelude or traditional hymn, not simply to please mixed musical tastes, but to express "the goodness of Creation and the wholeness of Redemption," to accept the world and transform it.

Moreover, the participatory power of familiar pop music can stir a congregation of mixed musical tastes and abilities to sing along. "We have a good choir, but it's small, and we don't have much time to practice," notes one of its members, "so we keep it simple, and encourage everyone to sing along. If you don't know the words, they're printed out right here" in the Sunday worship guide. Likewise, she adds, some liturgical roles are left open to volunteers each Sunday, for example, to help serve Communion. "Every time the kids are waving their hands and saying, 'Me, me, me!' That's wonderful," she smiles. It immerses children in practicing the mystery of the Eucharist in ways that prove performative, playful, and profound. It expresses the universal truth that a small church embodies most clearly: "Everyone is needed."

Opening up the liturgy is just one piece of a larger puzzle of "the old church we had to deconstruct before we could build this new one," Pastor Wendy explains. She refers to "the triad of believing, behaving, and belonging" reordered in ways that recall the "nonlinear, art-form" rearrangement of belonging first in Alto Church to welcome young adults in Silicon Valley.[16] "You belong here just because you're a beloved child of God," Wendy sums up. "That comes first, and coming to behave and believe as members of this community will follow."

A great deal of organizational and administrative work was needed to restart the congregation, Dan notes, but so were "grief work and reimagining, before we could put the old church to rest and really raise up something new." That included downplaying established practices and principles, but not doing away with them. "We kept asking why and why not?" Dan recounts. "We want to be creative and approach things differently, so we're not going to start with listing all the *shalt nots*: No drinking, no cussing, no dancing in here." Adds Wendy,

> We want you to be who you are, and to bring all of who you are into this place. If we have to say "no" to something, we do it individually and face-to-face, not with lots of written rules against this or that.
>
> That can be challenging. We're now in the process of facing problems like polyamorous relationships that come up when you start being gay-affirming.
>
> Most mainline denominations don't have much of that worked out theologically, except maybe what covenant relationships should look like one way or the other: Tell the truth, be honest, take care of others like you want them to care for you. Don't use them. That's real, and it's something people come to us for guidance on."

In response, Wendy affirms, "I don't want our first answer to be "No, don't do that!" I want it to be, "First, I want to listen to you—*and* to God and to Scripture and to the church, and I want us to start a conversation about it," instead of foreclosing conversation by clerical fiat or divine commandment.

Such conversation unfolds within "a culture of consent" that Wendy and Dan set out in terms of a moral covenant, not merely an interpersonal contract. "We talk about it and cultivate it as basic human respect for each other, not just liberal politics" says Wendy. That includes children. "We don't hug kids here, unless they want to be hugged. We offer multiple ways of engaging, and we let them choose, whether to be hugged or high-fived, or do a thumbs-up," she notes. "We don't believe you should be told what to do as an adult, or be in indentured servitude to church committees. You should be free to choose responsibly and give your consent to take part."

Does this hugging norm apply to passing the peace in the liturgy? "We talked that through with everyone after a year of just doing it," replies Wendy. They discussed it in terms of theology and practice, citing scripture and pondering creation in God's image as well as invoking Mr. Rogers. "I like you just the way you are," Wendy sweetly intones, "because God made you, and there's good in you, no matter what." Worshippers agreed to ask first, when in doubt, before hugging and shaking hands. And now they do, reminded every so often of their need for consent and their freedom to choose. "We offer instruction along with invitation," Wendy explains. "We invite you to hug your neighbor or shake hands or just say hi when we pass the peace, and we instruct you to please ask first if you're not sure."

The pastors of Intown Church likewise invite worshippers to consider taking on a new spiritual practice, or renewing an old one, often in step with the liturgical seasons of the church calendar. "We're not here to tell you what you need spiritually," Dan cautions. "But we are here to tell you about this or that practice, so you can choose wisely," be it daily devotions, contemplative prayer, or weekly visits to a shut-in senior. "If you're a head person, try a heart practice, and vice versa. We're offering suggestions, not directives, but we're also encouraging people to stretch themselves as we get to know them better." In that process, Wendy adds, "we push back on the church being here to meet *your* spiritual needs. If that's what you expect, you're bound to be disappointed and let down. We can't know everything you need. That's your work to do with God. Tell us what's going on, tell us what kind of feedback you need from us. We're ready to talk with you and help you discern your path."

Personal moral agency and mutual responsibility go hand in hand, by this account, guided by conceiving membership as discipleship within the story of finding one's own way to "follow Jesus and walk with Christ." Individual freedom of choice becomes incorporated within a community of character formation in liturgical practice, Wendy stresses. "We want you to know you're not alone, and we want you to come to know yourself by coming to know Christ. We're all here to do this together. It's not the church's job to meet *your* needs. It's our job to find out what *we* need and bring it to God."

Remaking Membership

Pastors Wendy and Dan recognize that many church visitors or newcomers ask what the church can do for them in terms of an exchange or transaction—for example, finding friends or feeling better in return for regular attendance and donations—or the self-improvement of completing a course of moral education, spiritual exercises, or cultural literacy. "But what we're really engaged in doing is incarnating the Body of Christ," stresses Dan by contrast. "The world is full of information you can access on your phone. You can hear sermons online, and read books of theology. But you can only incarnate faith together in community. You can try to be a good person on your own, but it's not enough."

Transactional churchgoing, joining, and leaving prove particularly problematic for young adults today, notes an older core member of Intown Church thinking of his own children in their twenties and thirties, because they have "so many more options and demands, too. You've got organized sports, shopping, shows, kids' birthday parties, brunch with friends, going to the gym and working out. Everything's open on Sundays now." At the same time, he notes, "Their lives are so busy, they're always trying to catch up. They're doing chores on the weekend, cleaning the house, washing clothes, doing yardwork, whatever. Career has taken over" the lives of his college-educated children in their twenties and thirties, observes this father. "They're working 24/7. They're online morning and night, texting at lunch and dinner."

Such changing ways of life, concedes this astute parent, "go along with a lot more money and pressure up here" on higher rungs of the job ladder, "while things down below are getting worse." Too many young professionals "have bought into the phony idea that you can have it all," he thinks, but even those who know better find themselves trying to manage too much to do in too little time. "Church becomes just one more thing to do, so what's it doing for you?" he asks. That question has no good answer, he suspects, when upper-middle-class "success is defined by achieving and earning, not by going to church. If you've got an extra hour, go to the gym, earn the burn, and look better, too. Then go out drinking with friends and play cornhole. That's as good as you get to feel," he adds, with a nod to rites of barroom fun and games.

By contrast, the "holier-than-thou" aspect of many American churches puts off educated young adults by its "judgmental, hypocritical side," fears this baby boomer parent, not so much by condemning the barroom vices of old-time religion as marking off selfish sinners in the world from would-be saints in the pews. "Why should I come into a church," he asks, "if I can't be myself there?" Few educated young adults today think of themselves as worldly sinners in need of a road to repentance, he observes. Of his own children, he attests, "In fact, they're good kids, even though they left church in their teens. You can count on them not to cheat, lie, or steal. We taught them to be kind, to be responsible for themselves and their actions, and they are."

Why worry, then, that one's good children no longer go to church? "It's like there's something missing," answers this church elder, "some kind of spiritual awareness or caring. I'd love them to have a relationship with God," he sums up. "But I can't judge them without judging myself. I got away from church when I was in college, and I only came back when my kids got old enough to make me think twice about it. So I'm hoping that aha moment will come for them, too." He pauses, then adds with feeling, "And when I came back with my kids as a single father, there were older people in the church who loved me and accepted me. They cared for us. That's what I'm trying to do now, to pay it back and pass it on to the generation coming up. Go and do likewise!" he urges. "Show people you love and you care."

Many young adults at Intown Church affirm this recognition of communal integrity open yet strong enough to embrace diverse religious backgrounds, move individuals beyond their self-concern, and make members of a living body. "I was raised without church," attests one, "so authenticity and community are what really matter to me," as practical ideals of his own, drawn from hip parents at countercultural odds with their respectable Episcopal and Catholic families of origin. Without childhood memories of church music or hymns to revive, he says, "I can still sit in church, singing along to 'Time after Time,' and find myself crying, thinking of all the people we've lost."[17] Agrees his Methodist spouse, "I like to sing along with the pop music, *and* I appreciate the hymns that connect me to my grandma. I like that balance." More broadly, she adds, "Church connects us. Most of our lives are pretty self-serving, self-focused. Here you can let that go, because it's not just about you. You can pray about your family, pray for everyone. You can tear up. You can re-center and be grounded."

Does authority, true or false, enter into this process of communal grounding and moral re-centering? "Our generation doesn't like being told you have to do this and that, because it's in the Bible," replies this young Methodist. "We don't like the hypocrisy of preaching 'love your neighbor,' while you're actually serving yourself first. We're trying to find some place to belong and feel at home, so we want to know where the boundaries are that we can trust. We want to help set those boundaries, so we can really make them our own," she stresses in behalf of a participatory priesthood of all believers. "Be part of the solution instead of the problem. Don't just stand around outside with your friends and blame everybody else on the inside for the problems," she frowns. "Here you feel encouraged to get into a deep conversation," she nods. "It pushes you to bring the gifts you've got into the mix and get moving together."

Individuals are free as can be to join or leave congregations in the denominational society of America today, Wendy and Dan agree, but genuine membership becomes binding in light of the Gospel truth embodied in a moral community. "You are who you are, and you claim your own identity," acknowledges Dan. "At the same time, this congregation is a Christian church, so we are seeking to follow Jesus, understand his teaching, and live it out in this body."

Where does this lead? "It leads to a good kind of life. That's what we believe, and what we seek," answers Wendy. "It leads us to working for justice for all persons, including gay persons and persons of color, and welcoming everyone equally into the heart of the church," she continues. "It leads to sharing and putting the good of all over the good of self and offering healing and liberation for the least of these. That means questioning capitalism and self-interest, racism and nationalism," Wendy pauses, then smiles. "It's almost as if all this is in a book! Or on a T-shirt!" she laughs. "If it's not for you, if you're Buddhist or nothing in particular, that's your choice. That's fine, and you're totally welcome anyway to come out to our community meals, popsicles in the park, or gay neighborhood meetings."

A committed member of Intown Church weighs its welcoming approach considering his own Methodist upbringing, "We're trying to remake membership for a new generation: 'Don't tell me what to believe, don't push me around.' Don't drown them in doctrine, don't try to regiment them, or march them out of a wicked world into the kingdom of heaven." Intown Church clearly aims "not to fence folks in or out," explains this older church member, while it continues to work out flexible boundaries and caring connections to the neighborhood. "You walk a delicate line, trying to practice what it means to belong to this body of worship as a community of faith. Yes, it *is* all about love, but's it's about truth, too," he underscores, and truthfulness to tradition, reason, and revelation as well as experience, even if the faithful cannot simply rely on revelation, rehearse tradition, or reason once and for all between universal truth and error.

> It's all about people, because we are called to serve God's people, but it's not all about *me* and finding a church to meet *my* needs. Jesus is the way, the truth, and the light, scripture says. Does that mean there's only one true faith, or can we truly find the way and the light through different kinds of faith?
>
> That's still an open question for someone like me, who grew up with sin and salvation, even if our kids know better and think everyone has to find their own way.
>
> "Lord, I believe. Help my unbelief." I still wrestle with that. It's not all just a "construct" we need to figure out in order to put the world together. (Mark 9:23–25)

We can be true to tradition, and re-create it, too, holds this lifelong Methodist. "When it comes down to doing church, be creative," he urges. "There's a big canvas you're free to fill in to show the love of God in the world. We're trying to do that here, to love our neighbors and work for biblical justice." Modern world-acceptance and protean self-awareness come together here with commitment to a community of character shared in learning to see and serve the good in common.

Breaking Bread and Taking Part

The process of remaking membership informs Intown Church's liturgical emphasis on the Eucharist over baptism and confession. "You don't see a baptismal font anywhere when you walk into the church, and you won't hear much about it either," notes a church member raised Methodist. That's no accident, she thinks, in an era when few Methodist congregations are adding new professions of faith by adult converts or baptizing a steady stream of believers newly come of age.

This eucharistic turn represents ecclesial ideals as well as demographic realities. "We are trying to bring down boundaries here," sums up this Methodist, "between inside and outside, believers and unbelievers, saints and sinners." Prayers of confession seem similarly downplayed, in the absence of Methodist hymnals or prayer books at Intown Church. Scant mention is made of them in its weekly worship guide, even when the minister recites them at the Invitation to Table. But listen to the lyrics of many of the pop songs in Sunday services, notes this attentive worshipper, and "you'll hear a call to all the dead and disappointed, and a promise to always be there for you when you feel down and troubled." Lyrics of life's burdens and loss, fears and wounds, give way to hopeful encouragement to "cast aside your doubts and fears," recognize that "we're accepted as we are," and be reconciled to ourselves and others through God's love.[18]

No altar call follows the sermon with verses of "Just as I Am" to tug sinners forward to repent and join the saints, adds this cradle Methodist. But "words of witness" are invited from any and all of those gathered, including silent prayers for release from affliction or addiction, harm or hardship. Younger adults take the lead among worshippers to write down such prayers on cards and post them on a large bulletin board at the back of the sanctuary. However reworked in popular music or psychology, from sin to sorrow or repentance to self-acceptance, human suffering and evil are acknowledged in such liturgical practice, and divine forgiveness and grace are proclaimed. "Imagine a world without war or hunger, with all people sharing all things and living as one," sings this liturgical critic, rehearsing John Lennon's anthem to a world without countries or religion. "Isn't that a picture of the New Jerusalem, and God's kingdom come?" she asks. "All you need is love? Yes, love of God and our neighbor, who is everyone, just like the Bible says," she declares. "Amen! We get it!"[19]

"Ask yourself where the young people are instead of church on Sunday," proposes a devout church member with children in their thirties who left church behind in college. "They're down the street having brunch with friends, talking about love and work, or music and politics. Some of them are even off doing Habitat for Humanity or helping out at the food bank. And they're just as good and loving and caring as folks involved in organized religion," he testifies. In light of this contrast and continuity, consider the Eucharist at Intown Church, he suggests. Baptized or not, all are likewise welcome at the Communion table, because "the Bread and Wine come from the hand of God," not a denomination, to be shared in the universal Body of Christ, not withheld by a parochial body of worship.

Upbeat pop music played during Communion may surprise or distract some church visitors or seniors, allows this keen observer. "But it livens things up. Look at the little kids all excited when they line up and come to the table. Then that serious, mysterious moment, and afterward people hugging on their way back to sit down." A high-church Episcopalian may hold back at the altar rail, he concedes, and a Spirit-filled Pentecostal may hold out for sharing the Lord's Supper in the intimacy of a smaller circle. But here high church and low meet and mix, as members of the church come to feel its liturgical coherence in concert and sense its depth of meaning in practice.

"I feel rested and relaxed after I go to church," agrees a regular attender in her twenties. "It's free-flowing, instead of feeling like I'm doing my duty even if it's an effort." She welcomes that relaxed feeling. So do other young adults, often by contrast to how pressed they feel for time, energy, and attention to get things done over the weekend, since crowded careers and busy households leave them little leeway during the week, even if they are not married with children.

At every Sunday service at Intown Church its members affirm the Creed, Pastor Dan points out. They hear the Gospel and recite the Lord's Prayer, addressed to "Our Maker" and vowing "Thy kin-dom come." On the other hand, he stresses, you need not be a Bible believer or professing Christian in order to come to worship or take Communion at Intown Church. "A scientist who grew up with no church started coming with his wife," Dan recalls. "He was coming for her sake. But after a few months he began taking Communion. Just trying it out, since everybody else was doing it. Then he came up and said he was feeling something, physically, without knowing what it meant. So he was going to keep doing it, if that was okay. Fine, we said, and he has."

Is this new communicant on the road to baptism? "Who knows?" answers Dan. What he is doing, at the pastors' invitation, is occasionally playing music with the choir. "He's a classically trained violinist who's never played pop music," Dan notes, "so this has become a spiritual practice for him. To give up his expert perfection to be present with people singing together in this room. To take part in something he doesn't 'believe in' but he's learning about by doing for the first time, and just maybe experiencing something like grace."

Stressing participation in worship carries over to participation in self-governance. In supervising children's behavior in worship, parents were first left to decide how best to watch over their own children, and only counseled case by rambunctious case. "But when the church playground got really wild," Wendy reports, "we had a big group meeting to collaborate on what to say when, including agreement on language parents can use with kids besides their own, so we're not just saying no or *making* them behave." That informed a larger process of coming to share recognition of good practices among children and their parents over "what goes on where."

"The altar and stage are for worship, not playing around or running around," Wendy sums up, "If you want to be quiet, you can go and get a clipboard to draw and color with your parents in the sanctuary. Or you can go outside if you want to make noise." Marking off the either/or social setting of these practices and activities doesn't obviate the need for act-specific rules and commands, Wendy realizes, but it frames them within the practical virtues of a good way of life in community. "We've tried to base the rules and structures on how people want to live together, asking those questions with people in the room. Then intentionally going further to listen to voices outside the church, not just inside." Participation in common prayer and moral deliberation situates rules within the mutual care and responsibility of a community everyone can share in drawing its boundaries and enjoying its freedoms.

Neighboring

During their first year at Intown Church, Wendy and Dan set out every week to meet forty new people in the local neighborhood around the church. What did they hear there? "People wanted a place for their groups to meet, since there's almost no affordable meeting space available nearby," Wendy found out. "They wanted us to help build bridges, especially between the aging hippies and the up-and-coming younger families in the neighborhood. And what about helping seniors aging alone in their homes with no family around?"

Where have such encounters and conversations led? "We have one of the biggest, most accessible spaces anywhere in the neighborhood," Dan answers. "We already have neighborhood yoga classes and meditation groups meeting in the church basement," led by community partners committed to balancing body and mind without promoting this or that faith tradition in the process. "We offer meeting rooms for nonprofit groups to get together for free, especially local groups for community service or social justice, people of color, and gay groups. We make office space available at bargain rates for people who work at home to meet with colleagues and clients."

The church considered renting out coworking space but decided against it after hearing from locals. "They don't want to rent desks all day," Wendy explains. "They want to have a place to take a break, get up from their computer spreadsheet at home, go out for a walk nearby and meet other people." That prospect has led to plans for a drop-in lunchroom. "Bring your own sandwich, and we'll make the coffee. Come as you are, or make a date to meet someone," Wendy suggests.

These community programs are taking shape in their own right, Wendy makes clear, yet they remain tied to the church as a body of worship:

> We're lining up partners for lunch-and-learn sessions and musicians for little lunch-hour concerts, maybe an arts talk once a week or practicing work-mindfulness meditation with a local teacher. We'll try things out and see what serves the community, whether or not it gets people into church.
>
> We can be your den mother without being your pastor. Sometimes that goes on for six months, then folks come to church. Then they don't come back for another three months, and then they're in. Sometimes they show up saying, "I'm not Christian, I'm not spiritual or religious. I'm just looking for community." Then three weeks later they'll ask me about developing a prayer practice.

Thus belonging comes first, for the sake of social goods that serve the larger community and inhere in its everyday practices. Then believing may follow or not, finding its own way at its own pace.

These moral practices surround and tie into the congregation as a community of worship. They lead some of the church's neighbors and visitors, though certainly not all, toward becoming members of its faithful. "We welcome people for who they are," Wendy stresses. "That's at the heart of our theology. It's not just hospitality. It's not just trying to get people into church. It's trying to get the church into the community, to serve the community. So we offer meeting space for free to groups that help seniors or AIDS patients, even if they're never going to join the church." Why? "Because restoration for the world depends on what's happening out in the community," she replies, "not just what's happening inside the church. Building the kingdom doesn't mean packing the pews full for an hour every Sunday. It means our valuing what you do for the world and helping you do it."

"If all your friends are inside the church," Wendy warns, "you're not following Jesus, because he's out there in the world." Seen in this light, "neighboring" is a spiritual practice. "Learn your neighbors' stories," urges Dan. "Get to know their joys and hopes, their grief and pain. Get outside the house and your own routine, walk around the block and go to the block party." This encompassing, responsive approach has freed Wendy and Dan from too much strategic thinking about church growth and preset programmatic planning to achieve it. "It let us loose to try things out as we go along," Dan explains.

> You're supposed to know your demographic target and fit your niche. But our mix of young singles, gays, and families has grown up naturally. We're a hetero couple in our thirties with two kids in grammar school. So we started by rubbing shoulders with families like ours, and we carried over some older adults from the old church.
>
> Relationships with young singles and gays emerged organically, because people want an intergenerational experience. Single people who don't have kids want

to interact with them someplace where they can be like an aunt or uncle, where I can know them and they can know me.

Other social dynamics are now at work across generations. "Kids can get to know someone older, too," Dan notes, "who's like a grandmother they love and lives around the corner. Parents can find healing from their own childhood wounds from church, by seeing how we take care of kids here, without silencing them or forcing them."

Are there any limitations or gaps in this complementary mix of young and old, singles and families in Intown Church? "If you had told me five years ago I'd be worshipping in a church with no hymnals and children running around all the time and playing on the floor right next to me, I'd have said you were crazy," smiles a middle-aged single woman with years of experience teaching teenagers. "But I've come to see that makes sense in this neighborhood, and that's what it means to do right by this community."

This effort includes drawing parents and others into shared discussions of how to help children calm down in church and play more peacefully outside. "They've learned from that, and so have I," reflects this teacher. "They're quieter, and I'm clearer about being in a community-centered church, where kids feel safe in this space and accepted as they are. I can't wait till we have a youth group and I can help with it." She appreciates the church's commitment to teaching the whole congregation through teaching their children. But she advises, "Don't try to explain everything," for example, about the Trinity. "At some point, it's a mystery, so say so. Don't make up bad theology that they have to reject or unlearn later on. Sometimes just say, we don't know." On the other hand, with so many visitors from different religious backgrounds or none at all, she urges, "Say what we're doing in church and why, what it means in practice, not just in theology."

"Not everybody wants to be around kids all the time," acknowledges Wendy. "We've been talking with young singles, and we're going to try out a Sunday-evening service, just once a month to start, with a local folk-rock band—sung liturgy, no sermon or reflection from us. They'll read scripture, do Communion, and stick around to mingle afterward." Adds Dan, "It's not a singles group. It's not aimed at college kids or competing with the Christian-rock megachurches over in Buckhead. We're building on who's already here in the church and still in their twenties, their friends, and who's in the neighborhood."

Young singles and couples without children have already formed self-selected small groups at Intown Church. They usually meet in their homes or go out for brunch or dinner, free from the childcare support that the church provides young parents. But some of these young-singles groups have now turned intergenerational, joined by "older empty-nesters free to jump in and stay out late," Wendy nods, "so we'll see whether the singles service will fly on its own. We know we don't want to leave anybody out, or shoehorn them into a box, by dividing things up by age or gender. That's why we don't have women's or men's ministries," she notes, then smiles, "although we do have an occasional high tea, where you can dress up and wear a big hat, whoever you are."

Young and old church members agree. "I'm glad we're not so divided here," says a young mother. "Yes, you can't do everything with everybody on Sunday morning, and we have separate Sunday school classes for kids in grammar school and middle school. But other groups get mixed up, so it's not all single or married, or the same age." Accordingly, she reflects, "That's why I hope we don't get too big, where the only people you know are in your small group or class. I don't want to be in a megachurch with a crowd of strangers. I want to be known."

What comes next for Intown Church? "Not getting much bigger, two or three hundred at most," hopes a loyal member in her forties. "But getting to know each other better. Not pushing people too hard too soon. But getting more committed to doing social justice, and doing more of it with people of color and gay people in the lead." What of young adults? "Keep listening to them! Keep asking them what they believe and don't believe, what they care about and wonder about. And what they hate, too, like all the church-growth hypocrisy, and people only counting if they're pledging. Take them seriously. Use your imagination," she urges church leaders and elders. "Lower the entry bars and put participation over performance. Don't be afraid of making mistakes," she sums up. "That's what we're trying to do here. Most churches don't bother, and that's why a lot of us don't bother with church."

The mix of young and old, straight and gay, wounded and privileged, at Intown Church has helped its pastors to "relax our own tactical, technical expectations for building a church, and our own anxiety about getting results." For example? "The young people we have here in their twenties are working first jobs and exploring careers," Dan answers. "They're still dating or looking for that right person, they're not all settled at home or work. They travel a lot. Some of them are doing good in Bolivia with CARE or in the Delta with Habitat. They're not going to be here every week, they're not going to volunteer for everything. They want a place to come home to, and not be pressured or hassled. We have to see that and work with it," he pledges.

How? "If we really do belong here," Dan replies, "we should become more aware of how the neighborhood got this way, how it got divided into two parallel neighborhoods, one Black and one White, by the railroad running through it, just a block away from us. If we do that," he proposes, "it becomes a Holy Spirit project of neighboring to bridge this separation, by sharing our space and resources, and opening our minds. 'Build the Wall!'

Atlanta already did, and we're living right next to it. Let's see what we can do about undoing it."

That is a worthy social goal and moral aim, members of Intown Church agree, especially given the congregation's homogeneity by education and occupation as well as race, for all its diversity by generation and gender identity, stage of life and marital status. Much like the neighborhood as a whole, the congregation consists largely of college-educated White professionals and managers, whether young or old, gay or straight, with a sprinkling of educated Blacks and Asians.[20] So instead of seeking to get bigger on the model of the megachurch, urge core members of Intown Church, "Let's go deeper."

Instead of simply making the church as useful as it can be for its neighbors in affording them space to meet, or as functional as it can be for its own members in teaching their children good moral values and habits, argues a key choir member, "Let's go deeper into the meaning of the Crucifixion and the Resurrection. That's not just about being good and behaving yourself, or using the pablum of positive thinking to pump yourself up," she judges. "It's about life and death, and what we have to hope for, once you get old enough to know life hurts. Once you lose someone you love to death or divorce. If 'God loves you, be good,' is all we've got, that's not enough to keep going to church," she warns. "I'm all for welcoming in the wounded and loving them, one hundred percent. Some of them have already been on the cross, and they need to meet a soft-focus Jesus," she grants. "*And* some of us need to be doing the hard work of spiritual formation, too, at some point," she concludes. "We've been blessed, and we need to push harder."

BODIES OF WORSHIP, COMMUNITIES OF CARE

The ideal of the congregation as a body of worship that lives out its prayers in a community of care inspires these exemplary cases in terms that reach from the Church as the Pauline Body of Christ to the Judaic People of God, and beyond to the Islamic *umma* and the Buddhist *sangha.* Americans are indeed great joiners, and all these churches open their arms wide in welcome, including the neighborly embrace of Intown Church and the "nonlinear, art form" model of Alto Church in welcoming all comers to belong before freely committing to believe and behave. Critics of this user-friendly approach of seeker churches as "Christianity Lite" can doubt its champions' claims to march in the vanguard of an evangelical revolution ushering in a new unity among born-again, spirit-filled Christians beyond denominations. But both can agree on the need for the faithful to stand up and pitch in to serve others as "the hands and feet of Jesus."[21]

Everyone wants to be seen and known, these congregations affirm, to belong to each other and to God, to find "a safe place to heal your heart" and an unselfish love to move you to be the best person you were made to be. Everyone is our neighbor, to love and care for on the model of the Good Samaritan, even when—especially when—they do not look or sound like us. In calling the People of God to become the salt and light of the earth, these churches embrace love and justice as personal virtues bred by communities of character that share their exercise in ongoing practice and teach them by example, face-to-face and side by side. Authentic self-fulfillment comes only through moral community: To be true to yourself, "get out of your bubble." Right and wrong acts cannot be abstracted from social relationships rooted in rites of common prayer and practices of mutual care and shared self-governance. Nor can they be contained within the church alone as a separate realm set against or above and beyond the larger society.[22]

Let the light of our love shine in the world, leaders of these relatively resourceful churches urge, in the face of its neediness and unfairness, its indifference and evil, if everyone is to know the faithful as children of God, not merely pious and privileged Americans of a particular color, creed, class, and generation sheltered in more or less affluent suburban enclaves. These churches seek to reach out beyond such boundaries to help the needy in neighborhoods nearby as well as distant lands. In these efforts they draw on the talents, skills, and experience of their members to do good, and feel good about doing it, in ways we have heard praised by rich and poor, preachers and pastors alike as essential to every walk and stage of life. In particular they draw on the activist drive and organizing ability of young adults and younger retirees in core volunteer groups to sustain key ministries with apt community partners.

At the same time, these churches care for their own members across generations, for example, in aiding seniors in decline and protecting teens at risk. They struggle with the brittle certainties and persistent anxieties tied to their ethical rigor and social advantage, evident in the leafy enclaves of both Pine Glen and Alto Church. They try to shelter their children from moral controversy and confusion. They meet temptation to uplift the poor by high-tech problem-solving and upbeat Boy Scout cheering to try harder. With color-coded economic hardship hitting closer to home at Hillside Methodist, and gender differences cutting closer to the heart of Intown Church, social outreach in missions and membership remade in worship come closer together in these two cases. Yet in studying scripture, caring for souls, and sharing in fellowship, all these churches enable their members to nurture community in the present, stay true to tradition, and face the future. So they seek to heed hard truths of human frailty and finitude, to answer the call of suffering and sickness, and to mourn together those they love and lose.[23]

As treasure in earthen vessels and a living body of faith, every congregation interacts with society as a whole. Its communion is shaped by the ages and stages of its members' lives, unfolding in social space and historical time. In turn it shapes their individual dreams and shared stories across generations in common prayer and practice, Sunday by Sunday and day by day, in light of the life to come in this world and the next.

NOTES

1. Median home prices in this neighborhood approach $600,000, and three-quarters of adult residents at work are college-educated executives, professionals, and managers, averaging some $100,000 in household income, with 60 percent of adults aged twenty-five to fifty-four in a population counted as 62 percent White and 15 percent Black by race, with 3 percent same-sex couples, according to 2016 census data at www.point2homes.com/US/Neighborhood/GA/DeKalb-County. Material quoted and paraphrased here and below is drawn from repeated rounds of participant-observation in these congregations in Atlanta from 2017 to 2022 and related research for Steven M. Tipton, *The Life to Come: Re-Creating Retirement* (Nashville: Wesley's Foundery Press, 2018), ch. 4; including interviews recorded with their members, leaders, and partners in selected service projects and congregations nearby. I am grateful for their hospitality, honesty, and insight.

2. David A. Roozen, William McKinney, and Jackson W. Carroll, *Varieties of Religious Presence* (Cleveland: The Pilgrim Press, 1983), ch. 2. Cf. Ernst Troeltsch, *The Social Teaching of the Christian Churches* (New York: Harper & Row, 1960); H. Richard Niebuhr, *The Social Sources of Denominationalism* (New York: Henry Holt, 1929) and *The Kingdom of God in America* (New York: Harper & Row, 1937); and Martin E. Marty, *The Public Church* (Chestnut Ridge, PA: Crossroad Publishing, 1981).

3. On the moral moods and motives of rites expressing common ideals, inspiring action, and shaping social settings, see Clifford Geertz, "Ethos, Worldview, and the Analysis of Sacred Symbols" and "Religion as a Cultural System," in *The Interpretation of Cultures* (New York: Basic Books, 1973), 87–141; and Robert N. Bellah, "Religious Evolution," *American Sociological Review* 29, no. 3 (1964): 358–74. Cf. Marla Frederick, *Between Sundays* (Berkeley: University of California Press, 2003); and Rick Warren, *The Purpose-Driven Church* (Grand Rapids, MI: Zondervan, 2010), chs. 13–15.

4. Rick Rojas, "Let He Who Is Without Yeezys Cast the First Stone," *New York Times*, 17 April, 2019.

5. John Wesley, *An Extract from the Rev. Mr. John Wesley's Journals*, Vol. 1, Evans Early American Imprint Collection (Naples FL: Readex, 2011), 113, www.redex.com/products/early-american-imprint-series-i-evans-1639-1800. Cf. Hebrews 11:1 and 2 Corinthians 5:7.

6. On the correlation between church attendance as a child and religious belief and participation as an adult, see Aaron Gullickson, "The Diverging Beliefs and Practices of the Religiously Affiliated and Unaffiliated in the United States," *Sociological Science* 5 (2018): 361–79. Cf. Robert Wuthnow, *After the Baby Boomers* (Princeton: Princeton University Press, 2007), chs. 3–4.

7. Cf. Stanley Hauerwas, *A Community of Character* (Notre Dame, IN: University of Notre Dame Press, 1981); and Robert N. Bellah et al., *Habits of the Heart* (Berkeley: University of California Press, 2008), chs. 2, 9.

8. Stephen Ellingson, *The Megachurch and the Mainline* (Chicago: University of Chicago Press, 2007), chs. 5–7.

9. See, for example, Kate Bowler, *Everything Happens for a Reason: And Other Lies I've Loved* (New York: Random House, 2018).

10. One-third of US college students experienced clinical depression in 2014, up from a quarter in 2010, reports Amy Novotney, "Students under Pressure," American Psychological Association, *Monitor on Psychology* 45, no. 8 (September 2014): 36–44.

11. See Rick Warren, *The Purpose-Driven Church*, chs. 17–19, and related "crowd-congregation-core" distinctions in the case of Alto Church in chapter 4.

12. Median detached-house prices in this neighborhood reached $460,000 by 2016, with median household income nearing $80,000 in a workforce of educated professionals and managers, including 80 percent college graduates and 40 percent with advanced degrees; in a population 85 percent White, 5 percent Black, and 5 percent Asian, with more than 40 percent aged twenty-five to forty-four, according to census data at www.city-data.com/neighborhood...Atlanta-GA; including fifteen same-sex couples per one thousand households, according to analysis of the 2010 U.S. Census by Gary J. Gates and Abigail M. Cooke, "Georgia Census Snapshot, Williams Institute, UCLA School of Law, 2010. Cf. Petra L. Doan and Harrison Higgins, "The Demise of Queer Space? Resurgent Gentrification and the Assimilation of LGBT Neighborhoods," *Journal of Planning Education and Research* 31, no. 1 (2011): 1–20. DOI: 10.1177/0739456X10391266.

13. David W. Stowe, *Song of Exile: The Enduring Mystery of Psalm 137* (New York: Oxford University Press, 2016). See Michael Baughman, ed., *Flipping Church* (Nashville: Discipleship Resources, 2016).

14. The four "sides" of the Wesleyan Quadrilateral—scripture, tradition, reason, and experience—define the core of Christian faith for believers, according to Alan K. Waltz, *A Dictionary for Methodists* (Nashville, TN: Abingdon Press, 1991).

15. "While the grace of God is undivided, it precedes salvation as 'prevenient grace,' continues in 'justifying grace,' and is brought to fruition in 'sanctifying grace,'" states *The Book of Discipline of The United Methodist Church* (Nashville, TN: The United Methodist Publishing House, 2016), with an Arminian stress on divine grace inherent in the natural order of creation, human conscience, and social relationships that enables acceptance of salvific faith. Wesley affirms a grace that "waiteth not for the work of man" in the Spirit's work of preparing persons for salvation, in "On Working Out Our Own Salvation" (Sermon 85, 1872 edition), General Board of Global Ministries, at http://gbgm-umc.org. Van Morrison, "Days Like This"

(Universal Music Publishing Group, BMG Rights Management, 1995) at https://lyrics.com/lyric/27055233/Van+Morrison/Days+Like+This.

16. Cf. Diana Butler Bass, *Christianity after Religion* (New York: HarperCollins, 2013).

17. Richard Hyman and Cyndi Lauper, "Time After Time" (Sony/ATV Music/Warner Chappell Music, 1983) at https://www.azlyrics.com/lyrics/cyndilauper/timeaftertime.html

18. Julia Beck and Michelle Leonard, "Alive" (Sony/ATV, 2012) at https://www.lyrics.com/lyrics/28036547/All+Sons+%26+Daughters/Alive. Cf. Carole King, "You've Got a Friend" (Sony/ATV, 1971) at https://www.azlyrics.com/lyrics/caroleking/youvegotafriend.html; and Mark A. Miller, "Christ Has Broken Down the Wall (Choristers Guild, 2011) at https://www.choristersguild.org/pdf-samples/cga1224.pdf.

19. John Lennon, "Imagine" (Downtown Music Publishing, 1971) at https://www.azlyrics.com/lyrics/johnlennon/imagine.html.

20. See note 12 above.

21. Cf. Ellingson, *The Megachurch and the Mainline*; Wuthnow, *After the Baby Boomers*; and Christian Smith, *American Evangelicalism: Embattled and Thriving* (Chicago: University of Chicago Press, 1998).

22. See H. Richard Niebuhr, *Christ and Culture* (Harper & Row, 1951), chs. 1–2, 6–7, on ideals of Christian conscience and community embodying visions of Christ *against*, *with*, *above*, *beside*, or *transforming* culture. Cf. Stanley Hauerwas contra Niebuhr's uncritical notion of culture unfairly favoring "Christ transforming culture" over "Christ against culture" as a Calvinist norm of socially engaged liberal Protestantism, in Hauerwas, "The Church and Liberal Democracy," in *A Community of Character*, note 5, 246–47.

23. Cf. Alexis de Tocqueville, *Democracy in America*, ed. J.P. Mayer (New York: Doubleday, 1969), 292; H. Richard Niebuhr, *Christ and Culture*; Stanley Hauerwas, *A Community of Character*; David Hollenbach, "Justice as Participation," in *Justice, Peace, and Human Rights* (Chestnut Ridge, PA: Crossroad Publishing, 1988), 72–83; and Steven M. Tipton, *Public Pulpits* (Chicago: University of Chicago Press, 2007), 425–42.

Chapter 6

The Good of Congregating

Can we draw sweeping conclusions across all kinds of US congregations—mainline and evangelical, large and small, urban and rural—and apply to all of them specific advice on how to respond to unchurched young adults? Hardly. But we can find common lines of self-understanding and practical insight across these resourceful middle-class congregations situated in the suburbs of Silicon Valley and metropolitan Atlanta. We can weigh the prospects and problems detailed in these accounts and ask how distinctive or representative they turn out to be compared to the congregations and communities we know best.

This comparison of exemplary congregations focuses on two crucial questions in practice. First, how do these congregations engage young adults through "contemporary worship," liturgy, witness, and community that resonate with self-expressive chords in tune with popular culture today yet transpose them to a new moral key? Second, how do these churches deepen devotional formation, theological imagination, and moral commitment as essential "next steps" that newcomers can take once they cross church thresholds opened wide by upbeat revivalism, therapeutic care of souls, warm fellowship, and hands-on community service?

This first line of inquiry led us to concentrate on the experience of young adults encountering, evaluating, and entering into these congregations, in dialogue with the practical insight of pastors, youth ministers, and "contemporary worship planners." Their dialogue turns on themes of personal autonomy and spirituality as authentic self-expression and self-exploration which we found at the center of reflection by parents and children on their religious upbringing across generations, traced in chapters 2 and 3. By turns diagnostic, discerning, and deliberative, this dialogue connects these shifts in self-awareness, social practice, and cultural understanding to congregational analysis of religious membership and participation in chapters 4 and 5, which is tied in turn to parenting, schooling, work, courtship, and marriage as shared moral dramas and institutional pathways leading to and from church.

This second line of inquiry led us to explore a range of cohort-specific and intergenerational worship, small groups, Bible study classes, and service projects tuned to young adults in particular but also knitting them together with older church members. These groups not only embrace teenagers on the move from high school to college and beyond. They also span transitions in early adulthood from courtship to marriage and to parenting children of one's own. They frame exemplary relationships and activities of prayer, study, and service that inspire moral moods and motives in forming practical virtues of adulthood in love and work in the world as well as worship and fellowship in church.

These two lines of inquiry reveal distinctive yet related patterns of representative practice and meaning running through Alto Church in the Bay Area, a mainline Presbyterian congregation transformed into a conversionist megachurch through a synthesis of evangelical and Pentecostal elements distilled from sources such as Willow Creek, Vineyard Fellowship, and Fuller Seminary. These patterns also run through a constellation of United Methodist congregations in Atlanta remarkable for experimenting with new approaches to young adults in liturgy and preaching, teaching, witness, and service in step with neighborhoods shifting in cultural outlook and social identity.[1]

LEAVING CHURCH

How do the problems and practices of exemplary congregations bear out the implications of national surveys of declining religious affiliation, attendance, and participation in tandem with spreading spirituality? Led by rising waves of young adults over the past two decades, unaffiliated Americans have more than doubled their share of all US adults from fewer than one in ten to more than one in five. Declines in congregational membership and attendance bear out the fact that fewer Americans today than in the past claim any religious affiliation, while those who do identify with a particular religion are now less likely to belong to a local body of worship. Despite doubling in proportion, religiously unaffiliated Americans remain less than a quarter of the US population. But only two-thirds of affiliated Americans, as defined by their religious identification or preference, actually belong to a congregation now, compared to three-quarters twenty years ago. Fewer still attend regularly. Three-quarters of all American adults now identify with a religion, but only half of them claim membership in a congregation. That poses a clear challenge to the institutions of American religion, since they depend on active and loyal members of congregations to thrive here and now, and to form the faithful over generations.[2]

To whom should congregational leaders and members turn in seeking to welcome others to join them? Why not turn to those brought up most strongly in the churches of their childhood, most vividly attuned to a "sacramental imagination" and most fluent in "speaking religion"? Even if they now stand outside church doors, these alums remain closest to church in personal, social, and cultural terms. Some "liminals" straddle the threshold, and others attend church now and then as "perpetual visitors" if not marginal members. A quarter of all Americans identify themselves as "spiritual but not religious," yet most of these "SBNR" adults actually identify with a religious group, a third of them Protestant. Conversely, half of all Americans call themselves *both* "spiritual and religious," even if many take no active part in a congregation. One in four US adults identify as "religious," yet do not belong to a congregation. One in three millennials identify with no religion. But two in three do, though many of them do not belong to a congregation or participate actively in it.[3]

In sum, the dividing line between churched and unchurched Americans turns out to be dynamic, not fixed, evident in the fact that half of Americans had left their childhood community of faith by 2010, but only a quarter have remained out of church. Fluid religious beliefs and varied spiritual practices mark those closest to the line, whether in or out of the pews. Many doctrinal doubters still believe in "spiritual energy" or "a higher power" if not a biblical God. Many Sunday nonattenders continue to pray and practice their faith "in their own way." Some do it online. "Religion is becoming a single-player experience," notes the founder of a prayer app offering daily devotions and bedtime Bible stories, "and I've never been one to be bound by church pews or service times. Just because I don't want to go to church doesn't mean I don't want to honor God."[4]

Fewer than a quarter of those who identify as mainline Protestants attend services every week, a third attend occasionally, and the rest seldom or never attend. Fewer still are active in church groups or other religious organizations, although half say they pray daily and three-quarters weekly. Only one in five self-identified mainline Protestants qualifies as a typical "Sunday Stalwart" by weekly church attendance, active participation, and daily prayer. But two in three qualify as "somewhat religious" by such measures, clustered by belief and practice into three more or less equally sized and like-minded groups of the "diversely devout, relaxed religious, and spiritually awake."[5]

Accordingly, many mainline congregations in search of renewal and revival lean toward bringing such reportedly religious yet largely inactive Americans back to church and inspiring them to take an active part in congregational bodies of worship and witness. For many of these "somewhat religious" Americans share the criticism of most unaffiliated yet spiritual Americans. They still believe in God, they report, but they "just stopped believing" in church teaching. They still trust in life's ultimate meaning and goodness, but they stopped trusting in church authority bound by "too many rules" and more devoted to money, power, and playing politics than "meeting spiritual needs."

BELONGING AND BELIEVING

In responding to young Americans who no longer profess to believe or belong in church, social circumstances matter, agree congregational leaders. But survey data do not tell the whole story of a congregation's past or determine its future. The membership of each local church and its social setting go hand in hand through their history. But they find themselves in a present moment that brings together comparable decisions churches have made and choices they face.

Asked about young adults in or out of the pews, parents in these churches think first of their own children, coming of age or already grown, still at home, away at college, or off at work. Particularly in Silicon Valley, they weigh the impact of competitive demands exerted by elite schooling, professional work, and sky-high housing costs on church and family life alike. "God forgive me," says one, "for wanting my son to get into Harvard more than heaven." Excelling at school and work can come first at the expense of parenting and churchgoing, they know, as well as leading a life of integrity and care.

Alto Church focuses its evangelically engaging yet spiritually fluent outreach on attracting young families and single young adults swimming in the sea of an exceptionally educated, mobile high-tech workforce. In leafy suburban enclaves of Atlanta, well-established churches like Pine Glenn nurture touching contemporary worship and actively attentive youth groups to hold close their own children coming of age through adolescence and hold together churchgoing families across three generations. They pray they can continue drawing the next generation back to the warm embrace of the church with their parents and grandparents, if only their offspring can finish school, launch careers, and afford to buy houses nearby.

Beyond the beltway, Hillside Methodist reaches out to working parents on the go and in need of welcoming worship and comforting community, supportive childcare, and collaborative volunteering to help their needier neighbors nearby. Intown Church, by contrast, welcomes young singles, couples, and parents of school-age children with wide-open arms of personal acceptance, liturgical verve, and spiritual dialogue in tune with an artsy, educated local neighborhood, straight and gay, seeking community and commitment freed from fundamentalist authority and sectarian bounds.

Families and congregations need each other in order to thrive, all these church leaders stress. Neither can form faith or focus spirituality on its own. However outstanding a congregation's Sunday school classes, youth groups, and worship services, its leaders emphasize the need for parents to nurture their children's faith by practical example at home, not just by bringing them to church. The family is the first school of faith or indifference, by this account, no less than the first school of justice or injustice, spiritual awareness or moral hypocrisy. Faith is nurtured or neglected through the interactive drama of parents teaching their children what is true and good by doing or not doing, by doing as they say or not; and by praying together daily, occasionally, or not at all.[6]

Both parents practicing their faith together enact a common vision of religious coherence and integrity, by contrast to the binocularity of one parent at odds with the other on creed, code, denomination, or tradition—or more deeply divided on the need for religious practice, belief, or belonging at all. When it comes to growing up faithfully, congregational leaders emphasize the primacy of parents in shaping their children's sense of what is really real, what is possible, and what to go by. They do so through the everyday drama of prayers and parables they bring to life. These firsthand stories and sermons in action underlie survey data on the high odds of children raised by two churchgoing parents winding up in the pews, compared to the offspring of just one churchgoer or of the unchurched.[7]

Young adults will stay in church or return to church, congregational leaders confirm, if it meets their "needs," defined in spiritual, moral, and psychological terms that echo yet shift key terms featured in surveys of religious affiliation. "Everyone needs to belong," notes a youth minister in Alto Church, for example. So they know from "self-help culture," by contrast to knowing the love of Jesus "because the Bible tells me so," experienced in worship and fellowship no less than revealed in scripture. "Start with belonging, not believing," these pastors counsel, in welcoming unaffiliated young adults, particularly from religiously mixed, relaxed, or noncommittal families. Instead of pressing them for repentance, conversion, and conformity, embrace them with tender loving care, congenial concern, and spiritual enthusiasm, as new friends and newborn Christians, trusting in God's grace to move them forward in faith.

This updated "nonlinear, art form" stance takes a functionalist view of religion yet seeks to go beyond it. "No one gets healed alone," these ministers point out, with a nod to therapeutic settings from singles groups to seniors centers. Yet faithful congregations can uniquely heal souls and unify God's people, they add, unlike other groups devoted directly to healing minds, sparking friendship, or building community. They grant that we can attain cultural literacy and learn moral values outside the realm of religion, as half of Americans now agree. We can live by "good moral values without believing in God." We can complete elementary moral learning by churchgoing in childhood much like we attend grammar school, complete the curriculum, and then graduate. But only in church, they stress, can we come to love God and our neighbor.[8]

These congregational leaders lift up the church as a loving community of care and shared spiritual energy instead of a clerical hierarchy for imposing moral rules and judgments on the laity. As such, congregational community inspires us to "put on love," kindness, and humility as virtues that require daily practice to transform our lives. By graceful example, promise pastors, such ongoing, imitative practice gradually enables us to become part of the church as a living body, and so grow closer to God as members one of another. Through shared participation in the music, movement, and common prayer of Eucharistic worship in particular, they stress, we interact to cocreate the reality of the church as spirit incarnate, by contrast to the polished performances of preachers, musicians, and choirs delivered to a passive audience. We do likewise in the interplay between the church as a body of worship and witness to the larger community in active partnership with its unchurched neighbors across a full range of civic, educational, artistic, and spiritual activity.[9]

OPENING UP, REACHING OUT, WELCOMING IN

What does it mean to "put belonging before believing and behaving," as these congregational leaders advise in response to unchurched, uncommitted young adults? They concentrate on the shared spiritual experience of heartwarming revival and moving worship, while they downplay creedal professions of faith and baptismal vows of sanctified behavior. They offer care for souls scarred by fire-and-brimstone judgment in the past. They open up engaging dialogue for minds moved by religious questioning and curiosity in the present, and put off by partisan politics and apocalypse preached from the pulpit.

In Alto Church, for example, the "stuffy and staid" feeling of traditional church services and settings gives way to the upbeat Christian rock and uplifted hands of contemporary worship in a "casual café" for young singles. This rebirth relies on embracing mixed motives as well as milieus. Everyone "needs to belong to be healthy," notes a youth minister, and the church recognizes the therapeutic, romantic, and lifestylish resonance of its warm welcome, including its popular perception by young singles as yet another "self-help option" to enhance health and personal well-being. Yet the church offers belonging before believing in a caring community inspired by the exemplary love of Jesus Christ, pastors vow, and the indwelling presence of the Holy Spirit. So it testifies to the Gospel truth of a creative, redeeming God who will wait for each person to freely accept this life-changing love. On one hand, it espouses an ideal of the church that transcends purely inward mystical means to enhance individual wellness and authentic spirituality. On the other, it breaks through sect-like narrowness and the outer shell of "hard-core conservative churches" enforced by fundamentalist dogmatism, rigid moral authority, and political partisanship.

Rooted in revivalism and the Protestant priesthood of all believers, Alto Church proclaims a "new evangelical revolution" to bridge denominational differences and enact "small-c catholic" ideals of one true Church to unify Christian faith. This church is devoted to dialogue with doubt as well as healing souls and awakening spirits. It aims to overcome suspicion of sanctimonious hypocrisy by openhanded transparency and trustworthiness, for example, in making public its budget and balance sheet every month.[10] It aims to extend its helping hand as an unselfish community, by contrast to worldly institutions driven by self-centered competition at work, efficiency in administration, or profitability in the marketplace.

At its best this seeker-friendly approach rejects a sectarian sense of superiority, while staying alert to its own "Christianity Lite" challenges of "discipleship without discipline, love without obedience, and emotionally powerful worship experience without biblical authority." It holds up the possibility of exercising genuine moral and spiritual authority as pastor or parent in the exemplary integrity of practicing what you preach with humility, fairness, and love. The congregation pledges the loving support of a tight-knit family to members caught in the throes of personal conflict, illness, and loss. It calls spiritual seekers to become faithful church members through commitment and service within the Body of Christ. It asks the church to be true to its biblical covenant (Deut 6:4–9) through inspiring its members to integrate their own divided lives by becoming one with God. It invites them to unify themselves as God's people in a divided society by serving others firsthand and face-to-face.

In answering these challenges in practice, churches need to face their own moral ambiguity and tensions, Alto Church leaders acknowledge. This clearly pertains to their fundraising campaigns and political alliances for a younger generation wary of mass-media evangelism and mushrooming megachurches pursuing "money and power instead of spiritual truth," no less than pastors marching in lockstep with political partisans and religious lobbyists.

More deeply, as Fred Heiden observes, "there are rules everywhere" in the hardworking world of higher education and professional careers in Silicon Valley. So churches find themselves reacting by reflex to young adults seeking freedom, intimacy, and community in the realm of spirituality as well as leisure and romantic love. Contemporary congregations face pressures to be "fun and free," to stand apart from rulebound, performance-driven regimens of work and schooling pervasive in everyday life, no less than they stand out from the staid and stuffy services of conventional churches and their preachy authority. Instead of prizing church growth, giving, and congeniality as priorities, Heiden urges, Christians should congregate to worship God, first of all, and put this practice first in order to form God's people. Instead of struggling to obey or deny act-specific rules and commandments, by this Pauline account, church members should "put on love, which binds all together in perfect unity," through praying together and practicing what they preach to enact the Gospel story (Col. 3: 12–17). "Clothe yourself in mercy and humility, gentleness, and patience," exhorts Paul, as practical virtues formed by living together within a community of character that inspires each member to learn and teach by shared example.

This exemplary moral vision of the church underlies Heiden's diagnosis of baby boomers' responsibility for the spiritual drift of their children by failing to live out their faith fully. Instead, they "played" with spirituality and religion alike, he fears, betraying the prayerful power and moral integrity of faith in practice. They diluted the formative influence of daily devotional life to yield no more than good intentions and trust in a "911 God" to call in emergencies, instead of nurturing an "impassioned spirit for God" to light up every day and guide us through it.

All of these congregations aim to open up the church to the world around it in the local neighborhood and metropolitan area, by reaching out to those in need nearby if not nationwide and worldwide as well. They aim to welcome in their neighbors as biblical "strangers," members of a larger moral community to share, participants and partners in good work and mutual care, who can become friends of the congregation even if they do not join it. At the same time, each congregation aims to send its members out into the surrounding society to serve others, make friends, and join their fellow citizens in discerning and doing the good in common.

Pine Glen, for example, reaches out to resettle refugees from around the world in a nearby gateway city. It underwrites a church school in West Africa, packs weekly lunches for poor students and families across town, and serves hot meals to the homeless at a partner church downtown. Given its significant social scale and resources, it joins with a wide range of religious, civic, and public partners across the city and the country. It contributes volunteers and expertise as well as money to these joint ventures, much like Alto Church in Silicon Valley, even if its web of projects, programs, and partners is less far flung on the ground and less finespun online.

By contrast, Hillside Methodist Church, though smaller and more modest in means, finds itself in the middle of a neighborhood in need that it can serve face-to-face across the lines of race, ethnicity, and economic class. Church volunteers and donors join with other local congregations and community groups to sustain a food pantry, clothes closet, storehouse of school supplies, and an office for emergency aid to pay rent and utility bills. In the absence of a local downtown, civic center, or high school, the church "helps give this place a heart." It provides a meeting place for local civic groups and residents to gather across the lines of subdivisions separated by freeways and divided into neighborhoods with largely Black, White, or Hispanic populations.

With few college-aged singles nearby and many young families crowding into starter homes, Hillside weds its focus on local mission to meeting newcomers' needs for full-time childcare and preschool programs. It extends fellowship for dual-career young parents from friendly dinners to small groups for mindfulness meditation and spiritual reflection. Not yet ready to multiply and divide worship into traditional and contemporary services, it relaxes familiar patterns of Methodist worship by diversifying its music, personalizing its preaching, and expanding weekly Communion at the center of Sunday services.

Free to find full-scale rebirth in an artsy intown suburb of young professional singles, couples, and families, along with a large gay community, Intown Church opened its doors wide to its neighbors just two years ago. "We are all love," it promises, "with no BS" or barriers to full self-expression and active commitment to social justice and compassion. Upbeat "radio music" and low-key sermons light up a liturgy with Holy Communion at the heart of participatory worship and community-building to share authority and shape boundaries within "a culture of consent."

Here local visitors are free to stream in and stream through. They find lots of leeway to choose their own path and pace of movement to remake membership, eased by pastoral care of souls left wounded or exiled from the churches of their childhood. With young singles, couples, and families intermixed in a small congregation, shared interests in spiritual practices, social causes, and creative arts hold sway over age-grading in forming the congregation's small groups and classes. So do the church's unusually warm and imaginative "neighboring" initiatives to play den mother plus pastor in collaboration with local organizations to host meditation and yoga classes, town hall meetings, art shows and folk concerts, gay-pride suppers and telecommuter lunches. Thus, the congregation seeks to wed worship and witness, church and world, love and justice, vowing, "Bring everything you have to worship. You can't upset us, and you can't upset God." Come as you are, stay if you want, and change as you will.

CONGREGATIONS IN SOCIAL CONTEXT

Circumstances matter, congregational leaders agree, including the character of the neighborhood and community surrounding a local church in tandem with the composition of its membership. How do such social differences, including race and class, help or hinder a congregation in seeking to welcome and embrace young adults today? However privileged and insulated Alto Church may seem in the affluent center of Silicon Valley, it encounters these questions in reaching out to help needy neighbors, to partner with less advantaged churches, and to hold onto members drawn away from the community by the lower cost of living elsewhere. These same questions also weigh on denominational leaders in Atlanta, particularly those responsible for supporting and evaluating local churches such as Pine Glen, Hillside, and Intown Church compared to other congregations across the lines of race and class, age and generation. How do these differences bear on young adults in and out of church?

Many suburban churches in metro Atlanta grew up in the postwar boom years, planted in new subdivisions at every exit of the freeways that spread out from downtown as the city's white-collar economy mushroomed from regional to national scale. "But they couldn't keep growing like that," explains Chris Burns, a regional Methodist administrator who once served as Pine Glen's youth minister and went on to lead several other Atlanta congregations. "They got older as parents stayed on and retired, and kids left town even if they didn't leave church."

White flight drew new color lines, and newcomers shifted social attitudes. "Apartment blocks and shopping centers came in, people came from all over, and neighborhoods changed," notes Chris. "So did the world." What made Pine Glen different? "It was one of the earliest in-town suburbs in the 1950s," he replies. "It got developed all at once from farmland, with big ranch houses on big lots, a big public school, but no apartments or through traffic." With shopping centers, highways, and competing churches set outside its perimeter, the neighborhood came together around the Methodist church and K–8 school at its center, and the church grew into a kind of "county-seat cathedral." It attracted educated middle-class White families with local roots and resources to help many of their children return to settle down after they finished college, married, and began careers and families of their own. "The school got better and better, the streets stayed quiet, and the neighborhood renewed itself," Chris notes. "It got pricier, but it was worth it."

Granting Pine Glen's special circumstances, can we learn any larger lessons from its efforts to continue congregating across generations? Does it offer a model for mainline churches struggling to hold on to their own children, and attract young singles and families? "Contemporary worship works at Pine Glen, because it's traditional, too," answers Chris. "It's not a bright, shiny hook to pull teens in off the street. It builds on solid programs for preschool and grade-school children that the church has put plenty of effort into over the years to serve the whole community." Isn't that exemplary, however exceptional? "You have to start from where you are," counsels Chris Burns. "Pine Glen celebrates multigenerational families. It's not alone in that. But it's been able to carry it through so well, it's almost like an exception that proves the rule."

What is the rule? "It's not just programs," replies Chris Burns. "It starts with paying attention to young adults. Ask why they're missing from church, and what they're doing instead." For example? "Check out in-town neighborhoods in Atlanta on a Sunday morning, and you'll see lots of young singles having brunch with friends at a nice café around the corner, and couples without kids taking a walk in Piedmont Park or along the Beltline. You're not going to round them all up and get them to church," he shakes his head.

Then Chris leans forward. "But, you know," he says, "last year 300,000 people walked across Northern Spain on the Camino de Santiago. Many of them were young and unchurched, yet they're finding something powerful and meaningful doing that, something spiritual and mystical." Much the same holds true, Chris adds, for others nearby in weekly yoga, meditation, and exercise classes spread across Atlanta. "We need to learn from that," he suggests. "Young people, children of the baby boomers, want something deeper than pop music or pop gospel. They want to travel along an arc of faith that stretches further than the fashion of the moment. They want to find a longer, truer path."

How can this path of spiritual community be opened up for young adults today? "Ask the question, 'Why?'" urges Chris Burns. "Go all the way back to Deuteronomy 6: Why do we want to do this? Why do we want to find God, follow God, listen to God?" Why indeed? "Most of us today don't really fear God," he allows. "We don't want to obey all of God's commands, and we sure don't want somebody else trying to tell us what to do in God's name," he adds. "But most of us *do* want to find a way out of 'bondage' or suffering, whatever addiction or difficulty we're stuck in. We want to be free!" he exclaims. "We want to find our way to a better place, 'a land of milk and honey,' where we can be who we really are with the people we really love. For sure, we want to do better and prosper. But we actually want to be with God, be closer to God. We want to be loved and loving with people who do the things Jesus did. And we want that for our kids, too."

For church leaders over the past generation of declining growth, Chris suspects, such radical questioning of *why* has too quickly given way to asking *how* to turn things around, how to jump-start numerical growth or speed up programmatic progress. "We can be pretty pragmatic about religion in America, and focus on what works, what brings people in and what brings them back," he notes. This how-to stance informs many a megachurch today, he thinks. But it reaches back in the mainline churches to the urban development of revivalism, Sunday schools, and diverse denominations competing to save souls, with agencies and programs emerging in the late nineteenth century to help parents guide youngsters to come of age in church.

"But the churches can't do it all by themselves, if they ever could," Chris judges. The baby boom posted impressive but misleading benchmarks for church growth through the 1950s, followed by record rates of youths dropping out and stopping out since the late 1960s. "For a generation now we've been seeing more and more kids leave church, mostly kids who were never really in," Chris concludes. "Their parents gave them a pass, or brought them on Sunday every now and then, if they felt like it. Of course, they don't come back on their own. That's not surprising."

Does this reflect changes in ways of understanding religion among postwar parents as well as their children coming of age? Definitely, Chris Burns replies. "Assume that religion works to instill values of right and wrong, and help you learn to behave yourself. Then you should be able to get to that point, get that done, and get on with it." As a youth director, he reports, "I can remember losing some kids after confirmation, because they felt like they could check that box and move on. Sometimes their parents agreed, and you would lose them, too, after confirmation or high school graduation. Sometimes when the kids got their driver's license, you'd see them disappear along with their parents, who don't need to bring them anymore. Or the parents leave, but the kids self-select and come on their own to youth group, because that's where their friends are."

Rates of church attendance and membership stabilized as many 1960s youth reached middle age and dropped back in, Chris Burns notes, then new waves of "nones" began to rise over the past generation. But even if many baby-boom parents still state a religious preference and attend church more often than their offspring, he suspects, they nonetheless understand religious belonging and participation in more relaxed ways akin to their children. "It's a good thing to do, but it's not unique," he sums up. "Anytime the weather's nice and it's a long weekend, they're away at the beach or the mountains, if they can take the time off. Religion is always there, but on any given weekend, it's an option, too. It's not the defining gravitational center of who I am." Much the same holds true for defining the local community's center, Chris adds, where the Methodist church and small-town high school distant from downtown Atlanta gave way to consolidated school districts and multiplied churches spread across hundreds of miles and millions of households in the suburbs of the ninth-largest metropolitan area in the United States.[11]

What does such social and cultural transformation imply in practice for congregations ministering to young adults? "Make small-town America great again?" Chris asks in turn. "That's not going to happen anytime soon. But we can be much more intentional about helping young adults ask good questions and find real meaning in their lives, here and now. What do they want to find out about being a grown-up that their parents didn't teach them? About work and love and mortgages, too," he smiles. "Where are they coming from, what's their story? We can ask that, especially when the standard script isn't working. They lost their job, they're breaking up with the most important person in their life, their mother died, and they're really down."

Young adults on their own and in need of faithful attention and caring community can find themselves adrift, reports Chris Burns, in congregations tuned to young families "busy getting married, getting promoted, and having their second baby." If congregations are willing, he says, "we can recognize souls in need and open up to them. Sometimes they're hurting from life's hard knocks. Sometimes it's from having life-changing experiences and not knowing what to make of them, or what to make of your life. The questions to ask are just not on the radar of the upbeat megachurch you've been going to, or the sleepy church on the corner you drive by every day."

At the same time, observes Chris Burns, many social functions of congregations are now spread more widely through local communities, particularly educated middle-class neighborhoods with the resources to underwrite their aspirations. "Neighbors get together, they support one another. They have block parties and picnics, book clubs and ball games. They do yard sales and community service projects. They get their kids together for play dates. Everything except worship." Instead of seeing such efforts as competing with churches or distracting from them, advises Burns, "We need to come alongside these folks, and do it with them, then go deeper and draw it all together with God in worship. We don't need to reinvent the wheel or outdo them. It's in the common DNA of our creation," as spiritual beings who seek meaning and seek to know God.

None of this adds up to a "magic key for church growth, or five easy steps to a successful church," Burns cautions. But this outlook can point the way to clearer self-awareness of "what churches have to be about in a world where they can't take their place for granted." They're not pillars of the community or the cultural establishment anymore, "even if the building is still sitting there on Main Street with a big endowment. We have to show up and come together in the spirit to bring church alive. Think relationships, connections, and making meaning. Don't think big numbers and economies of scale," Chris stresses. "Be authentic, be available. Give young adults who come in enough time and space to find their own way. Don't load them down with too much stuff to do, just because they seem responsible. They're busy, too, even if they don't have kids to take care of and a lawn to mow."

On the other hand, "We're not just saying you're welcome, you're accepted, come on in and hang out, and we'll do your thing," Chris Burns shakes his head, much like pastors of Alto Church and Intown Church. "There are four gospels and you can interpret them any way you want to, as long as you keep the Creed in mind. We try to love everyone, and we welcome everyone who comes through the door. But sometimes we have to wrestle with how to be generous yet truthful, too, about entering into the body of the church and following Jesus, not just coming in and hanging out." This process of discernment requires faithful patience as well as creedal clarity, Burns reflects, since "wisdom is the work of a lifetime," and many young adults are still struggling to shoulder the burdens of functioning responsibly from day to day. "You can't really become part of Christian community without trying to be loving and caring," Chris judges. "We have to show them how, not just tell them they ought to. They can be very clear about their own spiritual needs beforehand, and what they want in a church. We have to help them find out what they really need and want. The only way we can do that is by showing them how we live and pray together."

What do we really need? "Take very little with you," answers Chris Burns. "That's what almost every expert advises when you're going on a long trip, whether it's a pilgrimage, a journey of self-discovery, or just a vacation. Invariably everybody takes the kitchen sink. Then you start walking, and you feel the weight of the world on your back. You realize what's important as you go, and what you can leave behind."

Does this advice assume some underlying gospel truth or law of human nature? "I'm assuming you want to live life as a good person, if not a good Christian," Chris replies. "So time will tell, if you take this path and stay on it. Maybe you really are 'spiritual but not religious,' and you really are happy and fulfilled staying home on Sunday morning, reading the *Times* over coffee, taking a walk, or watching the game with friends. I can't fault that," he allows. "But if you're asking why, and you can't find any reason good enough to get you out of bed on Sunday, then I'd say, 'Keep looking!'" he urges. "Start walking. Maybe you won't meet Jesus, but you'll meet yourself carrying way too much baggage, and you'll realize you can let some of it go. Try sitting in church, even if you tune out the sermon, and maybe you'll hear a hymn or feel the quiet, and find a little peace of mind," in a moment of spiritual awareness unbound by Christian conversion.

"Start by asking what you want to be saved *from*," Chris Burns invites, "instead of what you want to be saved *for*."[12] Churched or unchurched, "that gives you a place to ask questions about your life without having to believe in heaven or Jesus," Chris promises, in recalling a small reflection group he led during Lent a few years ago. "After a month one of the men said he wasn't sure he belonged here or believed any of this. He was here because of his wife and kids. You're exactly the reason we're all here around this table, I told him, and we have this safe space to share our doubts and our questions. You're helping us all be more honest about where we are with this."

Legalistic or philosophical arguments for or against religious faith are much less compelling now than a generation ago, Chris thinks, especially for educated young adults in or around mainline churches. "It's more experiential learning. You see how people in church are living their lives, you feel how they care about you, and you want to be around them and do this stuff, too. Belief grows out of that, not arguments." Through practicing together, Chris stresses, we come to share a way of feeling and seeing instead of reasoning one's own way into intellectual assent.

Rites of worship lie at the root of a wider web of moral and spiritual practice, by this account, reaching into the heart of each person and radiating out to the whole of life. However, as Chris Burns points out, "Ritual can't do it all. It's not a magic wand you can wave over everyone and work wonders," he explains in terms that echo Natalie and Pastor Dan. Moreover, he notes, young people prefer "experiential ritual over sermons that sound like lectures. They like rites of joy, not mourning." Chris raises his hands in praise, and exclaims, "Let's come and gather round the table, break bread, and have a big hug!" He then lowers his hands and bows his head, "Let's confess our sins, and say we're not worthy to gather up the crumbs under thy Table," he intones. "Not so much!" he laughs.

High church or low, congregations need both Sacrament and Word, Chris concludes, with a nod to John Wesley and Paul Tillich alike, particularly in bringing up children in the faith.[13] "My daughter became an acolyte at age ten," Chris recalls, "and she absolutely loved it, especially on Sundays when there's Communion. There's all these sights and sounds, all the solemnity and play in doing it." Decades ago, some Methodist pastors would move monthly Communion off the highly attended first Sunday of the month, Chris recalls, "because they didn't want it to hurt the offering plate. Now, especially in churches with young people, there's more participation when there's Communion, and there's more giving, too," he reports with a nod to Hillside and Intown Church.

Many churches need to work on rebalancing sacrament and word, Chris Burns counsels, especially if their prophetic voices turn too predictably political along partisan lines, be it conservative evangelicals alienating young adults by lining up rigidly with the religious right against abortion and gay rights, or mainline Protestants reverently rehearsing progressive programs of peace and justice. "Preach to the choir too much, and they'll start acting like they've heard it all before," he warns. "Been there, done that, got the T-shirt."

Conversely, Chris vows, liturgical immersion in the sights, sounds, space, and feeling of worship proves vital to raising children in the church. Whether it's incense and Handel's Messiah on Easter Sunday or lighting a candle and singing a prayer song before Sunday school, he promises, "That sacramental imagination and memory will never leave you." This indelible impression also belies Lockean assumptions of a childhood slate left blank for youngsters to decide on their own to believe or disbelieve in religious creeds and codes once they reach adulthood. "I've never understood parents who say they're going to let the kids decide for themselves when they're old enough," Chris marvels. "They're pretending they're not going to indoctrinate them, as if they're not already getting filled up with TV cartoons and video games. That's there from the beginning, so why not start with something real, too?" he asks, along lines underscored by Intown Church.

Diversity and inclusion are watchwords of mainline Protestant congregations, and Chris Burns affirms their significance for local churches seeking to embody the church universal. "Welcome everyone! We mean that. Love everyone as your neighbor and a child of God." At the same time, he recognizes, neighborhoods in metro Atlanta have continued to diversify by cultural politics and generation as well as race, class, ethnicity, and nationality. "People want to find a church where they fit and feel comfortable," he observes. "They don't want to fuss and fight."

Church leaders can recognize differences in the social composition and context of a congregation, Chris Burns advises, and not be driven by them. "You *can* be wise as a serpent and innocent as a dove," he says deliberately. "If you're surrounded by retirement communities and golf courses on the South Georgia coast, then tell the gospel story to engage seniors. If you're in a neighborhood in metro Atlanta with the highest concentration of gay-lesbian folks in the South, then act on that. Make a point of welcoming LGBT folks, because they *are* your neighbors, not just because it's good politics or smart recruiting. And push against good liberal bias, too," he proposes, particularly in more cosmopolitan neighborhoods. In a congregation anchored by educated young professionals committed to "accepting the other," for example, "you can affirm folks for really welcoming an interracial or same-sex couple, a homeless person, a funky single or artsy divorced person. But what if a well-dressed husband and wife with two neat kids come in for the first time, looking like they might be Republicans, and they get a cool reception. Call people out on it! Check your bias at the door."[14] Politically divided as denominations prove, and socially homogeneous as many congregations appear, judges Chris, local bodies of worship remain key communities of moral reflection, and we need to care for the coherence of their disagreement no less than the integrity of their consensus.

Leaving Church in Black and White

Which Americans are leaving church? Which churches? A veteran Black pastor in Atlanta considers these questions across racial lines considering his years as a denominational leader in United Methodism. African American young adults remain significantly more religious than other Americans of their generation, the Rev. Rick Martin knows well, and church leaders appreciate this crucial difference. At the same time, they see firsthand how much less likely Black millennials are than their elders to belong, attend, and take part in a congregation.[15]

Why so, pastors ask, and what should they do in response to this generation gap? Churchgoing has become more of an individual choice for members of this generation, they recognize. It's no longer a shared necessity or responsibility, something given as normal and normative to do together. Social conditions have shifted, Martin notes, along lines that lead individuals away from church, lifting Sunday blue laws, for example, and adding hours of weekly work needed to survive on lower rungs of the job ladder or to get ahead to the top. Alternatives to churchgoing have mushroomed in forms that range from televangelism and spiritual-growth podcasts to fitness training and streaming home entertainment. Related changes have made parenting more difficult, especially in working families headed by single mothers, he points out, while focusing better-off families less on church and more on meeting the middle-class demands of school and work, while choosing more widely among extracurricular activities.

"We see young people losing confidence in our churches," observes Rick Martin. "But it's not just the churches." It's a range of institutions, he adds, including the integrity of the family, the promise of the job market, and the good of government. "Look at the relationship of these young people to their parents. Think about who's raising them," he stresses, with an eye to the growing difficulties that rising generations have faced since the 1970s in finishing school, entering marriage, and finding steady jobs with living wages to sustain families of their own. Such obstacles threaten most directly those coming of age without college degrees and those facing discrimination due to race and class.[16]

Once, "all roads led to church," standing at the center of the Black community, many ministers recall, and serving it as school, town hall, aid society, healthcare center, concert hall, and social club. Racial discrimination and exclusion from taking part in these institutions of the larger society underlie this multipurpose history, they recognize, and real progress has been made by opening up such participation since the civil rights era.[17] But now these social institutions, activities, and relationships have multiplied and divided for many Black millennials, church leaders worry, in ways that narrow their vision of the church as less central and essential to the community as a whole, if not more insular and out of step with it.[18]

"Once upon a time, church was all there was to do on Sunday morning," recalls Rick Martin. "Now you can take your kids to a volleyball or soccer game," go work out with friends, or stay home and watch the NFL. "People are meeting their social and spiritual needs in different places," Martin judges, "and they're thinking differently about church in terms of their own needs. Pastors have to wake up to that. You have to deal with that tension. You can't just ignore it, or give in to it." Churches need to recognize the communal ties woven through many such activities, counsels Martin, bringing parents and children together with friends and neighbors in games, leagues, block parties, and clubs. Congregations can incorporate many such social activities and interests, he agrees with Chris Burns. But they should not seek in vain to compete against these venues by selling the soul of the church for a mess of pottage cooked up for the sake of sociable entertainment. That way lies "the pleasant irrelevancy of the church."[19]

Instead churches need to give up "the command and control system" of old-time religious claims to unquestioned authority and absolute truth, Rick Martin counsels. "We need to respect the questions young people live with today," rooted in personal maturity as well as social difficulty, and running along lines of social advantage and cultural outlook that divide the Black community across generations. "That's why they're looking for small groups," Martin says, "to ask those questions and think them over together," in light of spiritual experience they can discover as genuinely their own yet encompassing enough to share with others.

"Good pastoring is not so different from good parenting," Martin notes. "At some point you have to stop commanding and start discussing and explaining. You have to listen to them and go back and forth with them." Pastors can begin by asking, "What do you believe, and why? What don't you believe, and why not?" invites Martin, rather than trying to impose the Apostles' Creed on seekers or doubters. Instead, let them recite the Creed and question it together, and so "discover what it means, and how it means, for each of us and for one another," he promises. "You can take tradition to heart as the living words of the dead, not just repeat it as the dead words of the living," Martin sums up. "That's what our young people are hungry for."[20]

Ministry with young adults and youth can no longer content itself with "fun and games," Rick Martin stresses, if it ever could. "They are having to operate at another level now. Life has smacked them in the face," with challenges that many of their elders met later in life with stronger coping mechanisms and communal connections. Too often today Black youth and young adults struggle to pursue schooling, work, and courtship in the midst of hard drugs, casual sex, street gangs, prison culture, and few good jobs in metro suburbs as well as inner cities, before the COVID-19 pandemic made life harder still.[21]

The Black middle class and educated elite have grown from a talented tenth to a third or more, Martin grants, but the underlying moral needs that Black churches have long met still persist. "I am human!" he declares. "Church is the one place where you can say it and be heard, where you can stand up and be seen. It's the one place you can face racism and get beyond the original sin that this country still wants to deny and forget about." How can the church enable young Black men in particular to stand up and do right, to respect themselves and care for others? "We can't just leave it to the Muslims to speak to Black men about finding strength and dignity. We need to do better," he vows. Likewise, he adds, "We need to look into our own hearts to enable gays and the LGBTQ community to find their place in the Black church. They've always been there, they've always been in the family. But they haven't always been seen or accepted." In response to these changing challenges and enduring needs, urges Martin, congregations need to "wake up and get out of the box" to reach out to young adults face-to-face.[22]

Churches have long invited younger generations to join them in the status quo of a social establishment maintained by their elders, judges an astute Black pastor and longtime Methodist colleague of Rick Martin. Instead, the church must move from "the wrong side of history" to meet each new generation in the present by heeding "the stones shouting out in the streets" (Luke 19:40). "Black Lives Matter is a stone shouting out," he proclaims from the pulpit. "Me Too is a stone shouting out." So are advocates for clean drinking water, living wages, good schools, community policing, and adequate healthcare in Black communities across the country. Social movements such as BLM have emerged from the Black community but not from Black churches on the clergy-led model of the civil rights movement of a generation ago. A younger cohort of Black community activists, civic leaders, and professionals criticizes the church when it hangs back, for example, on marriage equality and women's rights. But they also welcome its moral partnership and social support in terms of love and justice that remain meaningful and moving to the unattached believers and "nothing in particulars," who far outnumber religious resisters and fervent atheists among Black "nones."[23]

The dynamic of congregating in worship and word should move us back and forth in dialogue, argues this veteran pastor, in order to move the church forward together across generations. Instead, he fears, generational division within the church resembles racial division in the larger society, particularly in its political polarization today. Consider civil rights and systemic racism shrugged off as matters of individual attitude and intention, he proposes, or economic hardship construed as the invisible handiwork of the market and the personal failure of the poor to try harder. These broken promises of liberty and justice for all, made by one nation under God, resemble in turn "the church's own broken promises to love all of God's children, and make disciples of all nations" (Matt 28:19–20). For the church itself is divided, he charges, over gay rights and marriage equality, women in ministry and politics in the pulpit, not only by long-standing arguments over infant or adult baptism and alcohol or temperance. "Can we hold our position but change our posture?' he asks. "Can we disagree, but see the humanity of the other person, and the Spirit of God moving in them as well?"[24]

If the good shepherd can go in search of one lost sheep (Luke 15:3–8), reasons a younger Methodist colleague of Rick Martin, "then we can go in search of our own lost young people without fearing for those already in the fold or abandoning them. If God has no hands but our own in this world, then we can reach out to our children and hold them close," he promises from the pulpit of a suburban Black church. "If we admit to losing our own way, we can go to them in exile. If we see the burden they carry, we can lift them up and help them homeward." Most of these "lost sheep" have been baptized, points out this minister in his forties. "They are no less the children of God than we are, each and every one of them, no matter how broken and messed up they may be, no matter how many times they have fallen and betrayed Him. Just like us," he confesses. "Even if we turn away from God, and forget who we are, God doesn't turn away from us," he promises. He abides in the church as our personal savior and redeemer.

"We are a church committed to connecting people to God and one another across generations," pledges this young pastor. "It's not a one-way street, with the young looking to the old to lead the way. It's the old looking to the young as well. It's a two-way street," with both sides responding to God's call in and through each other. This can serve as a counterexample, he offers, to the way one generation in America can stand in the way of the next and hinder it instead of helping it. If an older generation clings to power at the cost of progress for the young, it creates a crisis for the future. If the young feel blocked and betrayed by their elders, he warns, "they can lose their way and wander," without tradition to ground them or institutions to guide them. Instead, he promises, "If we live out the tradition faithfully by God's grace, we can celebrate the gifts of the young and encourage their prophetic witness to God's work in the world." Church elders can see God working in the world in new ways, and the young can learn to know the present they inhabit as part of the living story of the past they share in the church.

What stands in the way of such collaboration between generations? "Most denominational congregations are aging," replies this young pastor. "They're well-established and set in their ways. They want to grow, but they don't want to change," he observes. "They welcome the young into the same old place, and wonder why they don't stay, when all the seats are taken at the table up front for the leaders, and the new folks in the back need to fit in with the old taken-for-granted rules" that they don't understand. Look at black congregations in mainline denominations, prompts this pastor. "You'll find just a handful of young adults coming through the front door, almost none of them men." Why is that? "People want in, when they want what's inside. They value it, and they can't get it someplace else. They have to find that out themselves," he stresses. "You can't *tell* them they need the church. For what?" he asks. For community? For answers to life's big questions? "They can go to their friends for that, friends from work and school," he shrugs and shakes his head.

Compare a traditional church with its rows of pews facing forward to the pulpit, suggests this pastor, and the "coworking" open space of a contemporary corporate office. There managers and executives circulate as colleagues among desks, carrels, and conference tables set within the same walls. "It's all about techno-savvy interaction and communication" that college-educated young adults pursuing corporate careers now take for granted. "That's missing here," he notes, "along with the big screens and music you get everywhere in the megachurches," even as mainline Black congregations in metropolitan suburbs now appeal more distinctly to middle-class adults and feel more distant to and from their disadvantaged counterparts on the street.

Who's to blame? "That's exactly the wrong question to ask a lot of older church folks," replies this younger pastor. "Because they say the kids are shallow and selfish, and want everything their own way. The young folks can turn that right around at the old guard, who want everything to stay the way it's always been. Don't move the furniture around in the living room, because that's sacred," he chides. "If you want your own space, there's a corner in the basement where you can move the stack chairs around any way you want."

Younger adults with family ties in smaller Black congregations and local jobs in smaller markets are likelier to stay in church and struggle for a voice of their own, this pastor observes, while more mobile Black millennials linked to nationwide college networks and corporate job markets are likelier to look around and leave a larger "preestablished" congregation in metro Atlanta if it fails to fit. "Young Black folks are more educated than our parents, and a lot of us are better educated," adds this pastor. "That doesn't mean we're smarter," he smiles. "But we see things differently, even when you get past the resentment or superiority you can feel." More cosmopolitan or liberal views can prove problematic not only in principle—for example, on gay rights as civil rights or biblical abomination—but also when it comes to "who's in charge and why?" questions of practical authority in preaching, teaching, or decision-making in church.

"Whatever is happening outside has to come inside the church for younger folks," declares this young pastor. "That includes politics and injustice. We preach that. But some more traditional 'biblical' Black churches won't go there. That closes them off to young people. We can't be so heavenly minded, that we're no earthly good."[25] In fact, he argues, the Black church has always preached possibility and hope, even in slavery. "Keep breathing and keep going, for the sake of your children and their children. They refused to die back then, and right now I am living my ancestors' dream. Thank God for that, thank the church, and carry it on!"

This means "making your kids go to church, even when they don't want to," adds this pastor and father of teenagers, "and talking to them about what they don't like," What's that? "The extra stuff, the revivals, the Watch Night service," he replies. "Watch Night is more than a sleepover. It's about slavery and Emancipation," he stresses.[26] "I want my kids to know who they are, and where they came from. So we're reading slave narratives, from right here in Georgia. People who were enslaved telling their own stories. It's terrible and awful. But it's what you need to know and take to heart," he pauses for emphasis. "Whatever challenge you face in life, it's nothing like that. If they could make it from there, you can make it from right here. They had no rights. You have the right to vote. So vote every time," he smiles. "For everything. From president to mayor, from city council to school board and dogcatcher."

High demands for congregational commitment can put off young adults, acknowledges this young pastor. "They have less time to be in church every day and be committed to the choir, the usher team, the Bible classes." That tilts leadership toward older cohorts with higher levels of engagement. "They have more time, and they're more willing to give it. That's hard to fix," he concedes, "even if you want to incentivize young people to lead, because it's a practical problem, and it's about fairness, too." Should congregations change what they offer and ask of their younger members, short on time and long on ideas of their own? Consider Atlanta's mushrooming megachurches, Black and White alike, proposes this pastor in response. Note what's featured and what's missing in cases such as Northpoint Community Church, attended by some forty thousand members, mostly White suburban young families, couples, and singles.[27]

What do these megachurches do? "Weekend worship with great rock music, and Andy Stanley on stage talking just to you in the dark" of a huge theater, answers this pastor. "It's always well-prepared, well-scripted, and delivered heart-to-heart. Afterwards there are all these small affinity groups, if you want to go. That's it, nothing else," he emphasizes. "No choir, no Sunday school, no guilds or missions. No funerals. That's all gone. No leadership problems, either, since it's all top-down with paid staff putting on the show." Is this what young people really want, or what churches should aim to give them? "That's arguable," replies this pastor, since it falls far short of the priesthood of all believers, and it goes too far toward its own streamlined kind of clergy rule. "In the church we should be disciples and members one of another," he concludes. "Pastors can get in the way of that full discipleship by trying to call all the shots and do it all themselves."

What can mainline denominations do differently in response? "We need to start up churches led by young people for young people in the places where they live and work," answers this young pastor. "Start small. You don't need millions for a building. Start worshipping in someone's living room, then move to a local school gym when you get bigger. Meet for study or small groups at home, or meet remotely now with COVID." In fact, big mortgages for big buildings no longer make sense to many millennials, argues this pastor. "Don't spend the money on buildings. Spend it on people!" he urges. "Spend it on helping one another, and working for justice in the community. What nonprofit group asking people for money to do good sends out pictures of their big fancy building?" he asks. "Not one! They show you pictures of them feeding hungry kids and helping poor mothers."

Doesn't the congregation still center on the people gathered in worship around the book, hearing the Word and praising God? Yes, agrees this pastor, but the form and format of such gathering must change. "We thought the church would never change when it came to how we worship, but this pandemic has shown we can change. We can go online and think outside the box." Once COVID-19 contagion is finally contained, he judges, "We can choose to go back inside the box, or we can be reborn and remake the church with these new skills we have learned. If we trust in the light of the future, then we'll put our good work and mission over the size of the sanctuary and the number of people in the pews."[28]

Unlike the entertainment business, where tickets sold at every show provide an immediate measure of success, argues this pastor, "If we want to make a difference in people's lives, we need to change the metrics we're using. We need to open our eyes to see all the people out there in need that we can reach with our own hands, without the big budget or the big show of a megachurch." Over the course of the pandemic, he reports, his congregation of a thousand has continued to contribute more than a hundred thousand dollars to a charitable fund set apart from the church's general budget to aid church members and neighbors to pay their bills for groceries, utilities, medicine, and rent. "People give money out of the goodness of their heart for the church to give away because they value that," he attests. "Everyone knows that hotline fills up in ten minutes every month with hundreds of calls. They see the need, they see the Kingdom work being done, and they will not let that go." The process is personal, he notes, and it unfolds face-to-face. "Folks call and come in, we listen to their stories, and we pray with them. We help all we can, whether they come to church or not, because that's what we do."

Has the denominational landscape changed uniquely for African American congregations over the past generation? Not uniquely but notably, answers Rick Martin. "Black evangelical megachurches and 'Word Churches' have increased and multiplied outside Black denominations, while the Black presence in mainline denominations has spread," especially among the college-educated. Predominantly Black mainline congregations flourish, he notes, by "following the Spirit" in Spirit-filled, call-and-response preaching, enthusiastic worship, and powerfully moving music. They nurture warm fellowship and active mutual aid, vigorous evangelism and pointed political engagement.[29] These congregations support the principle of denominational integration across racial lines. But they recognize its practice as a "work in progress" at the congregational level. They remain committed to finding their own way and steering the course of their own church life. They support the denomination as a whole, without being captured by its internal divisions—for example, between "peace-and-justice liberals" and "conservative evangelicals" in United Methodism—or being deterred by its predominantly White congregations shying away from too pointed or frequent criticism of racial injustice.

"Don't blame the denomination for the decline and irrelevance of your own church," Rick Martin warns. "Don't make stuff up. The young people don't like the old hymns? Really? Then rearrange them and update them," he urges. "Add a men's jazz choir or a classical youth orchestra. Let bright young women volunteer as greeters out front, and young black men as ushers and security ministry. Let them both speak and read scripture from the pulpit. Rethink those roles all through the church, not just up front," he sums up, "You don't need to be whooping from the pulpit all the time," Martin allows. "But we do need to raise up the people and bring down the Spirit in our own sacred space. We need to speak to the historical experience of African Americans and face up to what folks are dealing with every day of their lives."

Steering this true course means distinguishing between "institution and incarnation," not just between Black and White church traditions, Rick Martin points out, with an eye to respecting denominational order but responding to changes in the everyday life of the local church and community to "make the Word flesh here and now":

> Pentecost is going on right now. The Word is being spoken in different languages we need to hear and understand. Some churches *are* getting smaller in this season. We need to find out how they can be smaller and stronger, instead of just struggling to get bigger, and then giving up and making excuses about all the resources we don't have. Play to your strengths, and respond to what's

present in your own people and community. Go with that. You don't have to get bigger to stay alive and flourish.[30]

Size and scale matter, Martin grants, but congregational integrity matters more. "You welcome everyone. You can do different small groups in a big church. You can do traditional and contemporary worship services at different times. You can 'target' young and old, singles and families." But churches shouldn't try in vain to be all things to all people like a department store, he cautions, or aim to target a niche market like a fashion boutique. Especially in more affluent congregations, pastors can feel the tug of a fee-for-services model of exchange and face the temptation to become a "spiritual concierge" of sorts, on call 24/7 and devoted to providing individualized spiritual services to key members of the congregation.[31]

Young or old, Black or White, what are people looking for in church? "Help, hope, and home," Rick Martin answers. That holds true across generations and stages of life, and it offers common ground for congregations to cultivate. "We all want to relate, young and old. Even pastors," Martin laughs. Offering-plate concerns turn pastors toward institutional givers, who tend to be older. But money matters to everyone, he stresses, especially in the Black Church, where money means freedom. "We're buying our own freedom. We own the property, so God can head the church, and we can take care of it ourselves as God's stewards."

Comparing genteel collection of offerings by passing the plate discreetly in the pews to answering the traditional altar call to come up front and give under the watchful eye of pastor and people, Martin underscores the common good inherent in the practice of each member of the church participating in the community and contributing to it. "Everybody can and should take part, because we're all part of the whole," he says. "Everyone actually wants to contribute, to put into the common pot, and share what you have. See and be seen. Don't hide it under a bushel. We're all part of the family, so I love and respect you enough not to exempt you from doing your part."

Full inclusion in the body of the church as members one of another, equally and infinitely valuable as children of God, transcends the inequality of worldly goods, Martin stresses, and it sheds light on personal moral example in face-to-face relationships. This extends to enabling children to come of age in the church and in the world, he notes. When his daughter turned eight years old, she pressed to join her mother in a pew up front in the sanctuary, Martin recalls, instead of being relegated to children's ministry in a separate classroom. That moved him to make his sermons more immediately engaging. "Don't take all day," he smiles, "and don't talk down to them!"

Age-grading can go too far, Martin reflects. "Children's ministry used to mean sitting next to your momma and learning how to worship in church.

Instead of separating young people out, let them hold hands with the older folks. Let them pray together, and fellowship together." Church isn't grammar school, "where you separate everybody out by age and grade," he reasons. "It's more like family, where young and old gather at table." There they draw together in prayer and communion all their separate rounds of activity in work and play, choir practice and Bible study. At the same time, he suggests, "You can do a small group for young mothers when you've got choir practice for their kids. Give them both a good reason to bring each other to church," while recognizing that young singles looking for partners want to meet and talk with one another rather than young couples with children.

Running through the diversity of Black churches and the integrity of the Black Church, Martin concludes, the common denominator of spiritual authenticity as a moral good comes home from cultural common sense to gospel truth: "People want to show up authentically in church today," like they want to do meaningful work and find true love. "They want to live out their deepest spiritual yearnings. They want to come home, where it doesn't matter how far or how long you've been away. There's a place for you at the table," he promises. "That's our story. It's a Bible story, the Prodigal Son and the Good Samaritan. It's the gospel truth: 'Blessed are they which do hunger and thirst after righteousness: for they shall be filled.' Everybody can come home" (Matt. 5:6). Authenticity as an existential virtue of seekers on the road to spiritual awareness comes home and becomes reincorporated in the body of the church as a forgiving, fulfilling family in redemptive communion.[32]

TRANSFORMING SELFHOOD IN COMMUNITY

Comparing congregations across the lines of race, class, and cohort in Atlanta rehearses and refocuses key themes from Alto Church in Silicon Valley. For many Americans congregational life no longer stands at the center of personal identity and local community, church leaders recognize as a social fact and a moral challenge. It's become more like a slice of life, a sector of social activity and relationship that individuals can choose to narrow, expand, or shape to suit themselves.

Why so? Manifold causes and conditions underlie such change, pastors say, embracing personal attitude and cultural outlook within new patterns of parenting, schooling, work, and leisure that range from more confessionally mixed marriages and single-parent households to freer participation by African Americans in the institutions of the larger society. Don't take young adults for granted or all of a piece, pastors advise, when it comes to creeds and codes, fear of God or grasp of doctrine. Pay attention to them instead, ask what they care about and hope for in life, why they're staying away from church, what they're doing instead and with whom. Give up "the command and control system" of trying to impose God-given authority and assert the truth of God's word and will. Test tradition instead, recite and question the creed, retell the gospel story and wrestle with the gospel truth to distill wisdom as the work of a lifetime.

What is religion good for? Note the range of functionalist views of religion today, suggest these pastors. Young adults see it as a way to make friends and strengthen social bonds, teach moral lessons and cultural literacy, cultivate good habits, and ground moral character and community. Listen for their underlying visions and doubts about the meaning of truth and goodness lived out together in the name of authenticity. Sense their longing for practical wisdom and trustworthy authority. From what are young adults seeking to be saved, pastors ask, or with what are they seeking to cope, particularly those not so securely credentialed at school, launched in careers, and married with children? Whether getting ahead or lagging behind, what more do they want and need to lead good lives, love others, and be loved in turn? Congregations can grow more intentional and insightful, their leaders promise, in enabling young adults to raise and answer these questions of meaning in their lives through prayer, communion, and mutual care, in the course of "becoming a grown-up" in love and work, in the marketplace and public square.

Congregations need to recognize the social functions served by circles of friends, neighbors, and colleagues at work and play, pastors agree, then "come alongside them" to deepen their shared community in worship and love instead of trying to outdo them in competition or flatter them by imitation. They need to affirm the full personhood and infinite value of each and every person—Black and White, rich and poor, gay and straight, young and old—by enacting peace and justice in an unfairly divided society too often heedless of "the stones shouting out in the streets." Let churches begin by healing their own internal divisions along each and every one of these lines. If they renew their commitment to the integrity and diversity of faithful tradition, then young adults will be free to come home to a place at the table.

Do common cultural dynamics mark congregations that draw and hold young adults in America today? They recognize the moral good of spiritual authenticity and the sway of autonomous selfhood at work and play in modern individualism. They are willing to engage in this common sense, their leaders promise, and they are committed to transforming it. How? Through "making Jesus real" in living out Word and Sacrament in love, they answer in Christian vernacular, animating the congregational Body of Christ in mutual care and service, and grounding the gospel truth of peace and justice in the experience of common prayer and worship. What makes such a congregation's worship and community meaningful? It is not the existential incandescence of each autonomous individual choosing to join in and take part, they stress, but the love of an incarnate God choosing and calling each person to come closer by the goodness of creation and the grace of redemption. Such recognition comes only through practice of Word and Sacrament sustained by participation, not by proclamation or profession alone.[33]

Such participatory practice proves challenging, as we have seen in each of our congregational cases. Why so? It seeks to unify a separate self in all its protean possibility and diverse social roles with one biblical God as creator and redeemer, and to form this self as a member of the congregation's body at the center of social life. But fewer Americans today inhabit a social world centered on the church. We hold sacred "separation of church and state," each governed by its own members. We prize freedom *from* "organized religion" in the same Constitutional breath as freedom from an established church that once secured free exercise *of* religion. We take denominational pluralism for granted, and we choose for or against congregations more strongly based on personal feeling and fit than parochial loyalty or family legacy.

We aspire more often to integrate our personality and unify our sense of self than to grow closer to God or unite our soul with the One. We recognize our many social roles as part of the drama of everyday life at home, work, and play in diverse activities and relationships: "Don't tell your boss everything you tell your spouse," we advise each other. "Don't treat your employees like children or your friends like clients. Don't expect your mortgage banker to forgive your debts like your parents do." Multiplied and divided selves require common sense to balance their distinctive social norms and styles, we grant, but rarely do they add up to an existential crisis of fragmented identity, demand an all-or-nothing flight to authenticity, or provoke an all-out fight for integrity of character.[34]

However smoothly we balance our diverse social roles, however coherently we stick to their scripted lines in cultural conversation, we do not institutionalize them equally or once and for all.[35] More Americans now see themselves as freer to come and go when it comes to church than to school or work, and freer to play the episodic role of "perpetual visitor," if not a marginal member or liminal guest, than either a Sunday stalwart or fervent atheist.[36] They may be spiritual seekers or diversely devout, present on the rolls but not in the pews of mainline churches. They may be more or less occasional attenders, but nonetheless free spirits, modern mystics, and religious individualists at heart, even when they fill a pew on Sundays.

This fluid sense of selfhood, particularly but not only among millennials and those declaring themselves "spiritual but not religious," reflects widening cultural convictions among Americans of an authentic inner self that runs deeper, rises higher, and reaches further than any religious institution. Churches can and should meet the spiritual needs of such free-flowing selves and enhance their fulfillment, report surveys of religious "nones," instead of trying to impose rigid rules on their conduct or make outsized demands on their time, money, labor, and loyalty.[37]

What can church do for me? These exemplary congregations are willing to engage that self-centered question in practice, first, by generosity of personal attention and unselfish spirit, welcoming the stranger and loving the neighbor for Christ's sake. By living out Christ's example of attentive care and unselfish love, these churches pray and pledge, they can soften up separate selves and bridge their buffered disengagement to spark creative self-expression, emotional fulfillment, and moral integrity. Beginning to dwell among such friends can turn the moods and motives of newcomers toward grateful affection for the kind of moral community that inspires such loving care in turn. That it comes through the common prayer and faith of a body of worship may seem dubious at first to the self-centered newcomer. But through time and effort shared in prayer, fellowship, and service, this interactive transformation can become a familiar kind of grace and harmony with God, however miraculous or anomalous it appears to the unpracticed observer.[38]

The congregation can thereby come to offer consolation and shelter from an unfair, unloving world. It can give inspiring witness and actual example of how serving God in this world helps transform its suffering and division by helping others as God's children. Thus the wide-open doors of Alto Church's "art-form café" greet newcomers with a heartfelt welcome instead of "linear" demands to accept fundamentalist orthodoxy and conformity in order to belong. Thus Intown Church's "radio music" welcomes visitors into a homey living room for worship with French-roast coffee and fresh-baked scones close at hand. Local yoga classes stretch and beckon in the basement, and community activists engage their neighbors in the auditorium.

By contrast to self-declared atheists, opposed in principle to religious institutions as false if not evil, most of America's "nones" today find mainline churches irrelevant and inattentive in practice to what concerns them most. Preachy and politicized, hypocritical and boring, conventional churches seem to offer them little chance to express and fulfill their innermost selves, to bridge the separateness and fill the emptiness they feel, to rediscover their creative spark and reawaken their joy in living, let alone come closer to God. They yearn to reconnect with others, dwell among friends, and make the world a better place. Can churches respond to such aims, couched as they are in terms of therapeutic thinking and the pragmatism of quasi-scientific common sense? Yes, they can, these exemplary cases promise, by recognizing the religious roots of aspiring to authentic selfhood, integrity of character and community, love and justice beyond kith and kin, and responsibility shared by all for our common fate. That holds true, however naturalized our language, romanticized our sentiments, and mysticized our outlook.[39]

Modern mysticism is not all wrong, in fact, or inimical to faith, as it morphs from the cosmopolitan culture of educated Western elites into the global culture of self-realization in work and play, romance and leisure. Nor is ethical individualism, however psychologized or contractualized it has grown from its biblical and civic roots in American culture, and however ideologically its branches have bent under the polarizing pressure of American politics for the past generation. Insightful and resourceful congregations can engage these cultural changes in meaningful conversation and prayerful practice, promise their leaders, if they disarm the divisive distraction of God as a member of this or that political faction. They can resist conscription into would-be culture wars waged by "God and Country" armies of law and order against the "moral chaos" wreaked by secularists and their progressive allies in the name of justice and equality.[40]

CHURCH, SECT, AND MYSTICISM

Now let's turn to the overarching moral visions and underlying institutional ideals that frame these stories of religious upbringing and spiritual insight told by baby boom parents and their millennial children come of age and raising children of their own. In this light let's weigh the meaning of these stories to clarify the challenges and opportunities they offer to congregational flourishing in mainline American religion today and assess the moral arc they paint across the canvas of American culture.

Looking over the cultural and social transformation of the religious landscape in Western Europe a century ago, the historian and theologian Ernst Troeltsch discerned a distinctively modern kind of religious individualism reweaving strands of traditional Christian mysticism in its interplay over centuries with ideals of the church embodied in Roman Catholicism and the sect in dissenting Protestantism.[41]

Seen as an ideal type, the Church institutionalizes grace and salvation resulting from the saving work of Christ as Redeemer, made flesh and fulfilled once and for all humankind forever. This endows the Church with the sacramental authority to transmit the remission of sins and sanctification of all souls. It enables the Church to embrace society as an organic whole through its ordained ministry, the revealed Word of God, and the holy sacraments. As Christ's living presence on earth and itself the fundamental sacrament, the Church comes before us and nurtures us like a mother, rather than emerging as the offspring of our voluntary association as individuals.

The Sect, by contrast comes together as a voluntary society of elect believers, who have come out of "the world" of the larger society and been born again by following in the footsteps of Christ as Lord, the moral example and lawgiver of biblical authority. You are born into a church, but you are called and chosen to join a sect. Its members live apart from the world in a strict community of love and holiness, in preparation for the Kingdom of God to come when Christ returns and completes the work of redemption.

Mysticism in the modern era dissolves fixed forms of church doctrine and sacramental worship, along with sect discipline and biblical authority, into a purely personal inner experience of Christ as divine spirit, spark, or principle. It goes its own way in the name of freedom of spirit and conscience. Appealing to individuals from educated, cultured classes in particular, it brings kindred souls into a fluid fellowship lit by unity with universal truth and led by the immediacy and intimacy of its felt experience. Mysticism redeems individuals through an ongoing process of spiritual illumination that culminates in the union of the soul with God in the ever-present moment.

All three ideals go back to the dawn of Christianity, Troeltsch thought, and all three interact and intertwine throughout its history, each with its own biblical warrant. The original community of Jesus and the Apostles centers on a free personal piety that inspires profound intimacy, communion, and spiritual fellowship without any organized worship or fixed social structure. "Only when faith in Jesus, the risen and exalted Lord, became the central point of worship in a new religious community, did the need for organization arise," Troeltsch judges. From the outset Christian fellowship and teaching typically take shape through ritual practice along the lines of church, sect, and mysticism intertwined in Christ as sacrificial redeemer, moral exemplar, and inner spirit.[42] The church embodies the Kingdom of God on earth in sacramental form, the outward sign of an inward grace. The sect heralds the lawful Kingdom to come, ushered in by Christ's return. In the mystical realm of the Spirit the Kingdom of God lies only and ever within us.

MODERN MYSTICISM

Throughout history these three types counterpoint one another, according to Troeltsch, and mysticism forms a welcome complement to the church and the sects. In the modern era it animates Christian piety as a living, creative movement of universal religious consciousness. But Troeltsch feared that modern mystical individualism also proves problematic to religious institutions in themselves and in their relationship to public life and its moral coherence:

> It is neither Church nor sect, and has neither the concrete sanctity of the institution nor the radical connection with the Bible. Combining Christian ideas with a wealth of modern views, deducing social institutions, not from the Fall but from a process of natural development, it has not the fixed limit for concessions and

> the social power which the church possesses, but also it does not possess the radicalism and the exclusiveness with which the sect can set aside the State and economics, art and science.[43]

Committed to an immediate, inward experience of the spirit, mysticism is indifferent to outward forms of religious worship, doctrine, and organization. At the same time, it takes them for granted. It is likewise indifferent to the larger society's political and economic organization through modern administrative, bureaucratic, and market-centered structures. It therefore relies all the more upon these structures in the absence of its own distinctive institutional arrangement, moral authority, and social discipline as a community of faith.

In the absence of a gospel ethic or ecclesial tradition of its own, modern mysticism reflects the morally mixed cosmopolitan culture surrounding it, especially among the educated and urbane middle classes, even as it senses itself transcending such bounds to represent the highest ethical ideals of humanity as a whole. As it comes to predominate in modern Europe by the twentieth century, thought Troeltsch, this type of religiosity takes fluid form in a "voluntary association with like-minded people," a purely spiritual fellowship of inner light and love equally remote from the magisterial church and the perfectionist sects whose crosscurrents mark the mainstream of Christian tradition.[44]

In mid-twentieth-century America, by contrast, social thinkers such as Talcott Parsons discerned an ethical individualism spreading cultural values of human dignity, rights, and progressive reform across society at large from essentially religious roots. As modern democratic government expanded to integrate the entire society more fully around such values, the not-so-secular city of the society itself, conceived as a societal moral community, became more and more like a universal if invisible church. The process of "Christianizing secular society" in America institutionalizes the ethical individualism Parsons identified at Christianity's own taproot, grounded in the idea of God's people in the biblical covenant of Judaic society.[45]

Modern denominational pluralism by this account carries moral visions of the sacred value, dignity, and autonomy of individual persons throughout American public life. It extends individuals' moral responsibility and calling beyond the tutelary authority of a magisterial church or the bounded body of a strict sect. It diffuses them across the social spheres of family life, schooling, and the professions to inspire good citizenship in a "nation with the soul of a church." Modern principles of religious freedom, voluntarism, and toleration combine with the generalization of traditionally religious values of moral duty, virtue, and responsibility to create "a common matrix of value commitment which is broadly shared among denominations, and which forms the basis of the sense in which the society as a whole forms a religiously based moral community."[46]

This generalizing process of ongoing reform marks a moral upgrading rather than breakdown at work in modern society, according to Parsons. A conscientious and truly self-governing sense of individual autonomy and mutual responsibility informs and expresses values institutionalized in the practice of democratic self-government under rule of law, civic rites, universal education, and middle-class family life, cemented by the Golden Rule mutuality inherent in Christian ethics.

This prospect of moral reintegration redeems religious individualism from Troeltsch's critique of modern mysticism. It recognizes no inherent tensions between an encompassing civil-religious faith in "one nation under God," the benign fluidity of modern culture, and the rationalized structural arrangement of modern social institutions administered by the state as a liberal constitutional regime to yield "liberty and justice for all." It promises the material progress and moral integrity of a complex society rooted in religious values that all citizens share.

American faith in flux in the twenty-first century can justify both a sense of promise and peril in response to the rise of such religious individualism across a wider range of carriers, and its ambiguous impact on their religious understanding and participation. It stretches from New Age spiritual seekers, through many mainline Protestants and Americanist Catholics sitting in the pews yet charting their own spiritual journeys, to softer evangelicals whose voluntarist piety floats free of fundamentalist faith, dutybound congregational community, and the rigor of prayerful practice.

Modern religious individualism redefines the traditional meaning of "spirituality" as a practical aspect and inner dimension of all religious life into its common usage today as a "spiritual but not religious" term of contrast. It counterposes spirituality as an autonomous personal realm of cosmic consciousness to "organized religion" as an institutional realm of social solidarity that seeks to form its members and sustain their lifelong integrity in an organic body bound by constraint instead of "letting them be" to come and go as authentic individuals in a voluntary association that frees them to choose their own path to meet their own spiritual needs.

At its best, modern religious individualism stresses the need for all doctrinal beliefs to receive personal reinterpretation, and for all religious liberties to lead to deeper self-understanding and greater social responsibility for the shared fate of humankind. The search for personal meaning and social relevance at the heart of the modern quest for salvation after heaven and beyond belief, especially among the more educated, has led spiritual seekers to explore forms of ritual practice, artistic expression, therapeutic care, and social activism well beyond the boundaries of traditional religious institutions.

More open and flexible patterns of membership in turn have made for more permeable boundaries and fluid types of organization in most major denominations, and in the freestanding congregations of their "transdenominational" offspring. There these changes have spurred conflicts over orthodox belief and biblical authority, active membership and faithful discipleship, as well as debates over church growth and decline across generations.[47]

At the same time, mounting evidence points to the unsettling effects of a this-worldly individualism severed from constitutive relationship to God or a purposive cosmos, and self-centered in seeking to serve strategic self-interest or emotional self-expression on the modern model of market exchange or therapeutic encounter. Thus the commonsense view of most Americans holds that "an individual should arrive at his or her own religious beliefs independent of any churches or synagogues." That is a sociological impossibility, to be sure, but a clear corollary of imagining human beings standing as separate individuals, each on their own two feet, instead of being embraced as members within the whole of social bodies, groups, and webs of relationship that enable us to become who we are.[48]

From this standpoint comes radical reconstrual of James Madison's deist remonstrance, for example, that the sovereignty of individual conscience and conviction requires free exercise of religion precisely to honor its divine Creator and the lawful order of nature and nature's God. Freedom of conscience to worship God and follow reason comes to be contested and recast as freedom of choice to pursue one's own interests and express one's own feelings. Thus contemporary common sense follows utilitarian principle. Since God does not either speak or write to us, Bentham asks, "How then are we to know what is his pleasure? By observing what is our own pleasure and pronouncing it to be his."[49] Unlike Benthamites in theory, modern religious individualists in practice find it difficult to sustain their own sense of moral integrity and responsibility, let alone transmit it to their children, if they do not share its practice in religious communities with some binding sect-like discipline or churchly authority.

Early modern Puritans practiced democratic self-government with striking social flexibility and freedom while remaining strictly grounded in cultural and psychological frameworks of doctrinal orthodoxy and rigidly disciplined personality enacted in their church, family, and schooling. Can modern societies that celebrate freedom in personal, political, and cultural terms actually institutionalize our freedom securely and fairly? Consider the constraining coordination of our disciplinary education and employment of specialized technical skills, habits of mind, and practical virtues tuned to occupational and bureaucratic life organized by modern business corporations and administrative states. Can this strategic order suffice to sustain the moral integrity of our way of life and uphold the responsibility we share for our society as a whole?[50]

Modern forms of instrumental individualism suit the social arrangement of efficient economic activity within a complex division of labor and bureaucratic administration set by strategic interests and procedural rules. Forms of expressive individualism fit lifestylish leisure to embrace emotional self-expression and satisfaction. Both sorts of individualism have coexisted from their outset with civic and religious ideals of the dignity and sacredness of each person that inform our moral rights and duties, practical virtues, and responsible relationships within traditions of biblical religion and civic humanism in American culture. The question critics pose is whether an individualism centered on the self as a nexus of interests and feelings and counted chiefly as a market actor or client-citizen of the welfare state, can actually sustain a public *or* private life coherently. If not, they ask, can civic and religious forms of individualism be critically reworked through congregational communities of shared moral practice and argument to ground in everyday experience a purposeful sense of human life for all of us? Can we mediate and rebalance the moral ecology of private life and public institutions by renewing genuine individuality in relation to a larger social whole and deeper cultural conversation?[51]

This challenge invites mainline Protestant churches in particular to pursue their ongoing reformation as faithful communities of character. Freedom of religious association emerges in the early modern West as fully legitimate on the strength of dissenting Protestantism's stress on thinking for oneself in the light of biblical revelation and individual conscience. Such congregations first feature strict standards of doctrinal orthodoxy and efforts to enforce moral purity grounded in the sect-like discipline of monks in the world. Then patterns of membership gradually grow more open and flexible in major American denominations, holding each person morally responsible for themselves and their own ultimate answers to religious questions.

These churches now face the challenge to reform themselves in ways that balance the religious individualism illuminated by the inward communion of modern mystics and spiritual seekers—and the exemplary moral vigor and prophetic witness inherited from Christian sects as ingathered elects composed of come-outers—with the social realism of the Church as the Pauline Body of Christ, the fundamental sacrament that precedes and nurtures every faithful person in redemptive relationship to God, love of neighbor, and seeking the good in common.[52]

SECTS AND SECULARISM

If the unity of modern society centers on a secular state inherently at odds with religious faith and community, by contrast to the moral integrity of the not-so-secular city, then there comes to the fore a very different ecclesiological ideal of a radically reformed church or sect. It stands against "the world" of the larger society. In its most aggressive stance, it seeks to "conquer the world for Christ" in theocratic form, or to establish a "Christian America" by force of law and votes if not by force of arms. More typically, in the revivalist American grain, it seeks to realize the ideal of the Sermon on the Mount in all its purity and usher in the Kingdom to come by calling each and every person to the altar of born-again conversion and moral transformation, and so save America one soul at a time.

A progressive social gospel assumes that faithful citizens can engage in public life to reform our institutions, aid individuals in need, and make our society more nearly just. But such Christian enthusiasm for secular political involvement distracts Christians from the church's first public task as an exemplary witness community of Christian virtue and love. So argue more radical reformers like Stanley Hauerwas. He fears that such naive political enthusiasm leads Christians to acquiesce in "the liberal assumption that a just polity is possible without the people being just," and to consider the disciplined formation of virtue in communities of faith "an inexcusable intrusion into our personal liberty." For the true Christian, Hauerwas declares, "the church is always the primary polity." Its first task is to make persons holy and genuinely just, not to make the society better, by forming in itself an exemplary "society built on truth rather than fear" bred by the state's coercive power and the market's anxious self-interest.[53]

Let the church be the church, urges this "Christ against culture" view, instead of imitating the secular social world surrounding it. The church fulfills its first responsibility to society by being itself, less an introverted sect than a church militant, an apostolic church radically reformed through exemplary *ecclesiolae in ecclesia*, small churches within the church as a whole, shaped by the shared concentration and intimacy of their communal life in worship, work, and witness. Such a church, "living in but not of the world" of the larger society and prepared to stand against it, enables the faithful to see the world for what it is. It enables them to recognize why America's secular political self-understanding is so limited, for example, by the emptiness of the individual freedom it prizes as an end in itself, and the narrowness of the contractual legal procedures it resorts to for strategic coordination in the absence of conscientious self-restraint and communally shared social responsibility.[54]

By contrast, what if the public order of American society today is seen not as a single moral realm, however open or closed to reform, but as a constellation of two or more "kingdoms," that is, more or less discrete domains, each with its own ideals and arrangement? Then religious institutions best serve as socially adaptive, mildly sect-like "sheltering communities" set within the formal framework of denominations. These sheltering congregational and cultural communities contrast, on one hand, with radically reformed churches or strong sects set against the society as a whole. On the other hand, they contrast with loose, fluid associations of like-minded religious individuals or modern mystics in denominational guise, fully in step with the secular city of the larger society and culture.[55]

Instead of accepting or criticizing the state and the economy within society as a whole, such sheltering communities conduct their own affairs with measured confidence that truly faithful believers will also be reliable employees, honest merchants, and dedicated professionals as well as law-abiding citizens. The faithful can focus on seeking to save souls, shape conscience, and nurture the family, since they trust that conscientious workers will prove trustworthy in business and charitable in aid when the market fails to provide for the needy. Such sheltering communities can "mediate" between individuals and big government, urging the state to support churches, not supplant them, in educating, caregiving, and providing for the poor.[56]

On the broad theological ground that surrounds this sheltering, mildly sect-like stance of the church to public life, we find traditionally evangelical Protestant emphases on freedom of worship and conscience protected by "church-state separation," and wariness of state power expanding to take over the social functions of churches and shrink their moral authority. Here, too, stand traditionally Lutheran notions of church and state as two kingdoms, each sovereign in its own realm; and the concern of "Catholic Whigs" for strong boundaries between the economy and government as well as church and state. We find evangelical support for setting up voluntary associations to help the needy instead of expanding state social-service agencies to do so, Catholic concerns for parochial schools and hospitals, and fundamentalists founding Christian academies to educate their own to keep the faith.[57]

Along this church-state frontier, politicized religious lobbies and parachurch groups combine with ideologically charged political-action committees and paraparty groups to blur and bend bright lines of church-state separation. To build religious voting blocs partisan campaigns and elected officials propose faith-based initiatives and government grants to support church schools and social programs, and they promise legislation and court decisions to protect free exercise of some religious convictions over others.[58]

The historic ideal of the sect rings true to Americans in standing for the voluntary association of faithful individuals within a Protestant priesthood of all believers joined in God's Word yet free to exercise their own conscience in the light of God's grace and will. The ideal of the sect resonates with our sense of democratic equality and full yet free participation in self-government under the rule of law. Because the sect actively seeks to form disciples and bind its members into the Body of Christ or People of God, its nurture and discipline prove particularly pertinent to the need of mystical individuals and spiritual seekers to become members of faithful communities.

At the same time, the sect remains fragile, despite or indeed because of all the binding demands it makes on individual members to sustain it. This holds particularly true in a denominational society with growing freedom to switch or leave behind ever more independent congregations if they ask too much or too little of us. Many of America's "nones" cite just such reasons for leaving churches they see as sectarian obstacles to their spiritual freedom and fulfillment. Many of the spiritual but not religious see no need to belong to communities of faith at all, however ecumenically open, in order to experience and express their spirituality.

Especially in a society seen as the contractual creation of come-outers who freely form an ingathered elect, strong sects run the risk of ignoring how deeply their elect members are actually involved in the complex moral order of the larger social world they oppose and how deeply that world enters into their own community. Mild, sheltering sects risk allowing that world to go its own unjust and unconscionable way in return for religious tolerance under the law, freedom of individual conscience, interpersonal support, and psychic solace for the righteous. So the ideal of the Church is a welcome counterbalance to the sect, given its sacramental and liturgical embodiment of the encompassing reality of redemption for the whole of God's people in one organic body of many different members.

CHURCH AND SOCIETY

Church-like ideals of religious institutions arise from distinguishing between the state and the society conceived as a diverse yet interwoven whole, rather than a set of discrete political, economic, and domestic moral domains. From this standpoint society makes up a much richer, more inclusive reality than the state. It is composed of many subcommunities of various institutional kinds: families, neighborhoods, schools, labor unions, small businesses, giant corporations, farm cooperatives, professional guilds, and a host of clubs and congregations. Each form of community must be free to exist and flourish in its own right, and each must be responsible to act justly and carefully as parts of society through which people participate in the moral community of society at large as a diverse body of interdependent communities. They are pluralistic, yet all of them are public in their concerns for specific social goods and the general welfare.[59]

So the church typically stands ready to engage society as a whole and wrestle with it dialectically, practically, and structurally, in the cautiously hopeful expectation that such engagement can make the world more humane and just. It respects yet seeks to press beyond the stance of the sect as witness community set against the world or as sheltering community adapted to it. By arguing across multiple moral languages and visions, the church is willing to engage the larger society more intimately and dialectically than the religious kingdom holding itself at arm's length from the political and economic realms.

The church, too, seeks to infuse in persons the virtues of faith, hope, and charity, first of all, for the sake of salvation and graceful human flourishing. To these ends, it seeks to pacify the play of interests in the marketplace and temper the balance of political power and the rule of law in governance. It aims to engage its institutional neighbors across society in argument as well as love, turning them toward social arrangements restructured to help instead of hinder persons in practicing these virtues and leading good lives.

The ideal of the Church has its characteristic flaws and dangers as well as its strengths. It is too ready to compromise with worldly powers and principalities in order to consolidate its own authority. It is too prone to sacrifice both prophetic witness and inner holiness in order to objectify doctrine as dogma and fortify hierarchy as clerical office instead of moral example. It does so in institutional forms historically at odds with modern religious pluralism and disestablishment. It also runs counter to the rise of de facto congregationalism in the West over the last century in popular churches, movements, and voluntary groups tugging away at denominational principles and structures in order to define their own faith, control their own resources, and go their own way.

Why leave church, or stay away from it? Survey responses from America's "nones" today echo long-standing criticisms of both the church and the sect, and they affirm axiomatic assumptions of modern mysticism. Churches are too worldly, they charge. They are too concerned with money and power, and too hypocritical and insincere in pretending to hold themselves above the world in transcendent majesty or to stand against it in sect-like purity and militancy, while actually following in its selfish footsteps. Churches are too political, they add, insofar as their moral advocacy and witness—whether to advance gay rights or gun rights, outlaw abortion or gender discrimination, raise wages or cut taxes—come down to lobbying for partisan policies and ideologies. Churches set too many rules for their members, protest the unchurched, and claim too much moral authority over them, through asserting the magisterial orthodoxy of churchly creeds, or claiming the absolute truth of biblical literalism revealed to the sect. Organized religion should meet the spiritual needs of individuals instead of denying or ignoring them. It should tell the truth that no one religion is completely true.

What can and should be done in response? In principle the sect as prophetic witness community and priesthood of all believers is needed to check the churchly tendency of clergy in charge to compromise with the powers that be and muffle individual conscience. The mystical ideal of deep spiritual experience within a radically loving community is needed to check the Church's tendencies toward self-protective paternalism and dogmatic authority. At once embodied and enacted together in effervescent rites of renewal, such experience is needed to release the Church excarnate from infallible abstraction and bring it back to the full range of its senses and callings.[60]

Only through institutional structures consistent with religious free exercise and disestablishment in a denominational society such as ours can we balance the mutual interpenetration of ideals of the Church, Sect, and Mysticism, united and reconciled as far as possible, yet still driven to develop dynamically by their inherent tensions. Precisely because the all-embracing, redemptive ideal of the Church is hardest to find or even conceive in a culture where individuals commonsensically come first and come together freely to form sects or spark mysticism, opening up American communities of faith to the spirit of the Church may well be the most valuable step we can take to revive our denominations and inspire both spiritual seekers and dwellers, in and out of church, to re-create and renew our congregations. Easier said than done? Yes, but no less worth trying to be true to tradition in the present by making the Spirit flesh in congregational communion, generation by generation, day by day.[61]

THE GOOD OF CONGREGATING

What good is congregating? Why go to church, for goodness' sake? Such questions took on new meaning for Americans, unchurched and churchgoing alike, when a viral pandemic in 2020 forced them to distance themselves, shelter in place, and stay home if they possibly could. Our need to keep in touch with one another, literally and figuratively, came into the clear and came close on every side, touching hands and hearts, hungering for a hug and kiss, holding back from a handshake.

Funerals filmed if not forgone made us feel the ache of failing to gather to mourn, come close to console, and join together to part ways with those we love. Weddings postponed or moved online made no less vivid how close we come together to celebrate love's joy and share its radiant communion. We congregate for all sorts of good reasons in all sorts of happy settings—backyard BBQs and birthday parties, school reunions and Rotary banquets, car shows and concerts, ballgames and ballets. But we congregate, too, in the face of crisis and consternation, in order to confess and lament, to seek and surrender, not only to give praise and thanks. We pray for understanding and peace of mind in the midst of unknowing and for grace in the face of despair.

In this prayerful drama, we remake time and space. We come to our senses. We open our eyes and hearts to what it means to die on the cross and rise from the tomb, to come out of slavery and into the promised land, to let go of self-centered suffering and follow the middle path. Through exile and uncertain passage, we find our way together from the forceful facts of cause and effect, infection and mortality, to the heartfelt arc of human motive and aim, at once wondrous and mysteriously made in God's image, born and reborn as a baby baptized, a soul saved.

We congregate not to feel better or come to know it all, but to find forgiveness, to come to know better, and do our best by the grace of God and the light of seeking the good in common. Again and again, we wash our hands, and put them together in prayer. We come together in common prayer to touch hands and hearts. For it is the hands of others that lift us from the womb and lower us to the grave, that give us aid in our labor, joy in our affection, and consolation in our sorrow, now and forever, world without end.[62]

NOTES

1. Cf. Stephen Ellingson, *The Megachurch and the Mainline* (Chicago: University of Chicago Press, 2008); Donald E. Miller, *Reinventing American Protestantism* (Berkeley: University of California Press, 1997); Gerardo Marti and Gladys Ganiel, *The Deconstructed Church* (New York: Oxford University Press, 2014).

2. Michael Hout and Claude S. Fischer, "Explaining Why More Americans Have No Religious Preference," *Sociological Science* 1, 24 (2014): 423–47; Gregory A. Smith et al., "U.S. Public Becoming Less Religious," Pew Research Center, November 2015; Aaron Gullickson, "The Diverging Beliefs and Practices of the Religiously Affiliated and Unaffiliated in the United States," *Sociological Science* 5, 16 (2018): 361–79; and Becka Alper, "From the Solidly Secular to Sunday Stalwarts," Pew Research Center, August 2018.

3. Andrew Greeley, *The Catholic Imagination* (Berkeley: University of California Press, 2001); Webb Keane, "Religious Language," *Annual Review of Anthropology* 26 (October 1997): 47–71; Cary Funk and Gregory A. Smith, "Nones on the Rise," Pew Research Center, 2012; Gregory A. Smith et al., "U.S. Public Becoming Less Religious," Pew Research Center, 2015; Michael Lipka and Claire Gecewicz, "More Americans Now Say They're Spiritual But Not Religious," Pew Research Center, September 2017, 1–6; Chaeyoon Lim, Carol Ann MacGregor, Robert D. Putnam,

"Secular and Liminal: Rediscovering Heterogeneity among Religious Nones," *Journal for the Scientific Study of Religion* 49, no. 4 (2010): 596–618; Michael Hout, "American Religion, All or Nothing at All," *Contexts* 16 (2017): 78–80; and Michael Hout, "Religious Ambivalence, Liminality, and the Increase of No Religious Preference in the United States, 2006–2014," *Journal for the Scientific Study of Religion* 56, no. 1 (2017): 52–63.

4. Hout, "American Religion," 2017; Gregory A. Smith, "In U.S., Decline of Christianity Continues at Rapid Pace," Pew Research Center, October 2019, 1–26; Katherine Boyle, "Silicon Valley has Digitized Everything but Religion. Will that Change?" *Washington Post*, 21 May 2020, quoting Steve Gatena, CEO of Pray.com.

5. Here and below, see Rich Morin et al., "The Religious Typology," Pew Research Center, August 2018; and Robert P. Jones et al., "Exodus: Why Americans Are Leaving Religion—And Why They're Unlikely to Come Back," Public Religion Research Institute, September 2016, 1–15.

6. Susan Moller Okin, *Justice, Gender, and the Family* (New York: Basic Books, 1989), 17–23.

7. Pew Research Center, "U.S. Teens Take After Their Parents Religiously, Attend Services Together and Enjoy Family Rituals," September 2020, 6–10; Carol E. Lytch, *Choosing Church* (Louisville: Westminster John Knox Press, 2004); Edward L. Schieffelin, "Performance and the Cultural Construction of Reality," *American Ethnologist* 12, no. 4 (1985): 707–24.

8. Gregory A. Smith, "A Growing Share of Americans Say It's Not Necessary to Believe in God to Be Moral," Pew Research Center, October 2017; Morin et al., "The Religious Typology," 46, 64–67. On "unbundling" religious doctrine and ritual from communal and spiritual experience as functional equivalents of congregational life, see Angie Thurston and Casper ter Kuile, *How We Gather* (Sacred Design Lab, Harvard Divinity School, 2015); and Tara Isabella Burton, "The Future of Christianity is Punk," *New York Times*, May 10, 2020.

9. On learning practical virtues in mainline congregations, see Richard R. Osmer, *Practical Theology: An Introduction* (Grand Rapids, MI: Eerdmans, 2008), compared to other social settings and cultural traditions detailed in Nancy E. Snow, ed., *Cultivating Virtue* (New York: Oxford University Press, 2014).

10. For example, cf. Menlo Church, "Finances at a Glance," at https://www.menlo.church/giving/ accountability; and Bob Smietana, "Megachurch pastor John Ortberg kept a family member's attraction to children secret. Then his son blew the whistle," *Religion News Service*, July 6, 2020.

11. The Metropolitan Statistical Area of Atlanta numbers more than 6.5 million inhabitants in 39 counties, according to the U.S. Census Bureau, "Largest US Metropolitan Areas by Population," 2012, www.census.gov/data/tables/times-series/popest/CBSA. Cf. Michael Hout and Claude S. Fischer, "Explaining Why More Americans Have No Religious Preference," 2014; and Charles Taylor, *A Secular Age*, 3–22.

12. See Max Weber, "The Social Psychology of the World Religions," in Hans H. Gerth and C. Wright Mills, eds., *From Max Weber* (New York: Oxford University Press, 1958), 280, positing that "from what" and "for what" believers wish to be redeemed depend on their image of the world and their stance in the face of it, set by

the founders and first followers of each world religion in response to the socially and historically specific forms of suffering they faced.

13. John Wesley, "Articles of Religion," Articles 13, 16–20, *The Book of Discipline of The United Methodist Church* (The United Methodist Publishing House, 2016), 68–70; Paul Tillich, *The Protestant Era* (Chicago: University of Chicago Press, 1953), 98.

14. Cf. Robert Wuthnow, *The Restructuring of American Religion* (Princeton: Princeton University Press, 1988), ch. 7, on divisive "religious realignment"; Penny Edgell Becker, *Congregations in Conflict* (Cambridge, UK: Cambridge University Press, 1999), and Penny Edgell Becker, "What Is Right? What Is Caring? Moral Logics in Local Religious Life," in Becker and Nancy Eiesland, eds., *Contemporary American Religion* (Lanham, MD: AltaMira Press, 1997), ch. 5.

15. Only 18 percent of African Americans identified as religiously unaffiliated in 2014, by contrast to 23 percent of all US adults, but the share of Black "nones" rose comparably from 12 percent in 2007, led by three in ten unaffiliated Black millennials (29 percent), compared to one in six Black members of Gen X, one in ten baby boomers, and one in fourteen born before 1946, with Black men likelier than women (22 percent versus 14 percent) to be "nones," according to Pew Research Center, "Black Americans Are More Likely than Overall Public to Be Christian, Protestant," April 2018. By most measures, Black millennials are more religious than other millennials, but less religious than older Black adults: 38 percent of Black millennials attend church weekly versus half of older Blacks and one quarter of other millennials; 26 percent participate in weekly congregational groups vs. 45 percent of older Blacks and 17 percent of other millennials; 61 percent pray daily vs. 78 percent of older Blacks and 39 percent of other millennials; and 75 percent are absolutely certain that God exists versus 86 percent of older Blacks and 48 percent of other millennials, according to Pew Research Center, "Black Millennials Are More Religious than Other Millennials," July 2018, 1–3. Five in eight African Americans born before 1946 identified with historically Black Protestant churches in 2014, as did 53 percent of all African Americans, but only 41 percent of Black millennials did. They were more likely to belong to a predominantly White evangelical, mainline Protestant, or Catholic denomination, particularly if they attended college or resided outside the South. See Pew Research Center, "5 Facts about the Religious Lives of African Americans," February 2018; Pew, "A Religious Portrait of African Americans," January 2009; and Melissa Deckman, "Generation Z and Religion," *Religion in Public*, February 2020, noting that 29 percent of Black Gen Z Americans report attending church seldom or never. Cf. Hart Nelson, "Unchurched Black Americans: Patterns of Religiosity and Affiliation," *Review of Religious Research* 29, no. 4 (June 1988): 398–412.

16. On race, schooling, jobs, and income correlated with births out of wedlock, deaths of despair, and voting patterns drawn by economic distress and polarized politics of grievance and blame, see Paul Krugman, "The Return of 'Family Values,'" *New York Times*, 4 May 2021.

17. C. Eric Lincoln and Lawrence H. Mamiya, *The Black Church in the African-American Experience* (Durham, NC: Duke University Press, 1990), chs. 1, 12; Yusuf Ransome et al., "Churches are Closing in Predominantly Black

Communities—Why Public Health Officials Should be Concerned," at www.brookings.edu/how-we-rise, May 2022.

18. See Darren Sherkat, *Changing Faith* (New York: NYU Press, 2014), chs. 1–3, on differences by race and generation in religious identification, switching, believing and belonging, based on General Social Survey data.

19. See, for example, Jared C. Wilson, "The Attractional Church's Growing Irrelevance," *The Gospel Coalition*, July 28, 2016, www.thegospelcoalition.org.

20. Compare Jaroslav Pelikan, *The Vindication of Tradition* (New Haven, CT: Yale University Press, 1984), 65: "Tradition is the living faith of the dead, traditionalism is the dead faith of the living. . . . It is traditionalism that gives tradition such a bad name." On religious and cultural shifts from commanding to reasoning modes of child-rearing, see Philip Greven, *The Protestant Temperament* (New York: Knopf, 1977) and Daniel Calhoun, *The Intelligence of a People* (Princeton. NJ: Princeton University Press, 1973). Blacks residing in metropolitan areas outside the South are most likely to be unchurched, and to view churches as "too restrictive morally," reported Hart Nelson, "Unchurched Black Americans," noting parallels in 1988 with White Americans most likely to leave church as male, more educated, and holding ethics of personal fulfillment over social responsibility.

21. Mary Pattillo-McCoy, *Black Picket Fences* (Chicago: University of Chicago Press, 2000); Elijah Anderson, *Code of the Street* (New York: Norton, 1999).

22. Cf. Angelia Davis, "Future at Risk: Historic Black Churches Face Challenge of Attracting Youth," CBS Channel 19 News, Columbia, South Carolina, February 2017, www.wltx.com.

23. Pastor Byron Thomas, "Wheat and Weeds in the Kingdom," Ben Hill United Methodist Church, Atlanta GA, 19 July 2020. See Ryan P. Burge, *The Nones* (Minneapolis: Fortress Press, 2021), 100–102; and Ryan Burge and Perry Bacon, "It's Not Just Young White Liberals Who Are Leaving Religion," at https://www.fivethirtyeight.com, April 17, 2021, 3–4.

24. Pastor Byron Thomas, "Wheat and Weeds in the Kingdom," Ben Hill UMC, 2020.

25. Cf. Oliver Wendell Holmes, Sr., "Some people are so heavenly minded they are no earthly good," quoted in wikiquotes.com; and Johnny Cash, "No Earthly Good," *The Rambler* (Columbia Records, 1977) at https://www.johnnycash.com/track/no-earthly-good-5.

26. Celebrated annually on the night of December 31, Watch Night or "Freedom's Eve" commemorates the gathering of enslaved and free African Americans in prayerful vigil on the last night of 1862 to await news that the Emancipation Proclamation had taken effect at midnight, states the New York Public Library *African American Desk Reference* (Hoboken, NJ: Wiley, 1999).

27. Ulrike Krampe Ingram, "Geographic Analysis of Two Suburban Mega Church Congregations in Atlanta: A Distance and Demographic Study," MA Thesis, Department of Anthropology, Georgia State University, 2005, 75–77.

28. Cf. Rick Warren, *The Purpose-Driven Church* (Grand Rapids, MI: Zondervan, 1995), chs. 1–2, 9, 11.

29. On the distinctive ethos and practices of African American congregations, see Lincoln and Mamiya, *The Black Church*, ch. 1; Robert M. Franklin, *Another Day's Journey* (Minneapolis: Fortress Press, 1997), ch. 2; and Peter J. Paris, *The Social Teaching of the Black Churches* (Minneapolis: Fortress Press, 1985).

30. Kennon L. Callahan, *Small, Strong Congregations* (San Francisco: Jossey-Bass, 2000).

31. On marketing congregational religion, see Max Heirich, "The Sacred as a Market Economy," unpublished paper, American Sociological Association, Montreal, 1974; and Max Heirich, "Cultural Breakthroughs," *American Behavioral Scientist* 19, no. 6 (1976): 685–702.

32. Cf. the "Black Sacred Cosmos" in Lincoln and Mamiya, *The Black Church*, ch. 1; the "Black Christian Tradition" in Paris, *The Social Teaching of the Black Churches*, ch. 1; and the nature and history of the "Christian Ethos" in Ernst Troeltsch, *The Social Teaching of the Christian Churches* (Harper & Row, 1960), 999–1002, 1004–6.

33. Richard Madsen, "The Archipelago of Faith: Religious Individualism and Faith Community in America Today," *American Journal of Sociology* 114, no. 5 (2009): 1263–1301.

34. Max Weber, "Science as a Vocation," in Gerth and Mills, eds., *From Max Weber*, 148–56; Michael Walzer, *Thick and Thin* (Notre Dame, IN: University of Notre Dame Press), 85–104; Charles Taylor, "What's Wrong with Negative Liberty?," in Allan Ryan, ed., *The Idea of Freedom* (New York: Oxford University Press, 1979), 175–93.

35. Walzer, *Thick and Thin*, 85–104.

36. Lim, MacGregor, and Putnam, "Secular and Liminal," 596–618.

37. Pew Research Center, "Faith in Flux," 2009; Cary Funk and Gregory A. Smith, "Nones on the Rise," 22–24.

38. Charles Taylor, *A Secular Age* (Cambridge, MA: Harvard University Press, 2011), 27, 37–42; Edward Schieffelin, "Performance and the Cultural Construction of Reality," 721–24.

39. Cf. Pew Research Center, "Faith in Flux," 2009, 5–9; Michael Lipka, "Why America's 'Nones' Left Religion Behind," Pew, August 2016, 1–4; Pew Research Center, "Why America's 'Nones' Don't Identify with a Religion," August 2018, 1–3; Rich Morin et al., "The Religious Typology," Pew Research Center, August 2018, 5–9, 22–32; and Jürgen Habermas, *Religion and Rationality* (Cambridge, MA: MIT Press, 2002), chs. 6, 8, on biblical ethics of justice and love and classical ideals of reason and dialogue in relation to the quasi-scientific pragmatism of modern common sense.

40. U.S. Department of Justice, "Attorney General William P. Barr Delivers Remarks to the Law School at the University of Notre Dame," October 11, 2019; Claude Fischer, "AG Barr Says Attacks on Religion Are Loosening the Hounds of Hell. Are They?" February 6, 2020, at https://madeinamericathebook.wordpress.com; Hout and Fischer, "Explaining Why More Americans Have No Religious Preference," 2014. Cf. C. B. McPherson, *The Political Theory of Possessive Individualism* (New York: Oxford University Press, 1962); John Rawls, *A Theory of Justice* (Cambridge,

MA: Harvard University Press, 1971); Michael Sandel, *Liberalism and the Limits of Justice* (Cambridge, UK: Cambridge University Press, 1982).

41. Here and below, see Ernst Troeltsch, *The Social Teaching of the Christian* Churches, vol. 1, 23–37, and vol. 2, 993–1013; Robert N. Bellah et al., *Habits of the Heart* (Berkeley: University of California Press, 2008), 243–48; and Steven M. Tipton, *Public Pulpits* (Chicago: University of Chicago Press, 2007), 424–42.

42. Troeltsch, *Social Teaching*, vol. 2, 993.

43. Troeltsch, *Social Teaching*, vol. 1, 381.

44. Troeltsch, *Social Teaching*, vol. 1, 381–82.

45. Talcott Parsons, "Christianity and Modern Industrial Society," in *Religion, Culture and Society*, Louis Schneider, ed. (Hoboken, NJ: Wiley, 1964), 273–98.

46. Parsons, "Christianity and Modern Industrial Society," 295, here and below. Compare Emile Durkheim, *The Elementary Forms of Religious Life* (New York: Free Press, 1995), trans. Karen E. Fields, 41–44, 418–48; and Emile Durkheim, "Individualism and the Intellectuals," in *Emile Durkheim on Morality and Society* (Chicago: University of Chicago Press, 1975), ed. Robert N. Bellah; Robert N. Bellah, "Religion and the Legitimation of the American Republic," in Bellah and Phillip Hammond, eds., *Varieties of Civil Religion* (New York: Harper & Row, 1980), 3–23. On the "nation with the soul of a church," cf. Bellah, "Civil Religion in America," in *Beyond Belief* (Harper & Row, 1971), 168–89; G. K. Chesterton, *What I Saw in America* (London: Hodder & Stoughton, 1922); and Sidney E. Mead, "The 'Nation with the Soul of a Church,'" *Church History* 36, no. 3 (1967): 262–83. On priestly and prophetic versions of civil religion pledged primarily to one nation under God or to liberty and justice for all, see Martin E. Marty, "Two Kinds of Two Kinds of Civil Religion," in Russell E. Richey and Donald G. Jones, eds., *American Civil Religion* (Harper & Row, 1974), 139–57.

47. Cf. Robert N. Bellah, "Religious Evolution," 39–44 on the "modern" stage of religious evolution; Bellah, "The Future of Religion," *Tricycle* (Fall 2004): 52–55, 114–15; and Robert Wuthnow, *After Heaven* (Berkeley: University of California Press, 1998), chs. 1, 7.

48. Gallup Organization, *The Unchurched American* (Princeton: Princeton Religion Research Center, 1978), reporting that 81 percent of Americans surveyed agreed that each individual should arrive at her own religious beliefs independent of any religious community. Cf. Robert N. Bellah, "The Meaning of Dogen Today," in William R. LaFleur, ed., *Dogen Studies* (Oahu: University of Hawaii Press, 1985), 150–58.

49. Jeremy Bentham, *The Principles of Morals and Legislation* (Amherst, NY: Prometheus, 1988), ch. 2, "Opposing Principles," note to para. 18.

50. Bellah, "Religious Evolution," 43; and Robert N. Bellah et al., *Habits of the Heart*, ch. 9. Cf. Michael Walzer, *The Revolution of the Saints* (Cambridge, MA: Harvard University Press, 1982), chs. 1–2, 4–6.

51. Bellah et al., *Habits of the Heart*, 243; Tipton, *Public Pulpits*, 443. On the genesis and implications of universal human rights, see Mary Ann Glendon, *Rights Talk: The Impoverishment of Political Discourse* (New York: Free Press, 1991); Hans Joas, *The Sacredness of the Person: A New Genealogy of Human Rights* (Washington DC: Georgetown University Press, 2013); John Witte Jr., *The Reformation of*

Rights (Cambridge, UK: Cambridge University Press, 2007); John Meyer, "Self and Life Course," 242–60, in John Meyer et al., *Institutional Structure* (Thousand Oaks, CA: Sage, 1987), 242–60; Emile Durkheim, *The Elementary Forms of Religious Life*, 418–44; and Jean-Jacques Rousseau, *Emile*, trans. Allen Bloom (New York: Basic Books, 1979), Book V, 45–66.

52. Bellah et al., *Habits of the Heart,* 243; Tipton, *Public Pulpits*, 443. Cf. Howard Thurman, *Mysticism and the Experience of Love*, Pendle Hill Pamphlet 115 (Wallingford, PA: Pendle Hill Publications, 1961), 1–23, affirming that to love one another in person as God loves us beyond all measure inspires the transformative Christian community of common prayer and mutual care in the midst of solitary suffering in a world bound by caste and class.

53. Stanley Hauerwas, "The Church and Liberal Democracy: The Moral Limits of a Secular Polity," in *A Community of Character* (Notre Dame, IN: University of Notre Dame Press, 1981), 74–78.

54. See Hauerwas, "The Church and Liberal Democracy," 246–47, footnote 5, on behalf of the church militant taking a "Christ against culture" stance opposed to the secularized state and contractarian polity of Rawlsian liberal democracy instead of cultural Christians naively assuming a stance of "Christ transforming culture" by misjudging how open American political liberalism proves to faithful moral transformation and reform. Cf. H. Richard Niebuhr, *The Kingdom of God in America* (New York: Harper & Row, 1937); and H. Richard Niebuhr, *Christ and Culture* (Harper & Row, 1951).

55. Cf. Peter Berger, "From the Crisis of Religion to the Crisis of Secularity," in *Religion and America*, Mary Douglas and Steven M. Tipton, eds. (Boston: Beacon Press, 1983), 20–22; and Christian Smith, *American Evangelicalism* (Chicago: University of Chicago Press, 1998), chs. 4–5, 7.

56. See Peter L. Berger and Richard John Neuhaus, *To Empower People: The Role of Mediating Structures in Public Policy* (Washington, DC: American Enterprise Institute, 1977).

57. Michael Novak, *The Spirit of Democratic Capitalism* (New York: Simon & Schuster, 1982); and Alan Peshkin, *God's Choice: The Total World of a Fundamentalist School* (Chicago: University of Chicago Press, 1986).

58. Tipton, *Public Pulpits*, 429–35; Michael Lee Owens, *God and Government in the Ghetto* (Chicago: University of Chicago Press, 2007); and Susan Jacoby, "Government-Subsidized Christianity," *New York Times*, July 8, 2018.

59. Here and below, see Tipton, *Public Pulpits*, 435–42; and David Hollenbach, "Justice as Participation: Public Moral Discourse and the U.S. Economy," in *Justice, Peace, and Human Rights: American Catholic Social Ethics in a Pluralistic World* (Chestnut Ridge, PA: Crossroad, 1988), ch. 5.

60. See Taylor, *A Secular Age*, 767–72, on the need to counter the modern disembodiment of mainline Christianity, its excarnate abstraction of God incarnate, and its homogenizing reforms to narrow the range of Christian lives in strategic step with secularism itself.

61. Troeltsch, *Social Teaching*, vol. 1, 9–11; vol. 2, 991–93, 1010–13.

62. James Stockinger, "Locke and Rousseau: Human Nature, Human Citizenship, and Human Work," PhD dissertation, University of California, Berkeley, 1990.

Bibliography

Abramowitz, Alan, and Steven W. Webster. "Negative Partisanship: Why Americans Dislike Parties but Behave Like Rabid Partisans." *Political Psychology* 39, no.1 (2018): 119–35.

Albanese, Catherine L. *A Republic of Mind and Spirit: A Cultural History of American Metaphysical Religion.* New Haven, CT: Yale University Press, 2006.

Allen, Jordan et al. "Coronavirus in the U.S.: Latest Map and Case Count." *New York Times*, July 4, 2022.

Alper, Becka. "Why America's 'Nones' Don't Identify with a Religion." Pew Research Center, August 8, 2018.

———. "From the Solidly Secular to Sunday Stalwarts." Pew Research Center, August 29, 2018.

Alwin, Duane F. "Cohort Replacement and Changes in Parental Socialization Values." *Journal of Marriage and Family* 52 (1990): 347–60.

Anderson, Allan et al., eds. *Studying Global Pentecostalism.* Berkeley: University of California Press, 2010.

Anderson, Elijah. *Code of the Street: Decency, Violence, and the Moral Code of the Inner City.* New York: Norton, 1999.

Aquinas, Thomas. *Summa Theologica.* New York: Benziger Brothers, 1911.

Arnett, Jeffrey, and Lene Arnett. "A Congregation of One: Individualized Religious Beliefs among Emerging Adults." *Journal of Adolescent Research* 17, no. 5 (September 2002): 451–67.

Bass, Diana Butler. *Christianity after Religion.* New York: HarperCollins, 2013.

Baudrillard, Jean. *The Consumer Society: Myths and Structures.* Thousand Oaks, CA: Sage Publications, 1998.

Becker, Penny Edgell. "What Is Right? What Is Caring? Moral Logics in Local Religious Life." In Becker and Nancy Eiesland, eds. *Contemporary American Religion.* Lanham MD: AltaMira Press, 1997.

———. *Congregations in Conflict.* Cambridge, UK: Cambridge University Press, 1999.

Bellah, Robert N. "Religious Evolution." *American Sociological Review* 29, no. 3 (1964): 358–74. Reprinted in *Beyond Belief.* New York: Harper & Row, 1970.

———. "Civil Religion in America." In *Beyond Belief.* New York: Harper & Row, 1970.

———. "The Roots of Religious Consciousness I. Primitive Religion"; "II. Historic Religion"; and "III. The Contemporary Relevance of Religion," delivered as the Beatty Lectures at McGill University in March 1974, "Relevance of Man's Religious Experience," in elaborated form at the University of California, Santa Barbara in April 1974, and at Boston University in April 1975. Unpublished papers, University of California, Berkeley, 1975.

———. "Religion and the Legitimation of the American Republic." In Robert N. Bellah and Phillip E. Hammond. *Varieties of Civil Religion.* New York: Harper & Row, 1980: 3–123.

———. "The Meaning of Dogen Today." In William R. LaFleur, ed., *Dogen Studies.* Oahu: University of Hawaii Press, 1985.

———. "The Future of Religion." *Tricycle* (Fall 2004).

———. "What is Axial about the Axial Age?" *European Journal of Sociology*, 46, no. 1 (2005): 69–89.

———. "All Souls Day." In Robert N. Bellah and Steven M. Tipton, eds., *The Robert Bellah Reader.* Durham, NC: Duke University Press, 2006.

———. "The History of Habit." In *The Robert Bellah Reader.* Durham, NC: Duke University Press, 2006.

———. *Religion in Human Evolution.* Cambridge, MA: Harvard University Press, 2011.

Bellah, Robert N., Richard Madsen, William M. Sullivan, Ann Swidler, and Steven M. Tipton. *The Good Society.* New York: Knopf, 1991.

———. *Habits of the Heart: Individualism and Commitment in American Life.* 3rd ed. Berkeley: University of California Press, 2008.

———. "Paul Tillich and the Challenge of Modernity." In Richard Madsen et al., eds. *Challenging Modernity.* New York: Columbia University Press, 2024.

Bentham, Jeremy. *The Principles of Morals and Legislation.* Amherst, NY: Prometheus, 1988.

———. *An Introduction to the Principles of Morals and Legislation.* Mineola, NY: Dover, 2012.

Bercovitch, Sacvan. *The Puritan Origins of the American Self.* New Haven, CT: Yale University Press, 1975.

Berger, Peter L. "The Sociological Study of Sectarianism." *Social Research* 21, no. 4 (Winter 1954): 467–85.

———. *The Heretical Imperative: Contemporary Possibilities of Religious Affirmation.* New York: Doubleday, 1980.

———. "From the Crisis of Religion to the Crisis of Secularity." In *Religion and America.* Mary Douglas and Steven M. Tipton, eds. Boston: Beacon Press, 1983: 14–24.

Berger, Peter L., and Richard John Neuhaus. *To Empower People: The Role of Mediating Structures in Public Policy.* Washington, DC: American Enterprise Institute, 1977.

Berry, Wendell. "Poetry and Place." In *Standing by Words.* Berkeley: Counterpoint, 2011.

Bevacqua, Ari Isaacman. "Bringing Yoga into the Workplace." *New York Times*, January 1, 2019.
Block, Daniel. "Is Trump Our Cyrus? The Old Testament Case for Yes and No." *Christianity Today*, October 29, 2018.
Bosman, Julie et al. "Who I Lost." *New York Times*, March 6, 2021.
Bowler, Kate. *Everything Happens for a Reason: And Other Lies I've Loved.* New York: Random House, 2018.
Bowne, Borden Parker. *Personalism.* Whitefish, MT: Kessinger Publishing, 2007.
Boyle, Katherine. "Silicon Valley has Digitized Everything but Religion. Will That Change?" *Washington Post*, May 21, 2020, quoting Steve Gatena, CEO of Pray.com.
Braunstein, Ruth. "A Theory of Political Backlash: Assessing the Religious Right's Effect on the Religious Field." *Sociology of Religion* (November 2021): 1–31.
Brown, Peter. *The World of Late Antiquity.* New York: Norton, 1971.
———. *The Body and Society.* New York: Columbia University Press, 1988.
Bunyan, John. *The Pilgrim's Progress.* New York: Oxford University Press, 1998. 1678 for 1st edition of 1st part, expanded in 1679, and 1684 for 1st edition of 2nd part.
Burge, Ryan P. "Plenty of 'Nones' Actually Head Back to Church." *Christianity Today*, February 6, 2018.
———. "Evangelicals Show No Decline, Despite Trump and Nones." *Christianity Today*, March 21, 2019.
———. *The Nones: Where They Came from, Who They Are, and Where They Are Going.* Minneapolis: Fortress Press, 2021.
———. "How America's Youth Lost its Religion in 1990s." Religion News Service. April 13, 2022.
Burge, Ryan P., and Perry Bacon Jr. "It's Not Just Young White Liberals Who Are Leaving Religion." April 16, 2021, at https://fivethirtyeight.com.
Burkert, Walter. *Homo Neccans: The Anthropology of Ancient Greek Sacrificial Ritual and Myth.* Berkeley: University of California Press, 1986.
Burton, Tara Isabella. "The Future of Christianity Is Punk." *New York Times*, May 10, 2020.
Calhoun, David H. *The Intelligence of a People.* Princeton: Princeton University Press, 1973.
Callahan, Kennon L. *Small, Strong Congregations.* San Francisco: Jossey-Bass, 2000.
Calvin, John. *Institutes of the Christian Religion.* Philadelphia: Westminster Press, 1960. Edited by John T. McNeill.
Campbell, Colin. *The Romantic Ethic and the Spirit of Consumerism.* Oxford: Blackwell, 1987.
Campbell, David E., Geoffrey C. Layman, and John C. Green. *Secular Surge: A New Fault Line in American Politics.* Cambridge, UK: Cambridge University Press, 2021.
Camus, Albert. *Summer in Algiers.* New York: Penguin, 2005.
Chaves, Mark. *Congregations in America.* Cambridge, MA: Harvard University Press, 2004: 108–28.

Chaves, Mark, Helen M. Giesel, and William Tsitsos. "Religious Variations in Public Presence." In Robert Wuthnow and John H. Evans, eds. *The Quiet Hand of God.* Berkeley: University of California Press, 2002.

Chesterton, G. K. *What I Saw in America.* London: Hodder & Stoughton, 1922.

Chetty, Raj et al. "Social Capital I: Measurement and Associations with Economic Mobility." National Bureau of Economic Research. Working Paper No. 30313. July 2022.

———. "Social Capital and Economic Mobility." *Opportunity Insights*. Harvard University. August 2022.

Cloud, Henry, and John Townsend. *Boundaries: When to Say YES, When to Say NO, to Take Control of Your Life.* Grand Rapids, MI: Zondervan, 1992.

———. *Safe People: How to Find Relationships That Are Good for You and Avoid Those That Aren't.* Grand Rapids, MI: Zondervan, 1995.

Cohn, D'Vera. "A Record 64 Million Americans Live in Multi-generational Households." Pew Research Center. April 5, 2018.

Coleman, John A. "Church-Sect Typology and Organizational Precariousness." *Sociological Analysis* 29, no. 2 (Summer 1968): 56–66.

Cooperman, Alan et al. "Interpretation of Scripture." Pew Religious Landscape Study, 2014.

Cremin, Lawrence A. *American Education: The National Experience, 1783–1876.* New York: Harper & Row, 1982.

Davis, Darren W., and David C. Wilson. *Racial Resentment in the Political Mind.* Chicago: University of Chicago Press, 2022.

Davis, Jim, and Michael Graham with Ryan P. Burge. *The Great Dechurching: Who's Leaving, Why Are They Going, and What Will It Take to Bring Them Back?* Grand Rapids, MI: Zondervan, 2023.

Deckman, Melissa. "Generation Z and Religion: What New Data Show." *Religion in Public.* February 10, 2020, at https://religioninpublic.blog.

Delbanco, Andrew. *The Real American Dream.* Cambridge, MA: Harvard University Press, 2000.

Diamant, Jeff, and Besheer Mohamed. "Black Millennials Are More Religious than Other Millennials." Pew Research Center, July 2018.

Dimock, Michael. "Defining Generations." Pew Research Center. March 1, 2018.

Djupe, Paul A., Jacob R. Heiheisel, and Anand E. Sokhey. "Reconsidering the Role of Politics in Leaving Religion: The Importance of Affiliation." *American Journal of Political Science* 62, no.1 (January 2018): 161–75.

Doan, Petra L., and Harrison Higgins. "The Demise of Queer Space? Resurgent Gentrification and the Assimilation of LGBT Neighborhoods." *Journal of Planning Education and Research* 31, no. 1 (2011): 1–20. DOI: 10.1177/0739456X10391266.

Douglas, Mary. *Natural Symbols.* New York: Pantheon Books, 1982.

———. *How Institutions Think.* Syracuse: Syracuse University Press, 1986.

Douthat, Ross. "The Return of Paganism." *New York Times,* December 12, 2018.

Dumont, Louis. *Homo Hierarchicus.* Chicago: University of Chicago Press, 1970.

———. *From Mandeville to Marx.* Chicago: University of Chicago Press, 1977.

———. "A Modified View of Our Origins: The Christian Beginnings of Modern Individualism." *Religion* 12, no. 3 (1982): 1–27.

Durkheim, Emile. "Individualism and the Intellectuals." In *Emile Durkheim on Morality and Society*. Chicago: University of Chicago Press, 1975, ed. Robert N. Bellah.

———. *The Elementary Forms of the Religious Life*. Trans. Karen E. Fields. New York: The Free Press, 1995.

Earls, Aaron. "Southern Baptists Experience Historic Drop in Membership." June 4, 2020. https://www.lifeway.com.

ECUSA Office of the General Convention. "Table of Statistics of the Episcopal Church." September 2020. www.generalconvention.org.

Edsall, Thomas B. "The Contract with Authoritarianism." *New York Times,* April 5, 2018.

———. "Trump's Cult of Animosity Shows No Sign of Letting Up." *New York Times*, May 7, 2021.

Ellingson, Stephen. *The Megachurch and the Mainline: Remaking Religious Tradition in the 21st Century.* Chicago: University of Chicago Press, 2007.

Emerson, Ralph Waldo. *Nature.* Boston: James Munro, 1836.

———. *The Essays of Ralph Waldo Emerson*. Cambridge, MA: Harvard University Press, 1987. Edited by Alfred R. Ferguson and Jean Ferguson Carr.

———. "The Over-Soul." In *Essays: First Series.* Boston: James Munro, 1841.

Erasmus. *In Praise of Folly.* New York: Penguin, 1994.

Erikson, Erik. "Life Cycle." In David L. Sills, ed. *International Encyclopedia of the Social Sciences.* New York: Macmillan/Free Press, 1968, vol. 4: 286–92.

Evans, Nancy. *Civic Rites.* Berkeley: University of California Press, 2010.

Finney, Charles Grandison. "The One Thing Needful." *The Oberlin Evangelist*, February 2, 1859.

Fischer, Claude S. *To Dwell among Friends.* Chicago: University of Chicago Press, 1982.

———. *Made in America.* Chicago: University of Chicago Press, 2010.

———. "Declaring You're a 'None.'" August 19, 2013, at http://madeinamericathebook.com.

———. "Explaining Why More Americans Have No Religious Preference." *Sociological Science* 1 (2014): 423–47.

———. "Latest News on 'No Religion.'" October 13, 2014, at http://madeinamericathebook.com.

———. "The Politics-Religion Vortex Spins." September 17, 2018, at http://madeinamericathebook.com.

———. "AG Barr Says Attacks on Religion Are Loosening the Hounds of Hell. Are They?" February 6, 2020, at https://madeinamericathebook.wordpress.com.

———. "Covid-19: Exceptionalism with a Vengeance." August 21, 2020, at https://madeinamericathebook. wordpress.com/2020/08/21.

Franklin, Robert M. *Another Day's Journey.* Minneapolis: Fortress Press, 1997.

Frederick, Marla. *Between Sundays: Black Women and Everyday Struggles of Faith.* Berkeley: University of California Press, 2003.

Freud, Sigmund. *The Future of an Illusion.* New York: Norton, 1961. Translated and edited by James Strachey.

———. *Group Psychology and the Analysis of the Ego.* New York: Norton, 1990. Translated and edited by James Strachey.

Fry, Richard, and Kim Parker. "Rising Share of U.S. Adults Are Living without a Spouse or Partner." Pew Research Center. October 2021.

Funk, Cary, and Gregory A. Smith. "'Nones' on the Rise: One-in-Five Adults Have No Religious Affiliation." Pew Research Center. October 9, 2012.

Gallup, George, Jr., and James Castelli. *The People's Religion: American Faith in the '90s.* New York: Macmillan, 1989.

Gallup Organization. *The Unchurched American.* Princeton: Princeton Religion Research Center, 1978.

Gecewicz, Claire. "'New Age' Beliefs Common among both Religious and Nonreligious Americans." Pew Research Center. October 1, 2018.

Geertz, Clifford. "Ethos, Worldview, and the Analysis of Sacred Symbols." In *The Interpretation of Cultures.* New York: Basic Books, 1973: 126–41.

———. "Religion as a Cultural System." In *The Interpretation of Cultures.* New York: Basic Books, 1973: 87–125.

Geller, Stephen A. "The God of the Covenant." In *One God or Many? Concepts of Divinity in the Ancient World.* Ed. Barbara Nevling Porter. Transactions of the Casco Bay Assyriological Institute, 2000.

General Social Survey. "Religious Affiliation and Behavior." 2018. www.gss.norc.org.

Ginsberg, Alan. "Howl." *Collected Poems: 1947–1995.* New York: HarperCollins, 2001.

Glendon, Mary Ann. *Rights Talk: The Impoverishment of Political Discourse.* New York: Free Press, 1991.

Gorski, Philip. *The Disciplinary Revolution: Calvinism and the Rise of the State in Early Modern Europe.* Chicago: University of Chicago Press, 2003.

———. "Why Evangelicals Voted for Donald Trump: A Critical Cultural Sociology." *American Journal of Cultural Sociology*, 5 (2017): 338–54.

Graham, Ruth, and Charles Homans. "Trump Is Connecting with a Different Type of Evangelical Voter." *New York Times,* January 8, 2024.

Grana, Cesar. *Bohemian versus Bourgeois.* New York: Basic Books, 1964.

Graybiel, Ann M. "Habits, Rituals, and the Evaluative Brain." *Annual Review of Neuroscience* 31 (July 2008): 359–87.

Greeley, Andrew M. *The Catholic Imagination.* Berkeley: University of California Press, 2001.

———. *Chicago Catholics and the Struggles within their Church.* Piscataway NJ: Transaction Press, 2010.

Greven, Philip J. *The Protestant Temperament: Patterns of Child-Rearing, Religious Experience, and the Self in Early America.* Chicago: University of Chicago Press, 1988.

Gullickson, Aaron. "The Diverging Beliefs and Practices of the Religiously Affiliated and Unaffiliated in the United States." *Sociological Science* 5 (2018): 361–79.

Habermas, Jürgen. *Religion and Rationality.* Cambridge, MA: MIT Press, 2002.

Hadaway, C. Kirk. "Is the Episcopal Church Growing (or Declining)?" *Domestic and Foreign Missionary Society.* 200. www.episcopalchurch.org

Hadaway, C. Kirk, and Penny Long Marler. "All in the Family: Religious Mobility in America." *Review of Religious Research* 35, no. 2 (1993): 97–116.

Haller, William. *Tracts on Liberty in the Puritan Revolution, 1638–1647.* New York: Columbia University Press, 1933, Vol. 1.

Haraway, Jennifer M. McClure. *No Congregation Is an Island: How Faith Communities Navigate Opportunities and Challenges Together.* Lanham, MD: Rowman & Littlefield, 2023.

Hatch, Nathan O., "*Sola Scriptura* and *Novus Ordo Seclorum.*" In *The Bible in America: Essays in Cultural History.* Ed. Nathan O. Hatch and Mark A. Noll. New York: Oxford University Press, 1982.

Hauerwas, Stanley. *A Community of Character: Toward a Constructive Christian Social Ethic.* Notre Dame, IN: University of Notre Dame Press, 1981.

Hedstrom, Matthew S. *The Rise of Liberal Religion: Book Culture and American Spirituality in the Twentieth Century*. New York: Oxford University Press, 2013.

Heirich, Max. "The Sacred as a Market Economy." Unpublished paper, American Sociological Association, Montreal, 1974.

———. "Cultural Breakthroughs." *American Behavioral Scientist* 19, no. 6 (1976): 685–702.

Hetherington, Marc J., and Jonathan D. Weiler. *Authoritarianism and Polarization in American Politics.* Cambridge, UK: Cambridge University Press, 2009.

———. *Leviathan.* Ed. Michael Oakeshott. New York: Collier Books, 1962.

Hofmann, Wilhelm. "Morality in Everyday Life." http://science.sciencemag.org, May 11, 2015.

Holifield, E. Brooks. *Theology in America.* New Haven, CT: Yale University Press, 2005.

Holland, Matthew S. *Bonds of Affection: Civic Charity and the Making of America.* Washington, DC: Georgetown University Press, 2007.

Hollenbach, David. "Justice as Participation: Public Moral Discourse and the U.S. Economy." In *Justice, Peace, and Human Rights: American Catholic Social Ethics in a Pluralistic World.* Chestnut Ridge, PA: Crossroad, 1988: 71–84.

Hout, Michael. "American Religion, All or Nothing at All." *Contexts* 16 (2017): 78–80.

———. "Religious Ambivalence, Liminality, and the Increase of No Religious Preference in the United States, 2006–2014." *Journal for the Scientific Study of Religion* 56, no. 1 (2017): 52–63.

Hout, Michael, and Claude S. Fischer. "Why More Americans Have No Religious Preference: Politics and Generations." *American Sociological Review* 67 (2002): 165–90.

———. "O Be Some Other Name." *American Sociological Review* 68, no. 2 (2003): 316–18.

———. "Explaining Why More Americans Have No Religious Preference: Political Backlash and Generational Succession, 1987–2012." *Sociological Science* 1 (2014): 423–47.

———. "Why Millennials Are Less Religious than Older Americans." Pew Research Center, January 2016.

Hout, Michael, Andrew Greeley, and Melissa J. Wilde. "The Demographic Imperative in Religious Change in the United States." *American Journal of Sociology* 107, no. 2 (September 2001): 468–500.

Hout, Michael, and Tom W. Smith. "Fewer Americans Affiliate with Organized Religions, Belief and Practice Unchanged: Key Findings from the 2014 General Social Survey." National Opinion Research Center (NORC). University of Chicago, March 2015.

Hunter, James Davison. *American Evangelicalism.* New Brunswick, NJ: Rutgers University Press, 1983.

Ingram, Ulrike Krampe. "Geographic Analysis of Two Suburban Mega Church Congregations in Atlanta: A Distance and Demographic Study." MA Thesis, Department of Anthropology, Georgia State University, 2005.

Jacoby, Susan. "Government-Subsidized Christianity." *New York Times*, July 8, 2018.

Jefferson, Thomas. "82. A Bill for Establishing Religious Freedom." June 18, 1779, *The Papers of Thomas Jefferson*, vol. 2, ed. Julian P. Boyd. Princeton: Princeton University Press, 1950.

———. "Virginia Statute for Religious Freedom." In Edwin S. Gaustad, ed. *A Documentary History of Religion in America.* Grand Rapids: Eerdmans, 1982.

Jelks, Randal M. *Benjamin Elijah Mays: Schoolmaster of* the *Movement.* Chapel Hill: University of North Carolina Press, 2012.

Joas, Hans. *The Sacredness of the Person: A New Genealogy of Human Rights.* Washington, DC: Georgetown University Press, 2013.

Jones, Jeffrey M. "U.S. Church Membership Down Sharply in Past Two Decades," Gallup Poll, April 18, 2018.

———. "U.S. Church Membership Falls Below Majority for First Time." Gallup Poll Social Series. March 29, 2021. http://www.news.gallup.com/poll/341963.

———. "Confidence in U.S. Institutions Down: Average at New Low." Gallup News Service, June 1–20, 2022, at https://news.gallup.com/poll394283.

Jones, Robert P., Daniel Cox, Betsy Cooper, and Rachel Lienesch. "Exodus: Why Americans Are Leaving Religion—And Why They're Unlikely to Come Back." Public Religion Research Institute (PRRI), September 2016, 7–11.

Jones, Robert P., and Robert Cox. "America's Changing Religious Identity." Public Religion Research Institute (PRRI), 2017.

Jones, Robert P., and Rachel Lienesch. "Beyond Economics: Fears of Cultural Displacement Pushed the White Working Class to Trump." *PPRI/The Atlantic Report*, 2017.

Jones, Robert P. et al. "The 2020 Census of American Religion," PRRI, August 7, 2021.

Jones, Robert P. et al. "PRRI 2022 Census of American Religion," PRRI, February 24, 2023.

Jung, Christian. *Meister Eckhardts philosophische Mystik.* Baden-Baden: Tectum, 2010.

Kant, Immanuel. *Kritik der reinen Vernunft*. Leipzig: Verlag von Felix Meiner, 1919. First publication date is 1781.

———. *Von einem neuerdings Erhobenen vornehmen Ton in der Philosophie.* Hamburg: Meiner, 1920.

———. *Groundwork of the Metaphysics of Morals.* Cambridge, UK: Cambridge University Press, 2012.

Kaye, Les, and Teresa Bouza. *A Sense of Something Greater: Zen and the Search for Balance in Silicon Valley.* Berkeley: Parallax Press, 2018.

Keane, Webb. “Religious Language.” *Annual Review of Anthropology* 26 (October 1997): 47–71.

———. *Christian Moderns.* Berkeley: University of California Press, 2007.

Kluckhohn, Florence R., and Fred L. Strodtbeck, *Variations in Value Orientations.* New York: Row, Peterson, 1961.

Kohlberg, Lawrence. “Moral Development.” In David L. Sills, ed. *International Encyclopedia of the Social Sciences.* New York: Macmillan Free Press, 1968, vol. 10: 783–93.

Kohn, Melvin. “Social Class and Parental Values: Another Confirmation of a Relationship.” *American Sociological Review* 41 (1976): 538–45.

———. *Class and Conformity: A Study in Values*. Chicago: University of Chicago Press, 1977.

Krugman, Paul. “The Return of ‘Family Values.’” *New York Times*, May 4, 2021.

Kruzman, Diana. “Houses of Worship Grapple with the Future of Their Online Services.” *Religious News Service.* February 14, 2022.

Lai, Whalen “The Meaning of ‘Mind-Only’ (wei-hsin): An Analysis of a Sinitic Mahayana Phenomenon.” *Philosophy East and West* 27, no. 1 (1977): 65–83.

Lazerwitz, Bernard et al. *Jewish Choices: American Jewish Denominationalism.* Albany: SUNY Press, 1998.

Lennon, John, and Paul McCartney. “All You Need Is Love.” 1967 Sony/ATV Music Publishing, 2009.

Lim, Chaeyoon, Carol Ann MacGregor, and Robert D. Putnam. “Secular and Liminal: Discovering Heterogeneity among Religious Nones.” *Journal for the Scientific Study of Religion* 49, no. 4 (2010): 596–618.

Lincoln, C. Eric, and Lawrence H. Mamiya. *The Black Church in the African-American Experience.* Durham, NC: Duke University Press, 1990.

Lipka, Michael. “Religious ‘Nones’ Becoming More Secular.” Pew Research Center, November 2015.

———. “Which U.S. Religious Groups are Oldest and Youngest?” Pew Research Center, July 11, 2016.

———. “Why America’s ‘Nones’ Left Religion Behind.” Pew Research Center, August 24, 2016.

Lipka, Michael, and Claire Gecewicz. “More Americans Now Say They’re Spiritual But Not Religious.” Pew Research Center, September 6, 2016.

Locke, John. “Ethica A.” In Mark Goldie, ed., *Political Essays.* Cambridge, UK: Cambridge University Press, 1997.

———. *Two Treatises of Government.* Ed. Peter Laslett. Cambridge, UK: Cambridge University Press, 1988.

Lucia, Amanda. *White Utopias.* Berkeley: University of California Press, 2020.

Lugo, Luis et al. "Faith in Flux: Changes in Religious Affiliation in the U.S." Pew Research Center, April 27, 2009.

Luhrmann, Tanya Marie. "Toward an Anthropological Theory of Mind." *Suomen Antropologi: Journal of the Finnish Anthropological Association* 36, no. 4 (Winter 2011): 5–69.

———. *When God Talks Back: Understanding the American Evangelical Relationship with God.* New York: Knopf, 2012.

Lytch, Carol E. *Choosing Church: What Makes a Difference for Teens.* Louisville, KY: Westminster John Knox Press, 2004.

Madison, James. "Memorial and Remonstrance." In *The Papers of James Madison,* vol. 8, ed. William T. Hutchinson and William Rachal. Chicago: University of Chicago Press, 1971.

Madsen, Richard. "The Archipelago of Faith." *American Journal of Sociology* 114, no. 5 (2009): 1263–1301.

Margolis, Michele F. *From Politics to the Pews: How Partisanship and the Political Environment Shape Religious Identity.* Chicago: University of Chicago Press, 2018.

———. "How Politics Affects Religion: Partisanship, Socialization, and Religiosity in America." *Journal of Politics* 80, no. 1 (2018): 30–43.

Marler, Penny Long, and C. Kirk Hadaway. "Toward a Typology of Protestant 'Marginal Members.'" *Review of Religious Research* 35, no. 1 (1993): 34–54.

Marsden, George. "Preachers of Paradox." In Mary Douglas and Steven M. Tipton, eds. *Religion and America*. Boston: Beacon Press, 1983: 150–68.

———. *Fundamentalism and American Culture.* New York: Oxford University Press, 2006.

Marti, Gerardo, and Gladys Ganiel. *The Deconstructed Church*. New York: Oxford University Press, 2014.

Martin, David. *Pentecostalism: The World Their Parish.* Hoboken, NJ: Wiley-Blackwell, 2001.

Marty, Martin E. *The Public Church.* Chestnut Ridge PA: Crossroad Publishing, 1981.

———. "Two Kinds of Civil Religion." In Russell E. Richey and Donald G. Jones, eds., *American Civil Religion*. New York: Harper & Row, 1974.

Marwell, Gerald, and N. J. Demerath III. "'Secularization' by Any Other Name." *American Sociological Review* 68, no. 2 (2003).

Marx, Karl "The German Ideology." *The Marx-Engels Reader.* Edited by Robert C. Tucker. New York: Norton, 1978: 146–200.

Masci, David. "5 Facts about the Religious Lives of African Americans." Pew Research Center, February 7, 2018.

Masci, David, and Michael Lipka. "Americans May Be Getting Less Religious, But Feelings of Spirituality Are on the Rise." Pew Research Center, January 21, 2016.

Mason, Lilliana, and Julie Wronski. "One Tribe to Bind Them All: How Our Social Group Attachments Strengthen Partisanship." *Political Psychology* 39, issue supplement S1 (February 2018): 257–77.

Mason, Lilliana, Julie Wronski, and John V. Kane. "Activating Animus." *American Political Science Review* (2021): 1–9.

McGavran, Donald A. *Understanding Church Growth*, 3rd ed. Grand Rapids: Eerdmans, 1990.

McNeill, William H. *Keeping Together in Time: Dance and Drill in Human History.* Cambridge, MA: Harvard University Press, 1997.

McPherson, C.B. *The Political Theory of Possessive Individualism.* New York: Oxford University Press, 1962.

McRoberts, Omar. *Streets of Glory.* Chicago: University of Chicago Press, 2005.

Mead, Sidney E. "The 'Nation with the Soul of a Church.'" *Church History* 36, no. 3 (1967): 262–83.

Meeks, Wayne. *The Origins of Christian Morality.* New Haven, CT: Yale University Press, 1993.

Merkur, Dan. "Mysticism." *Encyclopedia Britannica*, 2019. www.britannica.com/topic/mysticism.

Meyer, John W. "Self and Life Course." In John Meyer et al., *Institutional Structure.* Thousand Oaks, CA: Sage, 1987: 242–60.

———. "World Society, Institutional Theories, and the Actor." *Annual Review of Sociology* 36 (2010): 1–20.

Meyer, John W. et al. "World Society and the Nation State." *American Journal of Sociology* 103 (1997): 144–81.

Mill, John Stuart. *Utilitarianism.* New York: Oxford University Press, 1998.

Miller, Daniel R., and Guy E. Swanson. *The Changing American Parent.* Hoboken, NJ: Wiley, 1958.

Miller, Donald E. *Reinventing American Protestantism*. Berkeley: University of California Press, 1997.

Miller, Perry. "Errand into the Wilderness." *The William and Mary Quarterly* 10, no. 1 (1953): 4–32.

———. *The New England Mind*. Cambridge, MA: Harvard University Press, 1983.

Miller, Perry. *The Life of the Mind in America.* New York: Harcourt, Brace & World, 1965.

Mitchell, Harvey. "Reclaiming the Self: The Pascal-Rousseau Connection." *Journal of the History of Ideas* 54, no. 4 (Oct. 1993): 637–58.

Mohamed, Besheer et al. "Faith among Black Americans." Pew Research Center, February 2021.

Mojzes, Paul. Ed., *North American Churches and the Cold War.* Grand Rapids: Eerdmans, 2018.

Morin, Rich et al. "The Religious Typology." Pew Research Center, 29 August 2018. Pew Research Center, August 29, 2018, "The Religious Typology."

Murphy, Carlyle. "Interfaith Marriage Is Common in U.S., Particularly among the Recently Wed." Pew Research Center, June 2, 2015.

Nelson, Hart. "Unchurched Black Americans: Patterns of Religiosity and Affiliation." *Review of Religious Research* 29, no. 4 (June 1988): 398–412.

Neunheuser, Burkhard. *Baptism and Confirmation*. Chestnut Ridge, NY: Herder & Herder, 1964.

Newport, Frank. *God Is Alive and Well.* Washington, DC: Gallup Press, 2013.

Niebuhr, H. Richard. *The Social Sources of Denominationalism.* New York: Henry Holt, 1929.

———. *Christ and Culture.* New York: Harper & Row, 1951.

———. *The Kingdom of God in America.* Middletown, CT: Wesleyan University Press, 1988.

Norris, Pippa, and Ronald Inglehardt. *Sacred and Secular.* Cambridge, UK: Cambridge University Press, 2004.

North, Michael. "The Making of 'Make It New.'" In *Novelty: A History of the New.* Chicago: University of Chicago Press, 2013.

Novak, Michael. *The Spirit of Democratic Capitalism.* New York: Simon & Schuster, 1982.

Novotney, Amy. "Students under Pressure." American Psychological Association. *Monitor on Psychology* 45, no. 8 (September 2014): 36–44.

Obama, Barack. "Faith and Politics." *New York Times,* June 28, 2006.

Okin, Susan Moller. *Justice, Gender, and the Family.* New York: Basic Books, 1991.

Osmer, Richard R. *Practical Theology: An Introduction.* Grand Rapids, MI: Eerdmans, 2008.

Owens, Michael Lee. *God and Government in the Ghetto.* Chicago: University of Chicago Press, 2007.

Ozment, Stephen. *The Age of Reform 1250–1550.* New Haven, CT: Yale University Press, 1981.

Paine, Thomas. *Age of Reason.* Independence Hall Association, 1999. https://www.ushistory.org/paine/reason.

Paris, Peter J. *The Social Teaching of the Black Churches.* Minneapolis: Fortress Press, 1985.

Parker, Theodore. *Ten Sermons of Religion.* Boston: Crosby, Nichols and Company, 1853.

Parsons, Talcott.

"Christianity and Modern Industrial Society." *Religion, Culture and Society.* Louis Schneider, ed. Hoboken, NJ: Wiley, 1964: 273–98.

Pattillo-McCoy, Mary. *Black Picket Fence.* Chicago: University of Chicago Press, 2013.

Pelikan, Jaroslav, *The Vindication of Tradition.* New Haven, CT: Yale University Press, 1984.

Peshkin, Alan. *God's Choice: The Total World of a Fundamentalist School.* Chicago: University of Chicago Press, 1986.

Pew Research Center. "Many Americans Say Other Faiths Can Lead to Eternal Life." December 18, 2008.

———. "A Religious Portrait of African Americans," January 30, 2009.

———. "U.S. Public Becoming Less Religious." November 3, 2015.

———. "Importance of Religion and Religious Beliefs." November 3, 2015.

———. "Choosing a New Church or House of Worship." August 23, 2016.

———. "One-in-Five U.S. Adults Were Raised in Interfaith Homes." October 26, 2016.

———. "How the Faithful Voted." November 9, 2016.

———. "Sharp Partisan Divisions in Views of National Institutions." July 10, 2017.

———. "5 Facts about the Religious Lives of African Americans." February 7, 2018.

———. "Black Americans Are More Likely than Overall Public to Be Christian, Protestant." April 23, 2018.

———. "When Americans Say They Believe in God, What Do They Mean?" April 25, 2018.

———."Black Millennials Are More Religious than Other Millennials," July 20, 2018.

———. "Why America's 'Nones' Don't Identify with a Religion." August 8, 2018.

———. "Americans See Advantages and Challenges in Growing Racial and Ethnic Diversity," May 8, 2019.

———. "In Changing U.S. Electorate, Race and Education Remain Stark Dividing Lines." June 2, 2020.

———. "U.S. Teens Take after their Parents Religiously, Attend Services Together, and Enjoy Family Rituals," September 10, 2020.

———. "Parenting in America Today," January 24, 2023.

Pickvance, Ronald. "Degas and the Painting of Modern Life." *Journal of the Royal Society of Arts* 128, no. 5285 (1980): 250–63.

Pieper, Josef. *Leisure: The Basis of Culture.* San Francisco: Ignatius Press, 2009.

Plato. *The Laws of Plato.* Chicago: University of Chicago Press, 1988. Translated by Thomas L. Pangle.

Preston, David L. *The Social Organization of Zen Practice*. Cambridge, UK: Cambridge University Press, 1988.

Putnam, Robert D. *Bowling Alone: The Collapse and Revival of American Community.* New York: Simon & Schuster, 2000.

Putnam, Robert D., and David E. Campbell. *American Grace.* New York: Simon & Schuster, 2012.

Rainie, Lee, Scott Keeter, and Andrew Perrin. "Trust and Distrust in America." Pew Research Center, July 22, 2019, 6–28.

Ransome, Yusuf et al. "Churches are Closing in Predominantly Black Communities—Why Public Health Officials Should be Concerned." at www.brookings.edu/how-we-rise. May 2022.

Rawls, John. *A Theory of Justice.* Cambridge, MA: Harvard University Press, 1971.

Ricoeur, Paul. "The Image of God and the Epic of Man." *Cross Currents* 11, no. 1 (Winter 1961): 37–50.

Rogers, Carl. "A Therapist's View of the Good Life: The Fully Functioning Person" (1961). In *The Carl Rogers Reader.* Edited by Howard Kirschenbaum and Valerie Henderson. Boston: Houghton Mifflin, 1989: 183–96.

Rojas, Rick. "Let He Who Is Without Yeezys Cast the First Stone." *New York Times*, April 17, 2019.

Roof, Wade Clark. *A Generation of Seekers.* New York: HarperCollins, 1993.

Roof, Wade Clark, and William McKinney. *American Mainline Religion: Its Changing Shape and Future.* New Brunswick: Rutgers University Press, 1987.

Roozen, David A., William McKinney, and Jackson W. Carroll. *Varieties of Religious Presence.* Cleveland: The Pilgrim Press, 1983.

Rorty, Richard. "Religion as Conversation Stopper." *Common Knowledge* 3, 1 (1994): 1–6.

Roszak, Theodore. *The Making of a Counter Culture*. Berkeley: University of California Press, 1969.

Rousseau, Jean-Jacques. *Emile.* Trans. Allen Bloom. New York: Basic Books, 1979.

Sandel, Michael, *Liberalism and the Limits of Justice.* Cambridge, UK: Cambridge University Press, 1982.

Scharen, Christian. *Public Worship and Public Work: Character and Commitment in Local Congregational Life*. Collegeville MN: Liturgical Press, 2004.

Schieffelin, Edward L. "Performance and the Cultural Construction of Reality." *American Ethnologist* 12, no. 4 (1985): 707–24.

Schleiermacher, Friedrich. *On Religion: Speeches to Its Cultured Despisers.* Edited by Richard Crouter. Cambridge, UK: Cambridge University Press, 1996.

Schmidt, Leigh. *Restless Souls: The Making of American Spirituality from Emerson to Oprah.* New York: HarperCollins, 2005.

Sherkat, Darren E. *Changing Faith: The Dynamics and Consequences of Americans' Shifting Religious Identities.* New York: NYU Press, 2014.

Smart, J.J.C., and Bernard Williams. *Utilitarianism: For and Against*. Cambridge, UK: Cambridge University Press, 1973.

Smith, Adam. *The Theory of Moral Sentiments.* New York: Oxford University Press, 1976.

Smith, Christian. *American Evangelicalism: Embattled and Thriving.* Chicago: University of Chicago Press, 1998.

Smith, Christian, and Patricia Snell. *Souls in Transition: The Religious and Spiritual Lives of Emerging Adults.* New York: Oxford University Press, 2009.

Smith, Gregory A. "Most Americans Oppose Churches Choosing Sides in Elections." Pew Research Center, February 3, 2016.

———. "A Growing Share of Americans Say It's Not Necessary to Believe in God to Be Moral." Pew Research Center, October 16, 2017.

———. "About Three-in-Ten U.S. Adults Are Now Religiously Unaffiliated." Pew Research Center. December 14, 2021.

Smith, Gregory A. et al. "Faith in Flux." Pew Research Center. April 2009.

———. *Religious Landscape Study.* Pew Research Center, 2014. www.pewforum.org

———. "America's Changing Religious Landscape." Pew Research Center, May 12, 2015.

Smith, Gregory A. et al. "In U.S., Decline of Christianity Continues at Rapid Pace." Pew Research Center. October 2019.

Smith, Timothy L. *Revivalism and Social Reform.* Nashville: Abingdon Press, 1957.

Snow, Nancy E., ed. *Cultivating Virtue.* New York: Oxford University Press, 2014.

Soulen, R. Kendall. *The Divine Name(s) and the Holy Trinity.* Louisville: Westminster John Knox, 2011.

Stanton, Allen T. *Reclaiming Rural: Building Thriving Rural Congregations.* Lanham, MD: Rowman & Littlefield, 2021.

Staub, Dick. *The Culturally Savvy Christian.* Hoboken, NJ: Jossey-Bass, 2017.

Stein, Leigh. "The Empty Religions of Instagram." *New York Times,* March 6, 2021.

Stevens, Wallace. "Sunday Morning." *Collected Poems.* New York: Knopf, 1954: 66–70.

Stewart, Katherine. "Why Trump Reigns as King Cyrus." *New York Times*, December 31, 2018.
Stockinger, James. "Locke and Rousseau: Human Nature, Human Citizenship, and Human Work." PhD dissertation. University of California, Berkeley, 1990.
Stowe, David W. *Song of Exile: The Enduring Mystery of Psalm* 137. New York: Oxford University Press, 2016.
Strathern, Alan. *Unearthly Powers: Religious and Political Change in World History.* Cambridge, UK: Cambridge University Press, 2019.
Stroope, Samuel, Paul Froese et al. "Unchurched Christian Nationalism and the 2016 U.S. Presidential Election." *Sociological Forum*. February 21, 2021, https://doi.org/10-1111/socf.12684.
Sudnow, David. *Ways of the Hand: The Organization of Improvised Conduct.* Harper & Row, 1978.
Sulloway, Frank. *Freud, Biologist of the Mind.* Cambridge, MA: Harvard University Press, 1992.
Swidler, Ann. "Culture in Action: Symbols and Strategies." *American Sociological Review* 51, no. 2 (April 1986): 273–86.
Tamir, Christine et al. "The Global God Divide." Pew Research Center, July 20, 2020.
Taylor, Charles. "What's Wrong with Negative Liberty?" In Allan Ryan, ed. *The Idea of Freedom.* New York: Oxford University Press, 1979.
———. *Sources of the Self.* Cambridge, MA: Harvard University Press, 1984.
———. *Modern Social Imaginaries.* Durham, NC: Duke University Press, 2004.
———. *A Secular Age.* Cambridge, MA: Harvard University Press, 2007.
———. "The Diversity of Goods," *Philosophy and the Human Sciences: Philosophical Papers.* Cambridge, UK: Cambridge University Press, 2010, vol. 2: 230–47.
———. "Religion, the Spiritual, and Art." Art Gallery of Ontario, Toronto. November 30, 2016. https://www.ago.ca/events/charles-taylor-religion-spiritual-and-art.
———. *The Ethics of Authenticity.* Cambridge, MA: Harvard University Press, 2018.
Thompson, E. P. "Time, Work-Discipline, and Industrial Capitalism." *Past and Present* 38 (1967): 56–97.
Thoreau, Henry David. *Walden.* London: Everyman's Library, 1993.
Thurston, Angie, and Casper ter Kuile. *How We Gather.* Sacred Design Lab, Harvard Divinity School, 2015.
Tillich, Paul. "The Permanent Significance of the Catholic Church for Protestantism." *Protestant Digest* 3, no. 1 (Feb.–Mar. 1941): 23–31.
———. *Systematic Theology.* Chicago: University of Chicago Press, 1963, vol. 3.
Tipton, Steven M. *Getting Saved from the Sixties.* Berkeley: University of California Press, 1982.
———. "Moral Languages and the Good Society." *Soundings* LXIX, no. 1–2 (1986): 165–80.
———. "Social Differentiation and Moral Pluralism." In *Meaning and Modernity.* Edited by Richard Madsen et al. Berkeley: University of California Press, 2002.
———. *Public Pulpits.* Chicago: University of Chicago Press, 2008.
———. *The Life to Come: Re-Creating Retirement.* Nashville, TN: Wesley's Foundery Books, 2018.

Tocqueville, Alexis de. *Democracy in America.* Ed. J. P. Mayer. Garden City, NJ: Doubleday, 1969.

Trilling, Lionel. *Sincerity and Authenticity.* Cambridge, MA: Harvard University Press, 1971.

Troeltsch, Ernst. *The Social Teaching of the Christian Churches.* New York: Harper & Row, 1960.

Uscinski, Joseph E. et al. "American Politics in Two Dimensions: Partisan and Ideological Identities versus Anti-Establishment Orientations." *American Journal of Political Science* 65, no.4 (July 2021): 877–95.

VanderWeele, Tyler, Tracy Balboni, and Howard Koh. "Health and Spirituality." *Journal of the American Medical Association* 318, no. 6 (August 2017): 519–20.

Waltz, Alan K. *A Dictionary for Methodists.* Nashville: Abingdon Press, 1991.

Walzer, Michael. *The Revolution of the Saints.* Cambridge, MA: Harvard University Press, 1965.

———. *Spheres of Justice*. New York: Basic Books, 1983.

———. *Thick and Thin: Moral Argument at Home and Abroad.* Notre Dame, IN: University of Notre Dame Press, 1994.

Warner, R. Stephen. *New Wine in Old Wineskins: Evangelicals and Liberals in a Small-Town Church.* Berkeley: University of California Press, 1990.

Warren, Rick. *The Purpose-Driven Church.* Grand Rapids, MI: Zondervan, 1995.

Weber, Max., "Religious Rejections of the World and Their Directions." In Hans H. Gerth and C. Wright Mills, eds. *From Max Weber.* New York: Oxford University Press, 1946: 323–359.

———. "The Social Psychology of the World Religions." In Hans H. Gerth and C. Wright Mills, eds., *From Max Weber*. New York: Oxford University Press, 1946: 267–322.

———. "Science as a Vocation." In Hans H. Gerth and C. Wright Mills, eds. *From Max Weber.* New York: Oxford University Press, 1946: 129–56.

———. *The Protestant Ethic and the Spirit of Capitalism.* New York: Scribner's, 1958.

Wesley, John. "On Working Out Our Own Salvation." Sermon 85, 1872 edition. General Board of Global Ministries, at http://gbgm-umc.org.

———. *An Extract from the Rev. Mr. John Wesley's Journals*, vol. 1. Evans Early American Imprint Collection. Naples, FL: Readex, 2011. www.redex.com/products /early-american-imprint-series-i-evans-1639-1800.

———. "Articles of Religion." Articles 13, 16–20. *The Book of Discipline of The United Methodist Church.* Nashville, TN: The United Methodist Publishing House, 2016.

Whitehead, Andrew L., Samuel L. Perry, and Joseph O. Baker. "Make America Christian Again: Christian Nationalism and Voting for Donald Trump in the 2016 Presidential Election." *Sociology of Religion* 79, no. 2 (January 2018): 147–71.

Whitman, Walt. *Leaves of Grass.* New York: Library of America, 2011.

Wilde, Oscar. *Lady Windermere's Fan.* New York: Penguin, 2011.

Wilkins-LaFlamme, Sarah. "Digital Religion among U.S. and Canadian Millennial Adults." *Review of Religious Research* 64 (2022): 225–48.

Willette, Jeanne S. M. "Baudelaire and 'The Painter of Modern Life.'" https://www.arthistoryunstuffed.com, August 2010.

Wilson, Jared C. "The Attractional Church's Growing Irrelevance." *The Gospel Coalition*, July 28, 2016, www.thegospelcoalition.org.

Winthrop, John. "A Model of Christian Charity." in *Winthrop Papers: Volume II, 1623–1630.* Massachusetts Historical Society, 1931.

Witte, John, Jr. *The Reformation of Rights.* Cambridge, UK: Cambridge University Press, 2007.

Wolfenstein, Martha. "The Emergence of Fun Morality." *Journal of Social Issues* 1, no. 4 (1951): 15–25.

Wood, Richard L. *Faith in Action: Religion, Race, and Democratic Organizing in America.* Chicago: University of Chicago Press, 2002.

Wordsworth, William. "The World Is Too Much with Us." London: Longman, 1802.

Wuthnow, Robert.

The Restructuring of American Religion: Society and Faith since World War II. Studies in Church and State. Ed. John F. Wilson. Princeton: Princeton University Press, 1990.

———. *Acts of Compassion.* Princeton: Princeton University Press, 1991.

———. *After Heaven: Spirituality in America since the 1950s.* Berkeley: University of California Press, 1998.

———. *Loose Connections: Civic Involvement in America's Fragmented Communities.* Cambridge, MA: Harvard University Press, 1998.

———. "Reassembling the Civic Church: The Changing Role of Congregations in American Civil Society." In Richard Madsen et al., eds. *Meaning and Modernity.* Berkeley: University of California Press, 2002, ch. 10.

———. *After the Baby Boomers: How Twenty- and Thirty-Somethings Are Shaping the Future of American Religion.* Princeton: Princeton University Press, 2007.

Yeide, Harry, Jr. *Studies in Classical Pietism: The Flowering of the Ecclesiola.* Lausanne: Peter Lang, 1997.

Yoder, John Howard. *Body Politics.* Independence, MO: Herald Press, 1992.

Index

About the Author

Steven Tipton has taught sociology of religion, morality, and culture at Emory University and its Candler School of Theology, where he is Charles Howard Candler Professor Emeritus, former director of the Graduate Division of Religion, and a senior fellow at the Center for Law and Religion. A native of San Francisco, he studied literature, philosophy, and religion at Stanford University (BA, 1968), then coupled cultural sociology with comparative philosophical and religious ethics for a joint degree in sociology and the study of religion at Harvard University (PhD, 1979). This led to *Getting Saved from the Sixties: Moral Meaning in Conversion and Cultural Change* (University of California Press, 1982). Tipton then collaborated with Robert Bellah, Richard Madsen, William Sullivan, and Ann Swidler on *Habits of the Heart: Individualism and Commitment in American Life* (University of California Press and Harper & Row, 1985, 1996, 2008; 1986 Pulitzer Prize jury finalist) and *The Good Society* (Knopf, 1991). These works in turn informed his research for *Public Pulpits: Methodists and Mainline Churches in the Moral Argument of Public Life* (University of Chicago Press, 2008) and *The Life to Come: Re-Creating Retirement* (Wesley Foundery Books, 2018) as well as his collaboration with Madsen, Sullivan, and Swidler to edit *Challenging Modernity* (Columbia University Press, 2024). Over the years Tipton's research has been sustained by the generous support of the Lilly Endowment, Guggenheim Foundation, Louisville Institute, Henry Luce Foundation, Danforth Foundation, Ford Foundation, Rockefeller Foundation, Alfred P. Sloan Foundation, National Endowment for the Humanities, American Council of Learned Societies, Association of Theological Schools, and Emory University's Laney Graduate School and Center for the Study of Law and Religion.

www.ingramcontent.com/pod-product-compliance
Ingram Content Group UK Ltd.
Pitfield, Milton Keynes, MK11 3LW, UK
UKHW020145250726
13967UKWH00002B/869